THE BARBER OF DAMASCUS

THE BARBER OF DAMASCUS

NOUVEAU LITERACY IN THE EIGHTEENTH-CENTURY OTTOMAN LEVANT

Dana Sajdi

Stanford University Press
Stanford, California

Stanford University Press
Stanford, California

Printed in the United States of America on acid-free, archival-quality paper

Library of Congress Cataloging-in-Publication Data

Sajdi, Dana, author.
The barber of Damascus : nouveau literacy in the eighteenth-century Ottoman Levant / Dana Sajdi.
pages cm
Includes bibliographical references and index.
ISBN 978-0-8047-8532-7 (cloth : alk. paper)
ISBN 978-0-8047-9727-6 (pbk. : alk. paper)
1. Ibn Budayr, Shihāb al-Dīn Aḥmad, active eighteenth century. 2. al-Budayri, Ahmad, active eighteenth century. 3. Barbers—Syria—Damascus—Biography. 4. Arabic prose literature—Eighteenth century—History and criticism. 5. Literature and society—Middle East—History—Eighteenth century. 6. Middle East—Intellectual life—Eighteenth century. 7. Middle East—History—Eighteenth century—Historiography. I. Title.
DS97.6.B83S25 2013
956.91'4403092—dc23
2013005612

ISBN 978-0-8047-8828-1 (electronic)

For the barber's namesake

Contents

List of Illustrations and Maps ix

Acknowledgments xi

Note on Language and Transliteration xv

Introduction 1

1 The Disorders of a New Order: The Levant in the Long Eighteenth Century 14

2 A Barber at the Gate: A Social and Intellectual Biography 38

3 "Cheap" Monumentality: The Nouveau Literates and Their Texts 77

4 Authority and History: The Genealogy of the Eighteenth-Century Levantine Contemporary Chronicle 115

5 A Room of His Own: The "History" of the Barber of Damascus 145

6 Cutting the Barber's Tale: The Afterlives of a History 174

Conclusion: From Nouveau Literacy to Print Journalism 205

Epilogue 213

Notes 215

Glossary 261

Bibliography 263

Index 281

Illustrations and Maps

Figure 1 *A View of Eighteenth-Century Damascus* 15

Figure 2 *Damascus from Above Salahyeh* 15

Figure 3 al-`Aẓm Palace 24

Figure 4 The Fārḥī Palace 25

Figure 5 *A Turkish Divan—Damascus* 26

Figure 6 Reception hall in the Jabri house 27

Figure 7 *Cafés in Damascus, A Branch of the Barada River Flowing Between* 29

Figure 8 Opening page of the manuscript of *The Events of Damascus* 169

Figure 9 Margin notes in *The Events of Damascus* 171

Figure 10 Barbershop in Damascus 212

Map 1 The Levant 3

Map 2 Damascus, inside the city walls 23

Map 3 Damascus and al-Maydān 32

Illustrations and Maps

Acknowledgments

This book was written in fits and starts over a very long period of time and in a number of cities on several continents. Given the extraordinary temporal span and geographical expanse of the times and places of writing, the list of my debts is very long.

My first note of gratitude goes to Tarif Khalidi, who warmly received me in Cambridge in 1995 (and made me a much desired cup of Turkish coffee). Since then, we met few times, but our communication continued sporadically over the years. He read parts of the different iterations of my project to which he replied (extraordinarily swiftly) with the requisite encouragement, advice, and warnings. Similarly, Cemal Kafadar has always observed the project from a distance. At one point he asked me, "Where is the social history?" which question impelled me to reconceptualize my project entirely. Though the answer to the question caused significant delays, I continue to be grateful for the fact that it was posed at all.

Various colleagues have kindly read and commented on parts of the manuscript. I am grateful to Diana Abouali, Zeynep Altok, Aslı Niyazoğlu, Adam Sabra, Ali Yaycıoğlu, and the members of "The Space and Place Seminar" and "The Ottoman Studies Seminar" at the Research Center for Anatolian Civilizations, Istanbul, for their feedback. Three people, none from "the field," read the manuscript in its entirety. Jim Bowley, who allowed me to experiment on him as the "lay reader," wrote a wonderfully relevant and touching review. Robin Fleming, my colleague and "mentor" at the History Department at Boston College, took the interest and time to read all of my work, and to fix my eccentric English and bad punctuation habits. I will always be grateful for her professional support (and gardening tips!). As usual, Shahab Ahmed read yet another version of the manuscript with devotion and attention. Since he too lived with the barber for a long time, I am thankful to him that he was able to sustain interest and still ask pertinent questions till the very end. My indebtedness, intellectual and otherwise, to Shahab is historical and foundational: I effectively learned English from him.

There are many colleagues who have lent their support over the years and whose kindness restores my faith in humanity (and in email). I wish to single out Steve Tamari, with whom I had a 14-year professional email correspondence before we even met. He shared with me the notes of his own research and allowed me to "steal" his title, "The Barber of Damascus." Steve's collegiality and generosity are exemplary. Similarly, Zayde Antrim and I have historically shared the "Damascus fever," but we met "properly" only once. Zayde kindly read my work as it evolved and has been a true friend in need. Derin Terzioğlu, whose work I have always admired and whose relationship to "text" is one that I wish to emulate, also came through at very short notice. Michael Cook was an ideal employer and great supporter during a postdoctoral stint at Princeton. Richard Bulliet, my mentor at Columbia University, always inspired.

At Boston College, I am indebted to my students who read parts of the manuscript or helped me in my research. Sandy Williams and Stuart Pike, both wonderful thinkers and writers, read Chapter 2 and helped me edit it. Sophia Moradian turned out to be a fiend of a research assistant: she organized and systematized my digital library with extraordinary efficiency and generated this book's bibliography in no time. These and other students at Boston College have given me much joy and satisfaction in my profession.

I am grateful to Michael Swanton and Kerry Burke at Media Technology Services at Boston College, who helped me with image scanning and tossed around map ideas. However, it was a student, Emma Sobbota, who adapted the busy map of intramural Damascus and made it legible.

This project would not exist had it not been for the unique manuscript of the barber's history lodged at the delightful Chester Beatty Library, where the curator of the Islamic collections, Elaine Wright, lent her cooperation and support throughout. At the same library, I thank Francis Narkiewicz for facilitating the reproduction of images. Jan-Eric Ericson of the National Library of Sweden delivered to me what became the book cover image in no time. Andrea Schuler, the Aga Khan Visual Archivist at

MIT Roth Library of Architecture and Planning responded to my online general query for images—reproduced and published gratis—with exemplary efficiency. I am indebted to Gerard Degeorge for permitting me to reproduce an image from his book, and to Dorothée Sack, who has kindly allowed me to adapt her wonderful maps.

A series of small research expense grants from Boston College allowed me to go back to Damascus several times to continue my research and covered some of the expenses related to the research, writing, and publication of this project. I thank the Norma Jean Calderwood Chair in Islamic and Asian Art at Boston College, occupied by Sheila Blair and Jonathan Bloom, for generously underwriting the cost of the illustrations.

Kate Wahl, at Stanford University Press, has been an exemplary editor. The professionalism and efficiency that she, Frances Malcolm, and Tim Roberts have shown made the process relatively painless. I am very grateful to Tom Finnegan for his conscientious but noninterventionist editing. To the two anonymous reviewers I am much obliged. Their observations, I believe, improved the quality of this product, and their encouragement made for an ideal academic exchange of critical helpfulness. Any mistakes in this book are not theirs but solely my own.

My global network of friends who put up with me (and sometimes put me up) have been invaluable for my sustenance and wellbeing over the years. In Cairo, I always found a home with Nabila Masralli and Pascale Ghazaleh. In Montreal, Rania Urabi suffered the cold with me. In Berlin, Dyala Hamzah, Zafer Yenal, and Farish Nour were social and intellectual partners in crime. In Istanbul, Rachel Goshgarian, Sofia Georgiadou, Galina Tirnanic, Ekin Tuşalp, and Leah Long danced the nights away with me. In New York, Joseph Massad, Lale Üner, Moeen Lashari, Nisreen Alami, Hadi Ghaemi, Mahnua Leng, and Josh Zinner allowed me into their homes and hearts. Sarahleah Whitson (in Cairo, New York, Amman, and wherever else we have met in this world) has been a constant and consistent surrogate sister since I left home in 1986. In London, Izzat Dawazeh, "taken in limited doses," is a constant source of joy, silliness, wit, and even comfort. Finally, Johannes Walter, Sanja Sever, Diana Abouali, Ilham Khuri-Makdisi, Sahar Bazzaz, and Jim Bowley have given me reason to think of Cambridge-Boston as home.

My family in Jordan has always managed to send me love, empathy, support, and humor—even from thousands of miles away. My sisters, Azza and Luma, have got me through the toughest of times by making me laugh (often at myself). My father has always trusted my judgment, and my mother never tired of showering me with unconditional love. This family anchors me in the world.

Note on Language and Transliteration

All of the main primary sources used in this study are texts written in a combination of classical Arabic and various colloquial Levantine dialects. Aside from where immediately relevant, I have not noted colloquial morphology and syntax; however, I have rendered obvious colloquial vocabulary in bold typeface. Standard transliteration systems for classical Arabic are ill suited to rendering the sounds of Levantine colloquial, for which there is no standard transliteration system. I have attempted to use standard classical transliteration as the basis when transliterating Levantine colloquial but have departed therefrom to employ simple phonetic transliterations in bold font for colloquial sounds that the standard classical transliteration system cannot convey. These should be transparent to the reader familiar with Levantine dialects.

THE BARBER OF DAMASCUS

Introduction

A book in a dream means power.
He who sees a book in his hand in a dream will acquire power.

`ABD AL-GHANĪ AL-NĀBULUSĪ (D. 1731)[1]

It is not fitting that anyone who possesses even a small amount of knowledge should allow himself to be forgotten.

SHAMS AL-DĪN MUḤAMMAD IBN ṬŪLŪN AL-DIMASHQĪ (D. 1546)[2]

THIS BOOK ARISES from a footnote—note 13 on page 188 of Tarif Khalidi's book *Arabic Historical Thought in the Classical Period*—upon which I chanced more than a decade and a half ago.[3] Before I divulge the contents of that fateful footnote, a bit of background is in order. Envious of the feats of modern European historiography, which had managed famously to uncover the history and reconstruct the worldview of the sixteenth-century Friulian miller, Menocchio,[4] I set out to retrieve "commoners" from the history of the medieval Levant (by which I mean Bilād al-Shām—the area covering the present day states of Syria, Lebanon, Jordan, Palestine, and Israel, (see Map 1). Individuals wiser than me warned of the monumental obstacles ahead: our main (perhaps only) sources for the medieval period are histories written by *`ulamā'* (singular,*`ālim*, scholars of religion, who are equivalent to today's academics), largely about themselves and for themselves. The social historian, then, is left with only one textual window to the social history of the medieval past, and it is a window with a very limited aperture. Obstinately, and all-too-naïvely, I decided to prove that "*`ulam*ology" could not possibly be "almost all the social history that we will ever have."[5] I spent a year canvassing the historiographical production of medieval Levantine *`ulamā'* in the hope of delivering up the commoners, but to no avail. I was in a state of dejection when I chanced upon footnote

13, which mentions "'popular' historiography [by] . . . the 18th-century Damascene barber or the 18th-century South Lebanon farmer al-Rukaynī." Barber historian! Farmer historian! I immediately resolved to desist, once and for all, from lamenting the irretrievability of medieval Arabic-Islamic commoners—and from indulging in bouts of "source envy" of the European historians—and switched to eighteenth-century Ottoman Levantine history. Here, I discovered that the Damascene barber and South Lebanon farmer(s) were not the only commoner or unusual authors to write contemporary history; such chronicles were also written in the eighteenth-century Levant by a couple of soldiers, by a court clerk, by Greek Orthodox and Greek Catholic priests, by a Samaritan scribe, and by a merchant.

While I was conducting my research on these histories, there was an extraordinary occurrence: a serendipitous discovery of the original and unique manuscript of the chronicle of the aforementioned Damascene barber: Shihāb al-Dīn Aḥmad Ibn Budayr (fl. 1762).[6] The version that I—and the rest of the field—had been using is one bowdlerized and significantly altered in language and content by a scholar in the late nineteenth century. Given that Ibn Budayr's chronicle is the only one in Arabic-Islamic history known to have been composed by a barber, the discovery was most auspicious. I had finally found my Menocchio, or his Arabic-speaking Muslim counterpart.

Ibn Budayr was a barber who lived and coiffed—and, doubtless, circumcised and healed—in the prestigious neighborhood of Bāb al-Barīd at the very center of the walled city of Damascus, the most important urban metropolis in the Ottoman Levant. He was born into markedly humble circumstances: into a family of porters who lived as far away from privilege as can be, at the extreme outskirts of the extramural city. By means unknown to us, the porter's son somehow came to be apprenticed to a fashionable city barber who cut the hair and shaved the beards of some of the city's most illustrious saintly and scholarly figures. Ibn Budayr ended up servicing the same cultured and up-market clientele. Ibn Budayr's striking upward and centerward social trajectory might help in explaining his even more extraordinary achievement: the fact that he wrote a book. Thus, at the heart of this study is the "life and work," the aspirations and fears, of this remarkable eighteenth-century Damascene craftsman.

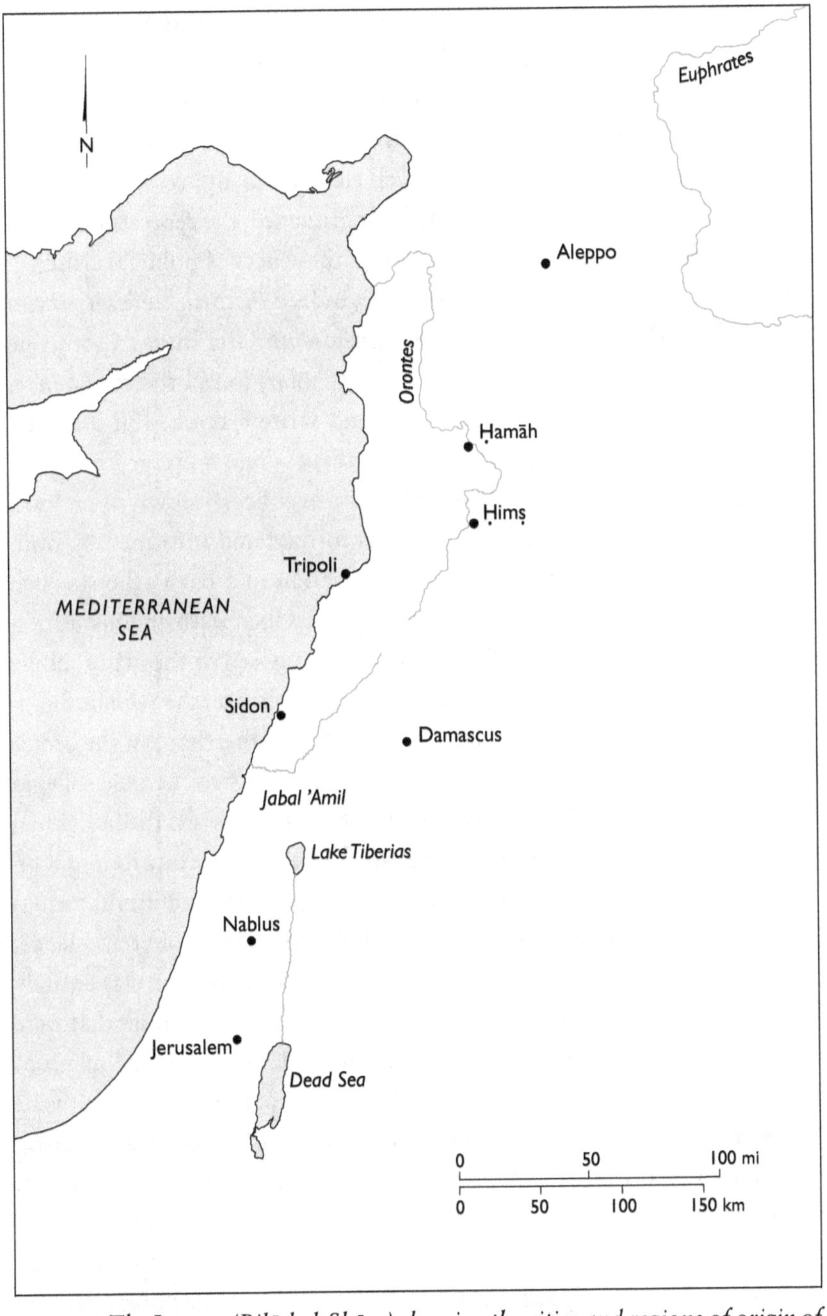

MAP 1. *The Levant (Bilād al-Shām) showing the cities and regions of origin of the chroniclers. Source: Esri data and maps, 2012.*

The Damascene barber lived in a highly urban environment and hobnobbed with men of letters.[7] He held conformist religious views, and his general social vision was markedly conservative. Nonetheless, he identified himself as a poor man—as one of "the small people"—and viewed his society as one composed of a tyrannical rich and an oppressed poor.[8] He was angry at, and in his chronicle actively criticized, the representatives of the state and the "notables." Even though these acts of political criticism might appear audacious enough, his true, indeed *historic*, audacity lay in the simple and remarkable fact of his *authorship*.[9] Ibn Budayr, someone without the training or certification of a scholar, found the confidence, the *authority*, to behave like an *`ālim* and write a book. Ibn Budayr's most remarkable act of mobility was his trespass into a literary, cultural, and discursive domain where no barber had ever been known to set foot.

Ibn Budayr's intellectual cosmos was formed and informed by both the oral and the written.[10] The barber's location in a barbershop, which in the Ottoman world was inextricably intertwined with the institution of the coffeehouse, allowed Ibn Budayr to be exposed to the art of public storytelling and other performative oral genres, such as the recounting of traditional epics. But the location of his master barbershop, in the center of the walled city of Damascus, where most of the city's venerable colleges stood, also permitted Ibn Budayr familiarity not only with the individual scholars who taught and studied there but also with their culture, and with their products—namely, written texts. Thus Ibn Budayr's cultural formation was neither "high" nor "low" (although sometimes, for convenience, these terms will be used in this study). Rather, his existence was entirely *appropriative*: he used and integrated disparate literary traditions that were at his disposal. This might also explain Ibn Budayr's "relaxed" relationship to text as well as to language. Ibn Budayr mixed the demotic with the higher registers of the Arabic language without anxiety or fear of being in violation of any rules.[11] He spoke, and reveals himself to us, in his own voice, in a book that he freely authored of his own will and in his own way.

The fact that Ibn Budayr wrote a chronicle, instead of some other type of book, is also significant since the genre by its very nature permits a high degree of *self-authorship*. Not only did the barber use the chronicle's capaciousness to portray himself in a certain "fashion," but he also used some of its other features to insinuate himself into the social worlds of the scholars and saints of his city. Indeed, the chronicle, at the hands of the barber, turned out to be a productive tool for social jockeying. Thus, just as Ibn Budayr managed to find for himself a physical location among the scholars in downtown Damascus, his literary appropriation constituted a self-instatement into their social world. Ibn Budayr, in other words, seems to have heeded the advice of the famous sixteenth-century historian, topographer, and scholar Ibn Ṭulūn quoted at the beginning of this chapter. The barber possessed some knowledge and subsequently did not allow himself to be forgotten. He authored himself.[12]

The barber's entry into the chronicle was not so benign. The mere entry of a craftsman into the scholarly form of the chronicle changes the very nature of the genre. Ibn Budayr admits to the text formal and literary features that are unaccustomed in the chronicle; he also introduces topics and protagonists that are equally unusual. The result is a subversion of the intention of the genre. In a significant departure from the conventions of the scholarly chronicle, under the authorship of the barber the state no longer functions as the raison d'être and cause célèbre of the genre. Ibn Budayr subjects the representatives of the state and the notables to merciless questioning and scathing critique. Although not radical in his vision of society—indeed, he implicitly invokes an older, more pristine social and moral order—he turns the chronicle from a complacent text into a platform of interrogation. Viewed from this perspective, Ibn Budayr and his chronicle may be seen to anticipate a definitive new figure of the nineteenth century and his equally definitive text: the public intellectual of al-Nahḍa (the Arab Renaissance) and his newspaper article.

A significant part of this book is a search for the sources of authority of the barber, what he did with that authority, how he used it, and to what end (Chapters 1, 2, and 5). This study will also trace what happened to the barber's authority (that is, his book) after his death, and how it was, in turn, appropriated (Chapter 6). But beyond the barber, this book is a pursuit of something larger. Ibn Budayr's appropriation is not singular, but rather a *symptom* of a phenomenon. He was not the only one who poached the genre of the chronicle for his own purposes in the eighteenth century. He was joined by other new authors whose social backgrounds were quite unusual for the genre of the chronicle: a couple of Shīʿī farmers from southern Lebanon, a Samaritan scribe from Nablus, a Sunni court clerk from Ḥimṣ, a Greek Orthodox priest from Damascus, and two soldiers also from Damascus. Thus, even though the core of this project is about the life and work of the barber, and about his chronicle's subsequent reception and bowdlerization, this study is also about an apparently unprecedented and historically significant social and literary phenomenon of the emergence of a group of unusual historians (Chapters 1 and 3). The barber, the farmers, the clerk, the scribe, the priest, and the soldiers were all representatives of this phenomenon, which I am calling "*nouveau* literacy."

NOUVEAU LITERACY IN THE EIGHTEENTH-CENTURY LEVANT

Nouveau literacy, then, is about the arrival of authors of unusual backgrounds into the space that had historically been arrogated to the *`ulamā'*, literally, "the people who know." These new authors chose to write contemporary chronicles, that is, records of the events that took place in their own lifetimes. Here, I will offer the conceptual contours of this phenomenon by considering the relationship between the social and literary dimensions of the genre, the intention behind and the conditions that facilitated its appropriation by these "random" individuals, and the connection between literacy and appropriation of texts. I propose that the emergence of these new historians is not necessarily connected with an increase in the level of technical literacy, the "mere" knowledge of how to read and write. Rather, it is a socially impelled appropriation connected to a subtly and significantly different quality: *cultural* literacy.

This study proceeds on the assumption that texts, or rather genres, are socially apportioned.[13] That is to say, the production and consumption of certain genres falls broadly within the purview of specific social groups, whereby these groups address their concerns and desires in the appropriate discursive space and simultaneously use the genre as a means for self-presentation and/or preservation.[14] The Arabic chronicle is about the establishment and legitimization of the Islamic order.[15] Organized annalistically by the Islamic Hijrī date,[16] the main subject of the chronicle is the accomplishments (and predicaments) of Muslim rulers whose very existence, and hence preservation, ensures the continuing existence of an Islamic polity.[17] The *`ulamā'* were the other buttress of that political order. As the bearers of Islamic knowledge, the guardians of religious and moral values, and the promulgators and executioners of Islamic law, their very existence was predicated on that of the state. As such, it is natural that the religious scholars would emerge as the primary authors of the chronicle.[18]

But a genre does not just engender a set of power relations and politics. Inscribed in it are specific literary demands having to do with arrangement, language, registers, and content that reflect the conditions of production and consumption, and the social practices surrounding the genre. The chronicle as a form was therefore initially located in the social space between *`ālim* and prince. In other words, it was *elite*. More significantly, it was *scholarly*. And it was intensely bound up with the authority of the preservers of Islamic knowledge (Chapter 4).

Given the entanglement of the chronicle with Muslim scholars, the coincidence of chronicles being authored by so many people of such different backgrounds in the eighteenth century is striking. Some of these new authors come from contexts that are not associated with literacy at all, such as the barber and the two soldiers. And if they come from literate traditions, such as two Shī`ī famers in southern Lebanon,[19] a Greek Orthodox priest from Damascus, or a Samaritan scribe from Nablus, their products are distinctly different within their respective traditions. They either represent an unprecedented attempt at chronicle writing (the Shī`ī farmers) or a new kind of participation in a historical discourse that is uncharacteristically non-ecclesiastical and is concerned with mundane and daily occurrences in their respective locations (the chronicle of the Damascene priest is set in Damascus and that of the Samaritan scribe in Nablus). It is not so much that non-*`ulamā'* never wrote chronicles before the eighteenth century, as we will see many singular examples in a later chapter. Rather, the issue is that in the eighteenth century *so many* non-*`ulamā'* wrote chronicles at around the same time. In other words, this is a phenomenon of *convergence* by people of diverse backgrounds on the genre of the chronicle in the eighteenth-century Levant.

Before drawing out the significance of the emergence of these new historians, a clarification about their social backgrounds is necessary. These authors come from backgrounds that are not dominant either socioeconomically, such as the barber, the farmers, the soldiers, and the judicial court scribe; or religiously and culturally, such as the priest, the Samaritan scribe, and the Shīʿīs. However, as we shall see, none of them were either entirely poor or powerless. Indeed, some of them managed to acquire riches and/or high positions. This brings me to my next important point: the phenomenon of eighteenth-century non-*ʿulamāʾ* chronicles is precisely about social mobility.

The Ottoman eighteenth century was a time of unusual opportunity, both economic and political. It was a time of fiscal and political devolution from the center, Istanbul, to the provinces. This devolution resulted in two crucial novelties: semi-independent rule and (almost) private ownership of land. As such, the eighteenth century could be legitimately seen as a new order, a time of social flux, in which political and social power was redistributed and led to the formation of new provincial households. The influx of wealth into Damascus is evidenced by the erection of magnificent public buildings as well as the construction of private palatial residences. Thus the change of Damascus' cityscape reflected the new wealth and power of a new elite. As new households and, subsequently, patronage networks came to be forged in the region, all these authors in our sample experienced or stood to experience entry into these networks and an amelioration in social position—whether as individuals or as members of a collective. Consequently, their authorship is impelled by, and was a product of, their desire to negotiate for or in new social positions. This was a moment of an extraordinary "opening" of a social structure in flux, and people took advantage of it. For such social transactions, the contemporary chronicle was strikingly suitable. Because it is a record of the events surrounding the author, the chronicle is author-centric and allows ample room for the self. Though by no means intended to be autobiographical, the contemporary chronicle enables the author to place himself in the world and in his present. In other words, it constitutes a potent instrument of self-fashioning. Hence these new authors whose positions had just improved or who had the opportunity to do better wrote *history* (*tārīkh*) to immortalize or display their now "new and improved" selves, but they wrote history as a *contemporary* document in order to seize the chance for, or to consolidate their hold on, a better position in their present. It is precisely the opportunity for, or the proof of, tangible betterment that motivated these new chroniclers. The new authors understood the words of their contemporary saint and scholar, `Abd al-Ghanī al-Nābulusī: a book meant power (or a desire and/or demonstration of it).

It is worth clarifying a few issues regarding those authors in our sample who do not come from traditions of literacy, such as the barber and the soldiers. It is important to remember that these new historians wrote books intended for *publication* (as opposed to private records—although there is one chronicler in this study whose text seems to have been intended as a private diary). A sense of how remarkable this is may be gained by juxtaposing this fact with our own time. Even by the standards of today, in the age of mass literacy, how many barbers or soldiers attempt (or dare?) to write academic, or even popular, books? I ask this question because the production of books by new groups is usually associated with the rise of technical literacy—the knowledge of how to read and write—among these groups. One of the main points of this study is precisely to dissociate book authorship from technical literacy. Such literacy is a precondition to consume a book, but it does not, in and of itself, provide the wherewithal to produce one. The production of a book necessitates the writer being confident that her authority is credible and receivable. She must be certain of a market for her product and confident that her role as a producer (as opposed to a mere consumer) is accepted as such. In short, this phenomenon is not about the sudden rise of literacy. Rather, it is about the *rise of authority* in new social groups. More specifically, it is about the rise of authority in the field of history among seemingly "random" individuals, who come from different backgrounds and who do not have any connection to one another. Somehow, there was something about the eighteenth century that gave license to a barber and a couple of soldiers to author books. As for the issue of technical literacy, whose measurement is notoriously difficult and inaccurate for the pre-print age, this study both assumes and will demonstrate that there was always a literate part of the population outside the circles of the *`ulamā'*.[20] Consequently, the phenomenon of the emergence of new historians has something to do with another kind of literacy: a cultural literacy. When we consider the whole sample of authors mentioned above—whether they come from literate traditions or not—the mere fact that they chose to write in a genre that is not originally theirs and that is historically associated with the *`ulamā'* betokens a knowledge on their part, no matter how rudimentary, of the culture of scholars and of the rules and regulations of scholarship that are woven into and demanded by the genre of the chronicle itself. Given that they do not come from the particular Islamic tradition of chronicle writing, these authors are therefore *recently literate* in the genre of the chronicle, and in the culture that surrounds its production and consumption. They have recently arrived (or are about to arrive) in new social positions and also in the particular literary or cultural sphere. In short, they are *nouveau* literates.

My coinage of the term *nouveau literacy* is clearly inspired by the expression "nouveau riche," which I am stripping of its derogatory implications and am using to denote new cultural wealth. In their arrival on the stage of historiography, these new historians are arrivistes in that they sport old literary habits and new cultural wealth. They come in with their "old baggage" and with their particular and distinctive linguistic heritage and literary traditions, which are unusual in scholarly forms such as the chronicle. The resultant gaffes and faux pas committed by these authors are not exclusive to form but also extend to content: some of these new authors unabashedly admit to the chronicle things that are not traditionally sanctioned. In their appropriation of the scholarly form and in their adding special seasoning from their own backgrounds, these authors offer not the accustomed chronicle written by an *`ālim* but something entirely new.

IBN BUDAYR'S *EVENTS OF DAMASCUS*

The published chronicle of the Damascene barber Shihāb al-Dīn Aḥmad Ibn Budayr is one of the sources most widely used by modern historians of the eighteenth-century Levant. The chronicle was edited and abridged in the late nineteenth century by the Damascene scholar Muḥammad Sa`īd al-Qāsimī (d. 1900), who, in his own words, "refined" the language and content of the chronicle. The effect of al-Qāsimī's editorial strategies on the narrative of the barber is the subject of Chapter 6. Here, it suffices to say that al-Qāsimī renamed Aḥmad Ibn Budayr by according him the sobriquet "al-Budayrī," which is the name under which the barber has subsequently become known. Al-Qāsimī's recension of Ibn Budayr's chronicle was edited by Aḥmad `Izzat `Abd al-Karīm and published in

Damascus in 1959 under the title *Ḥawādith Dimashq al-yawmiyya* ("The Daily Events of Damascus"), with the author given as Aḥmad al-Budayrī al-Ḥallāq.[21] The present study will use the original text, of which an apparently unique manuscript exists in the Chester Beatty collection in Dublin, Ireland. I will refer to the author as Ibn Budayr, the name that appears on the title page of the original unedited manuscript, discarding the sobriquet "al-Budayrī" that al-Qāsimī bestowed on the barber of Damascus.[22]

Ibn Budayr's chronicle covers the years 1154–1175 AH, that is, 1741–1762 CE. The framing unit of dating in the chronicle is the Hijrī year. The author does not include monthly entries, so the chronicle remains strictly annalistic. Once Ibn Budayr establishes the year, the chronicle is entirely event-led: he chooses what he deems to be worthy of recording and records the date and day of the event. The exception to this trend is the annual announcement of the advent of the month of Ramadan, probably on account of its religious significance as the month of fasting.

As is the habit of the genre, Ibn Budayr's history is overwhelmingly concerned with news of political import: the appointment and dismissal of rulers and other authority figures, and skirmishes and armed conflict on the streets of Damascus and the surrounding regions. Strongly local in flavor, Ibn Budayr's chronicle very rarely reports on political events beyond the Levant. The usual repertoire that constitutes the stuff of history is also found in the barber's chronicle: natural disasters, epidemics, unusual weather phenomena, and miraculous occurrences.

Strikingly recurrent in Ibn Budayr's chronicle—sometimes placed immediately after the annual entry—are lists of prices of produce and staple foods. Because food prices are a measure of the functioning of the market place and an indication of the justice of rule (or lack thereof), chroniclers have historically paid attention to food prices. In Ibn Budayr's case, the listing of prices is almost obsessive, and usually followed by a call for succor from God.

Unlike some chronicles of the period, the barber's chronicle does not include regular reports on the news of the annual pilgrimage caravan, and its progress to and back from Mecca, or the "Egyptian Treasury," which is the annual caravan carrying the "revenue" that the Egyptian province owed to Istanbul. The author reserves the mention of these caravans to moments when things go awry with them, as when a pilgrims' caravan is raided by nomads or afflicted by a natural disaster. We shall see how Ibn Budayr's exclusion of regular and recurring "normal" events lends his text a special urgent tone and a different political message.

Unlike the chronicles of the other nouveau literates in our sample, Ibn Budayr's text closely mimics the *`ālim* chronicle in that it includes biographies (*tarjama*, pl. *tarājim*). In the event of the death of a scholar or a saint—and in some instances family members and friends—he includes a biography of the deceased in the accustomed scholarly form and style. We shall see later that he puts the biography into good use. Also, as with the scholarly chronicle, Ibn Budayr offers poetic musings to commemorate special events, such as his visits to shrines or his picnic outings.

His barbershop must have functioned as a place of gossip about the goings on in the town. The other chroniclers in this study rarely relay news of sexual indiscretions, but Ibn Budayr does not shy away from reporting infidelities and juicy tales of sexual jealousies.[23] However, more often than not, his reports on sexual stories are in the vein of demonstrating the collapse of the moral order and are not impelled by the sheer joy of gossip.

It should be noted that Ibn Budayr's text does not include a beginning and a conclusion. Though the absence of a conclusion may be indicative of the sudden death of the author, the absence of the usual preamble (*khuṭba*) suggests that a part of the text went missing after the completion of the composition. Further, the author mentions having written a chronogram on the occasion of his son's death, "which has been placed at the beginning of [t]his book,"[24] but no such verses appear in the beginning of the book. This further confirms that the history is partly missing. Interestingly, because the bowdlerizer al-Qāsimī's rendition covers the exact same years and events, it seems likely that the editor used the same manuscript that I am using in this study (and in which, as we shall see, some marginal notes might have been al-Qāsimī's), or an identical copy of it. It should be noted that even though the original text ends in the year 1176 AH, the editor al-Qāsimī rightly claims that the barber added an extra year by mistake and ends his version with the year 1175 AH.

I have often been asked why I believed the barber—more precisely, why I believed that the author was a barber and not just an impersonator, an author pretending to be a groomer. My answer is, "There is just not enough razor and scissors in it."[25] Had the author been an impersonator, he would have set up the barbershop as a stage for the narration and included in it everything one expects from a barber and in a barbershop. We will see throughout that the barber's references to the craft and to his shop are entirely incidental. Ibn Budayr's focus is overwhelmingly on his city, and the events (and deaths) that took place in it.

The credibility of the barber himself with regard to the events that he narrates is attested by modern historians, who have made extensive use of his history as a source, and who have cross-checked the barber's information with other sources.[26] As is the case with any premodern text, Ibn Budayr records what seems to us incredible and fantastical, such as miracles of saints. However, it is very clear that in every instance of such "unusual" occurrences, Ibn Budayr is reporting from hearsay—although, of course, he himself is credulous of the stories.[27] The barber does show a proclivity toward exaggeration in tone, which is enhanced by his copious use of rhymed prose; but Ibn Budayr knows when to insert his emphatic eyewitness *I* when he thinks that his report might be taken with a grain of salt ("I saw with my own eyes al-Marja flooded as though it was a part of a sea.")[28]

Like in any other text (and because a text is, by definition, a public space), there is a great degree of active engagement in self-editing and self-fashioning by the author. A major theme in this study is the extent to which Ibn Budayr uses his chronicle to portray himself in the most complimentary fashion. We shall see how the barber is keen to show off his connections with the town's illustrious scholarly elite. However, what concerns me is not so much the veracity of his telltales about interactions with famous scholars and miracle-working saints but the very fact of his attempt to fashion himself, and the methods he employs to do so. Having stated this, I find no reason not to believe the barber. We will see that he has friends, high and low, and he accords them equal amounts of respect. In short, although Ibn Budayr is eager to emphasize his social strengths and hide his social weaknesses, he does not seem to alter or grossly misrepresent reality, at least not intentionally. After all, Ibn Budayr did not write in a vacuum and did not write anonymously. He envisioned an audience at whom he pitched the history of his city, which was also his audience's city. His lies would have been immediately found out, and the barber was no fool.

CHAPTER 1

The Disorders of a New Order

The Levant in the Long Eighteenth Century

It is worth reiterating that it is not so much the literacy of the eighteenth-century barber that is surprising, it is his authority. This chapter investigates the sources of the authority of our nouveau literates. What is it that impelled or gave confidence to a barber, a Greek Orthodox priest, a couple of Shī`ī farmers, a Samaritan scribe, a Ḥimṣi court scribe, and a couple of Damascene soldiers to *write*? What is it in the social and cultural landscape of the eighteenth-century Levant that prompted these people, whose professions, strictly speaking, fell outside the learned professions and especially history writing, to write chronicles? In short, this chapter is about nouveau literacy as a social phenomenon.

In search of the sources of the nouveau literates' authority, I focus on Damascus, the city in which the barber was born, and which was undeniably his own. Ibn Budayr's possession of the city is evident in his marking of the city's features: its neighborhoods, streets, bazaars, bathhouses, coffeehouses, shops, colleges, and mosques. In his chronicle, a cartography emerges in which the city is not just a list of places but a veritable habitat. It is home to all kinds of people: notables, scholars, merchants, soldiers, mystics, shopkeepers, prostitutes, and possessed individuals. It is a city where natural beauty and divine grace abound, but it is also a place of mysterious murders and curious suicides, of immoral revelry and marital infidelities. It is the hometown of the great Sufi thinker `Abd al-Ghanī al-Nābulusī, the poet laureate Bahlūl, and the impossibly seductive prostitute Salamūn.[1] Despite Ibn Budayr's anger over and frustration with the corruption and disorder in the city, the barber narrates his Damascus lovingly, proudly, and protectively.

Damascus is important not only because it is the barber's home. It happens to be one of the five most important cities in the Ottoman Empire and a chief provincial capital. It is the center of Ottoman rule in the region, and a recipient of imperial orders, benefits, and personnel. It is the node from

FIGURE 1. A View of Eighteenth-Century Damascus. *The image shows the centrality of the Umayyad Mosque. Oil painting by an anonymous artist. Source: Gerard Degeorge,* Damascus. *Translated from French by David Radzinowics (Paris: Flammarion, 2004).*

FIGURE 2. Damascus from Above Salahyeh. *Source:* Syria, the Holy Land, Asia Minor, &c. Illustrated. In a Series of Views Drawn from Nature by W. H. Bartlett, William Purser &c. With Descriptions of the Plates by John Carne *(London, Paris, and America: Fisher, Son, & Co., 1836).*

which imperial power is distributed and competed for. Thus, Damascus functioned as a microcosm of the empire and often mirrored its capital, Istanbul. In addition to its political significance, Damascus' cultural and social (hence, economic) wealth was abundant. Historically one of the most important knowledge centers in the Islamic world, in the eighteenth century it became the point of departure of the northern pilgrimage route to Mecca. In these capacities, Damascus was the center of religiously and intellectually motivated traffic. For all of these reasons, the first place to look for the sources of authority in the eighteenth-century Levant, even the authority of "unimportant" nouveau literates, is the Ottoman provincial capital par excellence, Damascus, in which a great deal was happening.

The Levantine eighteenth century represented a reconfigured social and political map, a new order of sorts. This order was constituted around the emergence of new households and networks, which afforded fresh opportunities to individuals and groups, and through which many experienced a change in social position or status. I trace the contours of this order by exploring the socioeconomic and political processes that undergirded it, and I locate in this new order a changed urban topography. It is inside the city of Damascus itself that I look for the manifestations of this new social topography not only in an altered cityscape of exhibitionism and violence but also in a more public sociability exemplified in a culture of the outdoors. This (more) public culture is evident in ostentatious buildings, some in imperial style, and in the visibility of new segments of society, such as women and minorities. In the eyes of contemporaries, including our barber, these changes represented not a new order but a condition of outright "disorder." I argue that the chronicles of the nouveau literates constitute part and parcel of this social and cultural change, as a literary disorder of the new order.

The barber and all the other new historians in our sample benefited from the changes in the region, whether as individuals or as members of a larger community. This enhancement in status afforded these individuals the confidence to celebrate, even flaunt, their rise, and it raised the stakes considerably. In a new position there was much more to lose. Whether to count their blessings, issue rebukes, or complain about the vicissitudes of time, these nouveau literates wrote chronicles to negotiate in a changed world. Having experienced social mobility, and prompted by hope and fear in their new positions, these authors used the publicness of the text to negotiate and exhibit their altered situations. Consequently most of their texts were public displays, inexpensive "monuments" to match the new urban architecture itself.

A RESHUFFLE IN THE SOCIAL TOPOGRAPHY

Despite (or perhaps because of) military defeat and territorial loss, the Ottoman Empire in the long eighteenth century has come to be seen as constituting a new order.[2] Politically, the clearest manifestation of this phenomenon is the externalization of the authority of the sultan to households outside his own. The capital city witnessed the rise of "vizier-pasha" households,[3] while the provinces saw the rise of powerful local gubernatorial families.[4] In the province of Damascus, local rule came tinged with a dynastic flavor. For much of the century, the al-`Aẓm family ruled the province with the exhibitionism, pageantry, and panache of a royal household.[5]

In many ways, the al-`Aẓm family represented a new creature. And the new creature came with a new fiscal deal: the *mālikāne*, a system of tax farming, which almost amounted to private land ownership.[6] The beneficiaries of this system were the governors and other members of the local elite, whether *`ulamā'* or commercial families. Competition over the purchase of rights over these tax farms, auctioned to the highest bidder, was the order of the day. "Wealth pulls along more wealth," as the Arabic proverb goes[7]; those who were able to offer advances for a *mālikāne* found generous reward.[8] Thus, in seeking to explain the eighteenth-century phenomenon of the rise of the notables (*a`yān*), scholars have determined that the new tax-farming system constituted an important economic basis that facilitated the social and political dominance of new figures and households.

Another economic factor that seems to have contributed to the changes in the eighteenth-century political landscape is the intensification of global trade because of European demand for cash crops such as cotton, silk, and grain. The emergence of port towns at the expense of traditional inland commercial centers reflected a shift in trade patterns toward the sea.[9] The point here, however, is that integration into the world market brought about what is usually expected of the integration into the world market: new avenues for political and economic power. The ascendancy of the tribal strongman al-Ẓāhir al-`Umar (d. 1775) is a case in point.[10] Having monopolized the cotton trade in Palestine, al-`Umar managed to garner the strength—and audacity—to challenge Ottoman rule from his newly fortified costal town of Acre. As we shall see, al-`Umar was ubiquitous in the region and consequently in the chronicles of the time. Often cast as the villain, but sometimes as the good ally—depending on who is reporting—al-`Umar eluded the representatives of Ottoman rule for a long time. Whether the good guy or the bad, al-`Umar rebelled with style,[11] which made him the subject of epiclike narrations of the variety we will encounter in Chapter 5.

The Levantine eighteenth century was also about a new sectarian order, which manifested itself in the rise to prominence of the Greek Catholic community. The origin of these dreaded schismatics—as the Greek Orthodox held them to be—dates back to the late seventeenth century, but their dominance in the subsequent century is intimately intertwined with their active role in the reinvigorated Mediterranean trade. Through conversion to Catholicism, this community sought to free themselves from the control of the Orthodox Patriarchate in Constantinople. Significantly, the community rose at the expense of their former co-religionists the Greek Orthodox, but by the end of the eighteenth century they had also superseded the local Jewish community, especially the Fārḥī family, who were hitherto the preferred custom collectors and financiers.[12]

Thus far, I have described the new order in terms of "rise" and "fall," which are the current terms in modern scholarship. However, these stories of rise and fall should not be seen as isolated trends in an otherwise unchanged society. Rather, I will argue that the emergence of new figures, families, and groups reflected a larger and deeper social flux, in which both the "middling sort" (say, a barber, a farmer, or a minor soldier) and the culturally nondominant (say, a Greek Orthodox priest or a Samaritan scribe) also experienced or stood to experience change in social position. In order to integrate nonnotables into the picture, one must readjust the view such that the focus is less on the fact and identity of the new elite and more on the *mode* and *place* of their operation, that is, on the dynamic of *family patronage* and its base, the elite *household*.[13]

The new order can be viewed as simply one of the appearance and dominance of new families whose households became the nodes and loci of social networks that extended beyond kin. The nature and extent of the power of the household differed according to occupation and social and/or political functions of the family. Whether these were large military-administrative households, smaller wealthy merchants, or distinguished *`ulamā'* families, they were generally rich, fiercely competitive, and decidedly local. However, for the perpetuation of their power, these families needed to cultivate connections further afield in the places that mattered most, often the imperial capital itself.

Although the shenanigans that went on between the local notables and their Istanbul patrons are known to the modern historian, it is the local character of these households that concerns us here. As nodes of social networks, these new households—whether in the provincial capital or in town districts—could not remain afloat solely by clinging to the rope extended to them from the capital city; they needed mooring buoys in their own ports. Notable families formed factions and forged alliances that necessarily crossed social functions and confessional lines. In their capacity as patrons, notables located beneficiaries nearby whose expertise, positions, or services facilitated their own rise, entrenchment, and even cultivation of their style. In other words, patronage, which was solicited from above and extended below, was the name of the game, and the new household necessarily "served as a bridge between elites and non-elites."[14] If lucky, the "non-elite"—say, an artisan, a soldier, or a minor scribe, whether Muslim or not—had the opportunity to be a useful client and become enmeshed in a web of favors and services that would bring him closer to the nodes of powers. Thus, an artisan, craftsman, or member of a nondominant community could participate in and was affected by the social jostling around him; he too had a stake in the new order.

Viewed this way, the emergence of the new notables, the Greek Catholic community, and/or rebellious local leaders cease to be isolated trends, that is, mere epiphenomena. Rather, they can be considered the tip of the iceberg. The famous tales of rise and fall that scholars have narrated to characterize the Levantine eighteenth century both mask and betray a larger phenomenon of social mobility—vertical and lateral—in which the non-elite and non-Muslims participated. In other words, the eighteenth century was about social flux, about a *reshuffling of the social topography.*

A reshuffle in social positions is rarely orderly. Even though the century was a time of opportunity, it was also a time of competition and fear. Many of the chroniclers saw their environment as a sign of God's wrath against the breakdown of the traditional order. It is no wonder that "lack of order" is *the* main theme in the chronicle of our barber, Ibn Budayr.[15] Though a beneficiary of this social flux, the barber never ceases to grumble about the disorders of the new order. Little did he know that he himself was contributing to this disorder. His book, which represents the new voice of the commoner in the field of historiography, was itself a disturbance in the literary order.

URBAN DISORDERS

As the social topography changed, so did the landscape of the city and the citizens' use of its spaces. New wealth and power sometimes exist to be exhibited. Damascenes, like their Istanbuli counterparts, did not shy away from displaying their new riches and social positions for all to see. They too were engaged in the business of *public display.*[16] This exhibitionist trend manifested itself in the erection of new public buildings and private palaces, whose interiors were exquisitely adorned—think the Rockefellers and their New York City family homes. The exhibitionism also extended to bodies as people started taking their assemblies from the privacy of their houses to the publicness of the outdoors. Whether they gathered in elite picnic spots or humbler coffeehouses, eighteenth-century Damascenes, Muslim or not, men or not, rich or not, seemed to spend—or desire to spend—much of their leisure time in public. And just as people competed in the display of power through public consumption, they vied for the control of sources of wealth. Factions coalesced around particular interests, which were often literally fought out on the street.

Violence was also public. Damascus (similar to Cairo and Istanbul) was undergoing a facelift, but not without some scars.

Private Mansions and Public Buildings: A New Cityscape of Power and Display

Perhaps the most apparent indication of the rise of new urban households is the appearance of their *houses* at the center of the walled city near the Umayyad Mosque, the main congregational mosque in the city (Figure 2).[17] As in Istanbul and Cairo, the residential patterns of the elites changed significantly in the eighteenth century.[18] In Damascus, a total of 17 new mansions—each representing a significant outlay of capital—were built inside the city walls in the eighteenth century, in comparison to a single mansion built in the two previous centuries (Map 2).[19] This is not to say there was no private residence building activity in earlier centuries, but it was on a different scale and in other locations. Termed the "Central Rectangle," this intramural space, although historically prestigious for its economic and religious significance, was not a residential area before the eighteenth century.[20] The movement of notable families, some of whom held mercantile interests, into the heart of the city may be indicative of not only their connections to the famous bazaars of the old city but also their will to "colonize" the center. Here lived 19 of the 28 most important Muslim families of Damascus.[21] In other words, in the eighteenth century the center of the walled city of Damascus emerged as a reincarnated residential uptown.

The most famous mansion in the Central Rectangle belongs to the most famous member of the aforementioned gubernatorial dynasty, As`ad Pasha al-`Aẓm (d.1757; Figure 3).[22] The process of the palace's construction, we are told, caused much havoc.[23] The governor had columns and rocks taken from old ruins, recently destroyed structures, and even standing monuments to be recycled into his new palace.[24] One of the buildings whose remnants were reused for this mansion was a ruined mill by the river Bānyās, the excavation for which caused "the river . . . to stop flowing for fully twelve days."[25] Inconvenience to the residents notwithstanding, the gubernatorial family did its utmost to show off. The series of complexes and smaller houses built by the al-`Aẓm family displayed not just new

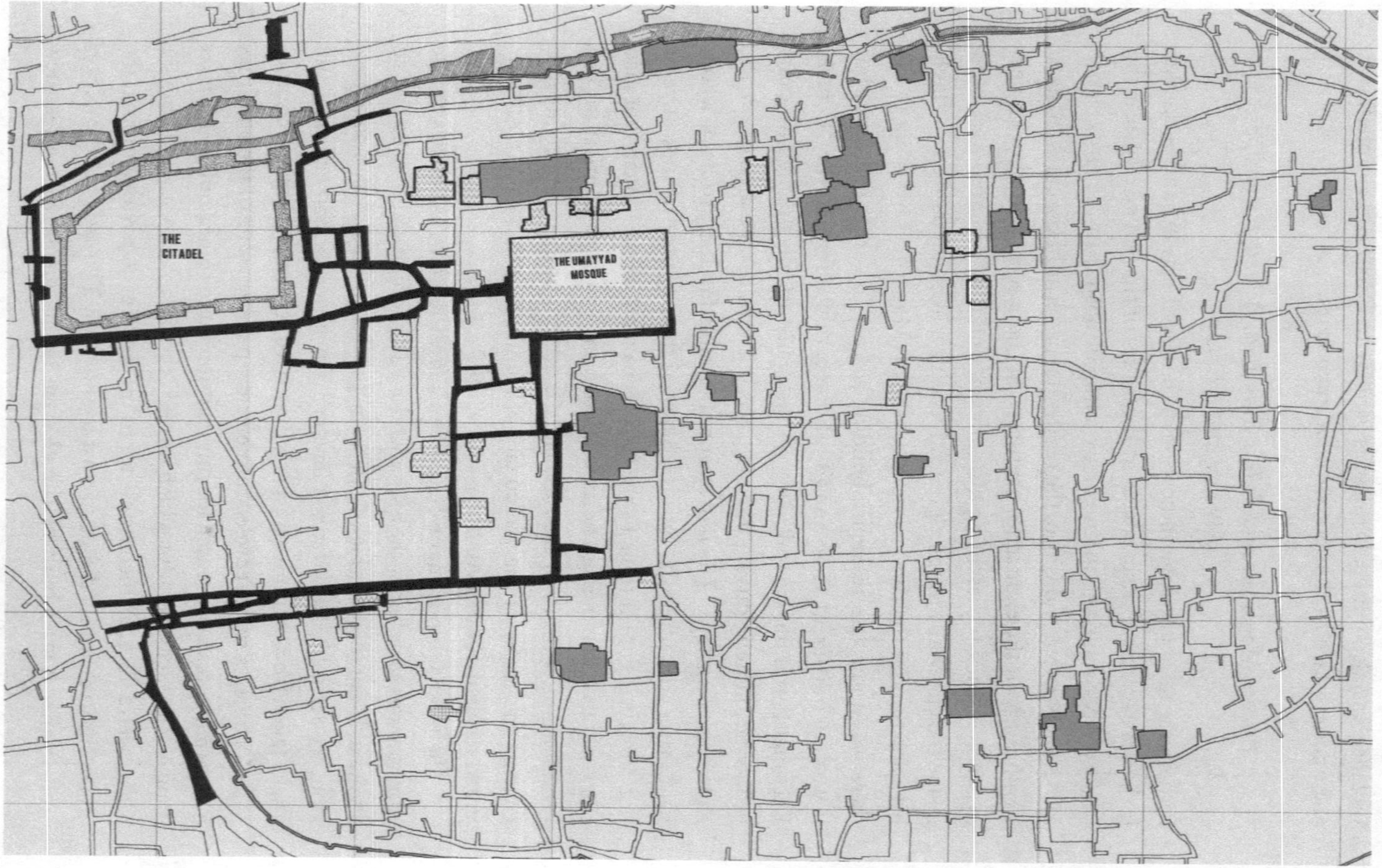
THE CITADEL
THE UMAYYAD MOSQUE

power and wealth but also a distinctive architectural style.[26] Though the architectural landscape of eighteenth-century Damascus awaits further study, there are several indications that the new mansions of the period are of a distinct Damascene style, a reworked version of Mamluk architecture and decoration interspersed with appropriations of both Ottoman and international forms, structures, and techniques.[27]

Inside the mansions of rising families, careful attention was paid to adornment and ornamentation. This is evidenced by the many eighteenth-century Damascene "period rooms" exhibited in international museums, and the painting depicting the exquisite courtyard of one of the grand Damascene houses by the traveler and artist Lord Frederick Leighton (Figure 4).[28] The views of Western travelers[29] and traveling rooms aside, native elites clearly took pride in their homes. The scholar and Sufi Ibn Kannān, the last Levantine `*ālim*-chronicler, characterizes the new reception room that he added to his house, a kind of addition that seems to have been fashionable at the time (Figures 5 and 6), as follows[30]:

In Dhū al-Qa`da, 1130 [1717 CE], the construction of the [reception] hall in our house . . . was completed. It came out to be of extraordinary beauty and grace. It was done in the best of brilliant paints, with ornamented bookcases, extensive calligraphy, the most elegant furniture, colored and decorated plaster, with an octagonal pool and a pretty fountainhead with copious water.[31]

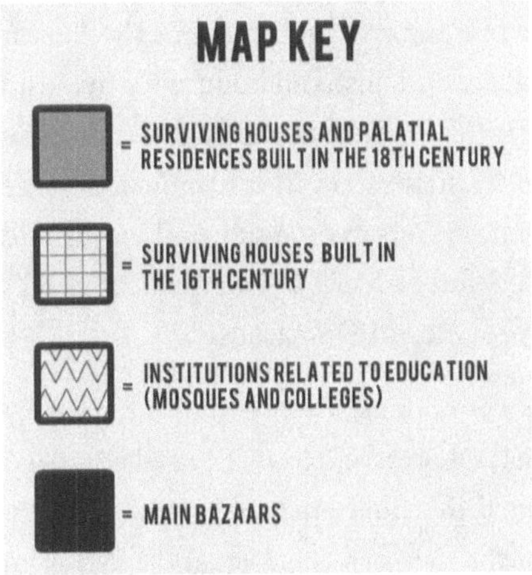

MAP 2. *Damascus, inside the city walls, showing the major bazaars and educational institutions in the city, and the palatial residences that were built in the 18th century. Source: Dorothée Sack,* Entwicklung und Struktur einer orientalisch-islamischen Stadt *(Mainz am Rhein: P. von Zabern, 1989). Scale: 200m/block.*

FIGURE 3. *Al-`Aẓm Palace, viewed from the courtyard. Source: Mohammad al-Asad, 1986. Courtesy of the MIT Libraries, Agha Khan Visual Archive.*

Although adding a reception hall is itself an indication of the acquisition of means to entertain guests at home, the furnishing further illustrates the degree to which the reception room was a showy affair. Ibn Kannān does not forget to mention his recent purchases of luxurious home decorations such as lanterns procured from French traders and copper trays engraved in gold and lapis lazuli.[32] Nor does he omit bragging about the "great house" in Aleppo that his daughter's second husband bought for her (and the fact of her entourage of retainers).[33] Ever attentive to such details, Ibn Kannān is keen to inform his readers/listeners about the opulence of the houses of others. With much interest, he reports the unusual wares and rare delicacies found in the house of `Abd al-Mu`ṭī al-Falāqinsī, who was the brother of the treasurer of the province of Damascus:

As for his [al-Falāqinsī's] house, there was nothing superior to it. It reportedly comprised seven buildings, with abundant flowers and trees, elevated pools and high fountains, and gilded halls painted in astonishing colors with wonderful and masterful engravings. None of the rich men could equal the masterful

FIGURE 4. *The Fārḥī Palace, as depicted in Frederick Leighton's painting* Gathering Citrons or Old Damascus: Jews' Quarter. *Source: Wikimedia Commons.*

design and management of his house, especially during his time as Master of the Army Kitchens. It was unprecedented. He had in his pantry every known variety of spice and condiment: pistachios, almonds, pine nuts, varieties of apricots, raisins, tamarind, pears, and other things. He had a place for sweets, a place for jams, a place for all types of waters, a place for borage, endives, and

FIGURE 5. A Turkish Divan—Damascus. *Source:* Syria, the Holy Land, Asia Minor, &c. Illustrated. In a Series of Views Drawn from Nature by W. H. Bartlett, William Purser &c. With Descriptions of the Plates by John Carne *(London, Paris, and America: Fisher, Son, & Co., 1836).*

cloves, and a place for aromatics, such as sandalwood, ambergris, musk, and other perfumes such as *shāhī*, Meccan, and the like. He had Egyptian mastic, and sweetmeats of pepper, clove, mastic, coffee bean, hazelnut, almond and date. Each storehouse had its own servant. He had a place for medicines—pills, pastes, antidotes and ointments—especially made for him by the apothecaries, so that if a doctor visited him, he could compound the medicine there and then. Everything that he had, including the medicines, was written down in registers on the responsibility of the concerned servant, so that he would not forget. The storehouse for balms contained sacks of roses, lilacs, pumpkins, and the like. Another contained varieties of honey and fat, and so on. Another place contained preserves brought from everywhere including preserves of walnut, pumpkin, citron and watermelon. These are made in the Levant, but if something were unavailable locally, he would bring it from its place of origin, such as preserves of coconut, ginger, and so on—each with its assigned servant. He had a place for strange pickles, such as *zaynī* grapes, and the like. He also had a storehouse for strange musical instruments. It was reported that he had a twin-pipe that produced twenty-four notes, and a box from the Land of the Franks

FIGURE 6. *Reception hall in the Jabri house. Source: Nasser Rabbat, 1983. Courtesy of MIT Libraries, Agh Khan Visual Archive.*

with a moving handle that opened to show a picture and figurines like singing girls playing tambourines and ouds, like ghosts without souls.[34]

There is no evidence to suggest that such a household, with its abundant provisions and wondrous items, represented a mainstream trend in Damascus. However, as in other parts of the empire, the report serves to show the degree to which the notables invested in display and the extent to which their investment was rewarded: they became the talk of the town.[35] It is clear that conspicuous consumption by the rich was the order of the day.

The building activities in Damascus, however, were not limited to private mansions. As in other Arab provinces, Damascene urban notables "increasingly took the initiative in commissioning publicly visible architectural monuments, from mosques to *madrasas* [colleges] to caravanserais to fountains."[36] The caravanserais (*khāns*) of the city are worth emphasizing. Perhaps indicative of reinvigorated international trade, at least six such new commercial establishments were built.[37] Historically, Damascus had not sought to emulate Ottoman imperial architectural styles, but of some of these new caravanserais, especially the one endowed by the same As`ad Pasha Al-`Aẓm, is noteworthy in this regard. Its unprecedented grandness and domed roofing attest to its identification with Ottoman style.[38] The caravanserai of As`ad Pasha, however, did not stand uncontested in its majesty.

Though not in the vicinity of the aforementioned caravanserai, the Qaymariyya mosque/college, built in 1743, competed with the governor's *khān*. The mosque's founder was none other than the Pasha's archrival, the treasurer of the province of Damascus, Fatḥī al-Falāqinsī (d. 1746). Known by his professional title al-Daftardār, he came to be famous for his many public endowments, which earned him the citizens' admiration.[39] The mosque also happens to be one of the few structures that were built according to an Ottoman architectural plan reflecting both al-Daftardār's strong bond to Istanbul[40] and his competition with As`ad Pasha for affection and favor from the imperial capital.

In short, the eighteenth-century intramural Damascus was a new old city. Public endowments and private mansions bespoke of new (and often competing) political and economic power. The change in the cityscape was indicative of new residential patterns in the center of town, and also of distinct architectural styles and rival parties attempting to outdo one another. And though the changed cityscape reflected competing interests, it was unified inasmuch as it was informed by a unitary will: the full and public disclosure and exhibition of the power of the new dominant urban households.

Public Visibility: The Culture of the Outdoors

It is not that the Damascenes had not gone on picnics before,[41] but in the eighteenth century this activity became, in a manner of speaking, discursively institutionalized. Going out on a picnic was now a favorite pastime, and the subject of writing and poetic celebration. Ibn Budayr, our barber-chronicler reported on picnics, both his and others'. Ibn Kannān wrote about having gone on at least 40 outdoor assemblies, some of which lasted several days. After his report on one of these occasions, the entry in his chronicle is telling: "As it is *the habit of the citizens* of Damascus, there were innumerable people [picnicking] at al-Rabwa."[42] Indeed, his

FIGURE 7. Cafés in Damascus, A Branch of the Barada River Flowing Between. *Source:* Syria, the Holy Land, Asia Minor, &c. Illustrated. In a Series of Views Drawn from Nature by W. H. Bartlett, William Purser &c. With Descriptions of the Plates by John Carne *(London, Paris, and America: Fisher, Son, & Co., 1836).*

composition of a topography of Damascus seems to have been an excuse to offer the reader a picnic guide.[43] In later times, this Damascene habit caught the attention of travelers, who depicted outdoor nocturnal revelers reclining under makeshift gazebos as the light of the candles shimmered and reflected in the waters of the Baradā River (Figure 7).[44]

Though Damascus had set promenade areas,[45] it seems that in the eighteenth century all the city was a (picnic) stage. Ibn Kannān would constantly characterize random structures, whether a functioning college or a ruined mosque, as "picnicable" or "agreeable" (*nazīh*).[46] In his capacity as a teacher, he even took his students out for a lesson in the meadows, an act that he claims was unprecedented in the city.[47] The great Sufi saint, `Abd al-Ghanī al-Nābulusī, supposedly in solitary seclusion at the time, would nonetheless join his friends for a banter by the river.[48] Clearly, like their fellow Istanbulis and Caireans, the Damascenes appreciated their verdant city and could not resist enjoying an airy spot or a spectacular view.[49] The celebration of life also occurred in the spaces of the dead. Cemeteries functioned as places of outdoor pleasure and were especially favored by women.[50] Who could deny his daughter the request to pay respects to her dead ancestors? (While at it, the daughter, of course, would secretly go on a rendezvous).

This outdoor culture is but an indication of a relative abandonment of privacy. If people, specifically men, had started showing themselves under the roof of the coffeehouse a couple of centuries earlier, now they did so under the sky. More strikingly, although women had been excluded from coffee shops, they now carried with them not only their coffee cups but also their hookahs and joined the reveling crowds at the banks of the river, something that our barber-chronicler deems unprecedented.[51] Some Christian women, according to our priest-chronicler, "transgressed all limits with their [improper] clothes and headdresses . . . and by smoking tobacco in houses, bathhouses, and orchards, and *even on the river banks while people passed them by*."[52] He adds that

> what is worse, they [the women] would go out to the hill every Saturday with the excuse of visiting graves, and gather in groups to drink *arrack* and wine, and to eat and drink, and take coffee, while the ill-bred men hung about and mixed with them. They engaged in every scandalous behavior, and pranced around, and trespassed all limits.[53]

The infamous prostitute Salamūn—apparently, the number of prostitutes increased in the eighteenth century[54]—even dared to wander about the streets in a state of intoxication.[55] On another occasion, a group of prostitutes paraded the city with hair exposed in gratitude for the recovery from poor health of a lover of one of the ladies of the night.[56] To some, this publicness of women was not just scandalous but a sign of the end times, a disorder in the gender hierarchy. Hence, just as privacy barriers were gradually eroding, so too was woman's place as exclusively limited to the private sphere or indoors.

Women's publicness was only one aspect of eighteenth-century social disorder. Our barber notes a different kind of disorder when he attends a musical performance in a coffeehouse. Much to his chagrin, the Jewish performers sit on stools taller than those on which their Muslim audiences are seated. Although one does not want to read too much into the observation of a single chronicler, the loosening of restrictions over minorities is evidenced in another instance. We are told that As`ad Pasha ordered the lifting of the poll tax from Christians. The Damascene priest who reported the annulment of the poll tax considered the exemption a release from "slavery."[57] He also celebrated the fact that his community was given permission to renovate the most important Christian monastery in Syria, Ṣidnāyā. While on the topic of minority monumentality, it is worth mentioning that among the most impressive palatial residences in the Central Rectangle are two that belonged to the Jewish Fārḥī family, the famous financiers,[58] one of which was depicted by the aforementioned painter, Frederick Leighton (in Figure 4). Like their Muslim counterparts, Christians and Jews became—or were perceived as—more publicly visible, and like their male counterparts, women belonging to these communities spent more time outdoors. These kinds of "public performances" on the part of the Muslim male's "others" led to anxieties about the social and moral order.

Violence and the City

Though Damascus, with its renovated mosques and churches, and its new mansions, palaces, and caravanserais, was considered by someone like Ibn Kannān as one large picnic spot, the city was not only about pleasure. The very same causes for the city's renewal resulted in intermittent and often violent skirmishes on the streets. Here, I show how violence was inscribed in the city, its architecture, and its very topography.

Thus far, in my discussion of the new palatial residences of Damascus, I have focused on the intramural city. For our purposes, eighteenth-century Damascus was actually divided into intramural Damascus, on the one hand, and its southeastern extension, al-Maydān, on the other (Map 3). To tell this story, we need to revisit the political economy of the city.

According to one scholar, the al-`Aẓm family was able to change the political economy, and hence the topography, of the city in service of their commercial interests.[59] The residential revival in the Central Rectangle seems to have been a result of their ability to reorient the city toward the north and west, allowing the inferior-quality grains produced in their lands near Ḥamā to find a market in the city.[60] Simultaneously, the

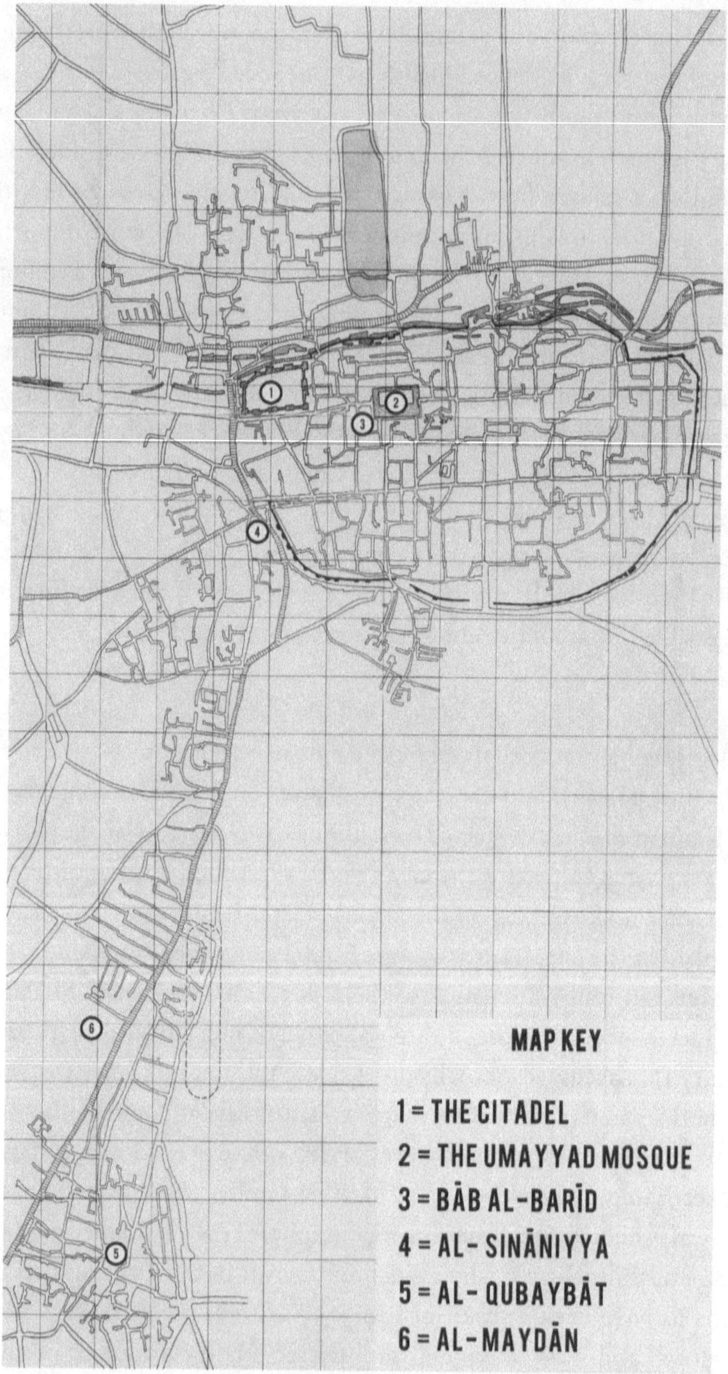

MAP 3. *Damascus and al-Maydān. Source: Dorothée Sack,* Entwicklung und Struktur einer orientalisch-islamischen Stadt *(Mainz am Rhein: P. von Zabern, 1989). Scale: 200m/block.*

al-`Aẓms were attempting to suffocate the grain trade that had traditionally taken place in the south, more specifically, in the extramural al-Maydān quarter. The family's attention to the market of long-distance trade over the market of daily comestible goods usually found in al-Maydān was a cause for discontent among the less privileged, such as craftsmen, peasants, and local traders.

The interests of the al-Maydān quarter were championed by a local paramilitary group, *al-yarliyya* (*yerli* in Turkish, i.e., local).[61] This group originated in the janissary corps: infantry battalions of slaves recruited at a young age and given superior military training. Once the reason behind Ottoman formidability, the janissary corps later lost its identity owing to the penetration of local, nonmilitary elements in the corps and conversely the blending of members of the corps into the local population through the acquisition of civilian jobs.[62] In the words of one scholar, "[t]he *Yarliyya* corps . . . was slowly being identified with Damascenes."[63] It is on behalf of and due to the discontent of the local population that the *yarliyya* janissaries showed insubordination on several occasions.

To balance the influence of the local corps, fresh troops, dubbed *al-qabīqūl* (from Turkish, *kapıkulları*, i.e., slaves of the Porte) were sent from Istanbul in the middle of the seventeenth century. Housed separately in the Citadel, this imperial corps generally served the interests of the governor, except in one case when the two groups joined forces to rebel against Ḥusayn Pasha al-Bustānjī in 1738. More often than not, however, the violence and clashes in Damascus occurred between the two janissary groups, as in the years 1708, 1718, and 1730.[64]

By the 1740s, the aforementioned Fatḥī al-Falāqinsī rose to prominence as the treasurer of the province, a position that was assigned directly from Istanbul and fell outside the power of the governor. In the treasurer, the localist Maydānīs and the *yarliyya* found a powerful patron. He became the representative of the newly underprivileged faction of the city against new interests as represented by the `Aẓms and their newly replenished imperial troops and mercenary contingents.[65]

This conflict was most disruptive during the governorship of As`ad Pasha al-`Aẓm, who in 1746 launched a full-fledged attack on the southern quarters of the city, including al-Maydān. Many leaders of the local corps and their innocent associates were killed and hundreds of houses looted or destroyed.[66] Not surprisingly, the ruling family prevailed. As for the treasurer, his "body was mutilated and dragged in the streets for three days."[67]

Even though this episode sealed the dominance of al-`Aẓms over al-Maydān quarter, the disturbances between the two janissary corps ebbed and flowed for the rest of the century and resulted in two dispatches of more imperial troops from Istanbul. By the end of the century the *yarliyya* corps had been downsized and coopted, and it did not launch any more insurgencies.[68] The last episode of military insubordination under al-`Aẓm rule, however, is telling. During the tenure of `Abd Allāh Pasha al-`Aẓm, which ended in 1807, the rebels were none other than the historical allies of the family and their military arm, the *qabīqūl*.[69] Though the revolt was successfully suppressed, `Abd Allāh Pasha was the last `Aẓm to govern the province of Damascus. In a manner of speaking, the rule of the Damascene "Medici" family was over.

LITERARY DISORDERS

The change in the political economy of the region paralleled a similar trend in the imperial center. The phenomena that we have just surveyed in Damascus were even more intense in Istanbul: the emergence of new households, the colonization of the banks of the Bosphorus with new private mansions, the emergence of a new outdoor pleasure culture accompanied by a change in sartorial fashions, new spectacular public buildings and private mansions, and violence on the streets.[70] But how do these interrelated phenomena reflect themselves on another public space, that is, the public space of the text? It seems that a new economy of literary texts, both historical and poetic, also emerged in this period and refracted and interacted with the new social and political realities.

In the Turkish-speaking world, one of the most noted eighteenth-century literary disruptions can be found in the realm of poetry. The eighteenth century witnessed the entry of vernacular forms into the literary canon. The most famous example is found in the works of the court poet Nedim (d. 1730), who in quotidian Turkish and a poetic form suited for song celebrated the new pleasure culture of the capital city.[71] This poetry was not about the classical private garden and the elite group assembled therein, but about public parks and fountains where regular people mixed, indulged, transgressed, and rejoiced.[72] The new public culture that took place in a new cityscape, therefore, effected a literary expression that changed the classical order of verse.

Even official Ottoman Turkish historiography changed in both tenor and form.[73] The new office of "court chronicler" (*vak'anüvis*) was established in the early part of the century. The holder of this office was to chronicle contemporary events.[74] Reflecting the phenomenon of the externalization of rule to households outside the Ottoman court, these official chronicles were written with a historical vision that acknowledged the new realities and facilitated the forging of a new consensus.[75] The chronicles by official historians rose to the status of best sellers among the learned elite, and their rise coincided with the decline of another historical genre, the biographical dictionary. The decline of the latter, it has been suggested, had to do with the diminished power of the social group that is typically (though not exclusively) associated with the genre, the *`ulamā'*.[76] This change in the order of Turkish historical texts is telling: the new economy of historical texts mirrored almost precisely the changed sociopolitical order.

The disappearance of the Ottoman Turkish biographical dictionary did not mean the death of biography, which had remained a staple of Islamic historiography.[77] Rather, in the imperial center, the biography merely migrated to the outdoors. In the eighteenth century, tombstones, which by now were elaborate artistic projects, began to bear more detailed biographies of the dead interred there. What ceased to be inscribed in books became inscribed in stone. In other words if the living promenaded by public fountains, the "dead were 'going public'" too.[78]

In this Istanbuli moment, then, the social topography that arose out of a new political order was reflected in an urban landscape now altered by recently built mansions, intricate tombstones, and resplendent fountains. In the process, or as a result of it, there emerged a new "textscape" that mirrored a new public urban culture and a polity that emanated from the Sultan's palace as well as a host of other notable households.

Moving from Istanbul to Cairo, the change in the content and form of literary texts in the seventeenth and eighteenth centuries is also clear. The "ordinary person" and his or her quotidian preoccupations, whether at work or at home, emerge as the topic of interest in books and compilations that defy generic categorization.[79] Also, a renewed interest in colloquial language dictionaries betrays an infiltration of the language of the ordinary person into texts.[80] In a manner similar to some of the voices that we will hear from the Levant in this study, ordinary Caireans in their books complained about the conspicuous consumption of the rich and powerful.[81] Thus, in Egypt there was a shift in the generic boundaries of the literary text and also its content, language, and interests, reflecting the emergence of a new "middle class."[82]

The Contemporary Chronicle/Diary in the Levant: "A 'Cheap' Sort of Monumentality"

The literary disorder that occurred in the eighteenth century Levant was about "going public" too. It happened at the hands of individuals not previously participating in written public discourse, or whose writings had been limited by genre, focus, and/or theme. In chronicling the events that occurred in their lifetime, most of the Levantine authors meant their texts to be public records. They managed to break the hegemony of the Muslim learned elite; they also demonstrated that *display* was not the exclusive prerogative of the elite. If the nouveau riche of Damascus managed to show off and negotiate through architecture, the less fortunate had the option to advertise and seek privilege through authoring a public text: a chronicle. This is how the nouveau literates came about.

The chronicles of the nouveau literates may be compared to some of the fountains constructed in Istanbul in the same period. (At this time, fountains proliferated in Cairo as well.)[83] According to a recent study, the fountain in Istanbul found patronage by sectors of society previously invisible in the domain of architecture, including craftsmen and artisans.[84] This is probably due to the fact that, of all architectural forms, the fountain was the easiest and least expensive for new patrons to appropriate. Endowing a public fountain was a quick and efficient way to both publicize and draw social capital. Fountains "were perceived as public trophies by individuals and social groups *rising* in power or *aspiring* to higher social prestige."[85] In other words, they constituted a "'cheap' sort of monumentality."[86]

Like the Istanbuli fountain and its pre-eighteenth-century patron, the traditional Levantine chronicle is an old form usually written by elite individuals. Like the Istanbuli fountain in the realm of architecture, the Levantine chronicle proved to be the most poachable of literary scholarly genres. Like the Istanbuli fountain, which is both a marker and seeker of prestige by the socially mobile, the Levantine chronicle of the nouveau literates is an advertisement and call for attention on the part of rising individuals and groups. In other words, both fountain and chronicle constitute public negotiations; the former is an intervention by new patrons in the cityscape while the latter is a disordering by new authors in the textscape.[87]

Let us now turn to Ibn Budayr's "fountain," to examine how the barber entered into textual space and used it for the acquisition of status and prestige. Although the portrayal of Damascus in this chapter is in part based on the barber's narration of his city, that is, on how he "made" the city, I will next show how the city "made" the barber.

CHAPTER 2

A Barber at the Gate

A Social and Intellectual Biography

Location, location, location . . .

—THE MANTRA OF REAL ESTATE AGENTS

For the barber Shihāb al-Dīn Aḥmad Ibn Budayr to write a book is an event of authorial boldness—"bold" because his profession is not historically associated with writing or learned culture. His boldness arose from a condition of social flux that prompted him to document a momentous history in a book of history. His chronicle is history-filled because it records the passage of events in time, and also because it discloses processes of historical negotiation, glimpses of how he managed change and adapted to it, how he displayed recently acquired privileges, and how he restyled himself in ways he thought appropriate for his new and improved social position. The chronicle, then, is the mirror of our nouveau literate in his new residence. It shows us the "turbans" he donned in braving an unfamiliar, sometimes frightful, and at other times welcoming, new world.

This, then, is the story of Ibn Budayr. More accurately, this is an attempt at constructing his social biography. Here, we will go on a journey in the footsteps of the barber as he traverses physical, social, and textual worlds. This biographical study of the barber is therefore an inquiry into the social conditions that allowed the man and the book to be. I consider the immediate circumstances that enabled this particular barber to become an author-historian. I attempt to tease out the social strategies he employs and discursive practices he appropriates as he treads, manages, and benefits from his new situation among the learned elite. The barber-author politicks in order to enter and acquire, and his politicking reveals the novelty of his (cultural) acquisitions. In order to understand the full significance of his maneuvers, we must first explore the society of a few highly placed individuals, more specifically scholars and mystics: their books, their educational certificates, their biographies, their séances and picnics, and even their dreams.

In this journey, the reader will meet scholars, saints, mystics, poets, barbers, a dyer, a weaver, descendants of the Prophet, paper makers and book binders, a spice shopkeeper, a son of a cook, a historian who also prescribed useful remedies, a teenager, a locksmith, women who smoked in public, and a few storytellers. Much of the information about most of these people is culled from a literary form that is part and parcel of the genre of the chronicle: the *tarjama*, or obituary notice/biography. For the purpose of this study, the *tarjama* is as important for its content as for its form. The obituary notice supplies us with information about people (and often places), and it can also be employed by its author to frame individuals, fashion them, and discriminate between them in significant ways. The *tarjama* was a powerful and empowering tool in the hands of the barber. If the book is the barber's mirror, the *tarjama* is his grooming blade.

Spatially, the journey starts in a Damascene neighborhood located outside the city walls, proceeds to the prestigious precinct of the Umayyad Mosque (also known as the Great Mosque) in the heart of the walled city, and ends in an unknown and unnamed coffeehouse. Along the way, the reader encounters the shop of our barber, as well as colleges, mosques, shrines of saints, picnic spots, and the road to Mecca. The divergence in these physical locations, hence the variety of cultural contents they represent, is quite remarkable. It should be remembered that the arrival of the barber in the world of the learned elite does not signify severance from other worlds or confinement to the new world. Indeed, social flux, by definition, is a breaking down of barriers, even if only momentary. The barber circulated in many realms where he acquired various literary forms: the *tarjama* of the chronicle and its high literary flourishes, the opaque language of mystical expression, supplications and healing formulas, popular singable *mawāliyā* verse, and stories of epic proportions.

SOCIAL MOBILITY: ARRIVAL

Ibn Budayr was born sometime in the first quarter of the eighteenth century, far from privilege. His distance from privilege is spatially reflected in the location of the neighborhood where he was born, al-Qubaybāt, which lay off the pilgrimage road to Mecca and was a good kilometer away from the walled city of Damascus where all power resided (Map 3).

Power in all its manifestations (political, economic, social, and cultural) was concentrated in a part of the walled city, the Central Rectangle. Located here was the main congregational mosque of Damascus, the great Umayyad Mosque, the palaces of the notable families of the city, the bulk of its commercial emporiums, and—as will prove significant for our purposes—the most important of the city's institutions of learning (Map 2). In one scholar's words, "the orientation [here is toward] . . . 'high' Islamic and imperial culture."[1] And Ibn Budayr was born, quite decidedly, outside this high and imperial culture.[2]

His father, as well as all the male members of his family, had been porters, or *`akkāmūn*, on the long and arduous pilgrimage journey to Mecca.[3] The job entailed carrying and serving pilgrims and attending to their camels. Possibly the only perk of the family business was the repeated performance of the pilgrimage, which would have accorded them the title of *ḥājj*, a title that carried some prestige.[4] Nonetheless, his relatives' repeated visits to Mecca remained in the first instance a business, and a "portering" business at that, which placed Ibn Budayr's family, quite literally, *under* other people. But Ibn Budayr's fate was quite different from that of his father. His final physical and social location would be much closer to the center of power and privilege.

On the death of his father (about whose economic standing the son was silent), the family moved from al-Qubaybāt, never to return.[5] Ibn Budayr bought a house in al-Ta`dīl, which lay to the southwest of the city walls, immediately south of the al-Qanawāt neighborhood, and at the outskirts of what has been designated as the "Localist Area" where the Arabic-speaking local population found affordable housing and jobs.[6] However, within this Localist Area, there is evidence that al-Ta`dīl may have been one of the higher-income neighborhoods.[7] This instance of evident upward and centerward mobility should not be taken, however, as a rags-to-riches story. At no stage in his life was Ibn Budayr materially well off. He mentioned that the purchase of the new house caused him financial distress.[8] He also never missed a chance to bitterly complain about the rising cost of living, especially the inflation of prices of basic produce, and consistently positioned himself as the spokesperson of the "poor," the "small people," and the "commoners."[9] In other words, though Ibn Budayr was socially mobile, he never ceased being a "middling sort."

Perhaps the most fortuitous thing that happened to the young Ibn Budayr is that he apprenticed at the barbershop of one Aḥmad Ibn al-Ḥashīsh (d. 1741). It is thanks to his master barber that, in the words of Ibn Budayr, things "opened up" for him.[10] The opening up in this context refers to the improvement in Ibn Budayr's material conditions, which is evidenced by the purchase of and move to the new house in al-Ta`dīl. However, just as the barbershop gave Ibn Budayr a better means of living, it also opened up a whole new set of social and cultural worlds.

Though sons were expected to follow in the profession of their fathers, changes in occupation were not unheard of.[11] The chronicle offers no indication as to the reason behind the young Ibn Budayr's departure from the family business of portering. According to Muḥammad Sa`īd al-Qāsimī, the late-nineteenth-century author of a dictionary of Damascene crafts and professions (and the editor of our barber's chronicle), a pilgrim-porter served the pilgrim and attended the mount (usually a camel) carrying the pilgrim. He had to possess the qualities of "endurance and strength and to walk deserts and rugged and hard lands."[12] Such hardships were made worse by the insecurity of constant threat of attacks by Bedouin marauders and highway robbers, and natural disasters, which occurred not too infrequently.[13] It would not be surprising if the sheer arduousness, dangers of the road, prolonged absences, and evidently low prestige entailed in being a pilgrim-porter led Ibn Budayr to seek a gentler and less taxing profession.[14]

Although palpably less physically demanding, barbering may not have been a much more socially prestigious profession than portering. A barber was not only a groomer (*muzayyin*) and shaver, but also practiced circumcision (*khitān*), bloodletting (*fiṣāda*), and cupping (*ḥijāma*).[15] Historically, the last two activities were considered base and undesirable and brought about social stigma.[16] However, studies on Ottoman guilds and medieval eastern Mediterranean cities offer a very different view.[17] The barber's craft and the associated guild were not only socially acceptable but enjoyed decidedly more prestige than other manual professions.[18]

Further, al-Qāsimī's dictionary of crafts expressly states that there were "classes" of barbers, those who owned their own shops and itinerants who practiced their profession in random outdoor settings.[19] The profession of barbering, then, at least in the Levant and Egypt, despite some of its unseemly aspects, seems not to have been perceived unfavorably.

Ibn Budayr eventually secured his own shop (that is, he qualified as a "classy" barber); it was in the best possible location in the city and frequented by the "best" kind of people. Interestingly, in his chronicle Ibn Budayr never mentions cupping, circumcision, or bloodletting, although he is quick to advertise his beard shaving and haircutting. So, even though we will never know whether Ibn Budayr practiced these less savory aspects of his profession, the fact that he omits any mention of them from his chronicle suggests that he knew how to present himself in the most favorable light. Ibn Budayr was evidently a barber with élan, a quality he seems to have acquired from Ibn al-Ḥashīsh, his master barber.

The master barber turned out to be an ideal mentor. Not only was he "a good and content man . . . companionable and affectionate,"[20] but he also serviced a particularly distinct clientele:

> During his lifetime, he barbered the Pole of his Time, he of the Sacred Station, Shaykh `Abd al-Ghanī al-Nābulusī[21]—may God sanctify his Sunnatic secret and grant us the benefit of his spiritual blessing. He also barbered Shaykh Murād al-Afandī al-Naqshabandī al-Kasīḥ,[22] and the Pillar of the Shāfi`ī rite Muḥammad al-`Ajlūnī,[23] and others like them, may God grant us the benefit of their spiritual blessings and the blessings of the purity of their breath.[24]

It would not be an exaggeration to say that these three scholar and mystic clients of the master barber together represented the pinnacle of social and cultural prestige in eighteenth-century Damascus: intellectual prowess, spiritual advancement, social prominence, and fabulous wealth. Such contact with the rarified clientele in the master barbershop may have influenced Ibn Budayr's choice to seek an education and as well to establish his barbershop in a particular physical location.

When Ibn Budayr established his own barbershop, it was at the heart of the walled city, in Bāb al-Barīd, in the Central Rectangle, the location richest in social and cultural capital (Map 2). And though much later in his life Ibn Budayr would set up another shop in a more modest area, al-Sināniyya, his long stay in Bāb al-Barīd proved significant.[25] It is not clear if the site of the barbershop in downtown Damascus was inherited from, or represented a move in the footsteps of, the master barber, but the apprentice seems to have succeeded his master in the tradition of barbering scholars and Sufis. So, whether it was the initial physical location of the master barbershop that determined the quality of Ibn Budayr's often prestigious customers and the location of his shop, or if it was Ibn Budayr's initial contact with the learned elite that enabled him to establish his barbershop in their territory, is unclear; however, what is noteworthy is that for at least 13 years,[26] if not from the beginning of his apprenticeship as a child, Ibn Budayr was on the home turf of the Sufi and scholarly elite, and it is at their lofty gate that the barber knocked.

THE INTELLECTUAL ITINERARY OF A "LEARNED ILLITERATE"

Fuqahā' ummiyyūn, literally, "learned illiterates," is a term that, I am told, has been traditionally used and is still used today to describe a particular social group in Fez, Morocco. These are the shopkeepers, artisans, and others who work and live in the proximity of the venerable Qarawiyyīn Mosque, the main congregational mosque of the city. Thanks to their regular attendance at the séances and free lectures offered at the mosque, these hangers-on end up well versed in matters of religion and Islamic law.[27] Though these learned men of the bazaar are clearly not necessarily illiterate in the technical sense (i.e., many, if not most, of them today probably know how to read and write), the expression "learned illiterates" is obviously employed to describe the dissonance between their occupational and/or educational backgrounds and the kind of the knowledge they possess. This expression is applied to those who are not expected to know as much as they do, and it seems well suited to our Damascene barber. Therefore here the term *learned illiterate* denotes an educated layperson and is used in juxtaposition to the *scholar*, whose very profession is knowledge, or "learned literacy."

Like the learned illiterates of modern day Fez, Ibn Budayr also had no business knowing what he knew. And since neither his family background nor his occupation placed an expectation on Ibn Budayr to be cultivated as he was, one assumes that he was inspired into this kind of knowledge because he shared the same physical space, and hence at least a part of the social and cultural world, of some illustrious scholars in town. In short, Ibn Budayr breathed the air of the high culture of the learned. And this air, naturally, contributed to the barber's constitution.

We do not know the details of the barber's education, but from what little that one can gather it is quite simply astounding. In addition to the first basic step of education of reading the entirety of the Quran,[28] he mentions having studied "theology (*`ilm al-tawḥīd*), jurisprudence (*fiqh*), grammar, rhetoric (*badī`*), and various sciences of religion (*al-`ulūm al-shar`iyya*)."[29] His main teacher in all of these subjects was one Aḥmad b. Muḥammad b. `Alī al-Sābiq (d. 1743). Not particularly famous, and with only one monograph in his curriculum vitae, al-Sābiq was nevertheless of sufficient standing to warrant an entry in Muḥammad Khalil al-Murādī's *Silk al-durar fī a`yān al-qarn al-thānī `ashar* ("The String of Pearls of the Notables of the twelfth Century [Hijrī]"), which is considered the authoritative biographical dictionary of the eighteenth century.[30]

Al-Sābiq, despite his evident deep influence on Ibn Budayr's life, was not the barber's only teacher. Ibn Budayr studied jurisprudence with two other scholars, one of whom was of stellar reputation, Muḥammad b. `Abd al-Raḥmān b. Zayn al-`Ābidīn al-Ghazzī (d.1754),[31] from one of the most important scholarly families in the city.[32] Among the positions that al-Ghazzī occupied was the Shafi`ī *muftī* (jurisconsult), that is, the highest judicial position in the legal rite to which the majority of the Damascene population ascribed. During his teaching career, al-Ghazzī held several teaching posts, including that of Hadith instructor/professor at the Great Mosque, a stone's throw from Bāb al-Barīd, where the barber practiced his trade for many years.[33]

Another teacher with whom Ibn Budayr studied was `Alī Kuzbar (d. 1751).[34] A well-known Shāfi`ī scholar, Kuzbar was "the founder of the fame and influence" that his family would achieve.[35] Like the aforementioned al-Ghazzī, Kuzbar also held a teaching position at the Great Mosque. With Kuzbar, Ibn Budayr mentions having studied two books, one of which he specifies as "by al-Shaykh al-Ḥiṣnī, called *al-Ḥiṣniyya*, which is a commentary on *al-Ghāya* [which is related to] the Shāfi`ī legal rite."[36] This happens to be the sole title in the whole of his history that Ibn Budayr actually cites. The fact that we know more about the teachers of Ibn Budayr than the books he read is telling and is a point to which I shall return.

The work that Ibn Budayr familiarly cites as *al-Ḥiṣniyya* is the *Kifāyat al-akhyār fī ḥall ghāyat al-ikhtiṣār* ("The Sufficiency of the Select in Explicating 'The Utmost Brevity'"), by the fifteenth-century jurist Taqiyy al-Dīn al-Ḥiṣnī.[37] As Ibn Budayr mentions, this is a commentary on the *Ghāyat al-ikhtiṣār* ("Utmost Brevity"), a summary work of positive law in the Shafi`ī legal rite authored by the eleventh-century scholar Abū Shujā` al-Iṣfahānī.[38] As works of *furū`* (positive law), both books, the original and the commentary, are meant to acquaint the reader not with the methodology of jurisprudence (*uṣūl*) and the derivation of law but with legal rules/rulings. In other words, *uṣūl* works are of concern only to the serious scholar-jurist while straightforwardly prescriptive *furū`* works are of a general, practical interest to any individual, whether of the scholars or the "laity," who aspires to lead a virtuous life.

As is typical of *furū`* books, *al-Ḥiṣniyya* deals with rules that have to do with both religious ritual and mundane nonreligious activities including prayers, marriage, divorce, fasting, sales, dietary issues, and more, each of which is the subject of a separate chapter heading. Particularly interesting is the author's introduction, which states the purpose behind the composition and sheds light on its intended audience while targeting people like Ibn Budayr:

> Know that the seekers of knowledge are as various as their aims . . . one kind seeks to dive in the sea . . . to procure the greatest pearls, and another [kind] who is satisfied with what he finds in utmost brevity. And of [this latter] satisfied [kind] there are two kinds: those with children and [who are] fatigued by work and those who are inclined towards God in an earnest and serious manner. The first [of this kind of people] is unable to be in continuous company of people [while] the [latter Sufi] path-traveler is busy attaining his aims and [spends] his night and day by himself in a state of anxiety. I desired comfort for each of them so that they may remain as they are [in resumption of their

activities] and so that they are freed from searching for what is needed. I hope to God . . . to facilitate that which leads to clarity and ease.[39]

Even though such justifications for authorship in book introductions tend to be formulaic literary devices,[40] in this specific instance Ibn Budayr represents the ideal target audience for al-Ḥiṣnī's book. The barber falls squarely within one of the two categories of intended readership: those whose familial and financial responsibilities compel them to work for a living, thus precluding the opportunities for them to pursue deeper knowledge. (The other category of intended audiences is the mystics.) This book is therefore made for the likes of Ibn Budayr. It is a basic textbook in law: jurisprudence "lite."

The introduction of *al-Hiṣniyya* is revealing in that it sheds light on the cultural divide between Ibn Budayr and scholars and so deserves a brief digression. Especially significant is the limit that the author establishes as the defining marker of the target audience, which is the *luxury of time.* It is not that artisans (and mystics) are less clever, or less comprehending, or are only capable of reading simple, brief books. Rather, they are defined by the fact that they cannot afford to spend time in the society of people (that is, scholars).[41] Extensive time investment in nonmaterially productive activities, most notably social interaction with other scholars, is a defining feature of the culture of scholarship. And though scholars may not be materially well off, their culture, in variance from that of our barber, is an expression of material comfort.

But to return to Ibn Budayr's intellectual itinerary: aside from the religious sciences, he seems to have been conversant in another field of knowledge, Sufism, or mysticism. Although in the eighteenth century the majority of male citizens belonged to at least one Sufi order, and though it was the Qādirī path that the barber followed, Ibn Budayr's knowledge of mysticism seems to have been not shallow. His employment of Sufi terms such as "*khamr sharāb al-malik al-jabbār*" ("the Wine of the All-Powerful King") and "*al-ghaybūba al-ilāhiyya*" ("Divine Trance") indicates more than basic literacy in the field.[42] These expressions are more sophisticated than would be expected from an average adherent and suggest a familiarity with written Sufi discourse. Consequently, there is great likelihood that Ibn Budayr's mysticism may have gone beyond social affiliation and ritual observance: it likely involved some serious reading too. There is no way of finding out what Ibn Budayr himself read, but we do know that books on Sufism were one of the most avidly read subjects in Damascus at the beginning of the century.[43]

Ibn Budayr's membership in the Qādiriyya Sufi order is noteworthy and deserves some reflection. The Qādiriyya, although historically important in Damascus (past and present Damascene members included the great fourteenth-century thinker Taqiyy al-Dīn Ibn Taymiyya and the aforementioned `Abd al-Ghanī al-Nābulusī),[44] was not one of the most popular orders among the Arabic-speaking population during the eighteenth century. During Ibn Budayr's time, the Sa`diyya, the Rifā`iyya, and the Shādhiliyya orders all enjoyed wider membership than the Qādiriyya.[45] However, significantly, the same order was popular among those college teachers who had mystical leanings.[46] Indeed it was a teacher, Ibn Budayr's main mentor Aḥmad al-Sābiq, who initiated the barber to the Path.[47]

The choice of Ibn Budayr to join the Qādiriyya order is worth exploring. Even though the association between particular craft guilds and certain Sufi orders is an established fact,[48] the state of our knowledge does not allow us to draw a connection between the barbers' guild and the order of which Ibn Budayr was a member. However, given the abundance of barbers in Damascus and the fact that the Qādiriyya was not a particularly popular Damascene order, one may conclude that the barbers' guild must have been associated with another order. (And curiously, Ibn Budayr never mentions fellow barbers aside from his master barber. As for the guild, he only once mentions the head of the barbers' guild, and then only in a cursory manner.[49]) So the barber's choice of a Sufi order favored by college teachers seems not to have been dictated by his profession, but rather by his immersion in the world of the scholars, some of whom were his companions and friends.

Several observations emerge from Ibn Budayr's intellectual biography. His long stint in downtown Damascus gave him the opportunity to study with and find role models in the famous and the elite among scholars, such as the aforementioned Kuzbar and al-Ghazzī, both of whom taught at the nearby Umayyad Mosque. Unfortunately, we are not able to reconstruct the exact circumstances in which the barber studied, for example, whether the lessons he attended were held privately at the barbershop or at the Umayyad Mosque, or even in one of the numerous colleges in the neighborhood and the city; whether they were acts of charity by these master scholars toward a poor apprentice boy, or held in a large class with many other students; and whether they represented an exchange of favors of barbering for learning. None of this is clear. What is clear is that the barber, by studying with these scholars, took advantage of the fact of his proximity to the center of the learned elite, and in the process he learned both their *knowledge* and the *culture* of that knowledge. Even his choice of Sufi order betrays the barber's desire to immerse himself in scholarly culture.

Ibn Budayr, then, was a learned illiterate. This attribute did not make him particularly special, since he was neither the first nor the last learned artisan. And though one may take the fifteenth-century scholar al-Ḥiṣnī's identification of his "working-class" readership as a literary device appropriate for introducing a book on positive law, current scholarship has established that cultivated artisans were not a rarity.[50] According to one modern historian, such a group already existed two centuries before Ibn Budayr in the circle of the Sufi popularizer and leader ʿAbd al-Wahhāb al-Shaʿrānī (d. 1565), which was composed of "illiterate Sufis and learned artisans."[51] Indeed literate commoners, those who were able to consume books, existed and continue to exist as in the example of modern-day Fez. However, what is striking about Ibn Budayr is that he *dared* to go one step further. He did not emulate the elite merely by reading books; he produced a book himself. To put it differently, by authoring a book, Ibn Budayr changed his status from learned illiterate to nouveau literate.

The competence to consume a book and the ability to produce one are not opposite sides of the same coin. Rather, they are two distinct moments connected by a complicated process, which along with aspiration takes the accrual of social and cultural capital necessary to become an author. Therefore the question is not one of technical literacy. Beyond learning how to read and write, it takes both ambition and the devising of various strategies for a person to successfully enter into textual space.

THE SOCIAL AND DISCURSIVE PRACTICES AND MATERIAL CONDITIONS OF THE *`ULAMĀ'* AND SUFIS

The phenomenon of nouveau literacy represents an entry by new authors. It is an entry into textual space that is accompanied by, as well as enabled by and conducive to, a parallel social movement. In the case of the barber, the social shift and the textual entry were remarkably close. His arrival into the mostly scholar-dominated textual space is concomitant with his arrival into their social world. To understand the meanings of the barber's authorship, a description of the discursive and social practices of the bearers of knowledge, be they *`ulamā'* or Sufis, is necessary.

The scholars were the practitioners of the religious sciences related to law, jurisprudence, Hadith, and Quranic exegesis. In other words, they attempted to know the Divine and His will through scriptures and the example of the Prophet. By and large, theirs was a textually based knowledge, and they are the learned literates par excellence. Mystics, or Sufis, on the other hand, attempted to know the Divine through a spiritual experience of Him. Theirs was an experiential knowledge. These two types of knowledge were not mutually exclusive. The matter was of degree of depth in one or the other type of knowledge, and there are several examples of people who were equally competent and/or active in both.[52]

One needs to reiterate that Sufis and scholars, historically and in general, do not represent a social class but rather are a diffuse group ubiquitous in every level of society. However, as shown by Michael Chamberlain in his study of the scholarly elite of medieval Damascus, knowledge was capital and constituted the main instrument by which the civilians of medieval Damascus accessed power.[53] To possess a highly valued commodity, such as religious/mystical knowledge, makes the possessor by definition a member of a cultural elite, whose commodity is often convertible in other spheres. It is not so much social origin or income that defines the savants but more the "social trajectory" and "group self-consciousness."[54] Like the French bourgeoisie, whom the historian Robert Darnton found to be an elusive socioeconomic category but who had a certain way of life ("'he lives, he speaks, he reasons *bourgeoisement*'"),[55] the Sufis and scholars, although not easily defined socioeconomically, were unquestionably culturally distinct and often visibly sartorially marked.

It so happens that the scholars and Sufis we will encounter in the next few pages represent the highest level of the social and cultural spectrum. The prominence of these figures is attributable precisely to the fact that they were powerful enough to be so well documented; they had sufficient authority to write about themselves and/or a sufficient following to record their deeds. The examples here perforce represent ideal types.

Texts and Chains

In opening up the world of the scholars, I will use the metaphor of the chain.[56] The image of the chain lurks behind the nature and process of the scholarly transmission of knowledge, and the scholars' descriptions of their achievements and of their social world. As it will be seen later in this book, the culture of transmission of knowledge was primarily oral and aural.[57] If a student wanted to be certified as having learned a book, he or she would, ideally, have to be taught the book by a scholar authorized to teach it, and to then recite back to the teacher what was learned from the text. In principle, it is only after this process that the student would receive an *ijāza* (a license to transmit the book) from either the author or someone authorized by the author, or even from someone who is separated from the author by generations (or even centuries) but ultimately connected to the author by a chain of authorities of transmission.[58] When a scholar describes his own scholarly achievement, his curriculum vitae so to speak, he writes it in the form of a *thabat*: a list of the books he has been authorized to transmit, along with the chains of transmission linking him or her to the original authors.[59] Thus the scholarly world is connected through chains of authority where the location of the scholar as an individual link in the chain is clearly indicated, and where the connection of that scholar to the scholars who are the links on either side of the chain is the result of personal contact and direct audition of the knowledge being transmitted. According to Steve Tamari, "[i]nclusions into chains of transmission meant admission into a social body that did not have a formal corporate existence but had a strong sense of identity and self-consciousness."[60]

These chains of authorities connect scholars across generations, that is, diachronically, and in a formal way. There is also a less formal—but no less significant—chain that connects scholars synchronically, meaning between contemporaries. The literary manifestation of this synchronic chain is the genre of the biographical dictionary.[61] The biographical dictionary is one of the most prolific literary genres produced by the Islamic scholars. Similar to a modern *Who's Who*, the biographical dictionary represents a compilation of biographies of people (except that the people it features are dead). The form of the individual biography is the *tarjama*.

The *tarjama* is an obituary notice devoted typically (but by no means exclusively) to a notable scholar. The notice recounts the scholar's academic achievements, what he studied, with whom he studied, where he taught, who his students were, and what his colleagues thought of him. Wherever relevant, the *tarjama* also lists idiosyncrasies, such as bad temper, unusual manner of dress, or strange habits, thus sometimes providing comic relief. The style is formulaic especially with regard to the titles of the deceased, which are expressed in rhyming, metonymous flourishes. The extravagant characterizations, in a manner of speaking, "entitle" the scholar. If a scholar makes it into a biographical dictionary, then his status as a scholar has effectively been acknowledged by his peers. In other words, to be in a biographical dictionary is to be *in*. (Ibn Budayr did very well to have teachers who made it into al-Murādī's *Silk al-durar*.) Aside from establishing the status of the scholars, the language used in the *tarjama* to describe the relationship between scholars of the same generation is a collegial vocabulary of fellowship (*ṣuḥba*), constant companionship (*mulāzama*), love (*ḥubb/maḥabba*), and benefit (*fā'ida*).[62] So just as scholars bind themselves across generations in formal chains of authorities, they bind themselves in the same generation through the informal chains of fellowship, love, and mutual benefit.[63]

The result of this complex of diachronic and synchronic connections is a relatively closed—or an *attempt at* a closed—world, where in and out are clearly demarcated by a whole network of chains that bind scholars and inhibit intruders. Between the *thabat* and the *ijāza* on the one hand, and the *tarjama* on the other, scholars provide us with a detailed map of both their social world and their respective locations within it.

The question, then, is: Who has the time to spend months and years studying with teachers, attend lectures of colleagues, pass afternoons in literary séances, and write books? It clearly must be those who are not in material need. The endowments of colleges regularly contained provision for student scholarships, and once a student graduated he found that some academic posts brought in quite a bit of money (as attested by the fact that 50 percent of those who held teaching positions in Damascus did not have to supplement their incomes by acquiring another job),[64] but in the Ottoman world the fact of being a scholar opened up several channels of revenue through patronage and links with state administration. By and large, the culture of the scholars and their lifestyles, tastes, and cultural products reflected distance from need.

Of course, not every scholar was wealthy (although we have many examples of *ulamā'* tycoons in the eighteenth century), but the sociability of the scholar was one that necessitated an investment of large amounts of time in activities that were materially nonproductive. As reflected in the *tarjama*s, frequenting (*taraddud*), visitation (*ziyāra*), constant companionship (*mulāzama*), and befriending (*ṣuḥba*) other, especially more powerful, scholars were a part of the game.[65] And though these activities, this social networking, entailed perhaps more spending than earning in material terms, they constituted other arenas of investment and reward. They were means of cultural capital. This is demonstrated in the revealing life of a particularly revealing scholar.

Picnics and Verse

The life of cultured pleasure of Ibn Kannān represents an ideal, almost a caricature of the eighteenth-century Damascene scholar.[66] Ibn Kannān received the full education of a scholar, was a teacher of jurisprudence, and was the leader of the Khalwatiyya order in the city.[67] A veritable polymath, he published in various fields outside the religious sciences, including history, geography, poetry, rhetoric, medicine, botany, and zoology.[68] Ibn Kannān was the last Levantine *`ālim* to have authored a chronicle (or perhaps his is the last surviving *`ālim*-authored chronicle). Luckily for us, his chronicle *al-Ḥawādith al-yawmiyya* ("The Daily Events") privileges the reader/listener with a close view of the daily life of a relatively successful *`ālim*.[69] Of a merchant background, Ibn Kannān seems to have been independently wealthy, as evidenced by the lavishly decorated and expensively furnished house that he owned. His life of leisure gave Ibn Kannān the opportunity to spend much of his time at lectures of fellow teachers and in literary salons and Sufi soirees, which were sometimes pretty expensive affairs.[70] When the weather permitted, Ibn Kannān and his companions combined business with pleasure, and like busy bees they conducted scholarly discussions and literary flitings amid the blossoms of the verdant gardens of the city.[71]

These literary picnics, especially "in the season of the roses," seem to have been the fashion of the times and are worth reflecting on. Such seasonal outings are notable for their frequency and their duration: they often lasted several days.[72] Such idyllic and seemingly idle pastimes, though indicative of the amount of spare time scholars had on their hands and their relative distance from need, were in fact arenas for competition that had some influence in a scholar's professional life. Aside from affording the enchanted *`ālim* the opportunity to appreciate the beauties of his city, it gave him the chance to capture and express that beauty in verse and prose, to display his skill at packaging or translating nature into literature. The picnic, therefore, was a chance for the scholar to show off his literary virtuosity, a necessary commodity for a scholar, and to test his peers' mettle through challenges to literary duels.[73] To rise to literary challenge was the mark of a fine scholar. In other words, literary picnics functioned as yet another informal instrument of both competition and certification.[74]

Remarkably, though Ibn Kannān mentions scores of gatherings in private houses, colleges, and the abundant picnic spots of Damascus, he never mentions having visited or gathered with his friends in a coffeehouse. As we shall see, the cultural elite had an attitude toward coffeehouses and eschewed them as places for the socially inferior, like our barber.[75]

Mystics and Dreams

I would argue that Sufism is a field homologous to and overlapping with that of the scholarly world. Many of the Sufis were themselves recognized scholars, and like the scholar the Sufi also seeks knowledge of the

Divine—in the Sufi's case, *experiential* knowledge. And like the world of scholarship, the world of mysticism is a hierarchy where people are located in stations according to their spiritual achievement. Also, the mystic seeker needs a teacher, a more advanced spiritual guide, who will initiate, train, authorize, and certify him through a *silsila* or *mashāyakha*[76] (the function of which is similar to *ijāza* and *thabat* in the scholarly world). The Sufi who attains the state of full and permanent consciousness of God is understood to have absorbed himself or herself in the divine self. A Sufi who has attained such a state of spiritual elevation is called a *walī*, that is, a "friend of God" or a saint. There is no process of canonization for Sufi saints; rather, the *walī* is recognized as such in his or her own lifetime. A saint functions as a conduit of the divine grace in which he or she dwells; this manifests itself in the capacity to perform minor miracles, such as curing sickness or predicting the future, and even sometimes the ability to intercede with God on behalf of others. Divine blessing and favour thus emanate from the person of the *walī* and may be obtained by being in his or her presence. The quest to obtain divine blessings from Sufis, whether from living saints or from the graves of dead ones, was a standard part of daily life in eighteenth-century Damascus.

Given that Sufism is about the knowledge of the Hidden Truth, dreams and visions are key in the process of spiritual pursuit. A dream is considered both a manifestation and a means of spiritual attainment and functions as a private passageway between the mystic-dreamer and the sources of spiritual authority. In short, a vision is proof of saintly authority; thus saints and spiritual seekers embark on "visionary careers."[77] The textual reflection of the centrality of dreams in Sufi life and practice is found in the existence of oneirocritical literature and dream log books.[78] In a later chapter, I will show the influence that these Sufi discursive practices may have had on the proliferation of first-person narratives in the seventeenth and eighteenth centuries. However, here I am more concerned with the social instrumentality of dreams and visions in Sufi practice.

"[D]reamers are shown things in their sleep appropriate to their spiritual station."[79] There is hierarchy even in the world of dreamers. A Sufi seeker, like Asiye Hātūn (fl. 1643), was encouraged to record her dreams so that they might be interpreted by higher authorities.[80] Yet when a Sufi saint, or near-saint, records his visions, the intent is markedly different. Let us visit `Abd al-Ghanī al-Nābulusī (one of the clients of the master barber) and his dream world.

Al-Nābulusī's spiritual authority was almost limitless. One of the main expounders of the doctrines of the famous Sufi intellectual Ibn al-`Arabī (d. 1240), al-Nābulusī was recognized for his intellectual and spiritual achievements, by both contemporaries and later generations, and his reputation reached well beyond Damascus and spread to other parts of the Islamic world. He became known, as Ibn Budayr correctly noted in a passage quoted above, as *quṭb zamāni-hi*, "the Pole of his Time," indicating al-Nābulusī's high Sufi station. However, before he became a mystic, al-Nābulusī attempted to get an appropriate teaching position but failed.[81] For this and other reasons, the scholar opted to withdraw from society. During his seven years of withdrawal from the world, al-Nābulusī became remarkably prolific, and it is precisely then that he launched his Sufi career. Having therefore failed in the "real" world, al-Nābulusī turned his investment into the spiritual realm, where his authority was not subject to the same kind of contestation by professional rivals for finite resources; the spiritual world did not have a limited number of positions.[82] In this way, Sufism sometimes functioned as an alternative field in which the cultural capital of scholarship was convertible. The desired position in the real world is compensated for by an even more prestigious Sufi station.

On the first day of his seclusion, al-Nābulusī started composing his dream chronicle, entitled *munājāt al-ḥakīm* ("Dialogue with the Wise").[83] But this chronicle was intended not for interpretation by a higher authority but rather as the proclamation of *being* that higher authority. The book constituted literally a publication of al-Nābulusī's experience with the Divine.[84] This kind of deployment of dreams to buttress and legitimize claims to spiritual authority and sainthood was not an innovation in and of itself and is wonderfully illustrated in the tragicomic life of the fifteenth-century failed saint Muḥammad al-Zawāwī (d. 1477). This man was a Sufi who seems to have had visions "inappropriate for his station" and wrote them in a book, *Tuḥfat al-nāẓir wa nuzhat al-manāẓir* ("The Gift of the Seer in the Promenade of Views"). Al-Zawāwī's attempt to persuade the world of his saintliness met with miserable failure (and he himself has been seen by modern scholars as a psychological case).[85] But for our purposes, in addition to the implied spiritual hierarchy, al-Zawāwī's dream chronicle drives home the point that authorship of dreams was not only a statement but also an instrument of and strategy for acquiring spiritual power. The unfortunate al-Zawāwī seems to have grossly miscalculated (i.e., his politicking was too transparent). Meanwhile, the wildly successful al-Nābulusī did not stop at authoring his dreams but composed a dictionary of dream interpretation, entitled *Ta`ṭīr al-anām fī tafsīr al-manām* ("The Perfuming of Humankind through the Interpretation of Dreams").[86] It is another strategic move that further confirmed his status. By positing himself as a decoder of other people's dreams, al-Nābulusī became the assayer of their spiritual experiences, the ultimate spiritual authority.

Between picnics and reverie, being an *`ālim* and/or a Sufi was not simply about acquisition and transmission of the relevant knowledge and attainment of an appropriate official position or Sufi station. These were complex and complicated cultures that entailed the employment of various discursive and social strategies. A necessary prerequisite for entry into these worlds is the establishment of connections with scholarly/spiritual authorities, both past and present, which ties had to substantiated through textual proof (*ijāza, thabat, tarjama, silsila*).[87]

Outside the text, away from discursive practices and in the social world, scholars had to engage in various social interactions in both institutional and informal settings in which their ability and authority were constantly being tried. Sufis had to delve into the "unreal" world and forge an interaction with a figure no less divine than the Divine, to then proceed to convince the real world of this private, unwitnessed, nonevident communication.

Pleasure in picnics and reverie in slumber thus masked two elaborate and overlapping "systems" of certification and distinction, which required laborious self-application and extensive investment in time and effort (and sometimes even money). As Chamberlain has suggested, achievement in these worlds required hard work and political astuteness.[88] To be a successful and significant player in the game of Sufis and scholars, one had to engage in intricate maneuvering, which, however, had to be carried out with precise finesse and cautious calculation. These practices and maneuverings served to perpetuate and simultaneously exclude; they were the elites' way of reproducing themselves.

FROM BAZAAR TO ACADEMY: THE CASES IN AL-MURĀDĪ'S *SILK AL-DURAR*

Before we move on to the barber and his situation in this complex culture, it is worth asking whether these practices of exclusion succeeded in the real world. Were the worlds of scholars and Sufis really closed? We will see later that commoners had already entered textual space as subjects in, and now authors of, historical genres. Here I have argued how the barber started out as a learned illiterate and ended up a nouveau literate. But to what extent could commoners actually manage to enter the world of academia and pursue successful academic careers or jobs in learned literacy? Though exact empirical research is impossible, a survey of al-Murādī's biographical dictionary may yield some answers.

Al-Murādī's dictionary is almost overwhelmingly devoted to the learned elite, whether of religious or spiritual knowledge.[89] In addition to his interest in the savants, it is noteworthy that the chain metaphor discussed above is evident even in the title of his work, "The String of Pearls." Being very status conscious, al-Murādī is keen to provide not only the positions and occupations of the deceased but also their sources of wealth. Most of the people included in the dictionary held professions that directly involved learned literacy (as opposed to basic or numerical literacy) or official positions (such as judges, jurisconsults, teachers, scribes, sermonists, historians, poets, Quran teachers and reciters, and saints). He also included physicians.[90] Of the 862 biographies, only a small minority of about 17 are of individuals who had careers in both learned literacy and the bazaar: a cook,[91] three spice-shop keepers,[92] one paper maker,[93] two book binders,[94] a book seller,[95] two textile weavers,[96] a locksmith,[97] and a few other professions.[98] Hence the image that emerges from surveying al-Murādī's dictionary is that there were cases of people who held artisanal jobs and at the same time had a reputation for learning. These cases, however, were extremely rare. Indeed, al-Murādī, as did the aforementioned author of al-Ḥiṣniyya, assumed that knowledge was a full-time commitment, the financing of which had to come from either an official position or one's own pockets.

This brings us to the subject of wealth in relation to knowledge-related careers. I have described how the culture of the scholars reflected a life of material comfort, but the question that arises is whether this culture was reflected in social reality. In this regard, the biographies of al-Shaykh Ḥasan and al-Shaykh Ismāʿīl al-Ḥā'ik in al-Murādī's dictionary are highly instructive.[99] Both Ḥasan and Ismāʿīl hailed from artisanal families. Both managed to make successful crossovers from bazaar to academia. Remarkably, these are the only two whom al-Murādī expressly mentions to have made this career change. According to al-Murādī, Ḥasan's father was a cook who made a bit of money through what was the brilliant idea of renting out crockery for weddings. His fortune grew so much that he brought up his son, Ḥasan, in a circumstance of "abundant means and ease of mind."[100] It was precisely this circumstance that allowed the son, an intelligent and industrious boy, to pursue an academic career and later become a teacher and preacher. Ismāʿīl al-Ḥā'ik, however, led a path diametrically opposed to that of Ḥasan. Ismāʿīl's father was a destitute weaver. Despite the father's need and desire for his son to help him in his occupation, Ismāʿīl refused to learn his father's craft and would instead escape the family shop to read Quran at the Umayyad Mosque. Ismāʿīl's lack of cooperation used "to infuriate and burden his father."[101] However, the son turned out to be a successful and respected scholar, who at one point held the all-important position of Ḥanafī jurisconsult of Damascus.

The implications of al-Murādī in his narration of these two instances of successful crossovers are clear. He posits an intimate relationship between wealth and a career in learned literacy. Wealth was a precondition for a career in knowledge. Given his father's means, it was natural and expected for the reasonably bright Ḥasan to take up an academic career. Ismāʿīl, however, was nothing less than extraordinary. He represented the exception that proved the rule (success in the pursuit of knowledge *despite* difficult material circumstances), and at the same time the ideal of committed passion in the face of social norms. Ismāʿīl was the prodigal son who was eventually vindicated. It is probably figures like Ismāʿīl who, for his uniqueness and perseverance, were most respected by the very same people whose social practices served to exclude people of a background like that of Ismāʿīl.

To sum up this brief survey of al-Murādī's biographical dictionary, I will reemphasize three points about the Damascene academy in the eighteenth century. The first is that there are very few artisans and craftsmen in the social world al-Murādī paints. Those who straddled an artisanal profession and a learned-literacy occupation were relatively few. Another point is that successful crossovers from bazaar to academia were also quite rare. But this exclusion of the working class, so to speak, did not result from a *conscious* attitude on the part of the practitioners of knowledge; rather it was due to time investment and commitments, both professional and social, that people of modest means, or according to al-Ḥiṣnī those "[who are] fatigued by work," simply could not afford. The third point to emphasize is that when it comes to a career in learned literacy, time is of the essence. And it took material comfort (or exceptional personal stubbornness) for a craftsman or a son of a craftsman to be able to afford the time investment permitting the switch from working class to learned class.[102] Although most of those who held teaching positions in Damascus did not belong to the dominant and rich scholarly families, like the Istanbul academy the Damascene counterpart had also become an aristocracy,[103] households reflecting the new order of the eighteenth century. In the words of Madeline Zilfi, in eighteenth-century Istanbul, when it came to *ʿulamāʾ* career, "[m]ore and more it was blood that told."[104]

Like the aforementioned Ismāʿīl and Ḥasan, the original social position of our barber Ibn Budayr was not one that allowed him to be conditioned into a career in learned literacy. However, unlike Ḥasan, Ibn Budayr's father did not come across a brilliant idea that brought in sudden wealth, and unlike Ismāʿīl, the barber's passion was not "excessive" enough to lead him to shake off his family responsibilities. In other words, Ibn Budayr had neither the material conditions nor the exceptional motivation to become a full-time scholar. Ibn Budayr may have been a more typical case of a learned illiterate. He was either unwilling or incapable of pursuing an academic career, but this fact did not stop him from writing a book.

To return to the main question of this chapter: Given the situation of the barber, what is it that led him to acquire the confidence, the authority, to write a book? It is Ibn Budayr's upward and centerward social movement, which threw him into contact with the learned elites and their social and discursive strategies. Now that his "learned illiteracy" has been established, Ibn Budayr will bravely break into the scholars' textual space and author a book to become a nouveau literate.

TRICKS UP THE BARBER'S SLEEVE

Ibn Budayr's book, which I have described as an appropriation, was itself full of further appropriative tricks and strategies. The barber's chronicle represents proof of entry into the textual space of the learned elite and their social world. It is a display of the barber's social and cultural capital. Beyond display, the book was also a vehicle by which to acquire even more such capital. It was a tool in the pursuit of social prestige. So, what are his various strategies?

Coif and Tell: Ibn Budayr's Tarjamas

Though Ibn Budayr, like other "learned illiterates," has read several books, there is certainly no indication of his ever receiving a scholarly authorization or *ijāza* to transmit any of these books, which is the basic certification of completing a formal course of study. After all, like other artisans, he has a full-time job and all kinds of financial responsibilities, including support of a mother (while she is alive), a wife, and at least three children.[105] The barber therefore cannot afford to go beyond the stage of being a part-time student. In other words, he has not entered one of those formal cross-generational vertical chains of scholarly authorities described above. However, what he *is able to do* is very significant. By authoring a chronicle, probably the most easily appropriated scholarly genre, and one that does not require prior authorization, Ibn Budayr is able not only to "produce" and fashion himself in the world of the scholars but to use many of their social and discursive practices.

One of the barber's most productive appropriations and one that bears multiple significances is his use of the *tarjama.* Ibn Budayr's chronicle reports about 67 deaths, most of which are written in the appropriate literary form. Significantly, and true to scholarly form, most of the subjects of his biographies are themselves scholars and Sufis. (The few non-elite personalities included in the barber's biographies are significant and will be treated below.) These are biographies of figures who generally constitute the cultural elite, though a significant number (about 25 of the 67 biographies) are of personalities with high enough status as to appear in al-Murādī's biographical dictionary. In his choosing to proffer biographies of the cultural elite, Ibn Budayr assigns himself a certain authority that is not unlike that of al-Murādī. The difference, however, is stark. Al-Murādī, having descended from one of the most venerable Damascene families known for its pedigree of education and wealth, is a legitimate arbiter of the cultural elite.

But how does Ibn Budayr manage to arrogate for himself the role of arbiter? It is simply through direct contact with the cultural elite. Just as biographical dictionaries describe relations of collegiality, Ibn Budayr, in his biographies of scholars and Sufis, describes convivial direct and personal relations with these (deceased) notables.[106] Let us take a few examples:

In Muḥarram, our *shaykh* and *lover—counted among the dearest of our companions*—Shaykh Muḥammad al-Azharī al-Miṣrī, known as Abū al-Surūr [the Father of Happiness], died. He was a great scholar and learned savant, unique in his age and singular in his epoch. May God, the Exalted, have mercy upon us through him and forgive him. *Ours was an old friendship and he had done us many a good deed.* Among these is the fact that if ever he visited me while I was depressed or grieving, I would quickly be restored to happiness, and he would not leave until I was laughing. . . . [107]

And:

On the 6th of Jumādā al-Thānī . . . The son of our *shyakh*, our teacher, *our friend, our refuge, our lover*, and our crown, who helped us in times of need, Muṣṭafā, the son of the deceased Shaykh, the Sea of Knowledge and the Concealed Secret, Muḥammad al-ʿAjlūnī, died.[108]

And:

On Friday, the 20th of Muḥarram, our *shyakh*, our teacher . . . the scholar of his time, unique in his age . . . Muḥammad b. al-Ghazzī, the Muftī of the Shāfiʿīs passed away. . . . I read Jurisprudence with him. We have not beheld any expression more pleasurable [than his] or meanings sweeter than in his speech.

And whatever poetry was uttered in his presence, he would be able to finish [the verses] and respond with more eloquent and better poetry.[109]

And:

The death of our *shaykh*, the knowledgeable scholar . . . Ismā'īl son of the Shaykh `Abd al-Ghanī al-Nābulusī . . . there was some companionship between us, and he was to us a friend and lover.[110]

And finally, one of Ibn Budayr's acquaintances was none other than the *naqīb al-ashrāf* (head of the "descendants of the Prophet," a group which will be discussed below):

The honorable and sublime scholar, the pious, the ascetic, the gentle, the modest . . . `Abd Allāh b. `Ajlān, *naqīb al-ashrāf* died . . . *there was some friendship between us , and he was a neighbor.*[111]

Although many a Damascene craftsman and artisan must have come into direct contact with the scholars, whether in a mosque, shop, or school or college, Ibn Budayr, by writing, established a competitive edge. He surveyed and "institutionalized" his social connections, therefore firmly establishing his position among the cultural elite in textual—that is, public—space. By using the form of the *tarjama*, the barber, in the manner of the scholar, was able to demonstrate veritable relations of friendship, benefit, love, and even laughter with the cultural elite. Of course, beyond establishing these connections, the barber's advertisement thereof must have served to further increase his prestige. Who would not want to befriend the friend of the right sort of people?

The appropriation of the form of the biography also allowed the barber to display yet another significant source and effect of cultural wealth: divine blessing (*baraka*). Ibn Budayr, like any other Ottoman of his time, took Sufism seriously, both in reading books of mysticism and in practice by being a member of a Sufi order. But the spiritual hierarchy in the world of mysticism divides the world into two: those who give divine blessing (the saints), and those who aspire to receive it (the seekers). Ibn Budayr, naturally, was on the receiving end. The chronicle contains a few instances of the author soliciting from Sufi saints the authorization to use certain supplicatory formulas that would deliver him from poverty, or help him cure a particular ailment.[112] However, it is significant that Ibn Budayr does not portray himself as just any other ordinary seeker of saintly blessings; after all, there is not much cultural capital to be gained from such an unremarkable location. Rather, he presents himself as someone who stands in an unusual location vis-à-vis the Sufi sources of divine blessing.

The learned (not only Sufis) were supposed to keep their hair short and were encouraged to get a haircut once a week. Therefore, "barbers plied a busy trade."[113] And Ibn Budayr gladly obliged and seems to have seen his trade as literally a blessing. Though other people struggled to be in the presence of Sufi conduits of divine grace, the fact of being a barber put Ibn Budayr in intimate and physical contact with them without his effort. Indeed, aside from his sobriquet (*al-ḥallāq*, "the barber") and the obituary of his master barber, our only clue to the fact that Ibn Budayr was a practicing barber is his mention by name of the Sufi masters among the customers that he coiffed at his barbershop. One of these was the prominent Sufi Yūsuf al-Ṭabbākh, who was very much one of the in people, occupying a good page in al-Murādī's biographical dictionary. Al-Murādī said of al-Ṭabbākh:

> Extraordinary virtue and spiritual power emanated from him, and he appeared like the sun in the middle of the day. It was said of him that he was one of the saints of the age, and the people hastened to kiss his hand and ask his blessing.[114]

And this is what Ibn Budayr has to say about this celebrated, sought after, and charismatic mystic:

> Among God's blessings upon me is that He afforded me the opportunity to sit with the saint, Yūsuf al-Ṭabbākh, in conversation, and to joke with him, and to *cut his hair*. I garnered his prayers as my spoils.[115]

Another coiffing encounter with a saint is this:

> The complete *shaykh*, possessor of manifest spiritual powers and of dazzling spiritual states, who had freed himself of the restrictions of the temporal world, and for whom night and day were one, who had drunk from the wine of the

All-Powerful King and was accorded recognition by the small and great alike, al-Shaykh Muḥammad Jabrī, who would sometimes be in trance and sometimes conscious, sometimes sober and sometimes intoxicated . . . held us in affection and often came by us. He was generally in a state of divine trance. May God be praised!—*I have barbered him several times* and was fortunate to receive his prayers and spiritual secrets.[116]

Ibn Budayr, in other words, was no ordinary petitioner for Divine favor. Although others hastened to kiss the hand of the likes of al-Ṭabbākh and asked their blessings, Ibn Budayr sat in the company of the saints, chatted and joked with them, and most significantly, *touched* them. He received their prayers in saintly gratitude for cutting their hair. To put it differently, if Jabrī and al-Ṭabbākh were "friends of God," Ibn Budayr was a friend of the friends of God, which was a source of considerable cultural wealth. The barber's unique location positioned him to be someone who had no less than a tactile connection with the saints. To touch is to claim.

So, given that the barber was neither scholar nor saint, he could not possibly enter one of those vertical chains of scholarly and spiritual authority through official licenses of *ijāza* and *silsila*. But what he managed to do is to insert himself in the *horizontal* chain of authority, where he displayed his social relations with the cultural elite. Through the language of love, companionship, and benefit, he ensconced himself among the scholars; and to the saints he was *palpably* close (albeit a closeness mediated by scissors and blade). The *tarjama* allowed Ibn Budayr to advertise and further cultivate his relations with the cultural elite. Ibn Budayr's story, therefore, was one of coif and tell.

Beyond formal textual appropriations in the barber's chronicle, the content also evinces Ibn Budayr's use of the social practices of the scholars and mystics.

The (Un)Enchanted Picnicker: Versifying Pleasure

Naturally, picnics were not the monopoly of the *`ulamā'* and saints. Picnicking and promenading in eighteenth-century Damascus, as in Istanbul, were very much in vogue. Ibn Budayr, like the scholar Ibn Kannān, mentions having gone out on *sīrān* (picnicking), but unlike Ibn Kannān, who had a dizzying outdoor schedule, the barber mentions having picnicked only a few times.[117] We may never find out whether Ibn Budayr simply could not afford to spend so much time enjoying the fresh air, or if he was a frequent picnicker. Regardless, Ibn Budayr's promenades are notable. In the manner of a scholar proud of his literary virtuosity, each time the barber described his pleasure in verse. Here is a particularly instructive example of the barber's commemoration of a day out in the beginning of the Spring:

> Oh, uncle, we have passed a day unsurpassed
> In teeming Marja of Damascus where there was not an empty space
> What a Thursday befallen of no misfortune![118]
> On the 18th of Rabīʿ al-Ākhir the cold departed
> Oh, literati (*yā hal al-adab* [*sic*]), relax, your constraints have left you.[119]

This form of verse is actually called *mawāliyā*, a typically Levantine form, sometimes uttered in colloquial, in a meter that is readily sung.[120] This kind of Arabic poetry is similar to the Turkish "şarkı" (a poem meant to be sung in local everyday dialect).[121] But unlike the Turkish counterpart, which was fashionable and used by even court poets such as Nedim, the *mawāliyā* never had the same success in elite Arabic-speaking literary circles.

It is interesting to see Ibn Budayr's participation in the social practice of versifying a picnic event and penning it in a chronicle, and watch him address his picnic companions as *ahl al-adab* ("literati"; also means, "polite society"). Thus Ibn Budayr, like a scholar, used the promenade as an occasion for poetic performance. He celebrated outdoor leisure time by showing off his literary virtuosity to a self-styled genteel circle. The performance, the supposed audience, and the reporting of the event in writing are all hallmarks of the scholar. However, Ibn Budayr's use of the *mawāliyā* form instead of more highbrow types of poetry betrays the novelty of his cultural wealth: a social gaffe?

Remarkably, this particular picnic event was not entirely enchanting for Ibn Budayr despite his poetic declarations. The passage immediately preceding the quoted lines is a prose description of the social constitution of the picnic area, which seems to have horrified the barber. The sight of multitudes of women eating, drinking coffee, and smoking in public deeply disturbed him. This is one of many instances in which Ibn Budayr expresses moral outrage, as will be seen later. For now, it is worth noting that Ibn Budayr's scholarlike social performance and self-designation as a member of the literati or polite society serve as attestations of his knowledge of the culture of the scholars. However the barber's nonscholarly origins are revealed as soon as he utters his verse, using a form not favored by elite types.

Dreaming Distinction: Prophetic Progeny

If lyricizing in picnics shows Ibn Budayr's attempt at the literary bravura of the scholars, it is his trespass into the dream world of the mystics that constitutes one of the barber's boldest moves. As mentioned earlier, Ibn Budayr was sometimes in the company of saints, whom he viewed with reverence and whose companionship he happily advertised, but he was always careful to never posit himself as being one of them. However, he manages to borrow one of their most significant legitimative practices: their dreams. Ibn Budayr's dream constitutes a remarkable strategy in which he attempts to convert acquired cultural wealth into nothing less than heritable legacy.

At one point in the chronicle, Ibn Budayr informs his readers that one of his sons "was titled by one of the titles of the Prophet," *al-sayyid* Muḥammad al-Mahdī (d. 1744).[122] The title *sayyid* is a marker of great social distinction that was the exclusive privilege of the descendants of the Prophet Muhammad (*ashrāf*, singular, *sharīf*), who constituted a distinct and respected community, and as we have seen, Ibn Budayr seems to have been acquainted with their leader. But the status of *sharīf* is not a happy germ that one catches through the society of the descendants of the Prophet; it is a title transferred through blood.[123] How did (could) Ibn Budayr, born without the particular cultural distinction, make a claim to such venerable descent? Ibn Budayr seems to recognize the boldness of his naming trick and its possible (mis)construance as an imprudent impingement, a faux pas. In order to preempt possible accusations of trespass, the barber informs the reader that his naming of his son was literally not "a transgression" (*bi-lā taʿaddī* [sic]). For Ibn Budayr's son's title was a result of an "inspiration from God the Almighty" (*ilhāman* [sic—with a final nūn] *min Allah ta`ālā*)![124] In other words, it is through a private vision, the ultimate authority—God himself—authorized Ibn Budayr to transform his children into Prophetic progeny.[125]

This is a fascinating maneuver on Ibn Budayr's part. The notion of private communication with the divine was far from alien in the Sufi environment, but it was generally understood as a rarified experience that came with considerable spiritual elevation (and at which sometimes the best of them, as in the case of the mentioned al-Zawāwī, failed). Although Sufis might invoke divine inspiration to legitimate and buttress claims to spiritual and social authority, Ibn Budayr's adoption of it for straightforward social climbing is altogether novel. Along with his superb courage, and the transparency of his politicking, it is precisely this strategic novelty that could almost be characterized as a classic marker of the arriviste.

The barber's vision may reek of a certain clumsiness, especially when contrasted with the dream life of al-Nābulusī, who having hailed from a wealthy scholarly family used dreams to convert his old, heritable wealth into spiritual capital. But the significance of Ibn Budayr's manipulation of the dream is his use of it to convert newly acquired cultural capital to claim a lineage, glorious and sanctified.

STRATEGIC DIFFERENCE: OLD LITERACY VS. *NOUVELLE RICHESSE*

It is the barber's knowledge of the social and textual practices of the scholars and mystics that seem to have enabled him to become an authority/author. And he used this authority to garner even more prestige through a variety of strategies despite some gaffes and faux pas that reveal his nouveau literacy. I have argued earlier that Ibn Budayr represents an example of upward social mobility. However, it should be remembered that he was never more than a man of modest means who consistently complained of insolvency and difficulty. So, how did the modest barber reconcile his social position (as improved as it may have been from that of his father) with his extraordinary cultural accomplishments?

In this regard, Ibn Budayr's attitude toward wealth is highly instructive: it is an attitude that makes "a virtue out of material necessity."[126] Recognizing that in *his* case material capital is not as easily accrued as cultural capital, Ibn Budayr took on the voice of his cultured scholarly companions and expressed distaste at the newly accumulated material wealth of the uncultured. Thus, at one point in his chronicle, the barber pronounces a janissary leader as, quite literally, "nouveau riche and of base origin" (*wa kāna hādha al-rajul muḥdith ni`ma wa fī aṣl-hi dunuwwu-hu* [sic]).[127] In this statement, Ibn Budayr distinguishes material wealth from cultural wealth and identifies himself securely with the latter. Indeed, he is never afraid or ashamed to identify himself as a poor man, as one of the "small people" in whose name he often spoke.

But if Ibn Budayr is disdainful of the nouveau riche, does he express any anxiety about his own nouveau literacy? Given what we now know about Ibn Budayr, one can read a certain anxiety in the obituary of his master barber, Ibn al-Ḥashīsh, whom Ibn Budayr called "my father," and which is worth quoting again here:

> During his lifetime, he barbered the Pole of his Time, he of the Sacred Station, `Abd al-Ghanī al-Nābulusī, may God sanctify his secret. He also barbered Murād Afandī al-Kasīḥ, and Muḥammad al-`Ajlūnī, and others like them.

These clients of the master barber are irrefutably the three most illustrious names in eighteenth-century Damascus. They combined scholarship and/or mystical authority with old money. This obituary of the teacher of his craft establishes the barber's own professional credentials through an old, historical connection with cultural capital. Having inherited nothing from his biological father, Ibn Budayr attempts to demonstrate that his cultural wealth is not recently acquired, but inherited from his surrogate father. In short, while although I have tried here to use Ibn Budayr as illustrative of the phenomenon of nouveau literacy, Ibn Budayr wants to demonstrate precisely the opposite, that he is "old literacy."

IN LIFE OR IN DEATH? THE BARBER'S FAMILY AND "OTHER" FRIENDS

The mention of the master barber, the surrogate father, brings us back to earth from the cloud of the cultural elite to Ibn Budayr's "other" friends and family: fellow learned illiterates, other surrogate fathers, fellow guildsmen, and children. To conclude the barber's social biography and understand the full import of his literary endeavor, we must complete the journey by visiting those of his associates, some very close, who fell outside the category of high scholars and saints. Not coincidentally, none of them are included in al-Murādī's biographical dictionary, and they came in various sorts and "forms." In making their acquaintance, we will be able to uncover the barber's other equally significant sources of cultural wealth. The place of these individuals in the barber's life also reveals to us different kinds of aspirations by the author, some of which are more mundane, immediate, and poignant than scholarly yearnings and lineage longings. This section exposes another side of the barber, not one constantly involved in sweet banter and convivial joking to the sound of clicking scissors, but a person in his full humanity: his aches and pains, his tragic losses, his surprising indifference to some people, and his immense respect to unexpected others.

The Apothecary of Remedies, the Historian al-Maqqār

Like Ibn Budayr, Muḥammad Ibn Jum`a al-Maqqār (d. 1744) is a figure known to the modern historian. His work *al-Bashāt wa al-quḍāt* ("the Governors and Judges of Damascus") is a list of governors and judges of Ottoman Damascus.[128] But al-Maqqār seems to have been unknown to his scholarly contemporaries, who do not cite his work. Nor is he listed in al-Murādī's *Silk al-durar.* However, to Ibn Budayr, al-Maqqār (or in Budayrian expression, "al-Maghghār") was a source of inspiration and cure. He was an esteemed fellow historian, and possibly a fellow craftsman,[129] that is to say, another case of a learned illiterate:

> On Thursday, our *shaykh* . . . Muḥammad al-Maghghār died. He was a knowledgeable man, delicate and blessed. He composed a great history and other works. I myself and others were witnesses to his sainthood. . . . If someone asked him about the [date of] death of an `*ālim*, or the [date of] rule of a governor, or an event in the past, he would raise his head to the sky for a little while and say "on such-and-such day, on such-and-such a month, in such-and-such a year."[130]

Clearly, it is both al-Maqqār's prodigious capacity for historical information and his manifest sainthood that impress Ibn Budayr. The passage also betrays Ibn Budayr's idea of what constitutes history in the hypothetical examples he proffers to demonstrate the skill of his friend: When did a *scholar* die? When did a *governor* rule? And what events happened in the past? For him the subjects fit for history are the scholarly and political elite, and larger historical events. Hence Ibn Budayr reflects the consensus of the scholarly elite in that they, along with the political/military elite, constitute the legitimate and exclusive subjects of the historical text. They are the very stuff of history. It is noteworthy that Ibn Budayr omits mention of any qualities of his friend that fall outside scholarly and spiritual prowess.

Al-Maqqār's sainthood—inasmuch as he is able to perform small curative miracles—is also significant and was witnessed by Ibn Budayr himself. The fellow historian licensed Ibn Budayr to use all kinds of supplicatory formulas to deliver him from physical and emotional distress. On one occasion, al-Maqqār chanced on Ibn Budayr and one of his sons on the street and seems to have immediately recognized the general disquiet from which the barber suffered. He licensed both Ibn Budayr and his son to recite certain words "from which many benefits" emanated.[131] On other occasions, the barber complained to al-Maqqār about "poor memory" and "knee pain," occupational hazards for a historian and a barber, respectively. Al-Maqqār repeatedly obliged by allowing Ibn Budayr (and, again, one of his sons) to recite certain supplications, which the *shaykh* himself had received from rather high spiritual authorities.[132]

Al-Maqqār performed important functions in Ibn Budayr's life, intellectual and spiritual or curative. Given al-Maqqār's "great history" (at least in the estimation of Ibn Budayr), one wonders if the friendship between them had any influence at all in Ibn Budayr's decision to undertake a history project. Though al-Maqqār's history, something akin to a list, is not as sophisticated as Ibn Budayr's chronicle, the latter clearly admired al-Maqqār and may have received a nudge of approval from him. But beyond collegiality between historians, to Ibn Budayr al-Maqqār was the saintly apothecary of curative remedies.

Fellow Guildsmen

On that day, three heads of guilds in Damascus died. ʿAbd al-Qādir, the head of the confectioners, and he was a godly man may God have mercy on him, the head of the barbers' guild, the master, Muḥammad al-Būshī, may God have mercy on him, and the head of *qāwūq* (head gear)-makers Muḥammad, may God have mercy on him.[133]

This is how Ibn Budayr reports the death of three guild leaders, including the head of his own guild. Though it is clear that Ibn Budayr bore no hostility to any of these fellow artisans, it is surprising that he does not accord them—especially the head of his own guild—proper textual respect in the form of *tarjama*s. The mention of these guildsmen is so cursory that one wonders if it is merely the coincidence of the three deaths on the same day that renders it a recordable, historical event rather than the value of the personages themselves. Though one may justify this omission as indicative of Ibn Budayr's purist attitude toward the "stuff of history" (as being exclusive to scholars and governors), Ibn Budayr clearly made some exceptions, as in this obituary notice:

Aḥmad al-Bābā, the head of the dyers' guild died, may God have mercy on him . . . he was nice looking, cheerful and good man, who smiled at whomever he met . . . he did not suffer from any lack, but was not arrogant . . . there was affection and friendship between us.[134]

What seems to have determined Ibn Budayr's choice in this instance is not the person's spiritual and/or scholarly knowledge but the degree of his friendship with the deceased. Nothing seems to distinguish the head of the dyers' guild from that of the barbers' guild except the degree of convivial ties to the biographer evident in this *tarjama*.

Finally, another head guildsman appears in the barber's chronicle. Fortunately, he appears in one of those few merry occasions recorded in the barber's chronicle, a picnic. In a cursory fashion, Ibn Budayr mentions having been invited to a promenade organized by, in a manner of speaking, one of the literati, *ahl al-adab*. The host is a certain Dāwūd al-Samrī (or al-Simarī), the head of the storytellers' guild (*shaykh al-ḥakawātiyya*).[135]

The relationship of Ibn Budayr to storytellers and their art is definitive and will be explored later. For now, it is important to emphasize that even though fellow guildsmen do appear in this craftsman history, their appearance is highly circumscribed.

Family: Son In the Image of the Father

In his chronicle, Ibn Budayr mentions two sons, a mother (upon her death), and a daughter (upon her birth).[136] The mention of family members like those of other associates is incidental and not purposive. They occur upon incidents of death (and birth in one instance), and events considered significant enough to be commemorated. For example, Ibn Budayr's younger son, al-Sayyid Muḥammad, is mentioned on both occasions when Ibn Budayr received supplicatory beneficial formulas from al-Maqqār. The son simply happened to be there. A further example is the mention of another son, al-Sayyid Muṣṭafā, who accompanied his father on two visits to the shrine of al-Sayyida Zaynab.[137] From these short references, one can surmise that the attainment of spiritual remedies from living spiritual authorities and blessings from graves of dead saints constituted commemorative events in Ibn Budayr's life. But more to the point, these references, as fleeting as they are, reflect the extent to which Ibn Budayr's sons were his companions outside the home.

The father was not just a friend and companion to his children. Ibn Budayr seems also to have been interested in giving them an education at least comparable to his. On the death of one scholar, Ibn Budayr offers an obituary:

> The practicing scholar, the memorizer and reciter [of the Quran], our *shaykh*, lover, and friend, `Alī al-Miṣrī, the Shafi`ī leader to prayers in the Umayyad Mosque, who is the Quran teacher of most of the scholars of Damascus, died . . . we befriended him through (*bi-wāsiṭat*) our son al-Sayyid Muṣṭafā, whom [al-Miṣrī] especially liked, and with whom he read the Quarter [of the Holy Book]. . . . Towards the end of his life, he spent a lot of time in our company in the barbershop and became dearer than most brothers.[138]

Ibn Budayr's son's education went beyond the Holy Book with the "elementary school" teacher of the Umayyad mosque. Like his father, al-Sayyid

Muṣṭafā also studied jurisprudence as evidenced by another biography in the chronicle.[139]

But this quotation is of particular interest because of its exposition of the degree to which Ibn Budayr's son was literally the conduit (*wāsiṭa*) in this particular social connection between the barber and the scholar. Also, it is important to note that this ʿAlī al-Miṣrī is of the few scholars and Sufis (in addition to the humorous Abū al-Surūr above, and al-Jibāwī below) who seem to have frequented Ibn Budayr's shop not for his barbering services but merely to socialize and engage in banter.

Perhaps nothing is more revealing of the barber's aspirations for and cultivation of his children than in his touching and anguished obituary for his son al-Sayyid Muḥammad al-Mahdī, who sadly passed away suddenly at a tender age:

> And among the things I lost was a youth lost to the plague. He was 14 years old and intelligent. He was one of the Signs of the All-Knowing Master. He had read the whole of the Quran, was possessed of goodness, religiosity, and a fine mind, and was a reader of books, such as *al-Durr al-thamīn*. His eloquence pleased the young and the old. He was snatched away within two days—Oh, my brothers!—as if he never was! He used to write for me and help me in the craft and in the hardships of life. Then the plague took him—as if he never was! Thus was the judgment of He who says to the thing, "Be! and it is"—"We are God's and unto him we return."[140]

This devastating loss betrays the degree to which the barber invested in the education of his children, both professional and scholarly. Like his father, the son read serious books. The title mentioned in the notice might be *al-Durr al-thamīn fī al-munāqasha bayna Abī Ḥayyān wa al-Samīn* ("The Precious Pearls Surrounding the Discussion between Abū Ḥayyān and al-Samīn") by Badr al-Dīn al-Ghazzī (d. 1576), Muftī of Damascus in the early Ottoman period.[141] The same author, it should be noted, also composed a work on scholarship and education.[142]

Although al-Sayyid Muḥammad was engaged in some scholarship through reading and copying for his father, unlike the "prodigal" son of the weaver mentioned in al-Murādī's biographies above he did not leave his poor father to his own devices in order to doggedly follow the path of scholarship. Ibn

Budayr's son was more normative and accepted being groomed to become a barber. Had he lived on, al-Sayyid Muḥammad in all likelihood would have been another learned illiterate, a barber with scholarly inclinations. Ibn Budayr, it seems, intended to produce a son in his own image.

BACK TO THE COFFEEHOUSE

Though we left the society of the high *`ulamā'* and Sufis to meet Ibn Budayr's more modest friends and his children on the street, in picnics, and at saints' shrines, our journey in search of Ibn Budayr and his book is not complete without entering the earthy place that functioned as a sibling institution to the barbershop: the coffeehouse.

The high *`ulamā'* held coffeehouses in contempt for being the gathering of the "riff-raff." The scholar Ibn Kannān never mentions having frequented a coffeehouse. Al-Murādī, the biographer of the elite, does not hide his low regard for coffee shops and their culture. His biography of a scholar and renowned poet, Aḥmad Shākir al-Ḥakawātī, is telling. Apparently, Shākir's poetry was excellent and prodigious enough to warrant a *dīwān* (collection into a book); however, the poet, owing to his own imprudence, ended up in the most undesirable of places. This is his story:

> He wasted his time in the practice of alchemy. Some people fell into the temptation [of alchemy] and squandered away their money. He did not desist from his habit until he died. This was the main reason for his poverty, the filthiness of his attire, his poor vision, and illness. . . . Thus, [his] conditions changed and fate threw him into troubles and calamities until he ended up in some coffeehouses, in the worst of places, telling stories, unusual tales, and jokes. [This is] despite his [original] respectability and his uncontestable literary prowess.[143]

Rather than remaining in his appropriate social position, in the séances and the picnic assemblies of the literati, Shākir squandered his wealth (and along with it, his prestige) to metamorphose into a coffee shop *ḥakawātī* (alternatively, *ḥakawī*, a storyteller). For al-Murādī, the literati's sojourns to the coffeehouse are a sign of descent straight into calamity. Ibn Budayr does not aver. On the death of Ibrāhim al-Jibāwī, the Shaykh of the Sa`diyya order, Ibn Budayr accords the famous mystic the appropriate characterization in a biography and ends with these remarks:

He was not arrogant and did not hold himself with [too much] esteem. Rather, he used to mix with everyone and would sit in the coffeehouses and souqs and talk to notables and commoners [alike], not counting himself a leader or a notable. . . . He was our friend and lover. He was delicate and he would sit with us in the shop and converse with us in sweet language. He would enjoy our banter, and would say, "I love you, by God, and you love us" . . . he would pray for us [with the effect that] much good and blessings occurred to us . . . and [once] we invited him, his children, some of his followers, and some dear friends to our house. [144]

This is yet another instance of a rather highly placed mystic frequenting Ibn Budayr's shop for company (not for barbering services). However, what is significant here is that the barber sees the mystic's socialization with commoners in cafes and markets not as socially reprehensible behavior (à la al-Murādī). On the contrary, it is a sign of a positive virtue: modesty. However, the very fact of Ibn Budayr's comment about the conduct of the mystic itself belies a shared point of reference with al-Murādī: a man of al-Jibāwī's station is not to be expected to mix with commoners in such places as cafes, markets, and barbershops. According to Ibn Budayr's logic, had al-Jibāwī "held himself with the" deserved "esteem," he would not have frequented coffeehouses, or for that matter his barbershop.

But what do coffeehouses have to do with Ibn Budayr? He received an education at the hands of *`ulamā'* and Sufis, in mosques and *madrasa*s. But he also received another kind of education, one usually disseminated at the coffeehouse:

Our father, mentor (*ustādh*), and instructor, Sulaymān b. Ḥashīsh al-Ḥakawī died—may God have mercy upon him! He augmented his age and time, and was singular in the arts of his time. He related the epics of al-Ẓāhir, Sayf, and Samar and `Antar,[145] in Arabic and Turkish. He had a prodigious memory and sound knowledge of every art, for all that he was illiterate and could not read and write: this is the highest degree of eloquence amongst mankind. He was a blond albino, extremely white-skinned. Indeed, he was a bottomless ocean, may God have mercy upon him![146]

What a far cry from al-Murādī's attitude to the poet Shākir's "descent" into the coffeehouse and its stories! For Ibn Budayr, the illiterate public narrator of popular epics is as much an ocean of knowledge as his *ʿulamā'* teachers. The barber's affinity to Ibn al-Ḥashīsh is not unexpected. Given his last name, the storyteller may have been the brother of Ibn Budayr's master barber, Aḥmad b. al-Ḥashīsh. If so, the connection serves to further reveal the "sibling" relationship between barbershop and coffee shop.

Ibn Budayr's acknowledgment of the storyteller is entirely appropriate, and it fittingly concludes our journey into the barber's biography for it opens up for us the barber's book, its form and content. Later on in this study, we will settle in the barbershop and coffeehouse in order to explore the literary aspects of Ibn Budayr's chronicle. There, we will measure the great debt that the scholarly history of the nouveau literate owes to the popular oral story of the illiterate. But before we move to the literary aspect of this study, further exploration of the larger phenomenon of nouveau literacy is in order.

CHAPTER 3

"Cheap" Monumentality

The Nouveau Literates and Their Texts

In his endeavor to write history, the barber was not alone. In the eighteenth-century Levant, a host of other non-*`ulamā'* chose to write records of events they witnessed during their lifetime. Whether coincidentally or not, Ibn Kannān (the proud owner of a remodeled reception hall and an enchanted reveler and picnicker) was the last Levantine *`ālim* known to have written a chronicle. The *`ulamā'* hegemony over the production of historical knowledge was finally completely broken; their "monopoly over time" had ceased. The text of the chronicle was now open to *other* people, those whose professions and lifestyles were not directly associated with Islamic learned culture: two soldiers from Damascus, a Shi`ī farmer and his son from southern Lebanon, a Ḥimṣi judicial court clerk, a Samaritan scribe from Nablus, a Damascene Greek Orthodox priest, and of course our barber of Damascus (Map 1). The convergence of so many people of such *different* backgrounds on the text of the chronicle cannot be attributed to mere coincidence. This is the "literary disorder" that is nouveau literacy.

Aside from variety of background among the new authors and their choice to write in the same genre of contemporary history, what else unifies our texts into a phenomenon? The answer, in one word, is language, which was decidedly *not* the language of the *`ulamā'*. The authors' indiscriminate use of the varied registers of Arabic, including "colloquial Arabic," is reflective of not only the degree of freedom that the eighteenth-century history text allowed but also the distance of its new authors from learned culture. Thus, after I traverse the Levant in search of our new authors' histories—their biographies, communities, and texts—I will consider their use of language. The exploration of the linguistic attributes of the nouveau literates' texts will take us to the next question: For whom were these histories written? A part of this chapter will offer tentative answers about the reception and circulation of our non-*`ulamā'* chronicles.

For now, let us remain within the realm of the social. Like the affordable "monuments" constructed by the newly arrived in eighteenth-century Istanbul, the chronicles of our nouveau literates constituted evidence of improvement in status, an entry of some sort, and an opportunity to garner more of that status, a negotiation of some sort. If the barber's arrival into textual space paralleled his journey into the worlds of the learned elite, then the other new authors' ventures, whether individually or as spokespersons for larger communities, also reflected entries, but into new households or new political configurations. In other words, although Ibn Budayr may have found a patron in the figure of the *`ālim* himself (and the Sufi), the other new historians found patrons in differing sorts of figures: provincial governors, district governors, and even minor subdistrict governors. Worse still—or even better, depending on whose side one is on—the Shī`ī farmers found patronage in what is usually seen as a most unreliable figure: a rebel. As with the text of our barber, (most of the) nouveau literates' chronicles were books, that is, public monuments. They were announcements of triumph, but they all masked a significant amount of discomfort born out of tireless jostling and continuous strategizing. Here, we will become acquainted with the motley crew of the new historians and their stories. As I treat the life and work of each author, and his community where relevant, I also expose his motivations and agenda. In other words, I explore what impelled and enabled these authors to write.

A PRIEST WITH A MISSION: MĪKHĀ'ĪL BURAYK AL-DIMASHQĪ (FL. 1782)

It now occurred to me to record (*u'arrikh*) what happened in my time in order that those who read it might remember me.[1]

Despite this note expressing a desire for self-memorialization on the part of our Greek Orthodox priest, Mīkhā'īl Burayk, his chronicle, which covers the years 1720–1782, is not about himself but about the Greek Orthodox community in Damascus.[2] Though the chronicle focuses on the tribulations of Christians, it barely treats theological or ecclesiastical matters. As such, to the best of our knowledge Burayk was the very first Orthodox priest in the Levant to write a secular (for lack of a better term) chronicle in the Arabic language.[3] Indeed, the author expressly posits his chronicle as a plain and simple "history of . . . Damascus . . . and the Damascenes," including its clergy and (Muslim) rulers.[4]

The most striking feature of Burayk's chronicle is the author's keen awareness of the momentous change that is taking place in his time. The priest recognizes a new order along with attendant opportunities and dangers. He is able to characterize the governorship of al-`Aẓm family as a new and dynastic regime whose protagonists are "sons of Arabs."[5] Of equal momentousness to Burayk is the defection of members of his community to Catholicism. To Burayk the schismatics adopted "the opinion of the Westerners (*ra'y al-gharbiyyīn*)" and "the inclination of the Westerners" or followed "a Frankish fancy (*hawā al-ifranj*)."[6] Let us examine how Burayk characterizes and negotiates these two phenomena.

It is most striking that Burayk is quick to read both opportunity and improvement in the rule of al-`Aẓm:

> I have read all of the histories of Damascus since its takeover by the Muslims until now, and I have not read one that reported the degree of wealth, strength, repute, power, and mention that the Christians have reached in the past ten years under the rule of As`ad Pasha Ibn al-`Aẓm. His name is As`ad [i.e., more felicitous], and good fortune (*al-sa`d*) is in his face.[7]

Burayk's unequivocal approval of As`ad Pasha al-`Aẓm's rule stems from a simple fact. According to Burayk, As`ad Pasha, who is the foremost representative of the new ruling household, lifted all the legal proscriptions regulating religious minorities under Muslim rule in their position as religious minorities. Although these rules were never systematically applied at all times and places, if we are to believe Burayk (and we have no reason to disbelieve him) As`ad Pasha granted Christians complete social freedom to the point that they were able to consume alcohol in public, and he allowed them to engage in commercial and building activities without "fear or envy" and visit religious sites "without restriction."[8] For Burayk, in his typically metaphorical style, this is a brave new world in which Christians of Damascus blossomed "like the flowers of April and May."[9]

But this auspicious moment brought about by the new order leads Burayk to be anxiously intent on preserving it. To his mind, the Muslim state has done its part, and now it is the turn of the Christian community to "behave itself" by not committing transgressions that may compromise its new (relatively) empowered position. Given his position of guardianship as a priest, Burayk takes it on himself to act as his community's moral compass by constantly surveying it and admonishing where admonishment is due.[10] In this he spares no one, although his severest criticism is reserved for his female co-religionists. This aspect of Burayk's guardianship is worth exploring precisely because it renders his strategies transparent.

The priest sees what he considers inappropriate behavior by women—whether wearing fashionable headdresses, or smoking and drinking alcohol and coffee in public—as a misreading by women of the recently ameliorated status of Christians. He says:

> As for the Christian women of Damascus, when they saw the opportunity [afforded in the relaxing of sumptuary rules] and felt sure of the rulers, they were deceived by Satan and filled with false pride. They transgressed all limits. . . . When they saw that God had been merciful to them and freed them a little from slavery, oppression, and excessive taxation, the devil deluded them, nay, they deluded themselves. . . . Truly, we say there is no harm or evil that is not caused by women.[11]

Misogyny notwithstanding, it is clear that Burayk sees the enhanced position of the community as a reason to worry about the moral order. For Burayk, the preservation of newly acquired privileges requires striking the right balance: women must not "transgress" by flaunting themselves and engaging in public diversions. In other words, the priest is conscious that the ameliorated position of the Christian community does not constitute limitless freedom, but one that is bound. If the Christians do not pay careful attention to preserve the new boundaries from within, a reversal of status might occur. For Burayk, the policy to be adopted by the community is clear: they must tread delicately and carefully.

If Burayk treats the relationship between his own minority community and the Muslim state with cautious and anxious optimism, he is rather indelicate and less hopeful about inter-Christian affairs. Understandably, the schism within the Greek Orthodox Church is threatening and distressful to Burayk. Ever frank and ready to take on responsibility,

Burayk does not lay the blame, or not all of it, on the schismatics. Rather, he unabashedly exposes his own church's dirty laundry. For example, he reports much to his dismay that the Patriarch of the church turned out to be a moneylender.[12] He also blames the Greek Orthodox for petitioning Muslim officials to impose taxes on the Greek Catholics, thereby inducing the latter to respond in kind.[13] In short, what worries Burayk is that the defection to Catholicism is only a reflection of the mismanagement of and ill-advised decisions by church officials, and disorder and corruption within the church itself. With a tone of resignation, Burayk shares with his reader this conclusion:

> Know, you who are reading this history of mine: if you see in your time lack of concord and lack of love among the bishops, and also among the priests, the monks, and the Christians [in general]; know, this is from long ago, as the histories have told us![14]

It is with a wistful and slightly fatalist tone that Burayk reconciles himself to inter-Christian discord. Perhaps this experience and sentiment explains the reason behind Burayk's leaving of the office of vicar and archimandrite of the prestigious Ṣidnāyā Monastery, in which position he served for only one year. He attributes his resignation from office to "excessive burdens and absence of organization."[15] Thus his acquiescent attitude toward problems within the Christian community is remarkably different from the more deliberative posture the author assumes regarding the position of the Christians in the `Aẓm-led Islamic order. Even if less hopeful about inter-Christian dealings, Burayk's insistent commentary on the affairs of the respective Christian communities—the Orthodox and the schismatics—betrays a clear and expected agenda: the unity of the Christian community.

Of all the chroniclers in our sample, Burayk possesses a most remarkable historical vision. Every one of our new authors notes the changes around them, but Burayk distinguishes himself in his ability to isolate and define what he saw as two separate new phenomena: the rule of the al-`Aẓm and the schism within the Greek Orthodox church. In other words, he identified a new order.

CULTIVATED AGRICULTURALISTS: ḤAYDAR RIḌĀ AL-RUKAYNĪ (D. 1783) AND HIS UNNAMED SON (FL. 1832)

This chronicle covers the years 1749 to 1832 and is authored by the Shī`ī farmer Ḥaydar Riḍā al-Rukaynī (henceforth al-Rukaynī Sr.) and completed by his unnamed son (al-Rukaynī Jr.).[16]

The Rukaynīs belonged to the minority Shī`ī community known as the Matāwila (singular, Mitwālī).[17] This agricultural community inhabited the mountainous area north of the Galilee known, both historically and today, as Jabal `Āmil, which included the Ottoman subdistricts of Bilād Bishāra, al-Shaqīf, and al-Shawmar.[18] Neither father nor son informs us where exactly in southern Lebanon they live, though the events of the chronicle take place overwhelmingly in the mentioned regions and end with al-Rukaynī Jr.'s migration to Damascus. This chronicle by father and son is the first contemporary chronicle in the Shī`ī tradition of Jabal `Āmil[19] and the only chronicle in Arabic-Islamic history known to have been written by farmers. Although it is easy for one to understand how an urban Greek Orthodox priest such as Burayk would be literate, the fact of the literacy of rural farmers requires some investigation. The only ready explanation has to do with the famous educational tradition of Shī`ī Jabal `Āmil,[20] which in the Ottoman period at least went well beyond an elite class of *`ulamā'*. We do not have a sense of numbers, but it is known that college-building activity continued throughout the eighteenth century.[21] However, as I have stated earlier, literacy, though a necessity for reading and writing, is not enough to establish authority. What is it that gave these farmers the confidence to author a chronicle?

Although the Shī`īs of Jabal `Āmil were always famed for their scholarship (even if chronicle writing was never their forte), they were not known for military and political power. This situation temporarily changed during one moment in the eighteenth century. Under the leadership of Naṣīf al-Naṣṣār (d. 1781), whose adventures and military achievements are ever more closely monitored and celebrated in the chronicle of the farmers, the Mitwālīs managed to become a serious nuisance to Ottoman authorities.[22] Thanks to al-Ẓāhir `Umar, who it will be remembered monopolized cotton trade in Palestine and rebelled against the Ottomans, the Mitwālīs, through a strategic alliance with him, managed to "piggyback" onto the stage of glory—albeit temporarily. This was no small feat since the region was rife with power struggles between various contenders representing the different confessional communities. By the time the Mitwālīs rose to power, the Maronite community under the leadership of the al-Khāzin family had occupied areas formerly inhabited by Shī`īs,[23] while the Drūz Shihābī family was consolidating its rule as an "emirate," a principality.[24] In other words, by choosing to ally with al-`Umar, the Mitwālīs managed to *survive* as a relatively independent community. It is the momentousness of this event that opened up the space for these farmers to write a history. Like the priest Mikhā'īl Burayk, the elevation of whose community under the rule of As`ad Pasha was one of the reasons impelling him to write, the Rukaynīs saw in the moment the opportunity to record the feat of survival.

One of the major enemies in the narrative of the Rukaynīs is the Ottoman state, which defined its own identity and legitimacy partly in opposition to Shī`ism.[25] Thus, *al-dawla* or "the State," which is the term the Rukaynīs used to describe Ottoman authorities, was not only simply a military threat but also a possible cause of extinction. As such, successful repulsion of the "state" becomes, in the eyes of the authors, not just a cause for celebration but almost a raison d'être. Here is how the chronicle depicts the most glorious episode in Mitwālī political history, the defeat of the highest representative of Ottoman rule in Syria, the governor of Damascus. This episode culminated in the occupation of Sidon by the joint forces of the Matāwila and al-Ẓāhir al-`Umar and is described in epic terms:

On 20 Jumādā al-Awwal,1185 [1771 CE], Al-Shaykh Nāṣīf, al-Shaykh Ḥamza, al-Shaykh Ḥamad al-`Abbās, al-Shaykh `Alī Fāris, and al-Shaykh al-Ẓāhir al-`Umar and his sons rode to Jisr Banāt Ya`qūb to fight the armies of `Uthmān Pasha, the governor of Damascus, along with two sub-district governors, those of Baṣṣa and of Mar`ash. They [Matāwila and al-Ẓāhir] inflicted a great defeat on these Pashas and they subjected the *dawla* to humiliation and disgrace because they [the governors] were utterly abased in a manner that had not happened in this age. They threw themselves, their horses and whatever they had with them into Lake Ḥūla. They were like Pharoah and his armies: "We drowned them in the sea"[26] "and they were unable to defend themselves."[27] They were overwhelmed by [the Mitwālī] battle cries and cowered in their places filled with despair and overcome by debasement. And they [the Matāwila] took from them [the governors' armies] booty of all kinds: canons and camels and horses and donkeys and sparkling swords and bedding and furniture and these became the property of people who had neither owned them nor would have inherited them. Their turbans and headgear were carried away on the surface of the water more quickly than stones [cast] from catapults, their munitions and gunpowder burned in a pillar that lit up the sky. Some were killed while the skin of others turned black. They were overcome by suffering and black tribulation and the *dawla* was laid low like `Ād and Thamūd. Of the armies of the *dawla*, which had numbered 10,000, only few survived, while all of the army of the Bishāriyya [i.e., the Matāwila], who were 300 horsemen, survived except for one man who was killed. His name was Shaykh Jabr of the Ḥamadiyya. As for the Bedouins who had fought alongside the *dawla*, they fled like rabid camels, and scattered in the wilderness asking for succor. Thus, their armies were subdued, laid low and humiliated like chaff blown by the wind, and they became bereft of joy and happiness. The downfall and defeat was that of the *dawla*.[28]

In this boastful passage, Rukaynī Sr. quits his customary terse and unembellished style and indulges in literary flourishes to document, emphasize, and glorify the military prowess of the Matāwila. Military prowess emerges in the authors' vision as the sole guarantor for the political independence, if not survival, of a small community. The passage also illustrates al-Rukaynī Sr.'s view of the Ottoman *dawla*. He likens the *dawla* to Pharoah, the Quranic symbol of the oppressive and illegitimate ruler. The author also compares the *dawla* to the people of `Ād and Thamūd, whose punishment by God, according to the Quran, is due to their denial of their prophets. In other words, the *dawla* is seen not only as illegitimate but also as religiously astray. The Rukaynīs' Shī`ī political identity and their view of the Ottoman *dawla* as politically and religiously illegitimate are neatly encapsulated in al-Rukaynī Jr.'s adaptation of some verses of traditional Shī`ī poetry predicting the appearance of the Hidden Imam:

If you see the two stars overlapping in
Capricorn in the morning and in the evening,
It is there that revenge will be taken from the Turks for the House of Muḥammad
and their oppression by their enemies.[29]

It is instructive to compare al-Rukaynī Jr.'s formulation of these verses with the original as preserved in the Shī`ī traditional literature, where the second line reads as follows:

It is there that revenge and the rightful inheritance of the House of Muḥammad
will be demanded from their enemies at the point of the sword.[30]

There is no mention of Turks in the original version. Thus al-Rukaynī Jr., in his formulation of an anti-Ottoman Matāwila political identity, adapted the Shī`ī eschatological tradition to the specific political situation of the Matāwila where the enemy is Ottoman Turks.

Although their hostility toward the *dawla* is evident throughout the chronicle,[31] the Rukaynīs' communal survival was also threatened by other regional confessional groups, especially the Drūz, who were consolidating their power under the leadership of the Shihābī family. Eager to delegitimize the Ottomans, the Rukaynīs nevertheless make no apologies on those occasions when the Matāwila actually ally with the Ottoman Empire against other groups. The dominant principle in such instances is unabashed self-interest. In another ringing panegyric, al-Rukaynī Jr. glorifies the military prowess of his people as they fight in alliance with al-Jazzār Pasha, the infamous Ottoman governor of Sidon, to defeat the Drūz chieftains of the district of al-Shūf.[32] Ironically, Jazzār Pasha would later kill the hero of our chroniclers, the Mitwālī leader al-Shaykh Nāṣīf al-Naṣṣār. These shifting alliances are exactly what compels the Rukaynīs to fill their chronicle with skirmishes and military events and to tirelessly note the power struggles in the region as though from a watchtower.

Hopeful for the perpetuation of their community and fearful for its extinction, the Rukaynīs saw matters as being not only religious (that is, ideological) but also pragmatic. It is no coincidence that the period covered by the chronicle is precisely the same in which the Matāwila community made a military, albeit short, presence in the region. In this two-in-one chronicle, the Rukaynīs' vision of authorship betrays the attitude that the individual author was not of significance. Rather, it was a project of collective memorialization of a distinct community, which had finally asserted itself militarily. This was a sign of a new time.

THE LOYAL SAMARITAN: IBRĀHĪM AL-DANAFĪ (FL. 1783)

Passover (*`Īd al-Fiṭr*) fell on the Friday. We carried out the sacrifice in the courtyard of the temple, without loud exaltation or extolment: the people were in a state of profound unease and anxiety such as never happened before.[33]

The passage indicates that the author of the chronicle from Nablus was a Samaritan. The Passover of 1771 was an unusually subdued affair as Nablus was under siege by the forces of al-Ẓāhir al-`Umar (the sometimes ally of the Matāwila community. Within the context of Nablus, al-`Umar is a villain writ large). Though the author does not identify himself in the text of chronicle, the manuscript of which is incomplete and untitled, there seems to be no doubt that the author is Ibrāhīm al-Danafī al-Sāmirī, known as al-`Ayyā, "the Tired One."[34] Ibrāhīm al-Danafī lived circa 1710–1783, and the chronicle covers the years 1770–1773.

The Samaritans were the subject of attention of many nineteenth-century Western travelers to Palestine, but most people today know nothing about the tiny community beyond the biblical reference to "the Good Samaritan."[35]

The Samaritan community has been numerically small throughout its history. Between the sixteenth century and today the Samaritan population was estimated not to have exceeded 600 individuals.[36] Several Samaritan communities existed in the sixteenth century, spread out among Nablus, Gaza, Damascus, and Cairo.[37] Today, however, the bulk of the community lives by the foot of Mount Gerizim in Nablus under the Palestinian Authority. A small part of the Samaritan community lives in Holon, which is in the metropolitan area of Tel-Aviv in Israel.[38] In terms of their religious doctrine, the Samaritans can be considered a schism from ancient Judaism. The most important difference between Samaritanism and first-century Judaism is the Samaritan reverence of Mount Gerizim (as opposed to the Jewish reverence for Jerusalem). Although Samaritans believe in the Torah as a whole, for them only the Pentateuch holds canonical force, and they reject the entirety of the oral law (the Mishna and Talmud). As such, all of their feasts are of Pentateuchal origin. Until the third century, Jews and Samaritans were not differentiated in religious terms and there is no definite point at which the schism took place. Samaritanism is similar to pre-Rabbinic Judaism, yet the Samaritans themselves do not identify as Jews.[39] The original language of the Samaritans was one of the forms of Aramaic and their script was palaeo-Hebraic. After the Arab conquest of the Levant, Arabic slowly replaced Aramaic, but the Samaritans continued using the palaeo-Hebraic script side by side with the Arabic script.[40] The contemporary Holon Samaritan community has adopted modern Hebrew as a vernacular.[41]

Ibrāhīm al-Danafī was one of the 200 Samaritans who lived in Nablus in the eighteenth century.[42] He was, in fact, a known social and intellectual figure in Samaritan history:

> In the 18th century—when the Samaritans had practically been reduced to the few families living in Nablus—there worked there the important commentator, grammarian, historian, and poet Ibrāhīm al-`Ayyā, one of the most famous of Samaritan literary and scholarly figures. . . . He is responsible, together with his uncle Meshālma b. Murjān, for the most comprehensive Samaritan commentary on the Genesis, Exodus, Leviticus and Numbers. Further, he participated in the exchange of correspondence with European scholars.[43]

Given his scholarly accomplishments, it comes as no surprise that al-Danafī wrote a chronicle.[44] After all, Samaritan scribes are known to have jotted down daily events on the extra folia of their codices.[45] However, this chronicle—intended to be a complete work, not just scribblings—is in fact the only extant chronicle written in Arabic by a Samaritan since the famous fourteenth-century chronicle by Abu al-Fatḥ.[46] The manuscript was found among the private collection of the Ṭūqān family of Nablus, to whom the author was intimately connected.[47]

The Danafīs were an originally Damascene Samaritan family who arrived in Nablus in the seventeenth century, where they entered the service of the Ṭūqāns, one of the three most important families in the city.[48] Al-Danafī served as a secretary (*kātib*) to Muṣṭafā Beg Ṭūqān, who was a standing contender for the position of *mutasallim* (subdistrict governor) of Nablus. As such, al-Danafī's profile seems to fit perfectly the impression of an eighteenth-century traveler who visited the nearby Gazan Samaritan community and observed that the Samaritans were rich and served as clerks to the local notables.[49] It was al-Danafī's patron, Muṣṭafā Beg Ṭūqān, who led the defense of Nablus against the forces of al-Ẓāhir al-`Umar. In this, Muṣṭafā Beg Ṭūqān was commissioned by the governor of Damascus and eventually rewarded with the district governorship. Thus Muṣṭafā Ṭūqān begins in al-Danafī's chronicle as Muṣṭafā Beg and ends up as Muṣṭafā Pasha.[50] This tripartite relationship among Tūqāns of Nablus, the rebel al-Ẓāhir al-`Umar, and the Ottoman authorities in Damascus is interesting. It complicates al-Danafī's text and drowns his personal voice. Let us untangle the various interests.

The rise of Muṣṭafā Beg and his being awarded the title "Pasha" (strictly speaking, the title denotes provincial and not subdistrict governorship) are indicative of the phenomenon of the rise of notable households. Muṣṭafā's family, the Ṭūqāns, were already well established in the city, but the assignment of the title by the Ottoman provincial governor constitutes a formal acknowledgment of the family and guarantees their primacy in Nablus. The title connotes an "Ottomanization" of the Ṭūqāns and perpetuation of their power. This is not unproblematic for the Nabulsis, who, given their situation far away from Istanbul, are not accustomed to direct imperial control and dearly value their semi-autonomy. However, Ottoman imperial acknowledgment is valuable not only for support in repulsing joint threats, such as that of al-Ẓāhir al-`Umar, but also for winning local rivalries. However, with assaults such as that of al-`Umar, the Tūqāns, despite themselves, have to cooperate with the Ottoman authorities in Damascus under whose jurisdiction Nablus falls. But, where is the author, al-Danafī, in all of this? The main intention of al-Danafī's text is none other than to mediate and balance the negotiations of his patron Muṣṭafā Beg with the enemy and with the Ottoman authorities. As al-Danafī's dealings in relation to his own position as a client and an important member of the Samaritan community, these lie entirely outside the text.

It is striking the extent to which the political vision and tone of al-Danafī resembles that of the Rukanynīs of Jabal `Āmil. The similarity between the two may be explained by the fact that the regions in which they lived were concerned with their respective relative autonomy and self-preservation. Al-Danafī's chronicle, like that of the Rukaynīs, displays a heightened value for the preservation of local independence through military force. In the case of Nablus, the immediate threat is from the villain-rebel against the empire, al-Ẓāhir al-`Umar. With a tone of bravado similar to that found in the al-Rukaynīs' chronicle, al-Danafī describes the defeat of al-`Umar's forces:

> The [Nābulsī] fighters attacked them [the soldiers of al-Ẓāhir al-`Umar]. They jumped out at them like monkeys, and surprised them with an attack, and fired their guns at them, and beat them and took their canons and munitions. The force of God drove them on and they took their banners and flags. On that day, over a thousand of them fell dead, and from our group, two people only.[51]

One wonders if al-Danafī's tally really measures up to reality (1,000 to two in favor of the Nabulsis!), but one may appreciate the self-congratulatory literary conceit on the occasion of a crushing defeat served to the formidable al-`Umar. Self-preservation, however, takes courage and shows of military power as well as shrewdness and guile. In the following passage, al-Danafī describes a meeting between Aḥmad Beg Tūqān (Muṣṭafā Beg's brother) and al-Ẓāhir al-`Umar:

> Al-Ẓāhir al-`Umar insisted that it was important and necessary that Muṣṭafā Beg be present before him. His Excellency Aḥmad Beg displayed complete manliness and told him, "We, oh, Shaykh, want to be like your children and to ally ourselves with you. We need your trust and to derive comfort and security from you. I will go in [to Nablus] and bring Muṣṭafā Beg to you," and he swore to him. Al-Ẓāhir thought that this was true and correct, so he dressed Aḥmad Beg with a sable fur and Aḥmad Beg departed. As soon as Aḥmad Beg left al-Ẓāhir's encampment, he called upon those who were with him to prepare them for war. . . .[52]

In other words, Aḥmad Beg unabashedly lies to al-Ẓāhir al-`Umar and deceives him. Al-Danafī, however, does not find this behavior cowardly and unchivalrous; on the contrary, he is evidently pleased to describe how al-Ẓāhir al-`Umar was persuaded into believing that Aḥmad Beg was conducting himself with "complete manliness" when in fact he was simply maneuvering to survive. Just as the Rukaynīs have no qualms about who the Matāwila ally with in order to preserve their independence, so al-Danafī has no qualms with his leaders' failure to conduct themselves honorably so long as they stay out of al-Ẓāhir al-`Umar's clutches.

The similarities between the Rukaynīs' and al-Danafī's chronicles end here, as the relationship of Nablus to Damascus was quite different from that of Jabal `Āmil to the provincial capital. Whereas the *dawla* (was the term used by the Rukaynīs to describe Ottoman authorities) is uncomplicatedly posited as the prime threat in the chronicle of the Rukaynīs, in al-Danafī the relationship between Jabal Nablus and the Ottoman Empire is much more ambiguous. Al-Danafī never once mentions Istanbul. The Sultan is mentioned not by his title but as *al-malik*—the king.[53] This absence of Istanbul along with al-Danafī's apparent indifference to the title of his sovereign reflect in the first instance a political distance between semi-autonomous Nablus and the center of Empire. Al-Danafī seems not to recognize, at least formally, being a part of the Ottoman Empire or under its rule. On the other hand, al-Danafī is forced to recognize the nearby representatives of the empire such as the governor of Damascus to whom al-Danafī, like the Rukaynīs, refers as *al-dawla*.

Al-dawla in the chronicle of al-Danafī functions as a handy dispenser of official positions for which the notables of Jabal Nablus, such as Muṣṭafā Beg, contend. Al-Danafī's concern, however, is to represent the relationship between Nablus and the Ottoman state as a relationship of equals. Indeed, al-Danafī would like us to believe that the state is more beholden to Muṣṭafā Beg than he is to the state. Thus, when the High Porte appoints `Uthmān Pasha al-Maṣrallī as governor of Egypt on condition that he suppress the revolt of `Alī Beg al-Kabīr in Egypt and al-Ẓāhir al-`Umar:

> `Uthmān Pasha, who was decorated with three *tūkh*s [Turkish, *tuğ*, a horsetail attached to a pole indicating rank], came to Damascus and established himself

there. He began casting canons and canon balls and gathering armies and publicizing that he was going to give order to Ṣafad and Egypt. When Muḥammad Pasha al-'Aẓm [the governor of Damascus] came back from the Hajj the two met and sent [a message] to Muṣṭafā Beg entreating him to fight al-Ẓāhir promising him two *tūkh*s [in return]. They asked of him courage and manliness, and relied on him to suppress al-Ẓāhir al-'Umar.[54]

Al-Danafī here leaves the reader in no doubt as to the nature of the relationship between Muṣṭafā Beg and the governors: their need for him is clearly greater than is his for them. Muṣṭafā Beg is effectively asked here to do the governor's job for them, and to display the qualities—courage and manliness—he is acknowledged to have and they, by implication, lack. Later, on the request of the two governors, Muṣṭafā Beg marches to Jaffa to preempt the occupation of the city by al-Ẓāhir al-'Umar. Having occupied the town, Muṣṭafā Beg writes to the governors concerned requesting the governorship of Jaffa for his brother, Aḥmad Beg Ṭūqān. Muṣṭafā Beg is, of course, effectively presenting the governors with a fait accompli, and they duly oblige. Muṣṭafā Beg then

established a thousand guards in it [Jaffa]. . . . He would borrow from the merchants in lieu of customs and spend it [on the city]. . . . After he had established order in Jaffa and among the soldiers, and after the investiture of his Excellency Aḥmad Beg, he [Muṣṭafā Beg] went to Nablus.[55]

Again, the message is clear: Muṣṭafā Beg and the representatives of the state are on an equal footing. Not only is Muṣṭafā Beg able to get what he wants from the state, but he is clearly fully deserving since he is doing the job of the state better than the state's representatives are able. After Muṣṭafā Beg's success in Jaffa, the area under his jurisdiction is extended on the condition that he pay a portion of the revenues to provincial capital. Al-Danafī is loathe to acknowledge that the conditions of the appointment clearly show that Muṣṭafā Beg is subordinate to the Governor: "He accepted this for himself in concern for the commands of *al-dawla* and indifference to those in authority."[56] In other words, Muṣṭafā Beg accepts the appointment in his capacity as one who obliges the state but is not obliged to it.

However, despite al-Danafī's strenuous attempts to represent Muṣṭafā Beg's relations with the state as being between equals, there comes a point when this pretense simply collapses. When the governor of Damascus, Muḥammad Pasha, is deposed, Muṣṭafā Ṭūqān—who now holds the title of Pasha—panics: "His Excellency, our *afandī* Muṣṭafā Pasha, was deeply distressed because he was dependent on Muḥammad Pasha in all his affairs."[57] In this moment of crisis, al-Danafī drops the pretense of equality and frankly acknowledges the politics of patronage. The Nabulsis could not do without Damascus.

It has probably become clear by now that the chronicle was likely not to have been commissioned by "His Excellency, our *afandī*, Muṣṭafa Pasha," and that it was written by al-Danafī to mediate and prop up his patron in the latter's negotiations. Given the intention of the text, one would not expect the author to be at the center of the narrative—and he is not. With the exception of the Passover, al-Danafī inserts himself in the text only four times; on each occasion he is either in the company of or acting on the instructions of Muṣṭafā Beg.[58] In an expectedly self-effacing manner, the author defines his relationship to his patron: "We accompany him to serve him."[59] Unlike Mikhā'īl Burayk's text, which is conscious of and written about the Christian community of Damascus, the "us" in the text of al-Danafī does not denote the author's co-religionists in Nablus. Rather, the collective in the text is the Ṭūqān-led Nabulsis.[60]

It is perhaps due to the fact that the author does not stray from his role as the servant of the notable and the voice of the citizens of Nablus that al-Danafī's strategies and politics with his own patron are hidden. However, external sources provide ample proof that al-Danafī was able to use his ties to the Ṭūqān family to bring benefit not only to himself but also to the rest of the Samaritan community. For example, al-Danafī interceded with the Ṭūqāns to bring home a Samaritan high priest who had been exiled a few years earlier. Also, he used a portion of his handsome income from the Ṭūqāns to buy a plot of land on Mount Gerizim where the Passover sacrifice might be carried out. Additionally, he built a Samaritan cemetery and repaired the temple and other sites revered by the Samaritans.[61] Although al-Danafī barely writes either himself or the Samaritans into the text of the chronicle, he uses the same relationship of patronage that makes his history possible to benefit his community, even while they both remain on the margins of the Ottoman Empire. Thus al-Danafī had every reason to be not only the "good" but also the "loyal" Samaritan.

THE ĀGHĀ'S MAN: MUḤAMMAD AL-MAKKĪ (FL. 1722)

Muḥammad b. ʿAbd al-Bāqī b. al-Sayyid al-Makkī (fl. 1722), who lived in the northern Syrian town of Ḥimṣ, wrote a chronicle covering the years 1688–1722.[62] The author seems to have worked in an unspecified clerical capacity at, or in relation to, the judicial court,[63] probably as a notary.[64]

Al-Makkī's chronicle is an oddity in the sample of chronicles treated in this study in that it alone was probably not intended as a public text. This is indicated by al-Makkī's manner of writing, which is in a staccato and telegrammatic style in which he limits himself to very short and abrupt sentences generally introduced by "verbal nouns." A random example (with verbal nouns underlined):

> The building (*ʿimārat*) of an upper room in the house of Umm Fakhrī, the dying (*wafāt*) of Muḥammad b. al-Ḥājj Khalīl al-Ḥamawī al-Dabbāgh . . . the coming (*majī'*) of the news of the death of Ibn al-Shaykh Yāsīn al-Ḥamawī al-Qādir, the falling (*wuqūʿ*) of the rock on the wife of al-Sayyid ʿAbd al-Qādir al-Ḥamawī al-Qādir, the *naqīb al-ashrāf*, and the dying of many, many people in Ḥamā . . . the falling (*wuqūʿ*) of the roof of the Great Mosque which had been built by al-Shaykh ʿAbd al-Ghanī al-ʿImād . . . the taking (*akhdh*) by al-Shaykh Yāsīn al-Ḥamawī of the marble column of the Māristān of Ḥimṣ. . . .[65]

This is a peculiar prose style, to say the least. Al-Makkī's policy of introducing each unit of information with a verbal noun is an unusual rhetorical strategy, which has the effect of rendering the text almost incapable of narration, but only of notation. Even though we may attribute his telegraphic style to his clerical functions at the court—i.e., his profession may have gotten the better of him—it is more likely that this text was meant not as a chronicle (*tārikh*) per se but as a diary reserved for the author's eyes only.

Al-Makkī's position at the judicial court places him in the very center of action, where Ḥimṣis from all walks of life come in to notarize their dealings and transactions. His diary teems with the affairs of all kinds of people, some of whose official transactions, such as sale contracts,[66] marriage contracts,[67] and public endowment deeds,[68] he quotes verbatim.[69] Since the court was his locus, he must have witnessed, drafted, recorded, or heard the names and legal concerns of hundreds of people (especially if it was the only court in Ḥimṣ).[70] Al-Makkī is remarkably eclectic about who or what he reports: his news ranges from the comings and goings of the town notables[71] to the death of a garbage collector,[72] to the marriage of a barber,[73] to a water-bearer's murder of his mother-in-law,[74] to the death of the neighbor of the author's daughter.[75] It is no exaggeration to say that Muḥammad al-Makkī, as a result of his occupation, knows just about everything worth knowing about everyone in Ḥimṣ. And although al-Makkī knows many people, he certainly has his favorites: he is a man who knows very well where his interests lie.

The "hero" of al-Makkī's diary is a certain Ibrāhīm Āghā. As the latter's title indicates, he is from the *aghawāt*, that is to say, from the military corps. More importantly for al-Makkī's purposes, Ibrāhīm Āghā, is a contender for and several-time incumbent as governor of Ḥimṣ. In addition to serving as a legal witness in Ibrāhīm Āgha's transactions, al-Makkī mentions several visits to and stays with Ibrāhīm Āghā. Indeed, the news of Ibrāhīm Āghā is ubiquitous in al-Makkī's text. Ibrāhīm Āghā's name appears far more often than any other in the diary,[76] and every mention of him is followed with blessings and praises *ad nauseam*—such as "May God preserve Ibrāhīm Āghā, his progeny, his siblings, his relatives, his followers, and anyone associated with him, by the honor of Muḥammad, his family, and companions, Amen, Amen, Amen!"—and often with the prayer, "May God perpetuate his rule!"[77] Al-Makkī relates not only the district governor's movements but also the comings and goings of Ibrāhīm Āghā's relatives, such as his mother and uncle.[78] It is noteworthy that al-Makkī's excessive interest in Ibrāhīm Āghā does not extend to the other governors who ruled Ḥimṣ in the thirty-year period covered by the chronicle. Ibrāhīm Āghā is al-Makkī's favorite, most likely because the latter lives in the favor of the former. It seems that al-Makkī is Ibrāhim Āghā's man at court.

Thus the relationship between the author and Ibrāhīm Āghā in Ḥimṣ resembles that between the Samaritan scribe, al-Danafī and Muṣṭafā Beg Ṭūqān in Nablus. Both these connections serve as regional variations on the same eighteenth-century Ottoman theme: the rise of notable households and attendant patronage networks. If the relationship between al-Danafī and his patron reflects a network that extends from Damascus to Nablus to affect locally the Samaritan community, the relationship between al-Makkī and Ibrāhīm demonstrates that the reach of these networks does not stop at the provincial capital but goes all the way to the imperial capital. The competition for the post of governor of Ḥimṣ is cutthroat and manifests itself in factions, which must be forged not only at the local and provincial levels but also in the capital.

Overriding decision-making authority in Ḥimṣ' political matters lies in the first instance in Tripoli (the provincial capital under whose jurisdiction Ḥimṣ falls), and ultimately in Istanbul. Al-Makkī carefully and ceaselessly monitors the political scene, both in Ḥimṣ and in Tripoli and Istanbul. Especially significant are the movements of the representatives of the local factions as they approach higher authorities in the provincial and imperial capitals: "Al-Ḥājj `Alī b. al-Aqra` and one of the Vizier's military officials traveled to Istanbul to attend to the interests of Ibrāhīm Āghā. May God satisfy his interests . . . and grant Ibrāhīm Āghā victory over his enemies!"[79]

Here, supporters of Ibrāhīm Āghā journey to Istanbul to lobby for support for the leader of their faction. Al-Makkī prays that God grant them success. When opponents of Ibrāhīm Āghā do the same, however, al-Makkī's response is very different: "Shaykh `Abd al-Fattāḥ al-Sibā`ī, Shaykh Ramaḍān al-Qā`ī, Sayyid Salīm al-Nafi`ī, and Sayyid Ramaḍān b. Sayyid `Alī b. Sayyid Zayn left for Istanbul. Each of them had an interest to attend. May calamity overtake the tyrant!"[80] Al-Makkī specifically prays for Istanbul to support Ibrāhīm Āghā against another contender, a certain Ḥaydar b. Dandash: "May God inspire the Sultan and his Vizier to appoint Ibrāhīm Āghā and depose Ibn Dandash soon."[81]

On the occasion of the appointment of Mustafa Afandī Köprülü as Grand Vizier in Istanbul (in 1689), al-Makkī eagerly reports the arrival of a messenger directly from Istanbul to inform Ibrāhīm Āghā of the news.[82] Two years later, al-Makkī writes:

> May God preserve for us the Vizier Muṣṭafā Afandī through the magnanimity of the Conveyer of the Divine Word, the Warner [Prophet Muḥammad]! Amen!

Amen! Amen! . . . The news reached us that the Vizier Muṣṭafā Afandī had been martyred. We ask God through the magnanimity of the Messenger of God that this news be false, through the magnanimity of the good Prophet![83]

Mustafa Köprülü, it would appear, must have been instrumental in the appointment of Ibrāhīm Āghā in Ḥimṣ—it is hard to imagine why else al-Makkī would pray so hard for the "preservation" of the Grand Vizier in Istanbul. The prayers for the preservation of Köprülü are themselves an expression of local factionalist politics: al-Makkī is effectively praying for the preservation of Ibrāhīm Āghā's interests in Istanbul.

We ask God the Great, Lord of Great Throne, through His Prophet, the Noble Messenger, that he perpetuate for the people the rule of Ibrāhīm Āghā, through the Master of the Messengers [of God]. May God inspire the Vizier through the sanctity of the Conveyer of the Divine Word, the Illuminating Lamp, that he soon appoint Ibrāhīm Āghā to rule . . . Amen! Amen! Amen![84]

Al-Makkī is not particularly subtle. Perhaps because of the private quality this text, the politics and negotiations it elicits are offered with exceptional candor. The author's aspirations and fears are simple and transparent: al-Makkī's position in the world is dependent on that of Ibrāhīm Āghā. The rise of the latter means the enhancement of the position of the former. Ibrāhīm Āghā's location, however, is determined by the will of the provincial governor, whose own position is decided by the Grand Vizier. Thus al-Makkī has to pray hard for a domino effect that will end up in his favor. This minor court clerk in a small town in Syria is invested in the bigwigs—or "big turbans"—of Istanbul.

FROM RAGS TO RICHES: ḤASAN ĀGHĀ AL-`ABD (FL. 1826)

Ḥasan Āghā al-`Abd was a Damascene soldier who wrote a chronicle covering the years 1771–1826.[85] He, like al-Makkī's Ibrāhīm Āghā, was from the military or paramilitary groups of his city. Throughout the chronicle, al-`Abd's interest lay in officialdom, ceremonials, intrigues, military skirmishes, and the movements of troops. The measure of his immersion in military affairs may be gauged from the fact that he almost never mentioned civilians, and that his references to the civilian part of the Ottoman administration—such as those who are involved in the religio-judicial-academic institution—were insignificant in comparison to his references to the military.[86]

Al-`Abd's case is remarkable.[87] He started out as a janissary officer and ended up in the position of no less than the *mutasallim* (district governor) of Ṣafad. As a district governor, al-`Abd was even referred to, albeit briefly and anecdotally, by a couple of other chroniclers of the period.[88] Al-`Abd's rise is the most extreme example of change in social position in our sample. Though all the non-*`ulamā'* historians I have discussed thus far were directly or indirectly touched by power, none of them experienced the kind of relative independent power that al-`Abd finally comes to possess. Indeed, some have suggested that al-`Abd is actually the progenitor of a powerful nineteenth-century Damascene family by the same name.[89] Though his rise is dazzling, it was not unheard of in the long eighteenth century. Whereas previously governors would appoint members of their own military households as district governors, the increased dependence of the governors on local military garrisons now results in the rise of local officers in the provincial administration.[90]

What is even more remarkable than the fact of al-`Abd's rise to power is the accompanying change of worldview and tone in his chronicle. As his position changes from the "have-nots" to the "haves," so do his politics. His chronicle's tone alters from critical outrage to satisfied observation.

Evidence that al-`Abd started out as a janissary officer is found in his statement: "I was formerly involved in the construction of the forts of the pilgrimage route."[91] The connection between the Damascus janissary corps and the pilgrimage route is a well-known eighteenth-century phenomenon resulting from a decision of the High Porte to invest the governor of Damascus with the responsibility of managing and administering the pilgrimage to Mecca while simultaneously exempting him from joining imperial campaigns. Since the Damascene janissary corps, along with other military groups in Damascus, proved troublesome and prone to mutiny, the governors decide to deploy Damascus janissaries to garrison the forts on the pilgrimage route to Mecca.[92]

Al-`Abd's rise in the Ottoman administration from a janissary officer to a district governor seems to have begun in 1813, when he accompanied the Damascus governor, Sulaymān Pasha al-Siliḥdār (r. 1812–1816), on the Hajj in the capacity of *urfā amīnī* (Turkish, *arpa emini*), or barley commissioner.[93] Thus by the time of the appointment as governor of Damascus of the former Grand Vizier, Muḥammad Darwīsh Pasha (r. 1820–1822), al-`Abd must have been a well-known local figure in the military-administrative circles of Damascus. The newly arrived ex-Grand Vizier, Muḥammad Darwīsh Pasha, clearly wants to consolidate his support of the local janissary corps, because within a few months of his arrival, in 1820 he appoints al-`Abd governor of the district of al-Biqā`.[94] Thereafter, al-`Abd participates in a battle for which he is duly awarded a sable fur.[95] On what seems to be a recommendation from the governor of Sidon, al-`Abd's loyal efforts culminate in Maḥmud Darwīsh Pasha's appointing him to the post of the district of Ṣafad at the end of 1821.[96] Stated differently, al-`Abd's rise is not only vertical, an upward movement through the ranks of janissary corps, but also a lateral move into a military-*administrative* network. For al-`Abd to be patronized by the current governor of Damascus, who himself previously served as nothing less than Grand Vizier, is most fortuitous. This twist of fate is rather unsubtly reflected in al-`Abd's change of tone from that of a victim to that of a winner. If al-`Abd's story of advancement is striking, the corresponding change of tone is even more so.

Between the years 1771 and 1812, that is, up to a year before his big promotion to the post of district governor of Biqā`, al-`Abd depicts a world without order. The rule of the successive governors of Damascus is often described as "tyranny," and/or "murder."[97] Almost all of the governors of Damascus and their deputies, starting with al-Jazzār Pasha (four-time governor between 1785 and 1804) and ending with Sulaymān Pasha (r. 1810–1812), are described as extortative, corrupt, violent, and oppressive.[98] For example, al-Jazzār's monopoly of power is so absolute that "not a single notable in Damascus remained with authority."[99] `Abd Allah Pasha al-`Aẓm (r. 1795–1798) "committed all kinds of oppression on the villages of Damascus . . . he introduced forced purchase . . . and extorted a lot of money."[100] Kanj Yūsuf Pasha (r. 1807–1810) "scared people with oppression and murder."[101] "The oppression was so great," says al-`Abd at one point, "that the rains dried up."[102] Damascus itself appears in this part of al-`Abd's chronicle as little more than a battleground for bloody skirmishes between the various military factions in the city, particularly the *yarliyya* and *qabīqūl*, and as torn by violent (and apparently random) political intrigues.[103] The absence of any security or order prompts common Damascenes to arm themselves,[104] the shops are closed frequently,[105] and invariably parts of the city are closed off or destroyed.[106] The city suffers extreme price inflation the effect of which al-`Abd describes as a "blaze of fire."[107] Clearly, for al-`Abd, Damascus has become a city where normal life is impossible.

It is not only through the local imperial order that the fact of empire deranges al-`Abd's city. As a result of the deployment of the Ottoman army against Napoleon in Egypt and Palestine, the Damascenes suffer the imposition of extra taxes for the financing of the campaign. Also, Damascus suffers from vandalism and looting by rowdy Ottoman troops stationed in the city on their way to join the French campaign.[108] Further, as a result of the Wahhābī revolt in Arabia, the Damascus Hajj caravan is prevented from performing the pilgrimage. In 1806, Al-`Abd reports how "the people grieved when the news [of the prevention from Hajj] arrived to Damascus." On another such occasion, al-`Abd says, "The caravan returned to Damascus in shame and disgrace."[109]

In sum, during the period up to 1812 al-`Abd presents Damascus as a theater where the collapse of imperial authority and legitimacy is enacted and its consequences felt. The Damascus representatives of imperial authority are described as violent, rapacious, and oppressive, and portrayed as failing utterly to maintain order and security in the city. Indeed, failure and chaos seem to accompany all the actions of the Empire. Thus, rather than defend the security of the empire, the imperial troops stationed in Damascus wreak havoc in the city. And even though the Ottoman Sultan is the custodian of the Ka`ba, the state is unable to ensure that its subjects can carry out the fundamental religious obligation of the Hajj—a situation that al-`Abd describes as nothing less than a "disgrace upon the state."[110] Al-`Abd's chronicle thus functions as the voice of a city that suffers from its being a subject of the Ottoman state, which, in its failure to fulfill its basic functions, emerges from the chronicle as ineffective, corrupt, and illegitimate.

Beginning in 1812, however, al-`Abd's tone is strikingly different. From this year onward, al-`Abd not only makes no criticisms whatever of the successive governors of Damascus but actually praises them. For each year between 1813 and 1814, he records the success of the Hajj caravan under the governor, Sulaymān Pasha al-Siliḥdār (1812–1815).[111] In 1816, he describes Ḥāfiẓ `Alī Pasha (1816–17) as possessing "an excess of sagacity and nobility."[112] In 1817, he praises the new deputy governor, Khulūṣī Beg:

> He ruled in the best possible way. The corrupt feared him, and life in the city became opulent and blissful because he would himself deal with the guilds and pricing matters and depended on nobody. Prices dropped and people's matters were put in order. He was above bribery from the millers and other guilds, and the people blessed him.[113]

When the new governor arrived later that year, he too turned out to be a model ruler:

> In [the month of] Sha`bān, Ṣālih Pasha . . . arrived . . . he was gentle and dignified and averse to bloodshed, he hated tyranny and transgression and ruled Damascus in the best possible way. During his time, people lived blissfully.

Sulaymān Pasha al-Izmirlī was appointed governor in 1819:

> He was a wise, complete, and just vizier who loved the people and hated oppression and transgression. He was clement and embodied the dignity of the Vizierate such that it was not heard that he oppressed anyone during the tenure of his rule.[114]

Al-`Abd's presentation of the relationship between the city and the imperial administration changes radically. This is exemplified in the brief bulletin for the year 1818. Only two events in the city are recorded. The first is an altercation between the *muftī* and the *qāḍī* (judge), which is successfully dealt with by the Pasha by way of an appeal to Istanbul. The second is a summary report of the successful performance of the Hajj. Both events convey the efficacy of the imperial order: the successful resolution of a conflict between the representatives of imperial authority, and the safe return of the Hajj caravan.[115] The staple events of the earlier years—inflation, injustice, and factional fighting—simply disappear from the scene. This transformation of Damascus, beginning in 1812, from a place of carnage and chaos ruled by corrupt representatives of the imperial order to an "opulent and blissful" city ruled by an unprecedented succession of just and wise men, is hard to believe. The problem with al-ʿAbd's account is that it is somewhat disconsonant with what we know from other sources. In his study of the history of Damascus in this period, George Koury writes:

The period 1804 to 1832 is characterized by a more frequent change of ineffective governors at Damascus than during the preceding period between 1783 and 1804. . . . The political situation of the Province of Damascus continued to deteriorate until Muḥammad ʿAlī Pasha, the *wālī* [governor] of Egypt, conquered Syria in 1832.[116]

Consequently, the stark contrast in al-ʿAbd's representations of the city from not-so-good to excellent is merely *a description of his own changed position.* His is almost a triumphalist narrative. Indeed the degree of triumphalism is indicated by the last event that this man, who started out as a janissary officer, reports in his chronicle. It is the event described in Ottoman official historiography as the "Auspicious Incident":

On the eleventh of Dhū al-Qaʿda in the year 1241 [1826 CE], the janissary *awjāq* [Turkish, *ocak*] was disbanded in Islāmbūl [Istanbul] and in the rest of the Ottoman lands by order of our Master, the Sultan Maḥmūd, may God make him victorious. It was reported to us that there was a great incident in Islāmbūl wherein approximately twenty thousand people perished. The disbanding of this *awjāq* was a great event because many rulers and sultans had wanted to do this but were not able, until God granted the great Sultan, king of the kings of the Arabs and non-Arabs, the just ruler, Maḥmūd Khān b. ʿAbd al-Ḥamīd Khān b. Aḥmad Khān, may God make firm the pillars of his Sultanhood, the capacity to disband them because they had rebelled against kings and viziers and the lords of the state to the point that they were feared by the old and the young, had come to hold decisive power, and the Sultan had become their ward. They did as they pleased and the wealth of the Ottoman lands became theirs. The fact is that the disbanding of this corps was a mercy from God to the country and to the people. The janissary corps did no good, but only harm.[117]

Ḥasan Āghā al-`Abd is by now the district governor of Ṣafad, that is, the representative of the Ottoman state in that district. From this high position in officialdom, he reports with great approbation the dissolution of the janissary corps by the Ottoman state. Though he was formerly a member of this corps, the corps being ever so prone to mutiny and insubordination now threatens his position. But what is especially revealing is al-`Abd's account of the Auspicious Incident which, as Bruce Masters observes without comment:

. . . reflects both the language and ideology of an imperial ferman [order] which reached Aleppo on 7 Dhū al-Ḥijja 1241 (14 July 1826) and Damascus on the 19th of the same month (26 July 1826) and which outlined the reasons in some detail for why the Janissary corps had been abolished. It seems most probable that the order was read aloud at the central court of Damascus where Ḥasan Āghā heard it and accepted his Sultan's explanation.[118]

In other words, Ḥasan Āghā al-`Abd does not just end his chronicle with a declaration of loyalty to the empire but effectively assumes its voice by paraphrasing the language and ideology of an imperial order. Al-`Abd's perception of the Ottoman state changes as he rises through the imperial ranks. Until 1812, when there is no indication of his occupying any position in the structure of imperial authority, he views the state as oppressive, corrupt, and illegitimate, and his chronicle speaks with the voice of a city that it is the victim of Ottoman rule. From 1812 onward, however, al-`Abd is rapidly incorporated into the state as a rising functionary and representative of the imperial order, and his relationship to the state is transformed accordingly until his voice and the voice of the state become one.

Initially, al-`Abd, like several other authors in our sample, speaks the language of the discontented commoner, portraying a collapsed social and political order. However, he then changes his tone and describes a restored order in which "life in the city became opulent and blissful," and he simply glosses over the very manifestations of disorder that earlier dominated his narrative. It is in this glossing over of disorder that al-`Abd reveals his agenda—which is to legitimize his own ascent in the new order. In the past, the state was bad, but now that al-`Abd has become a successful part of the state, the state is good, and there is no further need for the commoner discourse of discontent. The negotiations are over.

HISTORY AS STORY: ḤASAN IBN AL-ṢIDDĪQ (FL. 1771)

The author of the chronicle covering the pivotal events of 1770–71 is Ibn al-Ṣiddīq,[119] probably a soldier and member of the janissary.[120] Unfortunately, he refers to himself only once, at the outset of the chronicle:

> The poor slave, who acknowledges [his] culpability and inadequacy, Ḥasan known as Ibn al-Ṣiddīq, says: I have heard many *stories* (*ḥikāyāt*) which I found pleasurable. Had I collected [all of them], it [i.e., this] would have been a huge volume.[121]

The fact that Ibn al-Ṣiddīq considers his book a collection of "stories" is significant and is a point to which I shall return. For now, it is the identity of the author that is of concern. Aside from giving his name, the author does not offer any other information about himself. Even the usual authorial *I* accustomed in chronicles is completely absent from the text. The only clue to the author's identity as a soldier is his apparent closeness to the military events narrated, mainly regarding the constitution and movement of troops, the details of skirmishes and battles, and the content of missives and correspondence between influential figures. Also, at the beginning of the chronicle Ibn al-Ṣiddīq provides a list of appointees in higher posts of the *yarliyya* janissary corps, leading one to suspect that the author may have belonged to this particular corps.[122] As for his identity as a Damascene, not only does the author report with what seems like a firsthand knowledge of the city but he also displays a distinctly Damascene dialect in his text.

The background of Ibn al-Ṣiddīq as evidenced by his language and profession justifies the inclusion of his chronicle in this study, but the author's complete absence from the text poses a problem to its general hypothesis. Thus far, I have posited the chronicles of the non-`*ulamā*' as an effect of changed social positions, a change that prompted these previously silent individuals to negotiate in or for new positions, whether anxiously or complacently, through their authorship of chronicles. I have considered their books as a "cheap sort of monumentality" whereby the production of a book—by definition a monumental achievement for people who were not socialized into chronicle authorship—represents both a display of and a desire to improve or retain an enhanced social status. The problem with Ibn al-Ṣiddīq is that he, in a manner of speaking, *does not speak* but merely offers himself as a vehicle of narration. There is not a single point in the chronicle where one can detect a personal stake by the author, except for a general and insistent loyalty to Damascus, its governor, and the Ottoman Sultan. In his text, one is able to identify neither network nor patron nor a particular clique to which he belonged or wished to belong. One can easily state that this book was written almost entirely without the kind of personal investment, implicit or explicit, found in the other chronicles in our study. In short, there is neither consciousness of an enhanced social position nor obvious negotiation here. The absence of the author brings me to a related issue that has to do with the quality of this book and the reason for its inclusion in the present study: the fact that the text was conceived as a book of *stories*.

The title of the book, *Strange Marvels and Wondrous Events*, is reminiscent of the old Arabic genre of *`ajā'ib wa gharā'ib* (wonders and marvels), which are mostly fictitious tales of adventures of travelers, seafarers, and geographers and which culminated in such entertaining stories as *The Arabian Nights*.[123] However, there is very little fiction in Ibn al-Ṣiddīq's chronicle, which was deemed by a scholar to be "a very detailed and reliable account."[124] Yet the text's primary intention as made explicit in the quotation above is to tell *stories* (*ḥikāyāt*). This particular attribute of the text has led the same scholar to state, "One gathers from the expressions that Ibn al-Ṣiddīq uses and the warmth of his chronicle, that it was read before a group of people, possibly in *a coffeehouse where story-tellers related tales of adventures*."[125] As a result, this uniquely construed text subverts both the form and the function of two genres. Unlike the genre of the chronicle, this text does not proffer the authority of its chronicler as witness and narrator of real events. And unlike entertaining stories, the events of this text are not fictitious. The hybridity of this text and its connection to coffeehouse culture is important, as it displays qualities and issues utmost relevance to our discussion of the work of the barber later on. Despite differences in style and stated purpose, both Ibn al-Ṣiddīq and the barber of Damascus seem to have spent a lot of time listening to storytellers in the local coffee shop. The significance of this will become clear in Chapter 5.

Ibn al-Ṣiddīq's chronicle focuses on the events that culminated in a very brief occupation of Damascus by the Egyptian forces of the *mamlūk* (slave soldier) rebel ʿAlī Beg al-Kabīr of the new Qazdağlı household.[126] The expedition was led by Muḥammad Abū al-Dhahab, himself formerly a slave of ʿAlī Beg's.[127] In Ibn al-Ṣiddīq's chronicle many of the figures and groups mentioned in earlier discussions reappear. The main villains here are not only the Egyptian forces, "the wretches, the infidels . . . the pigs," but also their local supporters and allies, the ubiquitous rebel al-Ẓāhir al-ʿUmar, "the wretch and his sons, the pigs," and their partners "the group of accursed wretches, Naṣīf [sic] and his followers the Matāwila" (the heroes of the al-Rukaynīs' chronicle).[128] Even Muṣṭafā Beg Ṭūqān of Nablus, the patron of the Samaritan al-Danafī, makes several entries in this story, once in Damascus to be hosted and dined by the provincial governor himself. (A patron, too, is under obligation in such a relationship of codependence).[129]

Since as I have mentioned earlier there is not much to tease out in terms of politicking and strategies in Ibn al-Ṣiddīq's text, I focus here on a couple of reports in his chronicle that reveal the author's unique narrative style. However, it should be noted that the first of these reports is very much in the vein of a social critique. It is the closest the author gets to revealing an agenda of sorts.

The report in question is an entertaining, even comical, part of the chronicle. It represents a comment on the behavior of some of the notables of the town in the aftermath of the withdrawal of the Egyptian forces.[130] The butt of the joke is no less a rarified figure than the Friday preacher (*khaṭīb*) of the Umayyad Mosque, Sulaymān b. Aḥmad al-Maḥāsinī (d. 1773). As a background to the report, it should be noted that al-Maḥāsinī wrote two epistlelike single-event chronicles that deal with the occupation of Damascus by Abū al-Dhahab.[131] One of these epistles is a lampoon of the commander of the local janissaries, Ibn Jabrī, who while Damascus was under siege showed himself a coward and deserted the city under cover of night.[132] Ibn Jabrī was later executed for treason. This is how Ibn al-Ṣiddīq describes the circumstances of the publication of al-Maḥāsinī's epistle:

Everyone was happy for the execution of Yūsuf Āghā [Ibn Jabrī]—high and low, the grandees and the notables, and even those who had received favors from him and to whom he showed kindness and generosity. Even the Friday-preacher, Ibn Maḥāsin, who owed him [Ibn Jabrī] kindness and generosity, wrote about him an epistle [demonstrating] his unbelief and error . . . and showing his deeds to be more oppressive than those of Nemrod . . . [Then, al-Maḥāsinī] swore on pain of divorce to read it [the epistle] entirely and completely in the presence of ʿUthmān Pasha, the Governor of Damascus. He wrote it in 15 folios and claimed that it was an abridgement. . . . ʿUthman Pasha felt insulted, so he clashed with him [al-Maḥāsinī] and said to him: Oh, Afandī, is this what you will do when I am deposed from [the governorship of] Damascus. All the equanimity shown by ʿUthman Pasha in Damascus will be turned into unbelief, evil, and error?[133]

This is one of the rare moments in which Ibn al-Ṣiddīq shows personality and subjective judgment and betrays a stance toward one of his characters. Although Ibn al-Ṣiddīq on that same page objectively surveys the Damascene reactions to the execution of the commander of the janissaries and to the epistle of the Friday preacher, his facetious remarks about al-Maḥāsinī's sycophantic and faithless behavior is striking. Ibn al-Ṣiddīq not only recounts the humiliation received by al-Maḥasinī at the hands of the governor but also adds richness of detail by remarking on the length of the epistle and al-Maḥāsinī's exaggerated gestures and utterances, including his oath on pain of divorce. In this episode, Ibn al-Ṣiddīq makes life unfold before us as theater at which he laughs—and we, the audience, join him—from a distance.

Another example of Ibn al-Ṣiddīq's unique narrative style is an episode that takes place outside Damascus. We are now not in an urban setting but in the wilderness near the encampment of the Damascene army that has just occupied Jaffa. The army is dejected because the allied troops have not arrived and the promised munitions have not been found. The head of the janissaries must beseech a contingent to go on a reconnaissance mission. They oblige, but only hesitantly. Here is the rest of the story:

> They recited the *fātiḥā* [the first verse of the Quran] and proceeded at night for about four hours until the reached a bridge called `Awja. They did not see anyone so they returned to a tell and aimed to go there (*ḥawwalū* ***hūnīk***) in order to have themselves a cup of coffee (***yishrabūlhom*** *finjān qahwa*) . . . and to sleep an hour of the night. They did what we said. They rode their horses. Night faded away and daylight appeared to them. . . . While they were riding, a rabbit appeared to them for a reason only known to God. So, they directed their horses in chase of it [the rabbit], which ran to a hill and climbed down that hill to a valley. The horses followed suit. When they [the riders] looked up, they found about 200 horsemen from the Egyptian army.[134]

The cup-of-coffee detail, expressed colloquially (literally, "to drink themselves a cup of coffee"), is rich. The expression is typically used to denote the pressure of time: one does not have the opportunity to even have oneself a cup of coffee, a basic necessity. By using this colloquial expression, which denotes the mundane desire of the riders and the mention of their need to steal an hour of sleep, Ibn al-Ṣiddīq familiarizes and humanizes the dejected and tired cavalrymen, thereby provoking the sympathy of the audience. And what of the sudden appearance of the rabbit? One wonders how many army contingents in this world get so distracted by a rabbit as to chase it up a hill and down a valley! Here again, Ibn al-Ṣiddīq humanizes his warriors, who forget about their mission in pursuit of a small, harmless animal. However, there is also dramatization in the miraculous: the rabbit is what leads the riders to their enemies, who are taken by surprise and beaten. The episode resolves with the victory of the Damascenes over the Egyptians. The reader/listener cannot help but be pleased with the result of the encounter, as by now Ibn al-Ṣiddīq has successfully won our sympathy for the Damascene party.

Ibn al-Ṣiddīq's chronicle, then, is history disguised as drama narrated by an absent author. We will see history as drama again in this study when we come to analyze the literary qualities of the text of the barber. However, in the barber's chronicle the drama does not emerge from the banal details of human life: the alleged brevity of the epistle of the sermonist and his oath on pain of divorce, the need on the part of unwilling soldiers for a cup of coffee and an hour's nap, and the chase of a rabbit by an army. In Ibn Budayr's text, in contrast, the action is determined by the need for the epic and the heroic, which is narrated by an ever-present author. In Ibn al-Ṣiddīq's text, the author intimates distantly, quietly, and sometimes facetiously, while in Ibn Budayr's text, the author screams loudly and always earnestly.

IN PLAIN ARABIC

The modern editors of the nouveau literate's chronicles have noted how these works are composed in language that is "colloquial and weak (*`āmmiya wa rakīka*),"[135] "closer to the vernacular, (*al-`āmmiya*) than to the classical (*al-fuṣḥā*),"[136] "simple colloquial dialect,"[137] "full of grammatical and spelling mistakes" and making "profuse use of colloquial expressions,"[138] "riddled with colloquialisms,"[139] or, simply, "in the local dialect."[140] These editors' comments are highly instructive given that the modern editors of premodern histories are certainly not in the habit of drawing attention to the fact that a given work is written in what has come to be known as classical Arabic. In other words, our editors' pointed remarks about the works *not* being written in classical language, *al-lugha al-fuṣḥā*, betray an expectation on their part that the works *should* be written in classical, which modernity regards as the register appropriate to the written word, and that they should be devoid of colloquial language, *al-lugha al-`āmmiyya*, which modernity regards as a register appropriate only to speech.

In order to contextualize the linguistic uses by the authors in our sample, we must first untangle a few issues centered on these descriptions of the Arabic language. Today, Arabic is said to be problematically diglossic: on the one hand, the written Arabic that in English is usually referred to as Modern Standard Arabic, and on the other, the various spoken dialects. In today's Arabic, this distinction is made by referring to the written as *fuṣḥā* (literally, eloquent) and the spoken *`āmmiyya* (literally, common or vulgar).[141] But there is also a concept of a "classical Arabic" (which also in Arabic is referred to as *fuṣḥā*): an older, purer Arabic of pre-Islamic and early Islamic poetry and the language of science and letters of the

"Golden Age." The problem with these attributions is that they resulted from a particular language standardization movement that took place in the late-nineteenth and early-twentieth centuries, which we will treat in the last chapter of this study, and which canonized a Modern Standard Arabic as separate and distinct from spoken Arabic, with the result that the language became perceived as diglossic. To understand the effect of the linguistic usages by our new authors, a different and "restoredly" premodern understanding of the language is necessary. This may be obtained by going back to the literal meanings of the terms *fusḥā* and *`āmmiyya*, as eloquent and vulgar.

The very fact that the two terms *fuṣḥā*, "eloquent," and *`āmmiyya*, "vulgar," have always been juxtaposed or used in opposition implies that *fuṣḥā* is not only eloquent but also "refined," while *`āmmiyya* is not only "common" or "popular" but also not particularly articulate. As such, like any other language, Arabic had and has an elite register used by the educated and refined and a vulgar one associated with the uneducated masses. Though perhaps the most eloquent examples of Arabic were transmitted orally (such as pre-Islamic and early Islamic poetry), *fuṣḥā* quickly became associated with written texts, since it was by and large the educated who wrote most texts. Given its association with scholars, the register of the chronicle is expected to tend toward *fuṣḥā*—one might say to be *fuṣḥā*-ish. This said, it should be noted that the nexus between the oral and the written never really ceased.

Colloquial Arabic was, in fact, used in the writing of history even in the classical period, for example, in the great annalistic chronicle of al-Ṭabarī (d. 923), *Tā'rīkh al-rusul wa al-mulūk* ("The History of Prophets and Kings"), a work that almost came to define the genre. However, it is important to note that al-Ṭabarī's use of colloquial was localized and confined to the special circumstance of direct speech. As such, al-Ṭabarī effectively distinguished between two linguistic realms, the colloquial, used for the oral word even when committed to the written text; and another, classical, which al-Ṭabarī found appropriate for the narrative in text.[142] By the Mamluk period, however, the boundaries separating these two realms were not so fixed as before, as is evidenced by the chronicles of the generation of the Levantine historian al-Yūnīnī (d. 1326), in which some colloquial usages are not only found in direct speech but infiltrate the narrative itself.[143] Al-Yūnīnī's Egyptian contemporary, Ibn al-Dawadārī (d. 1335), wrote a universal history "in almost colloquial style,"[144] and in the generation after al-Yūnīnī the Damascene Ibn Ṣaṣra (fl. 1399) composed a chronicle dominated by colloquial language.[145]

The increasingly free use of colloquial in historical writing seems to have provoked a reaction on the part of many literati. Thus the Egyptian historian and historiographer al-Sakhāwī (d. 1428) commented with evident irritation at the history of his senior contemporary, Ibn al-Furāt (d.1405), "His book has many benefits . . . but he is not good at inflection . . . his grammatical mistakes are grotesque and his expression extremely colloquial." Of the history of Ibn Duqmāq (d. 1407), al-Sakhāwī said, "His compilations are useful, but colloquial in expression."[146] Al-Sakhāwī's comments are clearly built on the premise that there is a pure Arabic, the classical, the proper locus of which is the written word of the scholar, and a corrupt Arabic, the locus of which is the oral word of the commoner.

Critiques such as that of al-Sakhāwī seem to have made a greater impact in the Levant than in his native Egypt. Though the use of colloquial in Egyptian historical writing continued unabated,[147] Ibn Ṣaṣra's chronicle does not seemed to have spawned a colloquial tendency in Levantine chronicling; in fact, there does not seem to have been any subsequent Levantine chronicler who used colloquial as freely as did Ibn Ṣaṣra—or not until the eighteenth century. That the issue was still being contested, however, is evidenced by the fact that the sixteenth-century Damascene scholar Ibn Ḥanbal al-Ḥanafī (d. 1563) authored a language guidebook instructively entitled *Baḥr al-`awwām fī-mā aṣāba fī-hi al-`awāmm*, ("The Swimmer's Ocean in regard to that in which the Common People are Correct.")[148] The title of this work clearly implies that the common people—*al-`awāmm*—have a distinct *parole*—a "colloquial"—that is generally *not* correct, meaning, of course, that it is not correct in relation to something else that is recognized to be correct, this latter entity being the "classical." But Ibn Ḥanbal al-Ḥanafī is arguing here that the usage of the *`awāmm* is not necessarily incorrect; indeed, there are instances where their usage is correct but has not been admitted as such by the custodians of classical. Ibn Ḥanbal al-Ḥanafī's dictionary thus serves to break down borders obstructing the migration of colloquial—or, at least, some colloquial—into the written text; it effectively serves to legitimize the use of colloquial for writing. It is perhaps this sense of legitimation that manifests itself in the widespread reentry of colloquial into the Levantine chronicle in the texts of our eighteenth-century nouveau literates.

Although most of our chroniclers seem to have recognized a distinction between classical and colloquial, they all chose, in different degrees, not to assign classical to narrative and colloquial to speech.[149] To have drawn such boundaries would have limited their self-expression; subsequently, most of them chose not to conform to literary convention and thus earned the wrath of their modern-day editors. Only al-Rukaynī Sr. and the court clerk al-Makkī (the latter often unsuccessfully) attempted to preserve their respective texts from the colloquial. The priest, Burayk, and the son of the Shī`ī farmer, though capable of perfect classical rendition, chose not to heed the literary convention and wrote in whatever suited them. Unlike al-Makkī, whose principled consciousness of the literary conventions unfortunately exceeded his ability actually to employ them, and thus ended up impairing his self-expression, the soldier, al-`Abd, did not allow himself to be thus impeded; he made "respectful" gestures to the convention but otherwise wrote as he spoke. The Samaritan, al-Danafī, on the other hand, may have not even been aware that others would have considered his text as colloquial. As for the other soldier, Ibn al-Ṣiddīq, he told his history as a story and used the appropriate register of popular narrative: colloquial. Whether intentionally or not, in this way all of the nouveau literates produced linguistically hybrid texts that ignored literary norms. In these hybrid texts, the limits between the spoken and the written were left undefined.

It is, of course, difficult not to make the connection between the collective departure from literary convention in these chronicles and the fact that, for the first time, the authors of historical works come from social groups other than the *`ulamā'*. With the breaking of the *`ulamā'* monopoly over the production of the contemporary chronicle, the language of the chronicle is liberated from the literary convention set up by the *`ulamā'* themselves, which distinguished between the textual spaces appropriate to the classical and colloquial registers. Indeed, most of our authors wrote in what, in today's Levantine colloquial, is *bi-al-`arabī al-faṣīḥ*. This expression, *bi-al-`arabī al-faṣīḥ*, literally means "in eloquent Arabic" (*faṣīḥ* is from the same root as *fuṣḥā*) but is in ironic fact itself a colloquialism that is used to refer not to classical Arabic at all but rather to the idea of clear and expressive communication—that is, to "getting the point across" in whatever language is effective. It is to express something "in plain Arabic." This is what our nouveau literates did: they used language as an instrument, and not an end in itself. But to whom were these commoner and marginal authors trying to get the point across?

AUDIENCE, RECEPTION, AND CIRCULATION

Without exception, each of the chronicles treated in this study is found in only one or two extant manuscripts. The paucity of manuscript copies begs questions about the diffusion of these chronicles and leads one to suspect that they were not popular. While an ample number of extant copies of a certain text is indicative of wide circulation, a small number does not necessarily signify diminished value or lack of popularity, since survival of manuscripts can be a matter of sheer chance. Be that as it may, there is, unfortunately, little evidence, either internal to these chronicles or external to them, that allows the researcher to issue with certainty any judgment about audience and circulation. Alas, we may never know how these chronicles were received and who their audiences were; nonetheless, consideration of this question, no matter how conjectural, is necessary.

It is noteworthy that to the best of my knowledge these chronicles were not cited in contemporary or later texts—except for the barber's, which was bowdlerized by a scholar a century later. It is also worth emphasizing that their authors are apparently unaware of one another's works and do not refer to them. This is to say that these chronicles do not constitute a field in which specific reading/writing communities are participating in a clearly defined shared discourse with its specific terminology (as in the case of the works of the reformers and journalists of al-Nahḍa,[150] or of *`ulamā'* writings in the same or previous centuries). This is despite the fact that the chronicles elicit common general concerns, sometimes discuss the same figures, and are informed by a similar set of values. The absence of intertextuality among these chronicles and the dearth of extant copies may actually point to an unusual direction: to oral transmission (whether or not their authors intended them to be so). Meanwhile the lack of a singular and clearly delimited discourse may be indicative of multiple and varied—that is, open—audiences.

All of the chronicles in our sample, in varying degrees, ignore the limits between the spoken and the written, the colloquial and the formal. Indeed, both the barber's chronicle and that of the soldier Ibn al-Ṣiddīq are unabashed in their employment of straightforward storytelling techniques and styles. In other words, the likelihood is that they were intended for oral diffusion.[151] Given that their intention was oral transmission, it is not the fact of the paucity of the manuscripts but rather the fact of their very existence that is surprising. Viewed this way, one may logically propose that the mere fact that written records of these histories have survived at all is testament to their wide circulation. These oral stories were important enough to be written down.

The fact of the oral and colloquial aspects of the chronicles, coupled with the unusual backgrounds of their authors, is also indicative of the intended audiences for these works. These histories are not written for a closed circle of scholars and/or courtiers, the usual audiences for the chronicle. Each chronicler seems to have had one or more audiences. For example, the Greek Orthodox priest addresses not only his own confessional community but also his fellow Damascenes, irrespective of creed. Similarly, the Nabulsi Samaritan scribe's "we" signifies both his co-religionists and his non-Samaritan fellow citizens. And the barber, though keen to show off his social connections to scholars, is just as enthusiastic about his illiterate friends, and he is certainly not writing for the benefit of the governor and his court. In other words, these chronicles, unlike those in previous centuries, had several and diverse audiences, which sometimes but not always overlapped.

It is therefore precisely the openness exhibited in these chronicles, whether in terms of the language of the chronicle (colloquial and classical), method of transmission (oral and written), or multiple audiences (literate, illiterate, scholarly, confessional, civilian, military . . . etc.) that gives this trend of non-*`ulamā'* authorship of chronicles the shape and constitution of a distinct phenomenon. It is a phenomenon of circulation of a genre among different social groups, and a phenomenon that is definitively "popular." This popularity is not about the numbers of hearers/readers of a particular work but about the fact that it was people, regular people, who wrote or recited these works for other people.

We may never know whether these chronicles had enthusiastic audiences who in turn transmitted them orally or copied them into codices that are now lost. What is important here is that all of the nouveau literate historians, regardless of background, had the same idea: to write a chronicle. What is more, they felt confident that their histories would be received by a public, and they actually sat down and picked up the pen to write (or had a scribe write things down for them). The genre of the contemporary chronicle, then, regardless of the degree of success of any particular chronicle, became, in the eighteenth century, in a manner of speaking, a genre that could be owned by anyone.

But how did this happen? How did the chronicle cease to be the exclusive purview of the scholars and become a genre that was up for grabs? Thus far, I have treated nouveau literacy as a social phenomenon, as an effect of and instrument for the disorders of the long eighteenth century. Now, I will turn to the realm of the literary, and attempt to explain why the contemporary chronicle became the "popular" genre of choice. So let us turn from the chronicle as history to the history of the chronicle.

CHAPTER 4

Authority and History

The Genealogy of the Eighteenth-Century Levantine Contemporary Chronicle

The recording of contemporary events has been undertaken, in one guise or another, from the earliest period of Arabic-Islamic historiography itself. However, it took a thousand years for the writing of contemporary history to metamorphose to the point where the fully developed genre of the contemporary chronicle readily lent itself to being appropriated by a quite different cast of historians: the barber, the farmers, the court clerk, the Samaritan scribe, the soldiers, and the priest. Not only did the identity of the authors of the contemporary chronicle change, but so did the language in which the chronicles were written, from classical to colloquial Arabic. But where did the eighteenth-century Levantine contemporary chronicle come from? What is the place of this phenomenon in the history of Arabic-Islamic and Ottoman historiography?

This chapter traces the genealogy of the contemporary chronicle in Arabic-Islamic historiography, which is the genealogy of the writing of contemporary history in the eighteenth-century Levant. In the following, I attempt to identify the earliest ancestors of this genre in the notebooks of scholars in the eighth century, and to chart its subsequent appearances in guises such as the "*ta'rīkh*-diary" (chronicle-diary) and the *dhayl* (supplementary history), until we reach its unique Levantine manifestation of the eighteenth century. I will try specifically to trace the transformation in historical vision that led to the emergence of two defining features of the contemporary chronicle: the overriding interest in the here and now, and the pervasive authorial *I*. These two features are quite significant, as they indicate the transformation of history from a project about the past to a project about the present, and concomitantly the gradual release of the chronicler from the "clasp" of an elite scholarly community and his acquisition of relatively independent authority. In tracing the history of the transformation of the literary form, I examine a range of issues related to the writing of contemporary history, such as the historical impact of changes in institutions of knowledge, literary influences, and audiences and language.

ORIGINS: HISTORY, BIOGRAPHY, AND AUTHORITY

The eighteenth-century Levantine contemporary chronicle has a history as long as that of Islamic historiography itself. The contemporary chronicle's past is intertwined with, and sometimes disguised behind, the two main genres of Islamic historiography: the classic annalistic chronicle, as canonized by the *Tārīkh al-rusul wa al-mulūk* ("The History of Messengers and Kings") of al-Ṭabarī (d. 923),[1] and the biographical dictionary, as canonized by the *Kitāb al-ṭabaqāt al-kabīr* ("The Great Book of Biographies") of Ibn Sa`d (d. 845).[2] Typically, the annalistic chronicle is a record of *past* events usually related to matters of state and arranged chronologically around the Hijrī year, while the biographical dictionary is a collection of life stories usually of deceased scholars describing their qualifications and accomplishments. Despite their differing intentions, it is well known that the relationship between the chronicle and the biographical dictionary was organic in the development of early Islamic historiography. The basic form of the historical report in the early Islamic period consisted of an *isnād*—a chain of transmitters/reporters—and a *matn*—a text. It was held that the veracity of the latter depended on the integrity of the former. In other words, a text is true only if its successive transmitters actually overlapped in time and were known for accurate narration. Hence, in order to establish the integrity of the narrators in the chain of transmission, certain things had to be known about them—their birth and death dates, their qualifications, etc.—with the result that biographical dictionaries came into being primarily thanks to the Hadith movement.[3] The authority of a historical report derived from its *isnād*, the chain of *authority* to which it was shackled. With the passage of time, the chains grew too long and too unwieldy to carry around, and their presence ceased to be formally required in a chronicle. However, in order to legitimate historical knowledge, the burden of demonstrable authority remained. To legitimate himself as a historian, an author still had to demonstrate, by academic training and professional reputation, his possession of a pedigree of authorities. So to authorize—that is, to make one's knowledge public—a historian had to have been himself authorized by previous scholars. In other words, a historian had to be a *transmitter* of the knowledge of preceding authorities before he could legitimately be an *author.*[4] In our eighteenth-century Levantine chronicles, this is not the case. Our new historians present no credentials or authorization; they have somehow been released from having to establish that special link to previous authorities. Unhampered by the procedure of authorization by the scholarly community, present and past, the historian independently emerges as an author. Free from the obligation to establish before his peers the elite pedigree of authority, it becomes possible for *anyone* who is literate to become a historian. The history of the contemporary chronicle is therefore about the transformation of a literary-historiographical genre and of rules of scholarship as well as the transformation of audience/readership. Above all, as we shall see, it is a story of the liberation of the chronicler from the burden of history.

THE CONTEMPORARY CHRONICLE AS "*TA'RĪKH*-DIARY"

When, more than half a century ago, George Makdisi first discovered the diary of the Baghdadi scholar Ibn al-Bannā' (1005–1079), he thought it an exceptional case.[5] Effectively, *this ta'rīkh-diary is the first extant contemporary chronicle.* A comparison between Ibn al-Bannā's text and that of our Damascene *'ālim* Ibn Kannān yields striking results. To begin with, like Ibn Kannān, Ibn al-Bannā' was a teacher. Like Ibn Kannān's chronicle, Ibn al-Bannā's is a record of the events around him and is often written in the first person. Like Ibn Kannān, Ibn al-Bannā' fixed the date by establishing the first day of the lunar month.[6] The content of Ibn al-Bannā's text includes anecdotes, miracles and wonders, poetry, dreams and interpretations, and all kinds of events that concern the political, social, and academic life of the city. Although separated by seven centuries, the text of the Baghdadi teacher bears an uncanny resemblance, both in form and in content, to that of the Damascene teacher.

In a much later article, George Makdisi showed that the keeping of "*ta'rīkh*-diaries" such as that of Ibn al-Bannā' was, in fact, a widespread activity that went back as far as the eighth century.[7] And although these records were called *ta'rīkh*, history (or more accurately, history writing/chronicling), they were distinguished from the annalistic chronicle by the qualification of the latter as *ta'rīkh `alā al-sinīn* (history arranged by years). The distinguishing features of *ta'rīkh* (-diary) as opposed to *ta'rīkh `alā al-sinīn* (annalistic chronicles) and biographical works are that (1) *ta'rīkh*s are necessarily autographed; (2) they are title-less; (3) their dates are fixed by the lunar month, as opposed to the year as in annalistic chronicles; and (4) in terms of content and arrangement, in *ta'rīkh*s one finds obituaries and other events mixed together and arranged chronologically, whereas in the historical literature of the period obituaries were placed only in biographical dictionaries and events—mostly political events—were recorded in annalistic chronicles. Makdisi convincingly argued that all scholars kept *ta'rīkh*-diaries and that these autographed *ta'rīkh*s functioned as notes from which the scholars derived material for the composition of larger works. Having first recorded information in his *ta'rīkh*, the historian would later sift through this material and arrange it separately into biographies and events. If he wrote a chronicle, he would rearrange the events in an annalistic order. Hence, these "*ta'rīkh*-diaries" were used only as sources; they were not even drafts of which fair copies were made.[8] Makdisi emphasizes that these *ta'rīkh*-diaries "like our own present-day research notes . . . were not meant to be published."[9] It is the fact that they were not meant to be "*public* records" that is the rationale for Makdisi's appellation for them: "diary."[10]

If we accept Makdisi's convincing argument, the difference between Ibn al-Bannā's and Ibn Kannān's respective texts would be that the former was merely a means to an end and was not meant for publication, while the latter was an end in itself and *was* meant for publication; Ibn Kannān gave his chronicle a title and read it out in public.[11] However, it should be noted here that whether or not such was intended, Ibn al-Bannā's work *did*, in fact, enter circulation; as Makdisi himself demonstrates, it was used a century later by another Baghdadi scholar, Ibn al-Jawzī (1116–1200), who copied from and cited it in his chronicle of universal history, *al-Muntaẓam fī tārīkh al-mulūk wa al-umam* ("The Well-Ordered History of Kings and Nations"), just as al-Murādī used Ibn Kannān's chronicle as a source for his biographical dictionary, *Silk al-durar*. Further, Ibn al-Jawzī adopted two defining characteristics of the *ta'rīkh*-diary in his *al-Muntaẓam*: he organized the text by the month and united the hitherto formally separate categories of biographies and events between the two covers of a single book.[12] In fact, Makdisi shows that the use of *ta'rīkh*-diaries as sources by scholars subsequent to the author of the *ta'rīkh*-diary was absolutely standard practice at this time.[13] Indeed, Makdisi seems to concede that the author of the *ta'rīkh*-diary himself had in mind the possibility of an audience as "he recorded matters which were not meant for the eyes of members of other affiliations."[14] The implication is that *there was an audience* for these autographs, but that the audience was an intentionally restricted one—as was Ibn Kannān's.

THE CONTEMPORARY CHRONICLE AS *DHAYL*, AND CHRONICLER AS AUTHOR

Even as Ibn al-Jawzī was using the *ta'rīkh*-diary of Ibn al-Bannā' as a source for his universal chronicle, an important development was taking place in Arabic-Islamic historiography.[15] In his study of Islamic historiography, Chase F. Robinson singles out the eleventh century as a time of a "new confidence" that challenged the accustomed traditionalist ethos found in historiography.[16] Similarly, Tarif Khalidi speaks of the period between the eleventh and fifteenth centuries as a time that witnesses the emergence of a "greater measure of self-consciousness" on the part of historians:

> They [the historians] were now more likely to fancy themselves as actors on a stage which they once had only observed. . . . There are other signs of the historian's ego underpinning the narrative. The use of 'I say' (*qultu*) to interrupt the narrative and introduce the historian's personal comments or opinions on people and events becomes frequent enough to be noticeable.[17]

The twelfth century also witnessed what Dwight Reynolds, Christine Brustad, et al. have called a "flowering of autobiographical writing."[18] Khalidi specifically notes the appearance of autobiography in the context of contemporary history, for example, how "the universal history of the Ayyūbid prince Abū'l Fidā grows more autobiographical as he approaches his own days."[19] In short, the period in question witnesses a transformation in the self-perception and role of the author whereby he ceases to be exclusively, or even primarily, a transmitter on the authority of others. This period in Arabic-Islamic historical production is recognized as a break within the historiographical tradition. Claude Cahen calls it the "post-classical period,"[20] Ulrich Haarman speaks of a "dissolution" of literary forms,[21] and Khalidi states that this period "demarcate[s] a new attitude toward history."[22] This new attitude is well expressed in the declaration of the chronicler `Imād al-Dīn al-Kātib al-Iṣfahānī (d. 1201), secretary of state to Saladin (d. 1193): "My testimony is based on entirely what I witnessed . . . and *I have been concerned to record only what I myself experienced.*"[23]

In his survey of the history of Arabic historiography, Shākir Muṣṭafā identifies the new features of historical writing in this period as threefold: first, the unit of time in the annalistic chronicle is further broken down to the month, the day, and even to the hour[24]; second, historians are now increasingly concerned with contemporary events and turn their efforts from the production of universal histories to the authoring of what is called *dhayl* (the supplement)[25]; with the result that, third, the historian now emerges, in Shākir Muṣṭafā's acute characterization, as "the witness of the age."[26] Muṣṭafā shows that every chronicler in Egypt and the Levant between the mid-thirteenth and mid-fifteenth centuries recorded contemporary events, and no less than 17 of 41 chroniclers concerned themselves *exclusively* with contemporary and very recent history.[27] One of the first of these was the Damascene al-Yūnīnī (d. 1326), who is also the first to use colloquial Arabic rather unabashedly.[28]

A Damascene contemporary of al-Yūnīnī was `Alam al-Dīn al-Birzālī (d. 1339), who wrote a contemporary chronicle entitled *al-Muqtafā `alā al-Rawḍatayn* ("The Sequel to 'The Two Gardens'"). Al-Birzālī wrote *al-Muqtafā* (literally, "The Sequel") as a supplement (*dhayl*),[29] continuing the earlier history of Abū Shāma. Like al-Yūnīnī, al-Birzālī dealt only with the events of his own lifetime. In his study of al-Yūnīnī, however, Li Guo found that al-Birzālī's chronicle represented nothing less than "a new approach to *ta'rīkh*." The basis for Li Guo's assertion is the fact that, unlike al-Yūnīnī and his other contemporaries, "Al-Birzālī abandoned the customary form of equally divided event and obituary sections and combined the two indiscriminately into one strictly annalistic form based on a monthly chronological order."[30]

The alert reader will immediately recognize that, of course, this is not a new approach to *ta'rīkh* at all. In organizing his contemporary chronicle by the month, and by collapsing events and obituaries into a single narrative, al-Birzālī was doing exactly what Ibn al-Bannā' had done in his *ta'rīkh*-diary. What is new in al-Birzālī's chronicle is not the form—which was the existing standard form of the *ta'rīkh*-diary—but the fact of the *public* appearance of a text in this form. In al-Birzālī's *Muqtafā*, the *ta'rīkh*-diary emerges from its occlusion as a surrogate history serving as a source for later historians, and it comes forth into the world as the contemporary chronicle. In other words, the contemporary chronicle is now a history in its own right. It is instructive to note, in this regard, that al-Birzālī's chronicle was also known as *Ta'rīkh al-Shaykh `Alam al-Dīn al-Birzālī* ("The History of the Shaykh `Alam al-Dīn al-Birzālī"); that is to say, it is a work named after its author.[31] *Al-Muqtafā* is, effectively, the first known "*ta'rīkh*-diary" to acquire a title and put itself out for publication. Instead of being merely a source that may not legitimately make a public appearance, al-Birzālī's *ta'rīkh* was legitimated and transformed into a *book*. This is the point that Donald Little missed in his criticism of the *Muqtafā*:

> It is the most strictly chronological in format, being divided not just into years but into months as well; furthermore, obituaries of obscure scholars and functionaries are interwoven day by day . . . [the] very lack of organization and discrimination reveals an inability or disinclination to discern or assign importance to events.[32]

The apparent "lack of organization and discrimination" is a feature of all the eighteenth-century chronicles of the nouveau literates and is, of course, a direct consequence of the fact of the work being a contemporary chronicle. However, as Li Guo notes, the formal aspect of al-Birzālī's "new approach to *ta'rīkh*" was not immediately successful[33]; it would be another 200 years before a historian combined events and obituaries in the narrative in the *ta'rīkh*-diary manner.

The question to be asked, then, is, What is it in the period 1100–1500 that brought about the importance of the contemporary over the past, the priority of the here and now over received forms of categorization (into event and obituary), and above all, the audacious intrusion of the authorial *I*? Why did the writing of history in the Levant (and Egypt) change in the period 1100–1500? The most convincing answer offered is that the sheer shock of the onslaught of the Crusades and the Mongols in the Eastern Mediterranean brought about a new sensibility. Rosenthal writes, "At no other time in the history of the central regions of Islam did the rhythm of change from fear to hope and from hope to fear make contemporary happenings appear so worthy of the attention of the historian as it did then."[34] Similarly, Khalidi speaks of "the uncommonness of the hour . . . Whereas earlier historiography was largely an interpretation of a momentous past, the new historiography boldly projected its own present being of equal if not greater significance."[35] He cites the remarkable statement of the aforementioned ʿImād al-Dīn al-Iṣfahānī in the preamble to his biography of his master, Saladin:

> I, on the other hand, chose to date my history from a second Hijra . . . this Hijra being the Hijra of Islam to Jerusalem, undertaken by the Sultan Ṣalāḥ al-Dīn. . . . History would do well to be dated from this year. . . . Indeed, this Hijra is of more lasting significance than the first.[36]

Thus the contemporary chronicle became the vehicle by which to express the uncommonness of the time. The same condition applies to the writing of contemporary chronicles in the eighteenth-century Levant, except that what was uncommon about the eighteenth century was very different from what was uncommon about the twelfth and thirteenth.

This explains the preeminence of the contemporary over the past, but what about intrusion in history of the authorial *I*? The answer to this lies in far-reaching institutional transformations within the *ʿulamāʾ* class—the class from which the historians came—during the period 1100–1500. This is the period that witnessed the establishment and rapid proliferation of institutions associated with the *ʿulamāʾ*. The most important of these institutions was the *madrasa*, the proliferation of which was initiated by the Saljūq state and which were, subsequently, more often than not endowed and patronized by leading figures of the regime. The expansion of colleges went hand in hand with the *ʿulamāʾ*-ization of the state administration, as graduates of the *madrasa* increasingly entered state service, whether as high or petty bureaucrats (all of Saladin's biographers, for example, were *`ālim*-courtiers), or in the expanded judiciary that included state-appointed judges from all four legal schools and advisers to the *maẓālim* (extra-*shar`ī*) courts.[37] With the rise of these institutions, the *`ālim*'s vocation became a profession, and the *`ulamā'* themselves became an institution linked to the authority of the state—an institution, moreover, whose members were now fully expected to take stock of and administer the here and now. The historians of the period 1100–1500 thus represent a new institutionalized class of professional *`ulamā'*, of whom Khalidi observes:

> What was new was the high profile that these classes had acquired or have been given: as propagandists of the state, as regular recipients of state largesse or beneficiaries of the private endowments, as frequent employees on state business, as public preachers. One detects in these historians a greater measure of self-consciousness, with their own contribution to history considered worthy of mention alongside the exploits of their lords and masters.[38]

The historian thus becomes a confident professional witness of the times, and the *ta'rīkh*-diary of the *`ālim*, once just a prospective source for the history of the past, now becomes a legitimately publishable end in itself. When the contemporary chronicle becomes a book, its writer becomes an author who now openly and formally authorizes his own knowledge. However, it is notable that even now contemporary histories such as the *Muqtafā* were published in the form of the *dhayl* (supplementary history, literally, "tail"); even while not transmitting from earlier scholars, the contemporary historian still acknowledged the authority of his predecessors by formally positing himself as no more than the "tail end" of their project. Though the *`ulamā'* as historians had liberated themselves from the burden of history by writing about the present, and unshackled themselves from the yoke of speaking on a previous authority by disposing of the *isnād*, more often than not the contemporary chronicler still needed to attach himself to the *`ulamā'* of the past. In short, despite having acquired a greater measure of independent authority, the historian's authorship was still restricted. The historian, as a truly independent author—that is, a writer confident enough in his experience and his knowledge not to look back to previous works and authorities—will not emerge until the sixteenth century. Ibn Kannān, though he might mention the works of previous historians, would not posit his chronicle *al-Ḥawādith al-yawmiyya li-tārīkh aḥad `ashar wa alf wa miyya* ("The Daily Events from 1100 [AH]") as a supplement. The "liberation" of the *`ālim* from supplementary history and the concomitant empowerment of his authorship, however, also meant a dissolution of collective authority. The phenomenon of supplementary history reflects an attempt at continued monopoly of the *`ulamā'* over history, which they seem to have considered a collective sequential enterprise. The demise of the *dhayl* phenomenon signifies not only the birth of the independent author-historian but also the writing of history having ceased to be an exclusive group project, that is, an *`ulamā'* project. The birth of the author in historiography also meant the subsequent birth of a new author in it.

New Historian, New History, New Language

The first known entry of non-*`ulamā'* into the writing of history also took place in the fourteenth century, but in Egypt, not in the Levant. Although this particular history was not the beginning of a trend, it is nonetheless a fascinating solitary instance. Almost nothing is known about Abū Bakr b. `Abd Allāh Ibn al-Dawādārī (fl. 1335) beyond the fact that he was not an *`ālim*—there is no mention of him in any biographical dictionary of *`ulamā'*—but the grandson of a *mamlūk*, and the son of a man who was in the service of the Sultan Qalāwūn and whom Ibn al-Dawādārī seems to have assisted.[39] Ibn al-Dawādārī, though not himself a *mamlūk*, moved immediately in military society. Ibn al-Dawādārī authored a universal history entitled *Kanz al-durar wa jāmi` al-ghurar* ("The Treasure of Pearls and the Collection of the Finest"), which included contemporary history. His work displays a quite different vision of history from that found in the chronicles of his *`ulamā'* contemporaries.

> The chronicle of Ibn al-Dawadārī stands apart from other histories of the period in its lack of literary ostentation, its spontaneity, often comic, narrative tone, its relish for prodigies, dreams, omens, and "marvelous coincidences," its almost

colloquial style and its unaffected reflections on history and the exercise of power. . . . Ibn al-Dawadārī is oddly silent on the lives of the scholars. Instead, we are in the company of the mamlūk military elite as they march to battle or converse among themselves. This is anti-history.[40]

Although the *`ulamā'* simply ignored Ibn al-Dawādārī—no later historian cited him or his work[41]—and his intervention into the historiographical project did not immediately open up the space for non-*`ālim* historians, his chronicle is, in at least two dimensions, a harbinger for later developments.[42] First, Ibn al-Dawādārī's chronicle illustrates what happens to the concept and content of history when it is appropriated from the *`ulamā'*: its lack of ostentation, spontaneity, and comic narrative tone are something that many of our eighteenth-century chronicles authored by non-*`ulamā'* demonstrate. Second, there is the fact of Ibn al-Dawādārī's "almost colloquial style." The *`ālim* historians of the fourteenth century, such as the Damascene al-Yūnīnī, began to use colloquialisms in their narrative, yet Ibn al-Dawādārī's non-*`ālim* chronicle represents the first instance of a chronicler using colloquial so extensively. In the next generation, the Damascene Ibn Ṣaṣra (fl. 1399) would write a contemporary chronicle in largely colloquial language[43]; but this was the last chronicle known to be written in this register in the Levant until the eighteenth century. In Egypt, by contrast, the extensive use of colloquial in the historical narrative rapidly became standard practice. This movement culminated in the *Badā'i` al-zuhūr wa waqā'i` al-duhūr* ("The Marvelous Flowers and the Events of Epochs")—effectively, a contemporary chronicle masquerading as universal history—of the *`ālim* Ibn Iyās (d. 1524), who like most of the Egyptian *`ulamā'*-historians of his generation wrote in what Carl Petry has called "a blending of colloquial and formal language."[44] Even though Ibn al-Dawādārī's decision to use colloquial may well have been simply because of an inability to write in classical—Li Guo states that "there is no evidence to suggest that [he] . . . received any formal education"[45]—the same cannot be said of the Egyptian *`ulamā'* of the fifteenth to sixteenth centuries; Ibn Iyās was a student of no less a figure than the greatest scholar of his time, al-Suyūṭī (d. 1505). The decision of Ibn Iyās and his colleagues to use colloquial in writing history may, however, have been related to the third issue raised by Ibn al-Dawādārī's history, that of audience. For whom, after all, did Ibn al-Dawādārī, who moved in *mamlūk* circles, write his entertaining history of men-of-war, if not for the men-of-war themselves? Was it for the often half-literate *mamlūks* for whom Arabic was a second language and who, if comfortable with Arabic at all, would have been happier with colloquial?[46] Similarly, the fourteenth- and fifteenth-century scholars Ibn Iyās and Ibn Taghribirdī were *awlād al-nās*—descendants of *mamlūks*—who continued to have extensive links to *mamlūk* society.[47] Perhaps their histories were composed with audiences in mind similar to those of Ibn al-Dawādārī. Or perhaps other audiences for history existed beyond the *mamlūk* and *`ulamā'* classes. Certainly, there is evidence that some of the Cairo non-elite population, whether literate or semiliterate, may have constituted a potential readership/audience for scholarship in the Mamlūk period.[48]

Before we leave the Mamluk period, we will examine another remarkable solitary text that parallels that of al-Dawādārī in terms of its prospective value. It is not a history but a diary, by the Damascene Ibn Ṭawq (d. 1509)[49] who, like al-Makkī, seems to have worked in some capacity at a judicial court.[50] Similar to al-Makkī's relationship to his patron Ibrāhīm Āghā, Ibn Ṭawq also found a favorite person (and possibly a patron) in Taqiyy al-Dīn Ibn Qāḍī `Ajlūn (d. 1521), one of the most important scholars of Damascus whom Ibn Ṭawq calls "*sīd-ī al-shaykh*" (something akin to "my Lord the scholar").[51] Strikingly, Ibn Ṭawq is much more forthcoming than al-Makkī and even relates matters of personal/private import such as the occasion of his donning a new shirt, beating his slave girl, and later regretting it, or a domestic brawl in the house of his patron.[52] But the significance of Ibn Ṭawq's journal in our genealogy of historical writing is that it is perhaps the earliest (extant) manifestation of a nonscholarly diary, in contrast to Ibn al-Bannā's *ta'rīkh*-diary, which was composed as "research notes." Thus Ibn al-Bannā's text is the precursor of not only the contemporary history but also the mundane and personal diary. Ibn Ṭawq's journal, in turn, anticipates what will become a phenomenon of personal narratives in th seventeenth- and eighteenth-century Ottoman world, a brand of the contemporary chronicle dubbed *yawmiyyāt* (daily occurrences).

Shams al-Dīn Ibn Ṭūlūn, the Contemporary Chronicle, and the People

The later Mamlūk and early Ottoman period witnessed a divergence in historiographical production between Egypt and the Levant, respectively. Unlike Egypt, the fifteenth- and sixteenth-century Levant does not appear to have thrown up *awlād al-nās* historians freely using colloquial Arabic to write about contemporary and recent history. This may well have been for the simple reason of audience: "The Egyptian Mamluks and their sons (*awlād al-nās*) retained closer ties to the Mamluk sphere than those who went through their formative period in Syria."[53] In some ways, the Levantine historiographical tradition of the fifteenth and sixteenth centuries was more conservative than in Egypt; the Levantine *`ulamā'* continued to write history in classical Arabic for their fellow *`ulamā'*.[54] Nevertheless, a number of significant innovations were not paralleled in Egypt. These are seen in the most important chronicle produced in the Levant in the sixteenth century, the *Mufākahat al-khillān fī ḥawādith al-zamān* ("Bantering with Friends about the Events of the Time") of Shams al-Dīn Ibn Ṭūlūn (d. 1546), who wrote in the half-century immediately subsequent to the Ottoman conquest of the Levant.[55]

The importance of Ibn Ṭūlūn's history—which is a contemporary chronicle written as a *dhayl* to the contemporary chronicle of Ibn Ṭūlūn's teacher, `Abd al-Qādir al-Nu`aymī (d. 1521)—is witnessed in the fact that it was among the most widely circulated history books in Damascus in the two centuries after its author's death.[56] Ibn Ṭūlūn, an *`ālim* par excellence, was acutely conscious of being a member of a scholarly community: he cites previous authorities,[57] speaks of scholarly concourses and readings,[58] and, like Ibn Kannān, has a lot to say about colleges.[59] It is interesting to note, however, that in arranging his chronicle Ibn Ṭūlūn departs from the norm by resurrecting al-Birzālī's "*ta'rīkh*-diary" model; his unit of time is the month, and he mixes obituaries and events.[60] Ibn Ṭūlūn's contemporary chronicle constitutes a departure from the Levantine school, not only in form but in content as well. In contrast to Li Guo's characterization of the earlier Levantine chronicles as consisting of "a record of events . . . [and] a register of Muslim religious learning, as well as a selective anthology of the cultural and literary heritage of the time,"[61] Naila Kaidbey observes of *Mufākahat al-khillān*:

> [A] quantitative analysis of the text would disclose that the majority of the narratives report incidents of injustice against the *populace*[62] . . . The most distinctive quality of this chronicle is that Ibn Ṭūlūn appears to be the advocate of the people (*al-nās*) and not only of the *`ulamā'*[63] . . . Ibn Ṭūlūn emerged as the defender of the populace during those troubled times.[64]

In other words, Ibn Ṭūlūn's chronicle is less about the *`ulamā'* and more about the suffering of "the people." In this, his chronicle resembles that of the barber, Ibn Budayr, and the first part of the chronicle of the soldier, al-`Abd. Ibn Ṭūlūn's history seems to open up the Levantine contemporary chronicle for the part of the population that would take it over in the eighteenth century. The propensity toward "the people" is also found in the biographical dictionaries produced in sixteenth- and seventeenth-century Levant, which represent the bulk of the historiographical production of the period. Kaidbey has found that although the various biographical dictionaries diverged in their selection of the individuals preserved between their respective covers, the more inclusive among them registered "ordinary, sometimes frivolous, personalities." She also notes that these same dictionaries exhibit a more "popular narrative style," which along with their proclivity to include the ordinary man "might have made history more accessible to the less erudite."[65] Kaidbey's remark points to the possibility of a new readership/audience for contemporary history in sixteenth- and seventeenth-century Levant.

THE OTTOMAN WORLD: *YAWMIYYĀT*, SUFISM, THE SELF, THE QUOTIDIAN, CONVERSATION, AND COMPANIONSHIP

For the moment, though, it will be appropriate to turn from relating the development of the Levantine contemporary chronicle to literary activity in another place—the non-Arabic speaking provinces of the Ottoman Empire—and to another language—Ottoman Turkish. In a path-breaking article, Cemal Kafadar described the existence of a number of Ottoman works from the seventeenth century, which he termed "first person narratives."[66] They include diaries, travelogues, dream logbooks, letters, and captivity memoirs. Some of these works—the diaries, dream logbooks, captivity memoirs—are simply forms of the contemporary chronicle (they treat events contemporaneous to the author and rely on no authority other than that of the author as eyewitness), and even those that are not strictly contemporary chronicles share with them the underpinning authorial *I* that is a defining characteristic of the 18th-century nouveau literates' chronicles. For example, in Balat (Palatia) during the years 1661–1665, Seyyid Ḥasan (d. 1668), a Turkish-speaking Sufi, kept a record of his daily activities, which he entitled *Ṣoḥbetnāme.* As we now know, there is nothing remarkable about this in and of itself; Seyyid Ḥasan was simply doing something what Muslim scholars had done for a long time, keeping a "*ta'rīkh*-diary."[67] However, what is striking about Seyyid Ḥasan's chronicle is its unabashed personal, mundane, and quotidian quality; it is concerned with the self in the everyday. Therefore, although Ibn Iyās wrote a contemporary chronicle filled with entertaining tales, and Ibn Ṭūlūn wrote about the injustices inflicted by the state upon the common man, the dervish Seyyid Ḥasan wrote about *his* friends, *his* meals, *his* afternoon naps, and the social gatherings *he* attended.[68] The similarities between this first-person narrative Ottoman literature and the chronicles of our nouveau literates are striking: both groups of texts are author-centric. Is this author-centric narrative literature indicative of a larger trend in the Ottoman Empire in the seventeenth and eighteenth centuries?

The answer seems to be yes. Even without having undertaken exhaustive attempts to track down an empirewide production of contemporary chronicles, I have come across some noteworthy instances.[69] From Ṣan`ā' in the Yemen comes the chronicle of the scholar Yaḥyā b. al-Ḥusayn (d. 1688), entitled *Bahjat al-zaman fī ḥawādith al-Yaman* ("The Splendor of the Age Regarding the Events of Yemen"), which covers the years 1636–1687.[70] The Damascene scholar Ismā`īl al-Maḥāsinī (d. 1690) maintained a diary in which he kept a dated record of events that ranged from his planting a tree to social gatherings, to the appointment of officials.[71] Another Damascene *`ālim*, Muḥibb al-Dīn al-Ghazzī (d. 1704), wrote a "history arranged by daily events,"[72] now lost. An Ottoman bureaucrat by the name of Telḥīsī Muṣṭafā Efendi (fl. 1735) wrote a contemporary chronicle in Turkish in which he voiced personal opinions on contemporary issues ranging from Russo-Ottoman relations to women's clothing fashions.[73] An Istanbuli `*ālim* and teacher by the name of Ṣidḳī Muṣṭafā (d. 1791) wrote a contemporary chronicle in Turkish covering the years 1749–1756, whose concerns resonate with those of the Damascene scholar Ibn Kannān.[74] The Baghdādī scholar `Abd al-Raḥmān al-Suwaydī (d. 1785) wrote a chronicle covering six years of his life beginning with a touching account of how he and his family fled from plague-ridden Baghdad.[75] The Moroccan Sufi and scholar Aḥmad Ibn `Ajība (d. 1809) wrote a self-narrative about his accomplishments in both spiritual and religious knowledge.[76] Mulla Muṣṭafā (fl. 1805), who was an artisan turned religious functionary in Sarajevo, also left a record of contemporary events.[77] All of these are aside from the chronicles under study.[78]

The fact of the contemporary chronicle (whether a diary or a history) being an empire-wide phenomenon inevitably raises the question of intertextuality, especially between the Turkish and Arabic literary traditions. Certainly, the accomplished literati in the Ottoman Empire, regardless of ethnic background, were trilingual: in addition to Turkish and Arabic, they also knew Persian. The question of intertextuality in the literary discourses of the Ottoman world is a large one that warrants systematic and detailed study, and I am not going to attempt to answer it here.[79] What is striking, however, is the fact that roughly at the same time the Turkish contemporary chronicle made its appearance in the seventeenth century, the Arabic contemporary chronicle itself underwent further metamorphosis to appear, in two fundamental qualities, uncannily similar to its Turkish counterpart. This metamorphosis involved the adoption of smaller time units within the frame of which to chronicle events, with the result that the contemporary chronicle acquired a new name as a distinctive genre: in Arabic, *ḥawādith yawmiyya*, *waqā'i` yawmiyya*, and *yawmiyyāt*, and in Turkish, *yevmiye*, all meaning "daily events."[80] This narrowing of time frame was accompanied by a greater focus on the author himself: the *yawmiyyāt* is clearly distinguishable from its predecessors among contemporary chronicles by the fact of its marked author-centricity—the authorial *I* is more intrusive and the events fall even more directly within the ambit of the author's immediate daily experiences.[81] We have seen a concern with both the self and the quotidian in the late Mamluk diary of Ibn Ṭawq, but in the Ottoman world this became a standard literary preoccupation.

What was responsible for the narrowing of focus onto the self in the everyday? At least a partial answer may be ventured by returning to the Sufi Seyyid Ḥasan. Kafadar has suggested a possible connection between a standard literary activity in Sufi circles and Seyyid Ḥasan's writing of his *Ṣoḥbetnāme*:

> It is clear that recording the worldly and miraculous deeds, words and visions of one's *şeyḥ* was a respected activity in Sufi circles. Seyyid Ḥasan had in a way produced a work of that nature but inverted the process and recorded his own deeds.[82]

Interestingly, this inversion from the other to the self is accompanied by an inversion from the spiritual to the *quotidian*. The relationship between Sufism and *yawmiyyāt* is also seen in the earlier chronicle of a much more prominent Sufi than Seyyid Ḥasan, Maḥmūd Hüdā'ī, a native speaker of Turkish who wrote a chronicle in Arabic entitled *al-Tibr al-masbūk*, also known as *Vāḳi'āt* ("Occurrences"). The work chronicles a single year (1577–78) documenting the daily dialogues between the author as a novice Sufi and his *shaykh*, the founder of the Celvetiyye Order, Uftāde.[83] Ṣun'ullah Gaybī, a disciple of the Malāmātī *shaykh* Oğlanlar Ibrāhīm Efendi, also recorded his Sufi master's conversation in a work again entitled *Ṣoḥbetnāme*.[84]

But the Sufi connection to the *yawmiyyāt* took other routes as well. When the great Levantine Sufi 'Abd al-Ghanī al-Nābulusī had mystical dreams, he *chronicled* them in a work entitled *Munājāt al-ḥakīm* ("Dialogue with the Wise") where he "records the dates of each exchange [that] takes place, and he gives *mundane* details."[85] 'Abd al-Ghanī's dream diary fills all the criteria of a contemporary chronicle, and though the events he records take place while he is asleep rather than awake, they are no less "real" and meaningful to the author for that. Despite the long history of oneirocritical literature in the Islamic tradition (the first extant work on dream interpretation was authored by Ibn Sīrīn (d. 728) and the canonical Hadith collections contain oneirocritical sayings from the Prophet), first-person dream chronicles were uncommon before this period.[86] It is noteworthy that the aforementioned Sufi Hüdā'ī also recorded his dreams, and in addition he was a dream interpreter for the Ottoman Sultan Murad III, who would dictate his dreams and have them sent to Hüdā'ī by royal dispatch.[87] And at the same time `Abd al-Ghanī was chronicling his dreams, a woman—at last!—by the name of Asiye Hātūn, also a Sufi from the Balkan town of Üsküp (Skopje), was writing down hers.[88] These dream logbooks and dream chronicles in which the author records and explores the meanings of his or her dreams in the context of his or her life are of interest here because, by definition, they express the author's interest and absorption in his or her own consciousness and in the meaning of the events in his or her life. They are expressive, in other words, of precisely the concern with the authorial *I* that is fundamental to the contemporary chronicle.

Another route of connection between Sufi writing and the *yawmiyyāt* chronicle is the travelogue—though not all the travelogue writing of the period is connected to Sufism and some important travel narratives were written by Christians.[89] The similarities between the travelogue and the contemporary chronicle are clear: like the contemporary chronicle, the travelogue is concerned with the here and now in which the author moves, and it is necessarily suffused with the authorial *I*. The Ottoman period witnessed the production of a profusion of travelogues, a great number of which fall in the category of Sufi travel literature, a genre culminating, in the Arabic-speaking world, in the writings of `Abd al-Ghanī al-Nābulusī and his students.[90] These travelogues, which contain their authors' visits to Sufi shrines and *khānqāh*s (convents), their attendance of *dhikr* séances and meetings with Sufi *shaykhs*, are full of notices of the quotidian that we encounter in the *yawmiyyāt*. Even the *Siyāḥatnāme* ("The Book of Travels") of the famous Turkish traveler Evliyā Çelebi (fl. 1683)—whose journeys were, perhaps, less motivated by spiritual goals than by a fascination with other cultures—abounds with the author paying his respects at shrines, visiting Sufi lodges, and seeking the blessings of prominent Sufis. It is precisely this quotidian texture of Evliyā Çelebi's travelogue that prompted Suraiya Faroqhi to use it as a source for her book on daily life in the Ottoman Empire.[91]

What is suggested here, then, is that Sufism, the ultimate personal spiritual experience that was of such overwhelming social significance throughout the Ottoman world, contributed to the impulse to write about personal experience. Derin Terzioğlu has demonstrated how the rich Sufi vocabulary of self-transformation inherited by Ottoman Sufis was coupled with a legacy of biographical and hagiographical writings, and that these two things together formed the necessary tools that enabled Ottoman Sufi Nıyāzı-i Mıṣrī (d. 1694) to write his own biography.[92] But short of conscious self-writing, one can safely say that this general atmosphere of self-awareness and introspection necessarily drew attention to the immediate context in which life was lived, the context in which the Sufi sought to realize the larger truth of existence: the mundane, the routine, the quotidian, the here and now. This is the kind of attention to everyday life that we encounter in the *yevmiye* of Seyyid Ḥasan, and in the *yawmiyyāt* of our Ibn Budayr and al-Makkī.

The Sufi context also casts fresh light on the question of the audience of the *yawmiyyāt*. The title of Seyyid Ḥasan's diary, *Ṣoḥbetnāme*—in Turkish, "The Book of Conversation"; in Arabic, "The Book of Companionship"—is a very suggestive one. In his study *The Arabic Book*, Johannes Pederson prefaces his discussion of the social relations involved in the production of scholarship with the statement "Muslims love company and conversation."[93] Its essentialization aside, Pederson's statement is, in fact, expressive of some formal aspects of the production of books in the medieval Arabic-Islamic tradition; often, the medieval author legitimized writing his book by citing the "insistence of friends" in the preamble to his work.[94] Not only was the author's excuse for writing the book that he had to oblige friends or companions—even if this was only a literary device—but sometimes the book itself took the form of conversation, such as the *responsa* format of early Islamic legal texts, or the dialogue of Hüdā'ī's *Vāḳi`āt*. Both of these literary devices were, in truth, not disconnected from the reality of scholarly tradition and the social practices of the scholars. As shown earlier, premodern Islamic education was based considerably on the twin practices of conversation and companionship; in order to acquire knowledge, the student had to "become a companion to" his teacher (what was known as *muṣaḥaba* or *mulāzama*),[95] and the vocabulary of the transmission of knowledge is one of listening and narration (*rawā `an*, to narrate from; *sami`a `an*, to hear from; *qāla*, to say). In other words, companionship and conversation were a real part of the process of the production of knowledge, with the book being the final product. If we turn now to consider the possible audience of our *yawmiyyāt* in the historical light of companionship and conversation, we will find that these elements are of not merely literary but literal relevance.

Cemal Kafadar has commented on Seyyid Ḥasan's chronicle:

> The *Ṣoḥbetnāme*'s value lies, more than anything, in giving us that sense of companionship exactly as its title promises. What we know about the social structure and institutional aspects of Ottoman Istanbul is animated not only through the wealth of information about the material life and daily activities of some individuals, but about the ethos of daily life for a specific milieu—one that cannot be situated comfortably either in courtly or folk traditions. If unique personal experiences of a mystical nature are not recorded, perhaps it is because our diarist felt the true path to the good life to lie not so much in individual experiences as in communal harmony—a sensibility that was rather common in Sufism.[96]

In this highly suggestive passage, Kafadar relates the *Ṣoḥbetnāme* to Seyyid Ḥasan's "specific milieu"—to the group of people with whom the experiences of the individual author were in "communal harmony." Although Kafadar does not directly address the question of the readership/audience of the *yevmiye*, Suraiya Faroqhi picks up this point in a section entitled "Writing for a Restricted Circle: The First Person Narrative." Here Faroqhi suggests that all first-person narratives were authored for a restricted circle of people known to the author. Faroqhi's evidence is rather limited—she argues entirely on the basis of the fact that first-person narratives were generally not copied[97]—but there are other indications that her instincts are probably correct. Very astutely, Naila Kaidbey has noticed that the title Shams al-Dīn Ibn Ṭūlūn chose for his contemporary chronicle differs markedly from the titles of other historical works:

> *Mufākahat al-khillān fī ḥawādith al-zamān*: the word *mufākaha* suggests conversation of an anecdotal nature, not frivolous yet not as serious as *muḥādatha*. *Khillān* denotes companions and friends, not the general public or those in a position of authority. The audience and the paradigm of the text can, therefore, be discerned from the title. Although titles can be misleading, when compared

> with . . . the titles of Ibn Ṭūlūn's other works, *I`lām al-warā bi-man waliya min al-atrāk bi Dimashq al-kubrā* . . . one cannot help but speculate on Ibn Ṭūlūn's purpose in such a composition. Furthermore, the word *mufākaha* does not appear in other works of Damascus historians, contemporary or otherwise . . . was Ibn Ṭūlūn actually restricting his audience to the *`ulamā'* informing them about the injustice of their times?[98]

Certainly the title of Ibn Ṭūlūn's contemporary chronicle, "Bantering with Friends about the Events of the Time," has a quite different resonance from the title of Ibn Ṭūlūn's other historical work cited above, "Informing Mankind about the Turkish Governors of Great Damascus" (*I`lām al-warā bi-man waliya min al-atrāk bi Dimashq al-kubrā*). "Friends," to say the least, implies a much more restricted audience than "mankind," and "bantering" is a much less formal act than "informing." Though it is unclear who Ibn Ṭūlūn's friends were, his *`ulamā'* colleagues, as Kaidbey suggests, may indeed have been the restricted audience to whom his contemporary chronicle was directed.[99] It is noteworthy that Ibn Ṭūlūn's teacher, the famous `Abd al-Qādir al-Nu`aymī, wrote a contemporary chronicle entitled *Tadhkirat al-ikhwān fī ḥawādith al-zamān* ("Memento to the Brothers about the Events of the Time"), now apparently lost.[100] Its title, "Memento to the Brothers about the Events of the Time," is similar in its implied audience to Ibn Ṭūlūn's "Bantering with Friends." Al-Nu`aymī's contemporary chronicle is addressed to "the brothers"—by definition a close and restricted community. In terms of their close and closed audience, the contemporary chronicles of al-Nu`aymī and Ibn Ṭūlūn remind us, retrospectively, of the *ta'rīkh*-diary of Ibn al-Bannā' and, prospectively, of Ibn Kannān's *al-Ḥawādith al-yawmiyya*, which, as we have already noted, Ibn Kannān read out to a select audience of his *`ulamā'* friends, even as he was writing it.[101] The bilingual wordplay of the title of Seyyid Ḥasan's *Ṣoḥbetnāme*, "The Book of Conversation/Companionship," not only effectively translates Ibn Ṭūlūn's *Mufākahat al-khillān*, "Bantering with Friends," but also encapsulates the relationship among the author, the chronicle, and the audience.

Finally, I should note that Kafadar attributes the rise of the Ottoman first-person narrative to an "all-pervasive perception of rapid social change and dislocation"[102] in the post-Sulaymanic age with its "acute decline-consciousness, its sense of eroding stability, loss of control," which in turn led to "the inward turn or the concern with the self."[103] This anxiety expressed in text is also a characteristic of early modern social change.[104] The argument about changing times is, of course, the same argument about the "uncommonness of the time" that has been forwarded by Rosenthal and Khalidi to explain the rise of contemporary chronicling and autobiography in the period of the Mongol and Crusader invasions.[105] For the many authors who were practicing Sufis in the Ottoman Empire, this crisis loomed largest in the intellectual and physical onslaught of the seventeenth-century Kadızadeli movement against what they saw as heretical Sufi practices.[106] Ibn Budayr recorded Kadızadeli desecrations of Sufi shrines in his chronicle,[107] and though a scholar of the standing of `Abd al-Ghanī al-Nābulusī engaged the Kadızadelis in polemics,[108] the attack on Sufism may have led others, like Seyyid Ḥasan, to engage in "an even stronger search for solidarity in small and familiar circles"[109]—such as with the audience of the *Ṣoḥbetnāme*.

Ottoman Egypt: Popularization of History

Thus far, we have traced the genealogy of the Levantine contemporary chronicle up to the seventeenth century with a view to understanding the emergence of certain of its defining characteristics: to this point, primarily the qualities of author-centricity and the overriding concern with the here and now. However, two further and crucial defining characteristic of the eighteenth-century Levantine contemporary chronicle are the fact of the chronicle's appropriation by a barber, soldiers, farmers, a scribe, a clerk, and a priest; and the fact of the use of colloquial Arabic in the historical narrative. We have seen prospective possibilities in the Mamluk period in such texts as the diary of Ibn Ṭawq, and the chronicles of Ibn Ṣaṣra and al-Dawādārī. However, most of the chronicles considered thus far in the genealogy have been of the learned classes, *`ulamā'* of some description. However, in the eighteenth-century Levant contemporary chronicles were written by authors who were not *`ulamā'*. In other words, the eighteenth-century Levantine contemporary chronicle represents the popularization of history—by which I mean the participation in history of social groups that were hitherto excluded from it. This participation takes place both at the level of consumption of history by a popular audience and the production of history by non-*`ālim* historians, and it manifests itself not only in the changing identities of the authors but also in the changing content of history, which begins to include themes and registers untypical of traditional historiography. For immediate antecedents of the phenomenon of the popularization of history in the Ottoman Levant, we must turn back to Ottoman Egypt.

The "anti-history" of Ibn al-Dawādārī, with "its lack of literary ostentation, its spontaneity, its often comic, narrative tone, its relish for prodigies, dreams, omens, and 'marvelous coincidences,' and its . . . colloquial language," became a standard form of history in Ottoman Egypt. In discussing the changed form and content of the chronicles of Ibn al-Dawādārī, and the *awlād al-nās `ulamā'* Ibn Iyās and Ibn al-Taghribirdī, I have suggested the possibility of these chronicles being addressed to a new audience of consumers of history of a different cultural and educational background from the original *`ulamā'* audience, namely, members of *mamlūk* households. Similarly, Nelly Hanna has argued in regard to the chronicles of Ottoman Egypt that their language, style, and content "made them more easily accessible to a wider audience. . . . Many of the people who were involved in reading or listening to historical writing appreciated histories with a certain amount of entertainment."[110] She supports this argument for the popularization of history in Ottoman Egypt with two types of direct evidence unavailable for Mamluk Egypt. One indication of popularization is the number of history books that probate records have shown to have been owned by non-*`ulamā'* in early eighteenth-century Cairo. A second is the testimony of travelers in Egypt as to popular interest in history, including its public performance. In this context, Hanna cites the chronicle of the *`ālim* Muḥammad b. `Abd al-Mu`ṭī al-Isḥāqī al-Munūfī (d. 1650), who studied with notable scholars in both his hometown and Cairo. His *Laṭā'if akhbār al-uwal fī-man taṣarrafa fī Miṣr min arbāb al-duwal* ("The Pleasant Events of the Ancestors about those who Ruled Egypt") is a history of Egypt, from the Islamic conquest up to the year 1623, that combines historical narrative with amusing anecdotes some of which included "sexual details and obscenities." Hanna argues that al-Isḥāqī's chronicle was written to entertain—that is, to be popular. And popular al-Isḥāqī's history was, as is reflected by the numerous copies made of it.[111]

Even though al-Isḥāqī's was a history of events that took place before the author's lifetime, contemporary chronicles were also authored in Ottoman Egypt, including some composed in verse or rhymed prose, which were the preferred registers for oral recitation of dramatic narrative.[112] The Sufi-influenced *yawmiyyāt* genre, however, seems not to have caught on in Egypt, where the writing of history was dominated by what P. M. Holt has termed the "sultan-pasha chronicle,"[113] which Jane Hathaway effectively reconfigured as the "pasha chronicle."[114] The framework of the Egyptian "pasha chronicle" is provided by the tenures of the respective governors of the province:

> Each vice-royalty functions as a sort of limited *tarjama* [biography], opening with the dates of the governor's accession and deposition, and often closing with their *ma`āthir* [literally "feats"]: the monuments he left behind in Egypt. In some cases, the chronicler will briefly limn the pasha's physical characteristics.[115]

This is very similar to the chronicle of one of our soldiers, al-`Abd, where the framework is provided by the tenures of the governors of Damascus. The similarity with al-`Abd's chronicle is rendered all the more striking by the fact that Ottoman Egypt witnessed an important development in the popularization of the production of history. This was the appearance of contemporary chronicles authored not by *`ūlamā'* or bureaucrats but by soldiers. These chronicles are all written in colloquial—the increasing literary importance of colloquial in Egypt in this period is attested by the wave of colloquial glossaries produced at this time[116]—and contain eyewitness accounts. The pioneer of what Muḥammad Anīs has called *madrasat al-ajnād* (the soldiers' school) was Ibn Zunbul al-Rammāl (fl. 1552), who wrote a popular work on the Ottoman conquest entitled *Tārīkh akhdh Miṣr min al-jarākisa* ("The History of the Delivery of Egypt from the Circassians").[117] It was in the eighteenth century, however, that at least five such chronicles were composed by members of the `Azabān regiment; these are known collectively as the "Damurdāshī chronicles."[118] The contents do not differ meaningfully from the "pasha chronicles" Jane Hathaway characterized as containing political events, natural phenomena, obituary notices (*tarājim*), curious incidents (*'ajā'ib*), stories (*ḥikāyāt*), and personal observations.[119] However, a sense of the potential audience of these chronicles is obtained from this observation of 'Abd al-Wahhab Bakr: "All contain the type of anecdotes that appear to be coffeehouse entertainments to enhance the reputation of a few of the heroic characters of the chronicle."[120] In other words, the language, narrative tone, and content of these chronicles are resonant of the popular epics that were the staple fare of public entertainment at the time. Whereas the *'ālim*-chronicle of al-Isḥāqī represents the popularization of history at the level of consumption, the soldier-chronicles of seventeenth- and eighteenth-century Egypt represent the popularization of both the consumption and the production of the contemporary chronicle.[121]

In Ottoman Egypt, then, the contemporary chronicle emerges into the popular domain and becomes a cultural object consumed not only by the learned elite but instead by the general public. Clearly, the contemporary chronicle had come a long way from its origins as the *ta'rīkh*-diary, composed by an *'ālim* in classical Arabic for a close and closed audience; or as a "tail-end" *dhayl* history, deriving its legitimacy from its association with an earlier authoritative scholarly enterprise. Indeed, it is noteworthy that very few *dhayl*s were written anywhere after the sixteenth century—but there was no shortage of contemporary chronicles.[122] The contemporary chronicler spoke on his own authority, as an eyewitness, dramatizing events in his own colloquial voice. No longer was the consumption of the contemporary chronicle confined to the scholar in his study, or even to the nonscholarly but nonetheless limited milieu of the *mamlūk* household, or—as with the Turkish and Levantine *yawmiyyāt*—to the intimate circle of Sufi friends; rather, it had become a part of popular colloquial culture, drunk down by the common man in the public coffee shop alongside his pipe and his cup.

THE EIGHTEENTH-CENTURY LEVANT: THE ARRIVAL OF THE NOUVEAU LITERATES

It was in his autobiography that Ibn Ṭūlūn wrote, "It is not fitting that anyone who possesses even a small amount of knowledge should allow himself to be forgotten."[123] In the eighteenth-century Levant, Ibn Ṭūlūn's call was answered by an unprecedented array of individuals some of whom, by the standards of the *`ulamā'*, certainly possessed no more than a limited amount of knowledge but who did not allow themselves to be forgotten.

By the time the contemporary chronicle reached the eighteenth-century Levant, it had undergone a metamorphosis that rendered it singularly amenable for appropriation by the non-*`ulamā'*. Only two qualifications were now required for someone to compose a contemporary chronicle. The first of these, of course, was literacy. Although there has been no definitive study on literacy in the eighteenth-century Levant, research on probate inventories of early eighteenth-century Damascus has given some indication of literacy levels in the city. Ownership of books was not limited either to the *`ulamā'* or to the wealthy but included a limited group of merchants, tailors, tanners, druggists, confectioners, and barbers.[124] The literacy of some people who were not trained in the learned professions is not new in the Islamic urban context. A limited group of nonlearned literates, whom I have dubbed learned illiterates, had for a long time constituted a part of the population in cities such as Cairo and Damascus.

The second qualification to be a contemporary chronicler was the simple fact of being an eyewitness to the events in one's immediate milieu. No research or scholarship of past authorities was necessary; nor did the author have to link his work to that of a learned predecessor—the author of the contemporary chronicle wrote on the authority of his own *I*. Neither did the author's literacy have to extend to a command of classical Arabic; the contemporary chronicle freed itself of the obligations of "correct Arabic" and could acceptably be written in whatever degree of colloquial the author chose. The established content of the genre had long since gone well beyond just the latest news of ruler and scholar and come to include reports of injustices against the populace, marvels and wonders, sexual anecdotes and obscenities, afternoon naps and delicious meals. The focus on the individual that arose out of the common Sufi experience rendered the place of the author in the quotidian here and now as valid a subject for contemplation and interpretation as great battles and the rise and fall of dynasties. In other words, the contemporary chronicle was now a malleable enough genre for any individual who wanted to become a historian to join the chronicling project.

The chronicle had become open enough for any nonlearned literate to produce a book of history, and thus become a nouveau literate. If it was the social circumstances that impelled and gave confidence to socially mobile individuals to write, it was the chronicle's literary form as it emerged in the eighteenth century that made it easy for the nouveau literates to write in the particular genre. The social conditions allowed non-*`ulamā'* literates a certain degree of authority, yet the diminished level of authority required by the genre lent itself to being poached by the same people. To put it in "market" terms, the increased supply of authority in society seems to have met the decreased demand for authority in the genre itself.

Each chronicle examined in this book relates in a specific way to various elements in the genealogy that we have traced for the contemporary chronicle. The chronicles of the two soldiers Ḥasan Āghā al-`Abd and Ḥasan Ibn al-Ṣiddīq fit directly into the subtradition of military chronicles that go back, in terms of consumption, to the fourteenth-century chronicle of Ibn al-Dawādārī, and in terms of production to the sixteenth-century and Ibn Zunbul al-Rammāl, continuing through the Damurdāshī chronicles of Egypt. Al-`Abd's temporal framework is, like that of the "pasha-chronicles" of Egypt, the reigns of the governors of Damascus. Like that of his Egyptian counterparts, al-`Abd's language is openly colloquial. In contradistinction to the Egyptian school, however, al-`Abd offers very little in the way of marvelous and curious incidents; he is overwhelmingly interested in political and military events. His retrospective survey of the events surrounding his life through time renders his chronicle a history of the location of the authorial *I* vis-à-vis the world. In contrast, Ibn al-Ṣiddīq's *I* is almost absent, but his dramatic and entertaining style indicates a popular audience. Though his chronicle is not framed in terms of reigns of governors, the author's insistent focus on military and political matters including the tribulations and victories of the Damascene governor renders his text close to his Egyptian counterparts.

The contemporary chronicle of the two Rukaynīs is the first and only work in the history of Arabic-Islamic historiography known to have been written by farmers. It is, of course, significant that these were farmers from a rural region historically known for its colleges and for a tradition of learning.[125] It is also the first contemporary chronicle that is known to have emerged from the Shīʿī tradition of Jabal ʿĀmil, although an *ʿulamā'* autobiographical tradition already existed there. It also appears that, before the al-Rukaynīs, the ʿĀmilīs had shown no interest in historical genres other than the biographical.[126] The Rukaynīs' chronicle thus represents a double expansion in the generic scope of the contemporary chronicle: into a new social group (rural agriculturalists) and into a new regional and confessional community (the Shīʿīs of Jabal ʿĀmil). These novel spheres are reflected in the content of the Rukaynīs' chronicle; for example, the agriculturalists' overriding concern with crops and weather,[127] on the one hand, and the ʿĀmilī Shīʿī's iteration of a strong sense of regional and communal identity on the other. With the Rukaynīs, the contemporary chronicle becomes a communal testament. And though the Shīʿīs of Jabal ʿĀmil would, in the nineteenth and early twentieth centuries, eventually produce an entire corpus of historical writings expressive of their sense of communal identity, none of these later histories would be written by farmers.[128]

Mīkhā'īl Burayk was wrong when he said that there were no histories of Damascus prior to his[129]—but, of course, this is not what he meant. Burayk spoke often as a Greek Orthodox priest, and he was quite right in asserting that no Damascene Christian had written a contemporary chronicle before him. Until this point, Christian historians had been concerned with the history of the church and churchmen. By his appropriation of a historical genre that had hitherto been the exclusive property of the majority, Burayk posited the history of his community in imperial, as opposed to ecclesiastical space—in other words, in the same space as where the history of the Muslim community was lived and made. He also placed himself in the position of eyewitness and judge of all he surveyed, a vantage point apparently thus far reserved in Arabic historiography for Muslims. His chronicle is precisely about the struggle of his community to live beyond ecclesiastically defined space. His historiographical intervention thus simultaneously constitutes a radical expansion of the discourse of the contemporary chronicle, and of Levantine Christian discourse. Burayk's *The History of Damascus* announced the beginning of a series of contemporary chronicles reflecting a particularly Christian and sectarian communal awareness.

Al-Danafī's chronicle is, on the one hand, an example of a well-established subgenre of contemporary chronicling, the recording by a scribe of the events related to the common lifetime of the scribe and his master. This genre, as we have seen, goes back to at least the time of the scribes of Saladin, who clearly recognized that they lived in an exceptional time and in the service of an exceptional master who fought to preserve the autonomy of his followers in the face of foreign attack. On an altogether different scale, this was also the case with al-Danafī and his master, Muṣṭafā Beg Tūqān, who was seen by the chronicler as the hero fighting to maintain Nābulsī (semi-)autonomy against the Ottoman Empire and the attacks of al-Ẓāhir al-`Umar. What is striking about al-Danafī's chronicle is that, in form and content, it in no way associates itself with the most famous work of Arabic historiography in the Samaritan scholarly tradition, the *Kitāb al-tārīkh* of Abū al-Fatḥ—a universal history of the Samaritans from Creation till the advent of Islam, with which a scholar of al-Danafī's standing must undoubtedly have been familiar. Indeed, so complete is al-Danafī's assumption of the genre that were it not for the one instance where al-Danafī refers to the Passover we would not be able to tell that the author of al-Danafī's chronicle was, unlike the scribes of Saladin, not a Muslim, although this is in part because a "patron chronicle" such as al-Danafī's does not allow the same degree of insertion of the authorial *I* as, for instance, a *yawmiyyāt* work. Al-Danafī's is the first and the last chronicle of its kind in Samaritan historiography, in Arabic or otherwise.

Let us now turn to the only work in our sample that is not a history: the diary of al-Makkī. In arrangement, Al-Makkī's text follows the *yawmiyyāt*; indeed, it is the most "*yawmī*" (daily) of the texts under study. Like the text of the early-sixteenth-century chronicler Ibn Ṭawq before him, al-Makkī's journal does not seem to be directed at any audience at all, but to have been exclusively for the author's own consumption. In its specific configuration, this text is unique in our sample: it is almost indiscriminate in its selection of events to record, and almost devoid of narrative. Indeed, it has a nearly documentary quality—which is, perhaps, instructive in light of al-Makkī's apparent connection to the law court.

Whereas the barber Ibn Budayr, as we shall see, gave the *yawmiyyāt* the warm atmosphere of the oral popular tale, the court clerk al-Makkī imbued it with a cold and succinct archival tone. In al-Makkī's archive-journal, the role of the court is taken by the chronicler himself; al-Makkī records and sometimes passes summary judgment on the events in Ḥimṣ that come before the jurisdiction of the author's bench. Al-Makkī is the sole authority for the history in his diary; indeed, he is the entire court of history—witness, judge, and public gallery.

With the arrival of these varied nouveau literates into the space of historiography, is it then a mere coincidence that Ibn Kannān was the very last Levantine *`ālim* known to have authored a chronicle? Whether a coincidence or not, Muslim "clerics" effectively left the stage of contemporary chronicling, but they seem to have left the door ajar for Christian clerics and laymen to enter. One of those who knocked on the door was Ibn Budayr, the barber of Damascus. His chronicle also displayed a focus on the self in the quotidian here and now. Ibn Budayr's history is the most eloquent expression that we have of the popularization of the contemporary chronicle in the Arabic-Islamic tradition. Let us now return to the barber's chronicle, and to his context, the barbershop.

CHAPTER 5

A Room of His Own

The "History" of the Barber of Damascus

> Get up, examine the events of the age, and contemplate!
> And act according to your reason—in order that you *remember* them![1]
>
> —IBN BUDAYR

The act of authorship by the barber Ibn Budayr is something apparently unprecedented for a member of his profession.[2] The striking aspect of Ibn Budayr's decision is not, of course, the fact of the barber's will to memory, but rather his choice of the form of this memory: namely, a chronicle, or *tārīkh*, the scholarly form conceived and mostly perpetuated by the learned elite. In examining the barber's book, the immediate questions that come to mind are: Why does Ibn Budayr appropriate this scholarly genre to preserve his memory? How does he effect this appropriation? Is the barber's historiographical act merely mimetic of the scholarly form? Or does he draw on available nonscholarly memorial and narrative genres? In short, what does the barber do to the contemporary chronicle, and what does the contemporary chronicle do for him?

In attempting to answer these questions, I aim to show how this hair cutter, beard shaver, and circumciser trimmed and coiffed the elite literary form of the contemporary chronicle for his own ends. This chapter explores various aspects of the barber's history: his manipulation of the standard content of the contemporary chronicle; his specific use of literary registers, that is, rhymed prose, and/or poetry; and his use of language, meaning his negotiation between the so-called classical Arabic and Levantine vernacular. The treatment of the literary and linguistic aspects of the text allows us to make some conjectures about the barber's intended or implied audience.

The overarching goal here is to demonstrate how Ibn Budayr injects the elite chronicle form with elements of the popular oral epic so as to render the chronicle familiar to a new audience. This injection revalues the ethics/politics inscribed in the form of the chronicle and turns it from an order-establishing genre to one of contestation and dissent—even if his dissent is not of a radical sort. At the same time, the barber enables himself to become a protagonist, or an actor, in the reality of his here and now.

In order to appreciate the barber's manipulation of form in the chronicle, it will be necessary to briefly visit the contemporary Arabic literary landscape to consider other forms that were available to Ibn Budayr, but that he opted *not* to use. By comparing and juxtaposing the different genres and the politics therein, I hope to show that the intention behind Ibn Budayr's authorship is very grave indeed. For the barber, "remembrance" and "contemplation," which he saw as the components of history, are not a laughing matter. His somberness, it will be seen, is to a certain extent an indicator of his ethical stance and politics.

Finally, I move from the literary analysis of Ibn Budayr's book to its material aspects. Given that the text of the chronicle survives in a unique manuscript entitled *Ḥawādith Dimashq* or *The Events of Damascus*, I attempt to examine the manuscript for clues about the reception of the barber's history and its possible users, readers, and owners.

THE TEXTS

We recall that the text of the chronicle used in the study is not the version edited by Muḥammad Sa`īd al-Qāsimī in the late nineteenth century but is based on the unbowdlerized unique manuscript. It should be mentioned again that, like the edited text, the manuscript used here is also missing the opening and the end and covers exactly the same years: 1154–1175 AH (1741–1762 CE).

Since one of the purposes of this chapter is to identify and interpret Ibn Budayr's literary deviations from the scholarly form, it is instructive to introduce a scholarly chronicle against which the barber's history may be assayed. An appropriate point of comparison is the chronicle of his near contemporary Ibn Kannān, who represents an almost archetypical *`ālim*. His chronicle is entitled *al-Ḥawādith al-yawmiyya li-tārikh aḥad `ashar wa alf wa miyya* ("The Daily Events from 1111 [AH]") and covers the years 1699–1740. Unlike Ibn Budayr, whose chronicle seems to have represented his sole authorial act, Ibn Kannān was a prolific author who was thoroughly versed and proficient in the norms and culture of *`ulamā'* authorship.

IN THE BARBERSHOP

We have seen how the location of the barber in the city—in the heart of walled Damascus—was of the utmost significance. Ibn Budayr's location *in* the barbershop is just as significant. A haircut and good shave were not a prerogative exclusive to scholars, but that of perhaps the whole urban male population. Ibn Budayr's shop was an open and accessible place where even the poor found room,[3] and where males of diverse social backgrounds met and exchanged news, views, and gossip (often about politics).[4] Indeed, on various levels, the barbershop had a close association with the coffee shop and oftentimes even functioned like one. In Damascus, some barbershops were physically located next to coffeehouses[5]; in Istanbul, barbershops served as alternative places to coffee shops when the authorities closed the latter for what they saw as seditious activities.[6] The association between the two institutions was such that sometimes both barbershops and coffeehouses would be summarily commanded in the same breath to shut down.[7]

As a place primarily meant for socializing and entertainment, the coffeehouse was a stage where epic stories were narrated, music and dance performed, and shadow plays enacted.[8] And though, as we have seen, the urban elite and high religious functionaries remained contemptuous of it, the coffeehouse was nevertheless sometimes employed as a mise en scène for high literary culture: like the institution of the tavern before it, the coffee shop was often the locus of amorous encounters in Arabic love poetry.[9]

Though it is hard to verify whether the same kinds of performances took place in the barbershop as in its sister institution, one can state with confidence that the barbershop was a location where similarly various cultural discourses intersected, and where the custodians of textual scholarly literary forms sat—with beards freshly trimmed—next to the practitioners of oral popular forms. It is precisely at this juncture, at this social and discursive crossroads, that Ibn Budayr's chronicle was apparently conceived.

TĀRĪKH VS. *SĪRA*

Coincidentally albeit appropriately, the root for one of the Arabic terms for narration/story comes from the barber's very repertoire of activities: *qaṣṣa* means to "cut/clip/trim" but also refers to telling a story or narrating. Before exploring the history of the barber, let us compare the two narrative and memorial forms from which Ibn Budayr clipped his tale and which intersected in his barbershop: the chronicle (the *tārīkh*) and the Arabic epic (generally called *sīra*).[10]

Let us start with the genre that the barber's book most manifestly is: a chronicle or *tārīkh*. The chronicle is a narration of "real" events arranged around the passage of time. Given that it is a narrative of the real, the story is without a plot (at least apparently). Thus the narrative does not resolve but simply terminates.[11] Dating is the chronicle's defining feature. Given that the time referent—the Hijrī year—marks the birth of the Islamic polity and measures its progress, the chronicle's primary intention is the establishment and perpetuation of the Islamic political order.[12] It is an order for which the *`ulamā'* had many reasons to be grateful, not least for the fact that it allowed and supported their identity as the religious guides and moral guardians of the community.[13] Subsequently, the content of the chronicle is typically about the state, its practitioners, and their concerns.

Given the identity of its authors as *`ulamā'*, the chronicle has a natural relation to religious knowledge, more specifically to the science of Hadith, with its chains of authority and method of transmission.[14] This link is important inasmuch as some of the genres we will encounter later in this chapter constitute contrarian responses to it.

The appropriate language for the chronicle is textual or classical Arabic (*fuṣḥā*, or more accurately, *fuṣḥā*-ish) though colloquial dialects have always managed to leak into the text, especially during the Mamluk period. The use of colloquial in these scholarly forms, however, was not without contestation and admonition. As for the circumstances of its publication and dissemination, the chronicle was usually read aloud, most probably to a restricted audience, typically a group of scholars.

Another aspect of the chronicle that is worth reemphasizing is the author-centric nature of the text in the seventeenth and eighteenth centuries. The contemporary history text had come to reflect a greater measure of self-consciousness and is often pervaded by the authorial *I*. This is not a modern *I*; nor is it intentionally autobiographical, but indicative of a keen subjective awareness that events occurred around the self.

The term *sīra* (plural, *siyar*) usually means "biography" and comes from the verb *sāra*, to traverse or to journey. For most readers, the expression *sīra* immediately evokes the biography (or more accurately, hagiography) of the Prophet Muḥammad.[15] In this study, however, the focus is on the popular biographies of other heroes, most famously al-Ẓāhir Baybars, the Mamluk sultan known for his military feats against the Crusaders and Mongols; Sayf Ibn Dhī Yazan, the pre-Islamic Himyarite king who put an end to Abyssinian rule in Yemen; Abu Zayd al-Hilālī, the clever hero of the Banū Hilāl tribe; and ʿAntar Ibn Shaddād, the pre-Islamic poet.[16] The popular *sīra* is a highly fictionalized account of the life of such historically true, usually male, personalities. As expected of the epic genre in general, the *sīra* offers a narrative whereby the protagonist is able to overcome exceptionally challenging circumstances and emerge as a hero. Similarly, the early biographies of the Prophet, dubbed *sīra-maghāzi* ("biography-military expeditions"),[17] represent "the moral-historical epic of the life of the Prophet in his *heroic* struggle to found the Divinely-guided human Community."[18] In other words, the early Muslim community understood the Prophet to be, among other things, a hero. Unlike the popular epic, however, the representations of the figure of the Prophet quickly stabilized—at least, relatively—into the textual-historical corpus of Islamic knowledge, acquiring canonical status.[19] In the popular epic, the protagonist's formulaic set of roles distance him greatly from the actual historical figure whose biography the epic purports to narrate. Regardless, what concerns us here is not so much the authentic historicity of the figure/hero as the simple fact of his remembrance.[20] In other words, what is important here is that the epic, like the chronicle but in contrast to other narrative forms, is consciously memorial.

The Arabic epic is authorless and lodged in the collective memory. Given its oral nature, the content is fluid and often accretive.[21] It is publicly recited or sung from memory by a storyteller in verse, or prose. Its language has been described as a "classicalized colloquial": that is, a "colloquial language . . . which includes many words and phrases usually associated with the classical language."[22] This is a purely performative genre, one that is sung and narrated on the streets and in coffeehouses—and possibly in barbershops.

THE BARBER'S HISTORY

Ibn Budayr authored a text, that, like any regular scholar's chronicle, contains a narrative of "real" events arranged annalistically. The barber uses a host of literary devices, associated not only with the chronicle but also with other historiographical genres, such as the recurrent insertion of the scribal voice, as with *qāla al-mu'allif* ("the author said"),[23] *qāla al-rāwī* ("the narrator said"),[24] or the self-effacing interlocutive voice in which the author asks his audience to be lenient in judging his work as he is but a "weak slave" of God[25]; or the inclusion of *tarjama*s, which, as we have seen, proved of great social utility to the barber. Indeed, Ibn Budayr's chronicle has the standard literary equipment expected of the scholarly form and was explicitly declared by the author himself to be a *tārīkh* (a history).[26] However, behind the façade of *tārīkh* our barber has an epic *sīra* to tell.

Although the barber's text is organizationally and structurally a chronicle, remarkably—given the apparently irreconcilable formal difference between the two genres—the oral popular epic is to be found lurking in the background of his chronicle. It is precisely in the divergences of Ibn Budayr's text from the familiar genre of the *`ulamā'*-authored chronicle that we find the tensions between the popular and the scholarly, the oral and the textual, the "fictive" and the "real." A comparison of Ibn Budayr's chronicle with that of the eighteenth-century Damascene *`ālim* Ibn Kannān not only reveals the tensions present in Ibn Budayr's text but also better demonstrates the nature and effect of the barber's appropriation of the scholarly form.

The Content: "Everything Has Turned Upside Down"

In our examination of the content of the barber's chronicle, we begin at the beginning—that is, at the point where the chronicle opens. It will be instructive to first consider the opening of the barber's chronicle in its published version, which is, the reader remembers, the text that was "refined" by the *`ālim* al-Qāsimī. This version of the text begins with the following paragraph:

In the year 1154 [1741 CE], the governor of Damascus was `Alī Pasha of the Turks. This was eleven years after the investiture of our master, Ṣulṭān Maḥmūd Khān the son of Ṣulṭān Muṣṭafā Khān, may God support the throne of the state till the end of time.[27]

This is a standard way for a scholar to begin a chronicle—by announcing the order of the world and by calling on God to sustain that order. As holders of official positions in the judicial, academic, or administrative institutions of empire, the *`ulamā'* were beneficiaries of the state and thus acknowledged their benefactor by invoking the imperial order from the outset. Further, *`ulamā'* chroniclers made the imperial order one of the organizing principles of their text. Ibn Kannān, the *`ālim* and near contemporary of Ibn Budayr, begins not only the first but every year of his annalistic chronicle with a variation of the same formula reiterating the underpinning fact of imperial order.[28]

But this is not how Ibn Budayr's "unrefined" version begins. The original opening of the chronicle is quite different from the opening passage in al-Qāsimī's recension. Apparently devoid of feelings of obligation to empire, Ibn Budayr begins his chronicle abruptly, urgently, and anxiously:

The first day of 1154 [1741 CE] was a Saturday. The common people [*a`wām*] were saying that a great earthquake will take place in Damascus as a result of which many places will be destroyed and men will turn into women.[29]

The barber's chronicle thus begins by speaking in the voice of the "common people" raised aloud in an apocalyptic prophecy about imminent devastation in Damascus. The ensuing *disorder* will be so great that men will be turned into women. Ibn Budayr's chronicle is not about a world ordered securely from top down, but about disaster, violence, poverty, and disorder—indeed, about an inversion of the natural order.

This is not to say that the representatives of the imperial order who constitute a main (if not *the* main) subject of *`ulamā'*-history do not appear in Ibn Budayr's text; they most certainly do. However, *al-akābir* (literally, the "big people"), *al-a`yān* (the notables), and the *bāshā* (Pasha, the governor) enter the barber's text not to be commemorated and for their feats to be celebrated, but rather to be interrogated. Ibn Budayr explicitly speaks in the name of the *aṣāghir* (literally the "small people"), *al-`awāmm/ a`wām* (the commoners), or simply *al-nās* (the people).[30] It is in their name that he holds high officials accountable for a general state of disorder. He constantly demonstrates the officials' negligence and corruption in failing to fulfill their responsibility to regulate public space. For example,

> The unruly soldiers of Damascus have committed excesses, cursing of religion has increased, the commoners have been oppressed and no one listens to what they say, and the ruler of Damascus, his Excellency As`ad Pasha, . . . has not confronted any of these matters. Public order has dissipated. . . . He does not move a thing, but sleeps with the sleeping.[31]

Unruly soldiers, the cursing of religion, and the oppression of the commoners are all faces of the same phenomenon of disorder, which is unhesitatingly attributed to the indifference of the rulers. The manifestations of this disorder, according to Ibn Budayr, are a matter not only of unregulated streets but also of unregulated prices in the market place, and unregulated public morality. For example:

> High prices have attached themselves to Damascus . . . [a list of prices follows] . . . the people are sick and dumbstruck, women have become loose and men have melted, and all limits have collapsed. The notables are distracted . . . and each of them is busy with himself.[32]

Ibn Budayr's association of soaring market prices with public immorality ("looseness of women") and with emasculation ("melting of men") reflects the anxieties of the barber, as a self-appointed representative of the "small people," about the threat of his own further diminution and marginalization. The unregulated prices would drive him and other commoners into poverty (or further poverty), and the transgression of women translates into the narrowing of the space of one of the few privileges that his social position accords him, namely his patriarchal authority. Hence his constant reference to emasculation, whether through the images of "melting men," of "men turning to women," or what he calls "sullied manhood,"[33] serves to remind Ibn Budayr and his male barbershop audience that the state is squarely responsible not only for economic and material deprivation but also for social disempowerment. By comparison, it is instructive to note that such "riff-raff" as commoners, loose women, and melting men do not even enter the text of the *`ālim* Ibn Kannān. In the *`ālim*'s imperially ordered and refined world, such social trespassers do not threaten a scholar sure of his status; hence, they simply pass either unnoticed or unnoted.

The grim theme of death pervades both Ibn Budayr's and Ibn Kannān's texts. The chroniclers record deaths in the classical scholarly form of *tarjama*. The barber's use of the obituary notice closely resembles the scholarly model in terms of both the form and its customary subjects (biographies of scholars, saints, and male family members). However, I have also shown how the barber uses the *tarjama* very differently by elegizing the most unexpected individuals, such as the local *ḥakawī*, the popular epic storyteller. Given its relevance to the topic of our discussion here, the obituary is worth quoting again:

> Our father, our teacher, our instructor, Sulaymān b. Ḥashish al-Ḥakawi died—may God have mercy upon him! He augmented his time, and was singular in the arts of his age. He related the epics of al-Ẓahir, Sayf, and Samar and `Antar in Arabic and Turkish. He had a prodigious memory and sound knowledge of every art, for all that he was illiterate and could not read and write: this is the highest degree of eloquence amongst mankind. . . . Indeed, he was a bottomless ocean: may God have mercy upon him![34]

One suspects that this egalitarian attitude of what constitutes learning would not have been shared by Ibn Kannān, whose chronicle, of course, has no place for a *ḥakawī*. The fact of the commemoration of the illiterate popular-epic storyteller in the scholarly form of the *tarjama* is an eloquent reflection of the barber's appropriation and domestication of the scholarly form. By acknowledging the cultural contribution of Ibn al-Ḥashīsh, Ibn Budayr not only subverts the concept of knowledge but also allows textual space for a person who, historically speaking, fell outside the margins of the written word.

Another subject that recurs in Ibn Budayr's chronicle is food prices. He regularly provides lists, each of which is invariably followed by a complaint and an urgent plea.[35] This is not the case in the text of the *`ālim* Ibn Kannān, who mentions food prices very infrequently—about five times—in a chronicle that covers the span of 41 years.[36] Although accounts of street violence occur in both texts,[37] Ibn Kannān's chronicle is not the story of poverty, destruction, and disorder that is recorded in Ibn Budayr's text. Quite the contrary, the *`ālim's* text is characterized by a cyclical and stable rhythm of events regular and routine. Ibn Kannān unfailingly notes events that happen regularly, such as the beginning and end of the teaching cycles of the more famous Damascene teachers, the change of seasons, and the annual arrival and departure of the respective caravans of the Hajj and of the imperial treasury.[38] He also records events, which he routinely attended, such as literary salons and Sufi soirées. Among these regular events are what one may call "happy occasions," such as picnics, weddings, and circumcision parties, all of which sprinkle Ibn Kannān's text. Is there, then, anything regular, routine, or happy in Ibn Budayr's reports?

Though Ibn Budayr cannot have been unaware of the cycles ordering natural and civic life in Damascus—the changing seasons and the passages of the Hajj and treasury caravans—he does not stabilize his narrative around their rhythm. Indeed, even these regular events are mentioned by Ibn Budayr only when something unusual happens—such as a particularly successful or disastrous Hajj.[39] The barber's narrative, in other words, is inherently unstable. As for happy events, Ibn Budayr must have attended some such ceremonials—at the very least some circumcision parties in his capacity as a barber—but he actually reports only one wedding and one circumcision party, and even these were distinctly unhappy occasions.

The wedding reported by Ibn Budayr was given by the ill-fated treasurer and Ottoman official Fatḥī al-Falāqinsī for his daughter. Ibn Budayr, who probably did not attend the party, described the events of the seven-day wedding at disapproving length, concluding with the remarks

> On the last day of the wedding, they went too far (***badda`ū***). In doing so, their intention was to promote bad behavior (*qillat al-adab*), and they publicly performed vulgar acts, and behaved with excessive corruption and immorality.[40]

Similarly, the barber mentions the circumcision party for one of the sons of the governor Sulaymān Pasha al-`Aẓm in which, much to his horror, a mock all-male orgy reportedly occurred.[41] Such "happy" occasions thus were no more than pretexts for the rich and powerful to indulge in immoral behavior and conspicuous consumption.

Among the very few pleasant memories that Ibn Budayr preserves in his chronicle are his accounts of a couple of picnics, one of which, the reader will remember, did not particularly enchant our barber. While on the outing, he noted social disorder, remarking with displeasure how women were smoking and drinking coffee in public "just as men do."[42] As with the "loose women" that I noted earlier, this "irregular" behavior by women denotes their transgression into the territory of permissible behavior for men and threatens Ibn Budayr's patriarchal authority. This female transgression sounds a warning bell for Ibn Budayr; it threatens him with loss of male privilege and hence with disempowerment. For Ibn Budayr, then, most supposedly "happy" occasions are a reflection of social disempowerment, whether through emasculation or demotion of social status. Almost all of his reportages of celebratory public events are evidence of unregulated behavior and disorder, symptomatic of the collapse of the social order. For him, "everything has turned upside down" and "all matters are inverted."[43]

As might perhaps be expected from a barber, whose shop must have functioned as a brewery of gossip, his chronicle contains a regular record of what I will characterize as "tragicomic" sexual scandals that today might well make the front page of a popular tabloid. He tells the story of a woman who responded to her husband's taking a second wife by cutting off his penis.[44] There is also the story of a man who, upon his return from the pilgrimage, found that his wife was looking unusually beautiful. He concluded that the only possible explanation was that she must be having an affair, and so he promptly killed her.[45] Despite their entertainment value for the reader, many of these stories contain underlying political messages, such as the story of the man who, on discovering that his brother-in-law was having extramarital affairs, complained to the notables—whose response was to ignore him. He thus proceeded to the mosque, prayed on his own soul the prayers of the deceased, ascended the minaret, cried out, "Oh, Community of Islam, dying is easier than pimping with the state in this age," and jumped off the minaret.[46] In this story, the state's neglect of the appeals of the commoners and its failure to establish a moral order reduces its subjects to metaphorical pimping and prostitution, and to literal suicide. Of course, such sexual goings-on, whether the state's fault or not, are not a subject with which the "respectable" *`ālim* Ibn Kannān deals at all.

Now that we have examined the nature of what constituted "events" in each of the texts, let us finally explore how the authors of these events represent themselves in their histories. How do they treat themselves as the subjects and objects of their own tales? And given that of all the chronicles treated in this study Ibn Budayr and Ibn Kannān's texts happen to be the most self-referential, how does the I figure in their chronicles?

Although Ibn Kannān does not speak on behalf of the notables or scholars (as Ibn Budayr claims to represent the "small people"), it is clear that our venerable scholar saw himself as a member of high society. In describing companions during his various social and intellectual outings, Ibn Kannān refers to friends (*aṣḥāb/khillān*)[47] and also to the *akābir* ("big people")[48] and the *afāḍil* (the eminent/learned ones).[49]

The barber and the scholar's social identities notwithstanding, Ibn Kannān is not only self-referential but positively self-involved: he constantly refers to his lessons, his outings, his parties, and his concerns. Put differently, the scholar is both the subject and the object of his text. Though most of Ibn Kannān's reports about himself have to do with his incessant socializing—and he was one gregarious man—his enchanted existence was not free of worries. (He spent much of his life attempting to get "tenure" at the Khadijiyya-Murshidiyya College, a position he was finally given after much maneuvering.)[50] Despite his tribulations, our scholar's *I* is remarkably calm and unfussy. Perhaps this unruffled *I* comes from the centuries-old tradition of *`ulamā'* biographical and autobiographical writing. Following the etiquette of elite self-authorship, Ibn Kannān manages to remain composed, even introspective, in times of trouble: "I was in the `Adawiyya Garden. I did not accompany anyone and preferred to be alone. The heart was relieved [of troubles] caused by overt and covert sources, and from distractions, external and internal, [brought about] by companions."[51]

In this instance, Ibn Kannān's sophistication in his self-presentation is remarkable. This event constitutes an intentional withdrawal from society, which seclusion is not like the religiously motivated solitude of the mystic. This kind of retreat, expressly aimed at "collecting oneself" and establishing balance away from friends,[52] is entirely absent from Ibn Budayr's text.

As we have seen repeatedly in the discussion of the *tarjama*s found in Ibn Budayr's book, the barber's self-references are mostly incidental. In these biographies, though Ibn Budayr significantly presents himself, his self-insertions are only to the extent of his relationship to the subject of the biography. Outside the *tarjama*s, the barber speaks about himself only rarely. However, when his *I* emerges, it is striking: "I saw with my own eyes," "I myself saw," "I, the poor one, was among those who saw this," and "I (eye)witnessed."[53] This is an urgent *I*, reeking of incredulousness and "incredibility." The barber finds the events unbelievable, so he has to ascertain the fact of having eyewitnessed them, but he is also incredulous by the very existence of his *I*, so he has to repeat the fact of its existence ("I myself," "I . . . my own"). Thus, in contrast to the relatively poised Ibn Kannān, Ibn Budayr's self-presentation is emphatic precisely because it is hesitant. It is the insecure *I*, not supported by a tradition of textual self-presentation, an *I* unaccustomed to presenting itself. It is also an *I* that is limited to being the subject of the text and only rarely its object. This is, then, the *I* of the nouveau literate. And it is a remarkable and courageous *I* just for the fact of its emergence at all.

To sum up the comparison of the content of the texts of Ibn Kannān and Ibn Budayr: in contrast to the imperially ordered chronicle of the *`ālim*, which is about the regular, the normal, and the routine, Ibn Budayr's chronicle is a record of the fragility of existence in the face of poverty, violence, disorder, and the ever-present threat of "emasculation" and loss of privilege. And even though the two texts might share some themes, the barber's treatment of them is critically different from that of the scholar. Ibn Budayr strips the chronicle of its cyclical regularity and transforms the secure top-down gaze of the imperial order into a world of disorder viewed from the bottom up. As a testimony of a life experience, the chronicle of Ibn Budayr posits life as a constant struggle against adversity, as a test of perseverance, and, as we have seen repeatedly, as a test of his very masculinity and social position. This history, then, bears the perspective and the emotive experience of the popular epic.

If the popular epic gave Ibn Budayr a model after which to frame the events of history, the contemporary chronicle gave him the room to be. The chronicle gave Ibn Budayr the possibility of the *I*, the authority to speak in his own voice. And though the chronicle transported him temporally and spatially from the heroic tales in distant places into the concerns and issues of the here and now, it is the epic that helped Ibn Budayr to transform the chronicle from a site of *`ālim* complacency to one of contestation. In creating for himself a hybrid space, Ibn Budayr empowered himself to directly and poignantly use the chronicle to voice his discontent while simultaneously commemorating his heroic survival.

Language and Registers: Public Performance?

The epic aspect of Ibn Budayr's text neither begins nor ends with content but is actually most transparent in the languages and registers in which he wrote his chronicle. The issue of language and registers also brings us to the important question of the audience with whom Ibn Budayr was an interlocutor.

The primary register in most Arabic historical writing is prose with occasional interruptions of rhymed prose (*saj`*) and poetry (*shi`r*). These latter registers are generally used for a commemorative function whereby an extraordinary event is set apart from the rest of the narrative by the use of a different register. Often, these registers serve another function, namely the display of the kind of literary virtuosity expected of a scholar. Ibn Budayr uses poetry sparingly and only commemoratively, but his chronicle is unique in that *saj`*, rhymed prose, pervades his text (rhymed words are underlined throughout the discussion here). Ibn Budayr uses rhymed prose for reports on all manner of subjects, from a terrifying flood or a horrifying earthquake to speech between high officials, to street violence, or simply to animate the image of the definitively quotidian object, the sun: *wa ba`da dhālik ṭala`at al-shams wa <u>qandalat</u> wa zālat al-ghuyūm <u>wa ḍaḥikat</u>* ("After that, the sun came out and shone, and the clouds disappeared, and it laughed").[54] In Ibn Budayr's chronicle, then, the function of rhymed prose is not commemorative but rather lies in the aural effect of this register. The swift repetitive accent of rhymed prose serves to dramatize the narrative. By constantly breaking into rhymed prose narratives, Ibn Budayr raises the dramatic pitch of the chronicle and gives it the insistent dramatic quality suitable for the public recitation of the popular epic. Let us take the example of a reported exchange between two real political personalities (for the benefit of the reader who does not know Arabic the underlined words establish rhyme):

fa arsala al-Ẓāhir `Umar yaqulu min al-maqāl irḥam al-nisā wa al-aṭfāl wa hatk al-ḥuram wa al-`iyāl wa illā ista`antu `alay-ka bi al-maliki al-muta`āl fa-lamma waṣala-hu al-kitāb zāda Sulaymān Bāshā al-iktiyāb wa ḥalla bi-hi al-maṣāb fa-ṣāḥ "āh" mā `udtu anfa` fa-da`ūnī ilā Dimashq al-Shām arja` wa idhā muttu wa zāda nakadī idfinū-nī `inda waladī thumma innahu māt.[55]

Al-Ẓāhir `Umar sent a letter saying, "Have mercy on women and children, [and desist from] abusing ladies and infants; otherwise I will seek the help of the Exalted King [God] against you." When the letter reached him, Sulaymān Pasha grew dejected and was overcome by miseries. He cried out, "Aah! I am no longer of use, let me return to Damascus, and if my misery increases and I die, bury me next to my son," Then, indeed, he died.

This particular passage of rhymed prose was chosen intentionally as an example, precisely because it represents a point of tension in the chronicle where the epic form, generally lurking only in the background, here bursts out of the seams. The conversation is between al-Ẓahir al-`Umar, the local strongman and "arch-rebel" stationed in Acre, and the Ottoman governor of Damascus, Sulaymān Pasha al-`Aẓm, two sworn enemies who have been engaged in battle for years. Ibn Budayr narrates a story, which like the epic achieves dramatic closure. Also epiclike, the story adds fictionalized details to a real historical situation whose *dramatis personae* are real. Simply by the power of his speech, the rebel-hero al-Ẓāhir `Umar manages to inflict fatal depression on the governor Sulaymān Pasha, and consequently emerge victorious. Thus Ibn Budayr's usage of rhymed prose—a register unfamiliar to the chronicle—serves to render the chronicle suitable for recitation to an audience accustomed to listening to the epic tales of public storytellers, and for whom the chronicle in its usual register is an unfamiliar form.

This impression that Ibn Budayr's chronicle might have been intended for public performance is also corroborated by his particular use of the demotic and the classical. In general, the genre of the chronicle acknowledges the literary convention that classical Arabic is the language suitable for the realm of text, and that colloquial Arabic, which is generally assigned to the realm of oral speech, may enter the chronicle only under set circumstances. For example, Ibn Kannān, who wrote his text in morphologically and syntactically unmistakable classical Arabic, included in his vocabulary the occasional colloquial word in the vein of what one may call "narrative license." That is to say, when the word in classical Arabic is not expressive enough for the purpose at hand, Ibn Kannān allows himself the liberty of replacing it with a colloquial word.[56] This, however, is not the case in Ibn Budayr's chronicle, which privileges neither classical nor colloquial and does not assign them separate realms. Rather, Ibn Budayr altogether ignores the literary convention of the chronicle—that it be written in textual Arabic—for the benefit of writing in the register most suited to public narration: rhymed prose. Let us take the example of the story of the minaret suicide cited earlier. I will give the translation first:

On the fourth of Ramadan, a man threw himself off of the top of the minaret of the Qubaybāt neighborhood, and died. His name was Ḥasan Ibn al-Shaykh Yūsuf al-Rifā`ī. We asked about the cause, it was said to us that his wife's brother brought a woman of ill-repute to his house. He [Ḥasan] forbade him from doing this and said, "What actions are these? You corrupt our women and the children." He [the brother-in-law], being an ignoramus, chided him [Ḥasan] and wanted to beat him up. He [Ḥasan] went to the neighborhood notables, and told them about the matter. They shamed him, and distracted him with talk, as they were collectively plunged to the ears [with their own interests]. So, he went to al-Daqqāq Mosque, and performed the dawn prayers with the *imām*, then prayed upon himself the prayers of the deceased, climbed to the top of the minaret, and cried out, "Oh, Community of Islam, dying is better than pimping with the state of this time," and then, threw himself, may God forgive him and have mercy upon him.

In the transliterated passage, exclusively classical expressions are indicated in italics, exclusively colloquial expressions are written in bold typeface, and those expressions shared by both classical and colloquial are in regular typeface (and rhyming words are underlined):

wa fī rabī` shahr Ramaḍān **armā** *rajul* nafsa-hu min a`lā mādhanat ḥārat al-Qubaybāt wa māta wa kāna ismu-hu Ḥasan Ibn al-Shaykh Yūsuf al-Rifā`ī fa sa'alnā `an *dhālika* al-sabab fa-*qīla* la-nā anna akhū zawjati-hi **jāb** *imra'a* ilā bayti-hi wa kānat min al-**dāyrāt** fa-*nahā*-hu `an *dhālika* wa qāla la-hu **aysh** *hādhi-hi al-af`āl tutlifu nisa'*[sic]-na wa al-`iyāl fa *nahara*-hu wa *arāda* ḍarba-hu wa kāna mina al-juhhāl fa-*dhahaba* ilā akābir al-ḥāra wa *akhbara*-hum bi-*dhālika* al-*shān* **fa-ma`yabū-h** wa shāghalu-hu bi-al-kalām li-anna-hum **ghāṭsīn** *jam`an* ilā fawq al-*adhān* fa-*dhahaba* ila jāmi` al-Daqqāq wa ṣallā al-ṣubḥ ma`a al-imām wa ṣallā `alā nafsi-hi ṣalāt al-mawt wa *ṣa`ida* al-manāra wa nādā yā ummata al-islām al-mawt ahwan wa lā **al-ta`rīṣ** ma`a dawlat *hādha* [sic] al-ayyām *thumma* **armā** nafsa-hu raḥima-hu Allāh wa `afā `an-hu.[57]

The first point to note is that Ibn Budayr's syntax is recognizably classical. However, his vocabulary and morphology are mixed. He uses a number of words that are exclusively classical, and a number that are shared between colloquial and classical; but he also uses colloquialisms. Let us examine the dynamic of the relationship between the colloquial and the classical in Ibn Budayr's text. In one of the moments of direct speech—***aysh*** *hādhi-hi al-af`āl* ("What actions are these?")—the author begins with the colloquialism ***aysh*** ("What?"). Since Ibn Budayr could easily have used the classical interrogative *mā* instead of ***aysh***, his decision to use ***aysh*** indicates that he is actively giving primacy here to colloquial, perhaps to convey the texture of everyday language in this direct speech report. However, he does not finish his colloquial project but completes the sentence with the exclusively classical word *af`āl*, instead of an equivalent colloquial such as ***`amāyil***. The reason for this switch is simply the requirements of rhymed prose: *af`āl* rhymes with the last word of the next sentence *`iyāl*, and ***`amāyil*** does not. Thus Ibn Budayr uses classical here not because it is the language suitable for text but because he needs a rhyme. Although in this instance Ibn Budayr classicalizes the colloquial, there are in this same passage other instances where he reverses the process and colloquializes the classical. For example, in the phrase ***ghāṭṣīn*** *jam`an ilā fawq al-adhān* (literally, "collectively plunged to the ears," similar to the English "up to the ears in") Ibn Budayr substitutes the classical plural *adhān* for the colloquial ***adanayn*** in the colloquial idiom ***ghāṭṣīn la-l-adanayn***. Here, Ibn Budayr classicalizes the colloquial idiom, again for the purposes of rhyme. *Adhān* rhymes with *shān* in the previous sentence, but ***adanayn*** does not. In his negotiation between the vernacular and classical for the purposes of rhyme, then, Ibn Budayr is constantly doing one of two things: he is either using the language of the epic that, as mentioned above, has been characterized as a "classicalized colloquial" and with which the audience of the epic is of course familiar, or he is "bringing down" the classical language of the chronicle to that same audience who are not familiar with the language of the chronicle, by reversing the process and "colloquializing the classical."

Ibn Budayr's intentional disregard of the literary conventions of text, in making his chronicle a hybrid text that includes the formal elements of the epic, strongly suggests that he pitched his chronicle not to its conventional audience. Rather than a restricted scholarly audience convened at a literary salon or a *madrasa*, Ibn Budayr's may have been a public audience, a group of people who consumed the barber's chronicle along with their drinks in the coffeehouse, or to the sound of his scissors in his barbershop. Ibn Budayr, it seems, gave the customers of the *ḥakawī* a tale with a different flavor.

PATHS NOT TAKEN: THE IMPORTANCE OF BEING EARNEST

The *sīra*, however, was not the only performative or narrative form that Ibn Budayr had at his disposal. Both the *maqāma* (picaresque narrative) and the shadow theater (*khayāl al-ẓill*) were genres familiar—if not thoroughly popular—in Damascus at the time, but the barber seems to have blissfully ignored the former and chosen to categorically reject the latter. The exploration of these fictional literary forms is necessary, since the barber's decision to appropriate a form is as important as understanding his decision to reject or choose not to use another. This will also lead us to understand more deeply the motivations and politics of Ibn Budayr's *Events of Damascus*. More specifically, I will examine the politics of the genres of shadow theater and the *maqāma* through the place of laughter in these literary forms. By comparing the humor in these other performative genres to that found in the text of Ibn Budayr, I hope to place the politics of the barber in sharp relief.

The *maqāma* (plural, *maqāmāt*) is a narrative form that enjoyed wide readership/audition in Damascus.[58] Entirely fictional in purpose and conception, the *maqāma*, which means "assembly," derives its name from the reality of the gatherings of the literati.[59] And though there are several types of *maqāmāt*, the most famous and popular are those of al-Hamadhānī (d. 1008)[60] and al-Ḥarīrī (d. 1122),[61] which have come to be dubbed "beggar (Arabic, *mukaddī*)" or picaresque *maqāmas*.[62] The genre is constructed in successive closed episodes, each of which takes place in a different place or city in the Islamic world. The protagonists are a scholar and a wily rogue who meet and recognize one another at the end of every episode. A true chameleon, the rogue appears in various guises; however, his invariable quality and instrument is eloquence, through which he manages successfully to trick the scholar out of his wealth. It is only after the scholar falls for the trick that he recognizes the scoundrel.[63]

Evidently, the purpose of these "assemblies" is humorous entertainment, the primary object or victim of which is the scholar. Composed by a highly cultivated author for a literate audience,[64] the *maqamāt* are usually exercises in complicated linguistic acrobatics written in rhymed prose.[65] In addition to its satire of the *`ālim* (the guardian of values of Islamic society), the *maqāma* also parodies the definitive genre of his scholarship: Hadith. Each *maqāma* is introduced by a fictitious chain of transmission (*isnād*), the instrument of establishing the veracity of the Hadith report.[66] The effect of the structure and content of the *maqāma* is aptly summed in this statement:

> The lesson to be learned from the example set by his [the scoundrel's] behavior therefore constitutes an immoral doctrine that stands in stark contrast to the noble message proclaimed by the Prophet Muḥammad and codified in Ḥadīth literature. Thus, the inverse, even *perverse* relationship obtaining between maqāma and ḥadīth goes much deeper than any mere external or formal similarity between the two genres. We are presented in the *Maqāmāt* with the empty form of ḥadīth writings voided of all moral content.[67]

The *maqāma* thus stands in interesting apposition to the chronicle. The latter is an affirmation of the Islamic political order by the *`ālim* and the logical extension of his knowledge; the former, in contrast, is a poignantly humorous satire of not just the man but also his prudery and moral authority. It is a harsh—perhaps even radical—critique that presents the readers with the realities of their urban, highly mercantile, and rampantly corrupt milieu.[68]

Inasmuch as the *maqāma* is an indicator of a community gone astray from its ideals and emptied of ethics, it also deflates the heroic, as the genre's "entire artistic tension . . . is produced by portraying anti-heroic lives."[69] Thus the *maqāma* also situates itself in juxtaposition to the *sīra*-epic. Structurally, the epic, similar to the *maqāma*, is made up of episodes that all close with the survival of the protagonist.[70] In the *sīra*, the survival is solemnly heroic; in the *maqāma*, it is comically pathetic (because the scoundrel's survival is achieved by trickery). And though both genres present the audience with a bold subjective *I*, in the *sīra* the identity of the *I* is a "knight-errant"; in the *maqāma*, he is a "parasite-errant."[71] The *maqāma*, then, is a parody of the *sīra* and an invitation to laugh at the latter's seriousness.[72]

The coffeehouse was the site of performance not only of the *sīra* but also of shadow theater.[73] Unfortunately, very few shadow play scripts are extant today,[74] and those that survive are not of the category known as "*karākūz*," which happen to be the type that was most popular in both the Levant and Turkey.[75] The term *karākūz* (or *karagöz* in Turkish) comes from one of the main characters in Arabic and Turkish shadow plays. He is usually both the interlocutor of and foil for the other character, `Īwāẓ (Hacivat in Turkish). Surviving texts indicate that Turkish Karagöz theater had a fixed tripartite structure of preamble, dialogue, and main plot.[76] The fragmentary nature of the Arabic Karākūz texts and recordings does not allow us to issue similar generalizations about structure. However, shadow theater, whether Arabic or Turkish, is salient to us owing to the social world it presents and the kind of humor it contains.

Shadow plays usually present a host of stock characters who are based on ethnic, professional, and religious stereotypes.[77] The audience is therefore presented with an open social world away from the exclusivity and homogeneity of literary and scholarly assemblies. This is a world of the "plurality of life in the public domain."[78] The primary subject of shadow theater is not the Muslim ruler (of the chronicle), the heroic warrior (of the epic), or the scorned *ʿālim* and the chameleon trickster (of the picaresque narrative). Rather, shadow theater is about people from all walks of life, presented as caricatures and thus identifiable sartorially, linguistically, and professionally. Although, like the *maqāma*, satire and parody of pretentious cultivation are part and parcel of shadow theater,[79] the dramaturgy invites laughter not only through inversions like those found in the picaresque narrative but also through the bodily, the grotesque, the obscene, the sexual, and the scatological. This is a transgressive laughter that celebrates the flouting of all moral and social codes. It is a laughter of a world that according to the literary critic Mikhail Bakhtin is intentionally disordered.[80] It is a world turned upside down.

The mention of things "upside down" reminds us of the topsy-turvy state of the world according to Ibn Budayr. The barber's observations, however, are not celebratory or joyously encouraging but instead angry and somberly critical. It is the absence of transgressive or satirical humor in Ibn Budayr's text—indeed, of almost any humor at all—that marks Ibn Budayr's set of ethics.

It is quite ironic that the only reference to *khayāl al-ẓill* found in the barber's text is a play performance that takes place neither in the coffeehouse nor the barbershop but in the residence of the governor of Damascus during the aforementioned celebration of the circumcision of his son. Among the guests is a certain Ibn Tūmā, characterized by Ibn Budayr as the representative of the Greek Orthodox Patriarch. It is an event that the barber apparently did not attend but seems to report from hearsay:

> A shadow play was put on and someone made up one of the puppets, which was fat and tall, to look like Ibn Tūmā, and made up one of the puppets to look like a Jew. He then made the Jew sodomize (*yankiḥ ilā*) Ibn Tūmā, the Christian, in that gathering and assembly. All of them saw this and watched. They did things that [even] the ignorant do not do.[81]

The reported shadow play seems to have the familiar ingredients of the form: characters, or rather caricatures of particular groups (in this case religious groups), and the grotesque (an act of sodomy). It is difficult to credit the notion that Ibn Tūmā would be treated so insultingly at the governor's house, but the point here is Ibn Budayr's criticism of inappropriate and immoral behavior. He objects not only to the content of the play but also to the fact of the participation of the audience in such depravity. In short, shadow theater does not invite Ibn Budayr's victorious laughter but instead his disapproving moralizing and shocked outrage. The bodily, the grotesque, and the obscene do not make it into the barber's text, and when there is mention of sex it is in the vein of objection to moral laxity. In other words, Ibn Budayr finds the particular performance at the governor's house revolting, and he also seems to eschew the literary form and the values therein. Ibn Budayr does not allow this form to seep into his history, not even despite himself.

Ibn Budayr was certainly in possession of a level of education that would allow him a degree of appreciation of at least the literary qualities of the *maqāma*, but one cannot be certain whether he was familiar with it or not. He neither mentions the form nor employs it, despite the genre's copious capacity for critique. It seems both the nature of the genre and its intention are ill-suited to Ibn Budayr's project. First, the treatment of the main "characters" in the respective genres are not so much different as diametrically opposed. We know that the *maqāma*'s comic targets are both the heroic figure and the *`ālim*. Although the barber's text does not figure a particular hero, the *`ulamā'* enter his text to be celebrated, not satirized. Second, the thrust of the picaresque is not suitable for the existential condition of Ibn Budayr. The *maqāma*'s antiheroism and its satire of authority figures implies a distant self-critical impulse usually found in a relatively confident and secure society. This is not the society Ibn Budayr saw. On the contrary, what he saw is a society in shambles. Naturally, it in this context that the *sīra*, which has been noted to thrive in times of crises, appealed to Ibn Budayr.[82] In Ibn Budayr's eyes, his crisis-ridden society demanded the epic.

What about humor in the barber's text? Remarkably, in Ibn Budayr there is no room for the Bakhtinian "purifying laughter" of the plebs usually found in shadow theater,[83] nor for the inversive laughter wrought by the wiliness of the *maqāma*'s scoundrel. Indeed, the humor in Ibn Budayr's text, which I have previously termed "tragicomic"—such as the aforementioned episode of the minaret suicide, or the cutting off of a stray husband's penis—may not have been intended to induce laughter at all. If the humor was intended, it is neither enabling nor subversive but rather the humor of resignation and loss of control. It is not menacing laughter but exactly its opposite; it expresses the condition of being menaced. In short, it exemplifies the famous Arabic proverb "the worst affliction is the one that makes you laugh (*sharru al-baliyyati mā yuḍḥik*)." Thus, despite humorous episodes, the overall tenor of the text of the barber's chronicle is dead-serious. This brings us to the crux of Ibn Budayr's ethics.

Though by the mere act of writing in a form not legitimately his Ibn Budayr causes a literary disorder, his intention is not to wreak social disorder (à la shadow theater) or satirize an order (à la the *maqāma*). Quite the contrary, his message is one of restoration, of reinstatement of what he sees as a lost order. His tone is urgent and anxious at what he perceives to be social and moral collapse. For him, the terms of the social contract, so to speak, have been thoroughly violated.[84] This he does not find funny. Though the barber himself is socially mobile, he is not yet at a level of comfort that affords him the luxury of a distant glance at a society in flux. In his view, life appears chaotic. Any contemplation has to be earnest. Consequently, the genres of *tārīkh* and *sīra*, both earnest and memorial, suited his purpose to "examine the events of the age . . ." and to remember.

THE UNIQUE MANUSCRIPT: CLUES AND FINGERPRINTS

Let us now treat the important question of the reception of the barber's book. The foregoing literary analysis suggests strongly that his chronicle may have been intended for a new audience accustomed to listening to epic tales. Although there is no internal or external evidence to indicate that the barber's story was performed, the chronicle may have very well been picked up by a subsequent storyteller, who would have told it along with other chronicles such as that of the soldier Ibn al-Ṣiddīq, whose cadence as we have shown is also distinctly performative. But chronicles could not have lived very long in the oral realm, not only because their relevance to the here and now would expire with the passage of time but because the art of storytelling itself was soon to die.

Any questions regarding the reception of the barber's story will thus have to remain within the realm of the textual. So, let us examine the unique Chester Beatty manuscript for clues about readership, ownership, and circulation. The manuscript is of relatively good-quality paper. The script, in common *naskh* style, is neat and regular, albeit decidedly not intended for aesthetic appreciation. There are about 24 lines to the folio in a manuscript of 192 folios. The text is set within wide blank margins and is written in black ink. Occasionally, and only in the earlier parts of the text, red ink is used for some words and marks.[85] The ample size of the margins indicates the manuscript was intended as a clean copy (*mibyaḍḍa*) and not a rough draft (*miswadda*). This, then, is a copy that was ready for consumption or sale (Figure 8).[86]

As mentioned earlier, missing from the text is the customary preamble (*khuṭba*), which would have offered some indications about intended audiences. Given that the usual colophon is also absent, scribal identity and date of copy remain a mystery. However, since the script exhibits the same characteristics throughout the text, one may conclude that a single scribe copied the entire work.[87] A different hand (perhaps even more than one) appears in the title page and a few margin notes. What interferences are these? Who is their perpetrator? And what can we conclude from them?

Noteworthy among these marginal interferences is the title page, which includes the sentence *raḥima-hu Allāh* (may God have mercy on him) after the name of the author. This confirms the important fact that the text was copied and circulated even after the barber's death.[88] In addition to proof of circulation, as limited is it might have been, there is an indication that the book was actually read, evidenced by a statement of completion of reading (what I will call "reading testament") in one of the marginal notes. The author of this note does not identify himself but dates the conclusion of his study of the contents of the book to 1249 AH (1834 CE).[89] The other notes in the text provide markers for events and people mentioned in the text itself and function like titles in the margin. Most of these "title markers" indicate important figures in the cultural and political life of Damascus and some of their activities.[90]

The title page inscriptions and most marginal notes may well have been those of the editor/bowdlerizer of the chronicle, Muḥammad Saʿīd al-Qāsimī. The script in the notes often resembles al-Qāsimī's handwriting in other manuscripts, including the edited version of the barber's

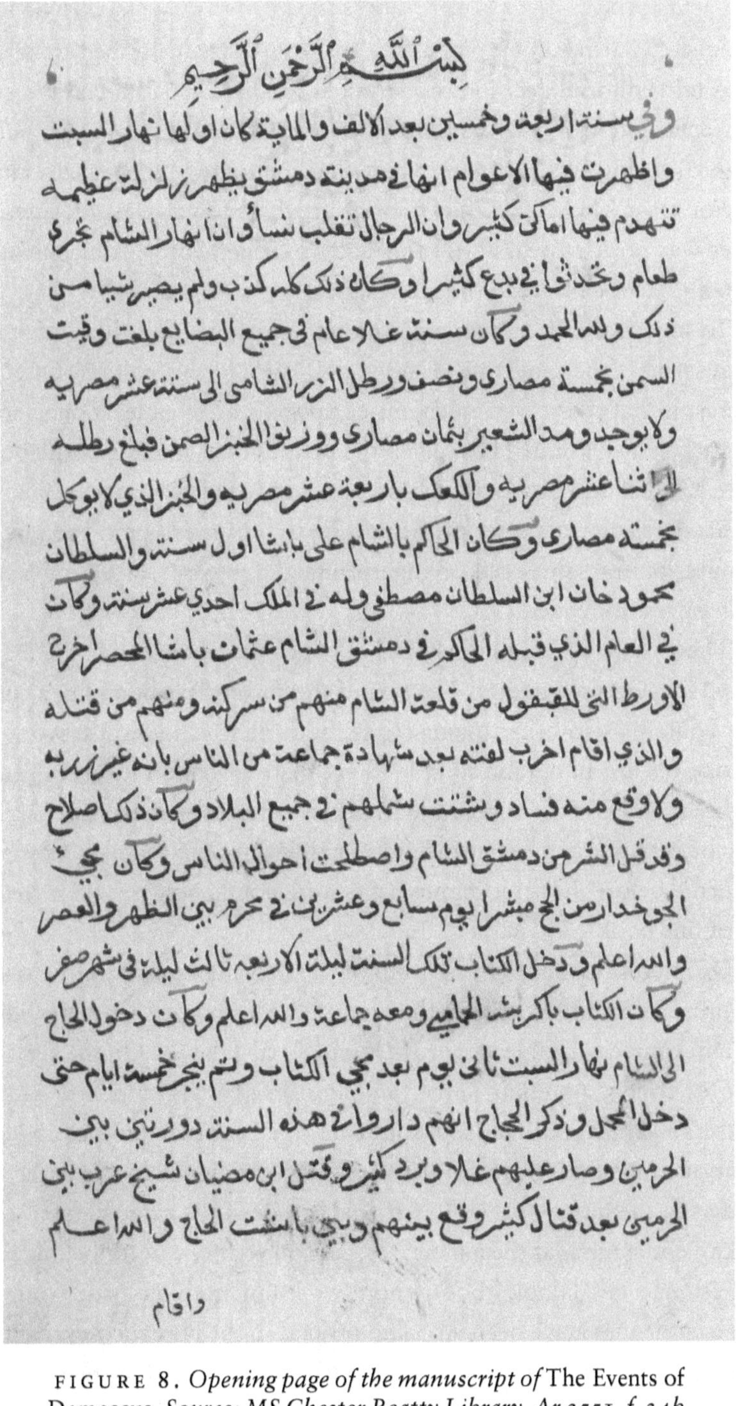
بسم الله الرحمن الرحيم
وفي سنة اربعة وخمسين بعد الالف والماية كان اولها نهار السبت
واظهرت فيها الاعوام انها في مدينة دمشق يظهر زلزلة عظيمه
تتهدم فيها اماكن كثير وان الرجال تنقلب نسا وان نهار الشام يجري
طعام وتحدثوا في بدع كثيرا وكان ذلك كله كذب ولم يصير شيا من
ذلك ولله الحمد وكان سنة غلا عام في جميع البضايع بلغت وقية
السمن بخمسة مصاري ونصف ورطل الرز الشامي الى ستة عشر مصريه
ولا يوجد ومد الشعير بثمان مصاري ووزنوا الخبز الصمن فبلغ رطله
اثنا عشر مصريه والكعك باربعة عشر مصريه والخبز الذي لا يوكل
بخمسة مصاري وكان الحاكم بالشام علي باشا اول سنة والسلطان
محمود خان ابن السلطان مصطفى وله في الملك احدي عشر سنة وكان
في العام الذي قبله الحاكم في دمشق الشام عثمان باشا المحصل اخرج
الاورط التي للقبقول من قلعة الشام منهم من سركنه ومنهم من قتله
والذي اقام اخرب لفتنه بعد شهادة جماعة من الناس بانه غير زربه
ولا وقع منه فساد وشتت شملهم في جميع البلاد وكان ذلك اصلاح
وقد قل الشر من دمشق الشام واصطلحت احوال الناس وكان مجي
الجوخدار من الحج مبشرا يوم سابع وعشرين في محرم بين الظهر والعصر
والله اعلم ودخل الكتاب تلك السنة ليلة الاربعه ثالث ليلة في شهر صفر
وكان الكتاب باكر بشه الحاميه ومعه جماعة والله اعلم وكان دخول الحاج
الى الشام نهار السبت ثاني يوم بعد مجي الكتاب وتم ينجر خمسة ايام حتى
دخل المحمل وذكر الحجاج انهم داروا في هذه السنة دورتين بين
الحرمين وصار عليهم غلا وبرد كثير وقتل ابن مضيان شيخ عرب بين
الحرمين بعد قتال كثير وقع بينهم وبين باشت الحاج والله اعلم
داقام

FIGURE 8. *Opening page of the manuscript of* The Events of Damascus. *Source: MS Chester Beatty Library, Ar 3551, f. 24b.*

chronicle.[91] Further, some of the "title markers" I have described are related to certain editorial decisions undertaken by al-Qāsimī and betraying his particular interests, such as the phases of the building of al-ʿAẓm palace (Figure 9). However, the margin note that contains the reading-testament date of 1249 AH (1843 CE) cannot be attributed to al-Qāsimī, since the latter was born 10 years after this date. In other words, someone other than al-Qāsimī also read the manuscript.

To sum up the discussion of the margin notes, it is quite likely that this manuscript is the same one used by al-Qāsimī for his edition. Of equal interest is that the very same manuscript was read by at least one person other than al-Qāsimī. Thus, given the posthumous interest in the book, there is indication of the circulation of not only the text (as text) but also of this particular manuscript. According to our investigation so far, the manuscript bears three sets of fingerprints: the copyist's, al-Qāsimī's, and an anonymous reader's.

There is, however, another level at which we can examine the manuscript: its place in a library. The text of the chronicle is bound in a codex that contains two other manuscripts, both of which are also works of history, but are autograph copies.[92] Since there is no indication of the date of the binding of the codex, any markers offered by these manuscripts may or may not be of relevance to our investigation, for they may have occurred before the three manuscripts were bound between the two covers of one book.

Of interest is that the first folio of the first manuscript in the codex contains an *Ex Libris* note in the margin: "This book is from the books of Ḥājj Aḥmad [illegible word] al-Ḥalabī [or al-Jalabī]." On the very last folio of codex, a similar name (among other names) appears: Aḥmad Jalabī al-Ṭarātī. This person could be one and the same as the just mentioned Aḥmad al-Ḥalabī (if we add a missing dot to the letter *ḥā'*, rendering the name al-Jalabī).[93] If this is indeed the same person, then we can conclude that the entirety of the codex at one point belonged to this Aḥmad (al)-Jalabī, about whom we know nothing aside from the fact that he may have been a scribal official in the bureaucracy, as indicated by his sobriquet (al-Jalabī, Turkish *çelebi*), and that the man was a serious history buff.

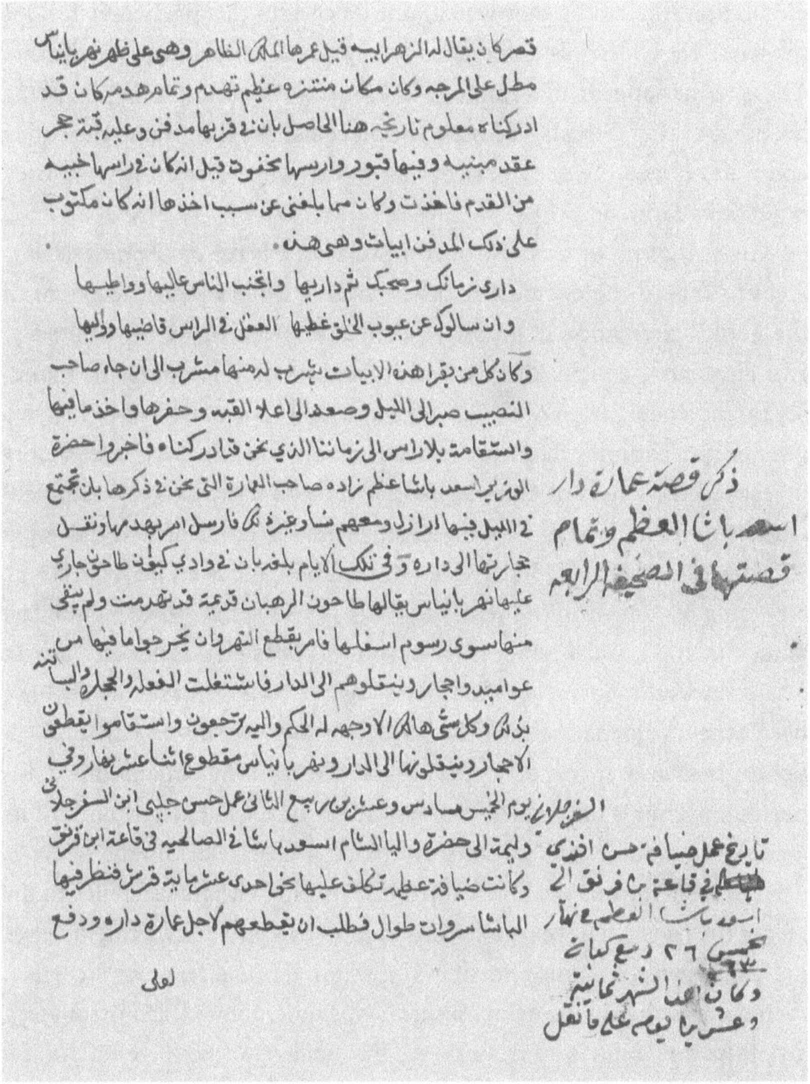

FIGURE 9. *Margin notes in* The Events of Damascus, *possibly in al-Qāsimī's hand. Source: MS Chester Beatty Library, Ar 3551, f. 81b.*

There are two other names on the last folio: Salīm Jalabī al-Sāyḥa (another scribal official) and ʿAbd al-Wahhāb Beg al-Tarazī. Significantly, this last name, which bears the sobriquet "the tailor," appears in what looks like a reading testament.[94] Even though the multiple set of fingerprints in this folio is exciting given that is suggests the possibility of wide circulation, the fact is that we cannot be certain this particular folio is related to the codex itself, or indeed to any one of the manuscripts therein. These names appear in a random fashion, as if a scribe were practicing his handwriting. For all we know, the placement of the folio in the codex could have been the deed of a frugal binder who recycled it from used notebooks or manuscripts.

Given that no other copy of Ibn Budayr's *Events of Damascus* survives (if indeed there were any other copies), evidence for the extent of the book's circulation is simply unavailable. As such, we are limited to two alternative conclusions derived from the examination of the manuscript and codex, both of which are modest. The less modest of the two possibilities assumes that the manuscript was bound a long time before it reached the hands of Chester Beatty, the collector, and was handled/read by at least all of those who left their marks in the codex: the copyist, someone who could be al-Qāsimī, the anonymous reader who wrote a reading testament in the year 1249 AH, two officials (bearing the last name "Jalabī"), and another person who was possibly a tailor (al-Tarazī). These readers/handlers left their marks on the codex, but there may have been others who made use of the codex without ever leaving any indication of their use. If this deduction is correct, then the circulation of this one manuscript is impressive and the variety of social backgrounds of its readers remarkable. A more conservative conjecture relies on the evidence derived from the margin notes in the manuscript without reference to the rest of the codex. The marginal scribblings bear the handwriting of three individuals only, including possibly al-Qāsimī. If this latter guess is correct, then the circulation of the manuscript was quite limited. Unfortunately, all of the foregoing is guesswork. As Ibn Budayr would have it, "*Allāhu aʿlam* [God knows better]."

A ROOM OF HIS OWN

Now that we have explored both the literary and the material aspects of Ibn Budayr's *Events of Damascus*, let us return to the question posited at the outset: When Ibn Budayr wrote his chronicle, what did he do to the chronicle and what did the chronicle do for him?

In the imperially ordered world of the *`ulamā'*, the chronicle was a form that anticipated its content. The structure of the form, which is built around the cyclicality and regularity of time, prefigured its content, which is also about the cyclicality and regularity of events. Indeed, the imperial offerings to the *`ulamā'* in the form of official positions gave the scholars a good enough life to remember the regular, the normal, and the banal. Ibn Budayr, whose position was far too low for him to pick the fruits of empire, lived in a world far away from that order, with the result that all he saw was disorder—a disorder he directly attributed to the negligence of the state. So when Ibn Budayr appropriated the chronicle, he disturbed the cyclicality of its content by literally turning it into a narrative of disorder. By furnishing it with both the formal elements and the emotive and experiential force of the epic, Ibn Budayr transformed the chronicle into a performance—one possibly delivered on a new stage, for a new audience. To this new audience, the barber performed the memory of a troubled existence, not that of a hero in the distant past, but of himself, the barber of Damascus, who like his audience struggles against the abuses and corruption of the rich and powerful in the here and now.

As for the question of what the chronicle did for Ibn Budayr: with its authorial *I*, the chronicle allowed him to speak. The contemporary chronicle allowed the barber to enter into—and register himself within—textual space. As the *`ulamā'* continued to immortalize themselves in biographical dictionaries, Ibn Budayr found in the chronicle an alternative space in which to immortalize himself. The contemporary chronicle gave Ibn Budayr a way to tell history as "his story," and in it he found a "room of his own."

CHAPTER 6

Cutting the Barber's Tale

The Afterlives of a History

Muḥammad Sa`īd al-Qāsimī (d. 1900) was an interesting man. He was a scholar and a teacher who belonged to what became a famous Damascene scholarly "dynasty,"[1] and a joyous host whose house was famous for literary and musical salons.[2] Though we are interested in al-Qāsimī mainly for his adaptation of Ibn Budayr's chronicle, his greatest achievement lay not in the intellectual realm but in the fact of his progeny: his son Jamāl al-Dīn al-Qāsimī (d. 1914) was one of the most important figures of the Islamic reform movement (*salafiyya*) in Syria, a movement that proposed a return to and search in the original scriptural sources for the revival of faith, state, and society.[3] Jamāl publicized his views and engaged in debates in various newspapers and journals, which had global circulation.[4] Print was Jamāl's medium. The times changed, and print became the sign of the times.

This chapter tells the story of the later reincarnation of Ibn Budayr's chronicle. It is about the adaptation of the text at the heavy editorial hand of Muḥammad Sa`īd al-Qāsimī. It will be remembered that al-Qāsimī's bowdlerized edition, which was completed sometime before his death (in 1900) and eventually printed in 1959, is the version of the work that is widely used by historians today. I juxtapose the two versions—the barber's original text and the amended al-Qāsimī version—with the goal of examining the editor's alterations; of identifying his motives, whether implicit or explicit; and gauging the overall effect of the bowdlerized text. We shall see that the editor's alterations, omissions, and additions are not simply about improving style and language. Rather the editor, though somewhat mindful of retaining the general meaning of the chronicle, paradoxically attempts to *revert* the text, from its original constitution as a hybrid product with a subversive message and a performative function, into a relatively orderly chronicle concerned with sultans and governors. In his attempt to make the text conform with the scholarly form, the editor reinstates the "state"—a strategy that facilitates the habilitation, if not the glorification, of the al-`Aẓm governors of Damascus. Al-Qāsimī's editorial power (further enhanced by the fact that the author, Ibn Budayr, was long dead) allows him to rid the text of the barber-author as *protagonist* with his insistent pleas and dramatic ways. The consequence of al-Qāsimī's editorial program is not only a text stripped of its original political import but also one that deprives the barber of all the sources of his social power. If the book had originally functioned as proof and showcase for Ibn Budayr's newly acquired cultural wealth, it is now a socially empty or "confused" text in which the barber and his language are so muted that they become, at best, a quaint backdrop. The *`ālim*, it seems, has no tolerance for the concerns and aspirations of a nouveau literate. Al-Qāsimī, himself a parvenu, may have been threatened by the barber's authority and thus had to "put the barber back in his place." To state it differently (and rather dramatically), the editor takes advantage of the fact of the death of the barber to kill him again, this time wiping him and his life out of the text. In addition to pushing the barber out of history, the editorial interventions by al-Qāsimī also betray something larger: namely, the transformation of history from reports on current events into a document about heritage or a collection of legacies. In other words, by the time al-Qāsimī edited the barber's chronicle, an idea of (a Damascene) *tradition* had been born. Meanwhile, "current events"—the original subject of Ibn Budayr's chronicle—had found another form: the newspaper.

Now, let us get to know Muḥammad Sa`īd al-Qāsimī and his times slightly better. Unlike his son Jamāl, the father Muḥammad Sa`īd did not produce scholarship in the religious sciences. In addition to his edition of the barber's chronicle, Muḥammad Sa`īd left three works, all of which are literary and/or historical. One of them is a biography of his own father, the eponymous founder of the dynasty, al-Shaykh Qāsim (d. 1867).[5] Another of his compositions is a book of variety and miscellanea in which the author collected all kinds of facts, events, wisdoms, and poetry entitled *Safīnat al-faraj fī mā habba wa dabba wa daraj* ("The Ship of Deliverance with regard to that which Proceeds, Advances, and Circulates"). Al-Qāsimī's third work may strike the reader as curious; it was described by one scholar as representing a "*genre inhabituel*."[6]

Entitled *Qāmūs al-ṣinā`āt al-shāmiyya* ("The Dictionary of Damascene Crafts"), this book is a dictionary of the arts and crafts of the city.[7] Clearly, al-Qāsimī's interests were not consonant with those of his peers and do not represent the preoccupations of his generation. What is it that prompted this *`ālim* to become interested in things as unusual as a history of a barber and the crafts and arts of his city?

It has been suggested that *The Dictionary of Damascene Crafts* had something to do with the *salafiyya* reformist agenda of the family. Initially proposed and later completed by the reformer son, Jamāl, the *Dictionary* is posited as representing a return to the sources of economic life in search of revival, parallel to the return to scriptures for moral renewal.[8] Although al-Qāsimī's dictionary may well have been related to the agenda of reform, one cannot help but see a connection between al-Qāsimī's preoccupation with the artisanal life in Damascus and his interest in a book by a craftsman, the barber Ibn Budayr. By the time al-Qāsimī was writing, the famed traditional crafts of Damascus were likely already disappearing, thus impelling the scholar to document them and their practitioners as folkloric legacies.[9] Also, there may have been something much more personal about al-Qāsimī's attention to the bazaar and the barber. It turns out that al-Qāsimī's own father, the aforementioned al-Shaykh Qāsim, was a barber too! Al-Shyakh Qāsim "worked as a barber in his youth, but . . . quit his trade [at age 40] to pursue a religious education."[10] In other words, Al-Shaykh Qāsim, the father of our editor, had much in common with Ibn Budayr. They were both *upstarts*.[11]

Indeed, the al-Qāsimī family and their agenda of reform have been studied in terms of the family's position in the city. They were "newcomers to the ranks of the ulama" with "middling status, modest wealth, and local posts."[12] They and other such families were pitted against the older, more established scholarly families who monopolized important positions. A case in point is Muḥammad Sa`īd's composition of "poetry that expressed his bitter resentment toward Damascus' wealthy elite."[13] In other words, the social background of al-Qāsimī and his position in the city seem to explain his interest in the barber. This is also consonant with his project of writing the *Dictionary*, effectively, an ethnography of the Damascus bazaar. Al-Qāsimī may have simply identified with the barber and the other craftsmen in the city. To put it in anachronistically, he may have been "a man of the people." But was he? It is only through examining al-Qāsimī's treatment of Ibn Budayr's chronicle that we will be able to discern his attitude toward the barber. But first things first: How did al-Qāsimī get his hands on the manuscript of the barber's history?

There are two reports about al-Qāsimī's "discovery" of the manuscript of Ibn Budayr's history.[14] The first story portrays al-Qāsimī procuring something from a spice vendor (*`aṭṭār*). The purchase was wrapped with a piece of paper, which al-Qāsimī could not resist reading—for he "was given to curiosity and loved reading."[15] Lo and behold, the paper wrap turned out to be a folio from Ibn Budayr's manuscript! Al-Qāsimī reportedly immediately returned to the spice shop to salvage the manuscript, and the rest was (literally) history.

The other story locates Ibn Budayr's manuscript in an auction sale of an extensive library at the Umayyad Mosque. The library had belonged to a local *`ālim*. Present at the sale were Muḥammad al-Qāsimī, his son Jamāl, and the educational reformer and founder of Syria's first public library, Ṭāhir al-Jazā'irī (d. 1920).[16] When Ibn Budayr's book was first auctioned, it was initially offered for little money. However, al-Jazā'irī, given his expertise as a book collector and educator, was the sole person to understand the value of the barber's book and resolved to buy it. But as soon as his intentions became obvious to other prospective buyers, another bidder wanted the manuscript. A tough bidding duel ensued, with the result that the price of the book rose from "ten to 300 *qurūsh*."[17] In the end, al-Jazā'irī prevailed. Being a personal friend of al-Jazā'irī, al-Qāsimī borrowed the book from his friend and made a copy for himself. The original was supposedly returned to al-Jazā'irī, whose library, we are told, has not survived.

Given that the associations between the Jazāi'rīs and the Qāsimīs are attested,[18] and that such auctions actually did occur at the Umayyad Mosque, the second story seems more plausible than the first. However, though the spice shop story is clearly a *topos* (which is not the same as saying it is necessarily untrue), the book auction narrative is not without embellishments, which render the account similar in sentiment to the former. Both stories posit Ibn Budayr's book as an undervalued and underappreciated work, serendipitously or miraculously appearing in a public place (spice shop, congregational mosque). An unusually curious *`ālim* (al-Qāsimī) or a sagacious expert (al-Jazā'irī) notices the manuscript and determines to save and preserve it regardless of the obstacles (the spice vendor dispersing the manuscript, the prohibitive price of the manuscript in the auction). In short, both stories satisfy all the narrative elements of a tale or a myth.

It is noteworthy that we have no evidence to verify either story. The only trace of an original copy is the Chester Beatty manuscript used in this study. As I have argued, this unique copy could have been that of al-Qāsimī's, however there are no clues whatsoever that the manuscript might have been owned by al-Jazāi'rī. But to return to the stories of the acquisition of the manuscript: though the report on the library auction may have a germ of truth in it, both stories intimate that a nouveau literate's work such as this was initially considered worthless—suitable only for wrapping paper at a spice shop or for auction at a minimal price at a book sale. Presumably, the diminished value of the work is due to the identity of the author: not a known *`ālim* but a lowly barber. But why does al-Qāsimī (or, depending on the story, al-Jazā'irī and in turn al-Qāsimī) save the manuscript? Is it because al-Qāsimī was interested in the work of a less privileged and less educated man? Is it because of some affinity that al-Qāsimī had for Ibn Budayr given that his own father was a barber? Ironically, it seems that al-Qāsimī's attitude toward the barber does not evince any such empathy. Despite the *`ālim*'s famed contempt for the haughtiness of the town's elites and the humbleness of his origins, his humility seems to have had limits.

Over a century elapsed between the time when Ibn Budayr wrote and al-Qāsimī edited his text. And it was not just any century, but one that brimmed with revivalism and reformist activities. Whether due to state-imposed reforms—like those of Muḥammad `Alī (d. 1849)[19] in Egypt or the Ottoman *Tanzimat* (1839–1876)[20]—or revival efforts by civilian actors, things changed significantly. Although state reforms are not irrelevant, what is of concern here are the reform efforts of al-Nahḍa, the social and cultural phenomenon of the late nineteenth and early twentieth centuries, a period characterized by deliberate efforts toward linguistic, intellectual, and spiritual rejuvenation.[21] Though not constituted of a single defined movement but rather of many ideological strands with various concerns and foci,[22] the Nahḍa can nonetheless be seen as a larger single entity because its participants were unified in their aim to effect an overhaul of society. During the time al-Qāsimī was writing, the movement for linguistic reform had already begun.[23] The motive for this particular aspect of the reform was not only the standardization of the Arabic language but also the Arabization of foreign words, simplification of syntax, and derivation of vocabulary for new scientific and social concepts.[24] The language had altered, but so too had its conduit. By the time al-Qāsimī was writing, the printing press had been thoroughly adopted and become the main technology for the dissemination of knowledge.[25] And Muḥammad Sa`īd was suffused with the thought and language of al-Nahḍa. He also kept up with the latest (printed) "scientific journals."[26] Indeed, he even produced a reformist son. Hence al-Qāsimī was *the* transitional figure par excellence. He straddled the scribal age of the chronicle and its various registers, and the print age of the newspaper and its Modern Standard Arabic.

CREATING ORDER: MUḤAMMAD SA`ĪD AL-QĀSIMĪ'S EDITORIAL INTERVENTIONS

In the prologue to his edition, after providing the requisite supplications al-Qāsimī offers the reasons for and intentions behind his edition:

> Most of the *Daily Events of Damascus* was written during the reigns of the two great *viziers*, Sulaymān Pasha al-`Aẓm and As`ad Pasha, who are the [more] notable of the great `Aẓm governors. [The book] was compiled by the noble (*al-fāḍil*) Shihāb al-Dīn Aḥmad Ibn Budayr al-Budayrī known as al-Ḥallāq [the Barber]. It contains wonders, and strange and extraordinary events. Due to the humbleness of its author (*li-basāṭati mu'allifi-hā*), he wrote it with colloquial tongue (*bi-lisānin `āmmiyy*). He exaggerated with the addition of words and rhymed supplications, which might bore the listener and weary the reader. So, I omitted the superfluous and kept the essence, and refined and corrected it as much as possible.[27]

Apparently, it is not the identity of the author of *The Daily Events of Damascus* that is of value to al-Qāsimī but the fact that the events took place under the rule of the two more "notable of the great `Aẓm governors." So it is the great among the great (the two most famous `Aẓm governors) whom the editor identifies as the subject of the book and the reason for its significance. The editor will frame and edit the reports on the `Aẓm governors in an attempt to habilitate them as main protagonists in the text and also as a source of Damascene cultural achievement and pride. As for the identity and the "humbleness" of the author of the chronicle, they are not just irrelevant for al-Qāsimī; they constitute a positive obstruction. According to the editor, the identity of the author determines the language and style of the work. Therefore the text is valuable because it provides information about great rulers (and other elite), but in its current form it is not publishable. So the worth of the chronicle is *not because of* but *despite* its author. For it to be suitable for consumption, the barber's text has to be mediated; it has to be abridged, refined, and corrected. The voice of the commoner-author has to be suppressed.

REINSTATING THE STATE: HABILITATING THE `AZMS

In a previous chapter, I described the disorderly aspects of Ibn Budayr's text. These are expressed in the author's overwhelming concern with social and moral disorder and also in the text's instability relative to the scholarly chronicle. Ibn Budayr's chronicle does not do what the genre of the chronicle generally does, which is to perpetuate the Islamic order. The barber's history does not make the state's annual rituals and rulers' reigns into regular reference points and organizing principles. It is a text that does not dwell on the regular and routine, but rather on unanticipated calamity and abrupt disturbances. Al-Qāsimī, not used to such chaotic and dramatic history characterized by a lack of gratitude to the state, attempts to normalize the text. Through omission, addition, framing, and minor reorganization, the editor reinstates the state back into the chronicle. While doing so, he habilitates the local rulers, namely, the `Aẓm gubernatorial dynasty. The result is a less querulous and less subversive text. Simultaneously, at al-Qāsimī's hand, the book of the barber turns from an urban chronicle of current daily events, *ḥawādith yawmiyya*, to a documentary record about the built legacies of the political elites of the time. In short, the text passes from the realm of news to the realm of *turāth*, that is, Heritage.

It is quite apparent that al-Qāsimī sees the representatives of the state as the appropriate topic of history and the Sultan's reign as its natural temporal marker. Recall from a previous chapter that the editor makes a significant alteration to the opening of the chronicle, which is worth quoting again here:

In the year 1154 AH [1741 CE], the governor of Damascus was `Alī Pasha of the Turks. This was eleven years after the investiture of our master, Ṣulṭān Maḥmūd Khān the son of Ṣulṭān Muṣṭafā Khān, may God support the throne of the state till the end of time.[28]

Let us again compare this passage to Ibn Budayr's original opening:

The first day of 1154 AH [1741 CE] was a Saturday. The common people [*a`wām*] were saying that a great earthquake will take place in Damascus as a result of which many places will be destroyed and men will turn into women.[30]

Though Ibn Budayr denies the rumor of the earthquake immediately after he makes this opening statement, he instantly follows it with the news of inflation and a list of ever-increasing prices of produce and staples. Then, and only after offering these two unnerving pieces of news (alleged earthquake and price inflation), does Ibn Budayr remember to mention the governor and Sultan:

At the beginning of the year, the governor of Damascus was `Alī Pasha, and the Sultan was Maḥmūd Khān, the son of the Sultan Muṣṭafā, and the reign was his (*wa kāna la-hu al-mulk*) for 11 years.[30]

There are two points to make about Ibn Budayr's mention of the governor and the sultan. The first is that such a declarative statement regarding the incumbent authorities is not a regular occurrence in the chronicle; nor does it open the text's annual entries. Rather, Ibn Budayr sees the reigns (and deaths) of high officials, albeit newsworthy (when an appointment or a death takes place it is recorded),[31] as not necessary for indicating the passage of time. In other words, the officials' authority is not reiterated year after year at the beginning of every year. Al-Qāsimī, except for the opening of the chronicle, generally follows the original version and does not forcibly insert the reigns of contemporary sultans and governors as an organizing principle at all annual entries. However, despite his general conformity to the text of the barber, the editor's treatment of these high officials is in political terms decidedly different from that of Ibn Budayr. This brings me to the second point about the passage above. Ibn Budayr's mention of political authorities is by and large devoid of celebration and usually does not include supplications for the longevity of the sultan and the empire. In contrast, in al-Qāsimī's version the editor offers prayers for the endurance of "the throne of the state" till eternity. In one instance, he adds, "may God keep this Ottoman state till the end of time, Amen."[32] Such warm feelings toward the Ottoman state are almost absent from Ibn Budayr's original text.

The reinstatement of the state into Ibn Budayr's chronicle by al-Qāsimī is even more striking when it comes to the `Aẓm governors of Damascus. One gets the strong impression that it is precisely because of the copious reports on the governors in Ibn Budayr's book that al-Qāsimī undertook his editing project. In his prologue, al-Qāsimī made the statement that Ibn Budayr's chronicle was "written during reigns of the two great *viziers*, Sulaymān Pasha al-`Aẓm and As`ad Pasha, who are the [more] notable of the great `Aẓm governors."[33] The reader's feeling of al-Qāsimī's strong interest in the `Aẓm governors is further reinforced by the editor's emendations of the sections that are related to As`ad Pasha al-`Aẓm's building activities, especially his famous palace and caravanserai. Not only does al-Qāsimī change the order of the narrative of the construction of the palace, but also he changes the intention behind the story.

In the barber's original version, the narrative of the building of the palace by As`ad Pasha is dispersed over several folios, given that Ibn Budayr was writing his history as a contemporary document—that is, he penned events as they happened.[34] The editor, however, aggregates these disparate episodes into one continuous narrative.[35] As he does this, he sometimes omits details that animate the barber's original passages and inform the narrative's aim. Almost the entire point of Ibn Budayr's narration of the construction is to demonstrate the conspicuous consumption of the governor, his unmitigated desire to own property, his greed in collecting and appropriating building materials, and the burden of inconvenience borne by the citizens of Damascus.[36] Although al-Qāsimī has no choice but to follow Ibn Budayr's narrative, he omits a few significant details. See for example how Ibn Budayr describes As`ad Pasha's preparations for the construction of his palace, which the barber reports in a partially rhymed passage, adding a dramatic tone to the story:

As`ad Pasha, the governor of Damascus, bought many properties: houses, orchards, and mills. He raised the price of wheat and barley while people were asking for relief and imploring for protection, but there is no one to help or guide the people.[37]

Compare how al-Qāsimī renders this event, which he does without the employment of rhymed prose:

As`ad Pasha, the governor of Damascus, bought many properties: houses, orchards, and mills, and other such things. This is before he embarked on building his house and caravanserai.[38]

Al-Qāsimī removes the comment about the suffering of the people and the dramatic tone in which it appears. He coolly prepares the reader for the next building project by As`ad Pasha: the famous caravanserai. But before we get to the respective reports by the author and editor about the construction of the latter building, let us visit one more instance in which the barber comments on As`ad Pasha's palace.

At the beginning of the year 1164 (1743 CE), the second piece of news that Ibn Budayr reports is about the persistence of price inflation in Damascus and "the entirety of Islamic lands." As usual, this is followed by a list of prices and a long complaint. The complaint is further followed by another grievance:

And the constructions of the rulers and notables of Damascus are ongoing . . . if a poor person wants to repair/build his house, neither builder, nor carpenter, nor piece of wood, nor nail, nor earth, nor tile, nor stone would be found for him. . . . As`ad Pasha diverted the water from the canals to his palace so that water was cut from fountains and canals. If one needs to do something or perform ablutions in a bathhouse or a mosque, he would have to bring with him a jug of water. This is something that our generation had not witnessed before and was not mentioned by those before us in Damascus.[39]

This is a clear indictment of As`ad Pasha, who selfishly monopolizes water and building materials, depriving the citizens of their natural "rights" to the same resources. According to Ibn Budayr, such imperviousness to the needs of the citizens is unprecedented. But al-Qāsimī, who is interested solely in the "great *viziers*," is bored by the barber's complaints and prefers to omit the entire report about the deprivation of the citizens. Though the editor retains the price list (which as will be shown below, he usually omits in other instances) and some of the earlier complaints, he decides to simply skip the whole passage and end his narrative with the curious statement: "to the end of what the historian said."[40] Al-Qāsimī—although he is not always able to avoid doing so—prefers not to present al-`Aẓms as excessive or unjust.

Let us now turn to As`ad Pasha's caravanserai and juxtapose the two versions. Ibn Budayr writes:

And in those days, his Excellency As`ad Pasha began building the caravanserai . . . after he had destroyed two caravanserais and some houses and shops, which he made into the single caravanserai. We ask God for assistance.[41]

In contrast, see how al-Qāsimī frames the fact of the building of the caravanserai (emphases are mine):

In those days of this year, his Excellency As`ad Pasha began building the caravanserai . . . *whose equal in the world is rare* (*`azza naẓīru-hā fī al-dunyā*). This is after he destroyed two caravanserais and houses and shops and made them into a single caravanserai *in this manner that is without peer* (*bi-hādhi-hi al-ṣifa al-latī la naẓira la-hā*).[42]

Ibn Budayr does not comment on either the beauty or the greatness of As`ad Pasha's building project. Indeed, the entire point of his statement is to complain about the conspicuous consumption of the Pasha and the latter's wanton appropriation of property. Significantly, the statement is followed by a plea to God for help. In other words, the barber views the Pasha's excesses as directly related to his own impotence and need for assistance. In contrast, al-Qāsimī relates the exact same facts but adds his own words, which contain a value judgment about the greatness of the building and deem it unequaled in the world. Thus, even though for Ibn Budayr the building is an indication of excess, for al-Qāsimī it is a source of pride. In short, Ibn Budayr's intention is entirely subverted. Throughout Ibn Budayr's treatment of As`ad Pasha's building projects (whether his private palace or his public caravanserai), he posits the governor as a Nemrodian figure, that is, a temporal ruler who indulges in impious excess.[43] For al-Qāsimī, these buildings represent great historical legacies for which the "great `Azm governors" deserve to be remembered. In other words, al-Qāsimī assigns the buildings by As`ad Pasha an entirely new meaning.

Given his partiality to As`ad Pasha, al-Qāsimī expectedly hates the archenemy of the governor, Fatḥī al-Falāqinsī. Indeed, al-Qāsimī hates the treasurer so much that the editor sometimes unabashedly inserts himself into the text to comment on al-Daftardār. After a report on the greedy behavior of al-Daftardār, al-Qāsimī cannot help but reassure the reader that the treasurer's end was nigh:

> The report about God's punishment of and anger against the mentioned al-Daftarī will come because: "God gives respite and does not overlook"[44] and "Deem not that God is heedless of what the evildoers work." (Quran: 14:42).[45]

Al-Qāsimī anticipates events and as well moralizes and judges through the addition, in one instance, of a proverb and in another of a Quranic verse. Such self-insertions by al-Qāsimī are not common, but they do appear sporadically.[46] Always a defender of the `Aẓms, al-Qāsimī's intervention in another instance reaches comic proportions. The report is about an encounter between the janissaries and the governor, As`ad Pasha. The latter was apparently trying to curb the janissaries' thuggish excesses. In reporting their defiance of the governor, Ibn Budayr, in his original version, quotes a statement presumably uttered by the janissaries in an assault on the governor's manhood. This formulation feminizes the name of the governor from As`ad to Sa`diyya: "They said, 'al-Sitt Sa`diyya' (Lady Sa`diyya) intends to deceive us and this matter does not frighten us."[47] Al-Qāsimī's rendition of this simple statement is slightly different: "They said, *due to their bad manners* (*min qillat adabi-him*) 'al-Sitt Sa`diyya'

(Lady Sa`diyya) intends to deceive us and this matter does not frighten us."[48] The insult to As`ad Pasha leads al-Qāsimī in retrospective rebuke to comment on the poor manners of those who made the statement. Al-Qāsimī was enamored with the `Aẓms, and it shows.

Al-Qāsimī's infatuation with al-`Aẓm governor may have held a contemporary value for the editor. Although al-`Aẓm rule of the province ended in the early nineteenth century, their power and influence as a faction in Damascus continued into the middle of the twentieth century.[49] It may be worth speculating that in the charged political environment in which the upstart, Muḥammad Sa`īd, operated, a good word about (and a pinch of glorification of) the `Aẓm governors may have gotten the editor "mileage" from their descendants, who were still one of the dominant households in his time.

But, to return to the texts: al-Qāsimī's intention behind his editorial project varies in significant ways from the author's original intention. For Ibn Budayr, the chronicle served as a platform for complaint about many things, including the excess and abuse of local governors. For al-Qāsimī, the worth of the chronicle is precisely its concern with the "great *viziers*"; his aim is *celebration* of their accomplishments, especially in the realm of building and architecture. For the barber, the monuments of As`ad Pasha were symbols of his corruption and ostentation; for al-Qāsimī the monuments were a symbol of greatness and a cause for celebration. By reinstating the state into the chronicle, whether through the alteration of its beginning or the reordering of the narrative while omitting some important details, the editor rehabilitates the `Aẓms, turning them from Nemrodian figures into Solomonic rulers. In other words, al-Qāsimī attempts to normalize Ibn Budayr's chronicle so that it may fulfill the requirements of the classical scholarly form: namely, the perpetuation of the Islamic state.

Concomitantly, the value and use of the barber's book changes as it undergoes adaptation in accordance with its editor's interests and needs. For Ibn Budayr, the chronicle served as a receiver and disseminator of current events and news, a public report of grievances about the calamities and afflictions of the time. For al-Qāsimī, the value of the book lay in its historicity. It is a container of events past. It includes reports about the governors' construction projects, the end result of which were sumptuous monuments, which still commanded the cityscape during the editor's time. The value of Ibn Budayr's book, then, is not what it told the scholar, al-Qāsimī, about the life and concerns of a man of "humble origins"; it lay in the fact that it informed about the monumental accomplishments of past Damascene rulers. (In addition, al-Qāsimī's attestation to the heritage-making power and legacy of the eighteenth-century gubernatorial family must have been music to the ears of the `Aẓms of al-Qāsimī's time.) At al-Qāsimī's hand, Ibn Budayr's chronicle is now a book on heritage. And in a book about heritage there is no room for lowly whiners.

"REFINING" AND "CORRECTING" IBN BUDAYR'S PROSE?

Surprisingly, though al-Qāsimī in his short prologue identifies language as the main deficiency in the barber's text, his corrections and refinements in that regard are not always necessary on the basis of language alone. The editor does correct grammar, such as adding appropriate case endings, standardizing the language (that is, using Modern Standard Arabic), and altering colloquial usages, but he does not do so consistently. Sometimes his "corrections" are superfluous and unwarranted. Many of his emendations are related to specific vocabulary items that are not a result of the author's "humble origins" but are due to the linguistic change that occurred in the intervening 100 years. Quite often, al-Qāsimī's emendations involve the Arabization of foreign words (in this case, Turkish) and glossing what seems incomprehensible or unfamiliar to the contemporary reader. Sometimes his editorial interventions are not about Ibn Budayr's incorrect language but rather serve to display the editor's own linguistic virtuosity.

To demonstrate how the editor alters the barber's language, I will juxtapose a paragraph from Ibn Budayr's original version with its counterpart in al-Qāsimī's recension. The excerpt is from a previously mentioned report on a parade of prostitutes celebrating the recovery from ill health of the lover of one of them. In order to be faithful to the Arabic original in both texts, I do not provide case endings unless they are visible in the text (for example, I do not add the accusative case ending to an indefinite noun unless the *alif* indicating the case is present). Let us start with the barber's version (the translation to follow is as literal as possible):

Wa mimmā ittafaqa fī dawlat As`ad Bāshā Ibn al-`Aẓm anna wāḥida min banāt al-hawā qad `ashiqat ghulām min abnā' al-turk fa-mariḍa fa-nadharat `alay-hā (sic) in ta`āfā taqra' la-hu mawlid `inda al-Shaykh Arsalān. Wa ba`da ayyām ta`āfā, fa-jama`at* ***shlikkāt*** *al-balad wa* ***ḥaṭṭat*** *sham` wa qanādīl wa mabākhir wa mashat fī aswāq al-balad wa dārū bi-al-qanādīl wa al-ghinā wa al-ṣafq bi-al-kufūf wa al-daqq bi-al-dufūf wa ***al-`ālam*** *wuqūf wa ṣufūf wa sārū wa hum makshūfāt al-wujūh mudalla`āt bi-al-shu`ūr madhūnāt al-wujūh wa al-nās tanẓur li-dhālik. . . .* [50]

It happened during the rule of the governor As`ad Pasha that one of the "girls of love" [prostitutes] fell in love with a boy from the sons of the Turks. He [the boy] fell sick. She vowed upon herself that if he were to recover she would recite on his behalf a *mawlid*[51] [in celebration] at [the shrine of] al-Shaykh Arslān. After a few days, he recovered. So, she gathered the whores of the city, and brandished candles and lanterns and incense burners and walked through the markets of the town and roamed about with lanterns and singing and clapping with the palms of their hands, and beating *daff*s.[52] And people stood still/up in rows while they [the prostitutes] walked around with their faces exposed and [were acting as] coquettes with hair [loose] and faces painted. And people were watching that. . . .

It is notable that the barber's version includes little colloquial vocabulary, but the syntax is sometimes demotic. This is indicated in the omission of words, the absence of which compromises meaning, but whose meaning nevertheless could be understood from context. For example, in describing the unveiled state of the parading prostitutes, he says "coquettes with hair" (*mudalla`āt bi-al-shu`ūr*) instead of "behaving provocatively with their hair loose." Ibn Budayr also sometimes uses terms in a particularly colloquial manner, such as his employment of the verb *ḥaṭṭa*. He uses it not in its more textual sense of "putting" or "positioning" but in the colloquial meaning of "intentionally exposing" or "brandishing." Similarly, to emphasize the public nature of the exposure of women in the parade, Ibn Budayr prefers to use *al-`ālam*, which literally means "the world," instead of "*al-nās*" (the people). When colloquially used, *al-`ālam* refers to "everyone" or "all the people" (similar to the French expression *tout le monde* or the English expression "for the whole world [to see]"). Some of the grammar in the passage is also colloquial. As an example, Ibn Budayr is impervious to gender distinction in the plural form of the verb. He uses *dārū* (they roamed about), the male plural form, instead of *durna*, the feminine plural form.

More than actual colloquial vocabulary and grammar, what gives the passage its colloquial flavor is the barber's use of rhyme. This is not rhyme intended to elevate the language to a higher register of Arabic or to display linguistic virtuosity, but rather to exaggerate and amplify. Listen to the cadence of the next sentence from the passage (noting the underlined rhyming words): *wa dārū bi-al-qanādīl wa al-ghinā wa al-ṣafq bi-al-kufūf wa al-daqq bi-al-dufūf wa al-`ālam wuqūf wa ṣufūf* ("they roamed about with lanterns and singing and clapping with the palms of their hands and playing *daff*s. And people stood still/up in rows"). Ibn Budayr is horrified by the behavior of the women and expresses it in the most dramatic fashion of ringing rhyme. Let us see how al-Qāsimī treats this passage (the translation that follows the passage is also as literal as possible, with the editor's emendations underlined):

Wa mimmā ittafaqa fī ḥukm As`ad Bāshā fī hādhi-hi al-ayyām anna waḥida min banāt al-hawā `ashiqat ghulāman min al-atrāk, fa-mariḍa, fa-nadharat `alā nafsi-hā in `ūfiya min maradihi la-taqra'anna la-hu mawlidan `inda al-Shaykh Arsalān. Wa ba`da ayyām `ūfiya min maradi-h. Fa-jama`at ***shlikkāt*** *al-balad wa hunna al-mūmisāt, wa mashayna fī aswāq al-Shām wa hunna hāmilat al-shumū` wa al-qanādīl wa al-mabāhkir, wa hunna yughannīna wa yuṣaffiqna wa yadquqna bi-al-dufūf, wa al-nās wuqūf ṣufūf tatafarraj `alayhi-nna wa hunna makshūfāt al-wujūh sādilāt al-shu`ūr. . . .*

It happened during the rule of the governor As`ad Pasha in those days that one of the "girls of love" fell in love with a slave boy from among the Turks. He [the slave boy] got sick. She vowed upon herself that if he were to recover she would recite on his behalf a *mawlid* [in celebration] at [the shrine of] al-Shaykh Arslan. After a few days, he recovered. So, she gathered the whores, and these are "prostitutes," of the city, and they walked in the markets of Damascus while they were holding candles and lanterns and incense burners while they sang and clapped and beat the *daffs*. And people stood still/up in rows watching them (the prostitutes) while they (were in a state of) exposed faces and loosened hair. . . .

Al-Qāsimī, by and large, remains faithful to the meaning, both in this instance and in most of Ibn Budayr's text. His linguistic changes are generally in the vein of glossing and explaining some terms. For example, he changes *dawla* to *ḥukm*. This alteration is probably an effect of language reform given that in modern Arabic *dawla* strictly means "state." The premodern sense of the term could denote both "state" and "rule," among other meanings; thus al-Qāsimī rightly changes the term to the usage that is more current in his time: *ḥukm* (rule or reign). Another interference is al-Qāsimī's gloss of the colloquial word (of Turkish provenance) *shlikkāt* (whores).[53] To this expression, he adds the explanatory phrase "*wa hunna mūmisāt*" ("these are 'prostitutes'"). Yet another explanatory addition by al-Qāsimī is related to Ibn Budayr's colloquial usage when words are omitted and meaning is to be derived from context (a characteristic of Ibn Budayr's text). Al-Qāsimī adds *sādilāt* (an active participle in the feminine plural form derived from the verb *sadala*, to "hang down" or "let loose") to Ibn Budayr's *al-shu`ūr* ("hair" in the plural) to indicate the state of the women walking about with loose hair.[54] Instead of the term *al-`ālam* (the world), which we discussed above as a colloquialism, the editor uses the term *al-nās* (the people).

But not all of al-Qāsimī's changes are necessary, even on his own terms. For example, both *ta`āfā* (Ibn Budayr's term) and *`ūfiya* (al-Qāsimī's expression) would be considered correct in Modern Standard Arabic. Also, his addition of "*fī hādhi-hi al-ayyām*" ("during those days") does not improve meaning or style. Similarly, al-Qāsimī's use of "*min al-atrāk*" ("from the Turks") instead of Ibn Budayr's "*min abnā' al-atrāk*" ("from the sons of Turks") does not constitute a correction or refinement. The editor's decision to use the verb *mashā* ("walk") instead of *dāra* ("roam about") is also uncalled for. In other words, contrary to his proclamations, not all of al-Qāsimī's editing decisions constitute corrections or necessary improvements.

Al-Qāsimī's intervention in grammar is sometimes, but not always, more essential than his vocabulary emendations. He appropriately adds the accusative case endings to the nouns *ghulāman* and *mawlidan*. One of his more redundant "corrections" is the adding of *lām al-qasam* (the *lām* of oath) and *nūn al-tawkīd* (the *nūn* of emphasis) to the verb *taqra'* (to recite), rendering it *la-taqra'anna*. Though the context of the verb is indeed that of a vow ("She vowed upon herself that if he were to recover she would recite on his behalf a *mawlid*"), al-Qāsimī's alteration to include the grammatical indication of an oath is grammatically unnecessary, even superfluous. Though al-Qāsimī, according to his own statement, is supposed curb Ibn Budayr's propensity toward exaggeration, he sometimes does not shy away from exhibiting his own linguistic flamboyance.

But the most puzzling grammatical interference by al-Qāsimī is his onslaught on the verbal nouns (*maṣādir*) in the text. Instead of keeping a gender-neutral series of verbal nouns used in the original ("*al-ghinā wa al-ṣafq . . . wa al-daqq . . .* " "[they walked around] singing and clapping and beating [the *daff*s]") he uses verbs: "*wa hunna yughannīna wa yussaffiqna wa yadquqna bi-al-dufūf.*" Admittedly, Ibn Budayr's usage is incorrect (from the perspective of Modern Standard Arabic) since he does use a verb to indicate simultaneous action (roaming *while* singing . . . etc.). However, al-Qāsimī's correction is severe. He could have chosen to correct the sentence by inserting just one verb, such as *wa qumna bi-al-ghinā' wa al-ṣafq . . . wa al-daqq . . .* etc. ("and started singing" . . . etc.). Instead, al-Qāsimī chose to change every verbal noun into a verb (*yughannīna, yuṣaffiqna, yadquqna*), which also required him to indicate gender in each verb. Though one is not able to ascertain the intention behind this particular alteration by the editor, its effect is rather significant as it serves to dilute Ibn Budayr's rhyming prose.

Compare Ibn Budayr's statement "*wa dārū bi-al-qanādīl wa al-ghinā wa al-ṣafq bi-al-kufūf wa al-daqq bi-al-dufūf wa al-`ālam wuqūf wa ṣufūf* (they roamed around with lanterns and singing and clapping the palms of their hands and beating the *daff*s while people stood still/up in rows)" to al-Qāsimī's "*wa hunna yughannīna wa yuṣaffiqna wa yadquqna bi-al-dufūf, wa al-nās wuqūf ṣufūf.*" Ibn Budayr's sentence achieves a balanced rhythm through a symmetry of verbal nouns and broken plurals (*al-ṣafq* *bi-al-kufūf wa al-daqq bi-al-dufūf*) and then reaches dramatic crescendo with the next phrase, which includes *wuqūf wa ṣufūf*. In al-Qāsimī's rendition, Ibn Budayr's (deliberate? and) balanced rhythmic rhyme is entirely undone. The editor not only modifies the verbal nouns (*ṣafq* and *daqq*) into verbs (*yuṣaffiqna* and *yadquqna*) but also omits the word *kufūf* (palms of the hands), which, though admittedly unnecessary, nevertheless rhymes with *ṣufūf*, *wuqūf*, and *dufūf*. Even if al-Qāsimī relents by allowing the terms *wuqūf* and *ṣufūf* to remain in the sentence, his interference interrupts the rhythmic cadence of the text and precludes its dramatic effect. More than language correction, it is the omission or dissolution of rhyme that is a consistent interference by al-Qāsimī.

Before we leave al-Qāsimī's treatment of language, it is important to note a couple of other editorial strategies that are not well represented in the passage quoted here, and that are of a "translational" nature. Turkish words and Arabified Turkish phrases appear infrequently in the barber's original version, but when they do appear al-Qāsimī translates them into Arabic. For example, as mentioned above, al-Qāsimī feels obliged to explain the term *shlikkāt* (from Turkish *şıllık*), which is still current today, by providing the synonym *mūmisāt*. In another instance, he substitutes the Arabified Turkish term *al-yaramāẓ* (Turkish *yaramaz*) with *al-ashqiyā'* (thugs or hooligans).[55] Similarly, he translates the term *sarkan* (Turkish *sürgün*) into *nafy* (exile),[56] and *ālāy* into *mawkib* (procession).[57] Interestingly, al-Qāsimī translates the term *shanak* (Turkish *şenlik*) to what is an odd construct relative to the original Turkish term: *a`māl nāriyya* (celebratory illuminations, but literally "fire works").[58] One wonders if this last Arabic expression—*a`māl nāriyya*—may have been a direct translation from the English "fireworks." Be that as it may, it should be noted that al-Qāsimī's Arabization of Ibn Budayr's text does not seem to be a strategy of political significance (say, an anti-Turkish sentiment). Rather, this is simply the language al-Qāsimī knew. In other words, it signals the success of one of the strategies of the aforementioned linguistic reform (undertaken by intellectuals and journalists): the translation of foreign words into Arabic.

The extent of the change of language is apparent not only in the editor's adaptation of foreign words but also in some Arabic vocabulary. Sometimes al-Qāsimī glosses what he deems to be archaic. For example, he explains the expression *`alāyif* by adding "*ayy ma`āshāt*" ("that is, salaries"),[59] and the term *tamassukāt* by qualifying it with the phrase "*wa hiya sanadāt*" ("and these are promissory notes").[60] This translation from Arabic into Arabic seems to also be an effect of the change of language over time.

Strikingly, sometimes al-Qāsimī's explanatory glosses supersede translation in the strictest sense. He translates Ibn Budayr's statement "the inedible bread" ("*al-khubz al-ladhī lā yu'kal*) to "dark bread" (*al-khubz al-asmar*), that is whole-wheat bread.[61] Although we do know that even the unprivileged considered whole-wheat bread unworthy and to be consumed only in the absence of alternatives, one wonders if the term "dark bread" is used proverbially by Ibn Budayr to mean whole-wheat bread (and understood by the editor as such), or whether it is al-Qāsimī's interpretation reflecting the biases of his own generation.

In exposing the linguistic alterations to which al-Qasīmī subjects Ibn Budayr's text, a few issues have become clear. When he is not bored by the subject and does not abridge and omit (something he does quite often), al-Qāsimī is by and large a faithful editor and attempts not to compromise meaning. However, it is also clear that Ibn Budayr's language is sometimes (but not always) problematic, even from the standpoint of postreform standardized Arabic. Though the editor does correct grammar and vocabulary, some of his linguistic alterations are in the vein of overcorrection. Other emendations do not evince linguistic incompetence on the part of the barber but are merely due to the change of language over time (in other words, it is the Nahḍa to blame!). In short, though it is true that Ibn Budayr uses colloquial vocabulary, syntax, and sometimes grammar, the editor could have treated it with a lighter hand. But more than the barber's "colloquial tongue," what rubs al-Qāsimī the wrong way is one of the main registers of the *Daily Events of Damascus*: rhymed prose.

ASYMMETRIES: DRAMATIC ABRIDGEMENTS

According to al-Qāsimī's opening statements, the "exaggerated expression" and the "rhymed supplications" of the barber are wearisome and boring. To al-Qāsimī, the barber is a complainer, and a rhythmic one at that. So, the editor simply cuts and expunges.

There are abridgements galore in al-Qasīmī's adaptation.[62] These omissions are various in length and content, ranging from brief one-sentence reports about a local event such as the death of an unknown girl[63] to a price list (in many instances),[64] to paragraph-long descriptions containing the news from neighboring regions,[65] to long passages the reasons for whose omission are not entirely clear.[66] Some omissions are quite minor, but these particular phrases in the original version are so important that they served as critical indicators in this study, as with the barber's charge against a hoarder from the ranks of the janissaries as "nouveau riche,"[67] which inspired one of the main concepts of this study; and the barber's statement that "everything has turned upside down,"[68] which is a title of a section in the previous chapter.

Among the variety of deletions, some of al-Qāsimī's abridgements are consistent and conform to his stated editorial goals, namely, the omission of "supplications," which we should read as "complaints" since supplications for succor usually come after complaints; and of the barber's rhymed prose, which not coincidentally is often the register in which the grievance is expressed. Earlier, I have shown how both grievances and rhymed prose are essential in the barber's original chronicle. In this section, I demonstrate the effect of al-Qāsimī's strategy of omitting urgent pleas and deleting rhymed prose or changing the latter into regular prose. These omissions imbue the text with a calmer, less dramatic, and stabler tone; yet they deprive it of its symmetric rhythm and balanced (albeit breathless) cadence. This program of expunging or suppressing critical elements in the chronicle further subverts or significantly changes the effect of the barber's intention.

As shown in the episode of the "prostitute parade," it is rhymed prose that lends Ibn Budayr's text equilibrium, even coherence. This characteristic is in ironic contrast to the general disorderliness of the text. Indeed, if Ibn Budayr's text lacks the banality, regularity, and orderliness of the scholarly chronicle, it achieves inherent balance through its consistent rhythmic beat. But al-Qāsimī insistently mutes the beat, thus upsetting the essential formal logic of the text. Let us revisit the familiar episode of the "minaret suicide." It is worth quoting Ibn Budayr's version again here (rhymed words are underlined):

*wa fī rabī` shahr Ramaḍān **armā** rajul nafsa-hu min a`lā mādhanat ḥārat al-Qubaybāt wa māta wa kāna ismu-hu Ḥasan Ibn al-Shaykh Yūsuf al-Rifā`ī fa sa'alnā `an dhālika al-sabab fa-qīla la-nā anna akhū zawjati-hi **jāb** imra'a ilā bayti-hi wa kānat min al-**dāyrāt** fa-nahā-hu `an dhālika wa qāla la-hu **aysh** hādhi-hi al-af`āl tutlifu nisa'[sic]-na wa al-`iyāl fa nahara-hu wa arāda ḍarba-hu wa kāna mina al-juhhāl fa-dhahaba ilā akābir al-ḥāra wa akhbara-hum bi-dhālika al-shān **fa-ma`yabū-h** wa shāghalu-hu bi-al-kalām li-anna-hum **ghāṭsīn** jam`an ilā fawq al-adhān fa-dhahaba ila jāmi` al-Daqqāq wa ṣallā al-ṣubḥ ma`a al-imām wa ṣallā `alā nafsi-hi ṣalāt al-mawt wa ṣa`ida al-manāra wa nādā yā ummata al-islām al-mawt ahwan wa lā **al-ta`rīṣ** ma`a dawlat hādha [sic] al-ayyām thumma **armā** nafsa-hu raḥima-hu Allāh wa `afā `an-hu.*[69]

On the fourth of Ramadan, a man threw himself off of the top of the minaret of the Qubaybāt neighborhood, and died. His name was Ḥasan Ibn al-Shaykh Yūsuf al-Rifā`ī. We asked about the cause, it was said to us that his wife's brother brought a woman of ill-repute to his house. He [Ḥasan] forbade him from doing this and said, "What actions are these? You corrupt our women and the children." He [the brother-in-law], being an ignoramus, chided him [Ḥasan] and wanted to beat him up. He [Ḥasan] went to the neighborhood notables, and told them about the matter. They shamed him, and distracted him with talk, as they were collectively plunged to the ears [with their own interests]. So, he went to al-Daqqāq Mosque, and performed the dawn prayers with the *imām*, then prayed upon himself the prayers of the deceased, climbed to the top of the minaret, and cried out, "Oh, Community of Islam, dying is better than pimping with the state of this time," and then, threw himself, may God forgive him and have mercy upon him.

This is a theaterlike episode. It contains instances of direct speech. A relative psychological depth is reached as the audience witnesses poor Ḥasan's escalating frustration. The story resolves with Ḥasan, rather dramatically—almost heroically—opting to end his own life in order to find peace from the prevailing moral disorder. The episode is further dramatized through the consistent use of rhymed prose.

In al-Qāsimī's rendition of the same report, the editor *omits all rhyme.*[70] Except for the last sentence of direct speech in which Ḥasan announces his intention to die, along with the reason for it, the editor deletes the earlier instance of Ḥasan's direct speech in which he rebukes his brother-in-law. The editor also cancels out the important detail of the reaction of the notables. Instead of "they shamed him and wasted his time with talk because they were collectively plunged to the ears (with their own business)," al-Qāsimī offers the rendition, "they ignored him because they were even more plunged." In short, though al-Qāsimī is, as usual, faithful to the meaning, he expunges the instances of direct speech that give the narrative a performative function, vivid details that intensify the situation, and the dramatic beat with which the story is delivered. In al-Qāsimī's text, there is no drama, no theatricality, just flat narration.[71]

In the foregoing narrative as well as in most of his text, Ibn Budayr adds colorful details that serve to intensify the effect of what is usually a distressful situation or a calamity. This brings me to the second omission strategy by al-Qāsimī: the deletion of complaints. A clear example of this is Ibn Budayr's narrative of an incident of a flood, in which episode the

> water groaned and growled, and flowed so fast that it swept away the birds . . . this is not to mention how swiftly and loudly the water had flowed, terrifying the young and the old alike, turning their hair white.[72]

This is a drama of suffering and distress, and this is why Ibn Budayr comes across as a complainer. Such "sketches" vividly portraying how people felt about and were affected by turbulent events in the city do not seem to concern al-Qāsimī. Let us visit a couple of instances in which Ibn Budayr expresses the collective suffering of the members of his neighborhood and examine the (non-)treatment of these events by the editor.

In the aftermath of a violent encounter between armed contingents in the city, the condition of insecurity was so intense that the vice-governor ordered the citizens to carry out a vigil to protect their respective quarters. Ibn Budayr describes the situation as follows:

> In the evening of Wednesday, the vice-governor instructed that the inhabitants of each neighborhood come out to the alleys and stay up all night. So, we lit up candles and lanterns and made coffee and stayed up at night while bolstering the gates [of the quarters] and sitting in the alleyways.[73]

Though al-Qāsimī faithfully reports the violent encounter preceding this story, he prefers to simply skip the event of the vigil, which he deems an unnecessary detail.[74] Another similar situation that Ibn Budayr reports regards a state of continuous alert and fear in the aftermath of a series of violent and bloody skirmishes in the city. He says:

> [During] the entire time [states of] dread would occur [and subsequent] closure [of the city] so that most of the [inhabitants of the] extra-mural houses moved into the city and the citadel. And [in] every neighborhood and quarter there were vigils at night [which people spent] awake, eating, drinking, laughing and playing [backgammon?] and [engaged in] distraction from calamities but with [the sense of] frightfulness and dread.[75]

This is a touching and honest report. Ibn Budayr's intention is to describe the intensity of fear precipitated by violence and by rumors of more violence. He does this while simultaneously relaying the human capacity to engage in amusing and distracting activities, even laughter, in the face of collective vulnerability and overwhelming sense of dread. This lively vignette, a transparent description of a Damascene predicament and the human emotions displayed therein, is in the eyes of al-Qāsimī entirely dispensable. He is satisfied with the abbreviated statement:

> [During] the entire time [states of] dread would occur [and subsequent] closure of the shops so that most of the [inhabitants of the] extra-mural houses moved into the city and the citadel.[76]

It should be noted that al-Qāsimī not only abbreviates the passage but also moves it to another part of the text. As mentioned earlier, this part of the story comes at the end of a series of reports of violent events, each of which is accompanied by a colorful portrayal of the predicament of the citizenry. Al-Qāsimī probably finds such portrayals exaggerated and repetitive, so he deletes most of them while reordering the text.[77] Indeed, such reordering and switching of events abounds in al-Qāsimī's text.[78] Al-Qāsimī, the scholar, is telling Ibn Budayr, the barber, "Enough! We got the point." In short, al-Qāsimī "shuts up" the barber and mutes his voice.

Al-Qāsimī's recension, then, is full of omissions of rhymed prose and episodes expressing intense grievance or dissatisfaction.[79] Despite his deliberate fidelity to the content in terms of events and meaning, the editor produces a text that varies in intention and effect from the original version. In his deletion of colorful and vivid details and passages, al-Qāsimī attempts to turn the chronicle of Ibn Budayr from one about the extraordinary and the calamitous to one characterized by relatively flat and toned-down narration. The result is simply an ineffective text. The adapted version is no longer performative. The breathless pace and urgent tone of Ibn Budayr's original content is perfectly balanced or complemented by the repeated use of rhymed prose, a register that gives the work a rhythmic quality suitable to its tumultuous content. The barber's use of rhyme and his reports of direct speech imbue the text with a theatrical quality that enhances and reinforces the dramatic nature of the events. In other words, Ibn Budayr's text achieves wholeness and stability precisely because of the harmony between a rhythmic form and a content of turbulence. It is rhythmic drama for calamitous times. Al-Qāsimī's omission of the main register of the chronicle results in an asymmetrical product. In other words, in an attempt to bring the stability of a scholarly chronicle to Ibn Budayr's text, the editor ends up upsetting or destabilizing its inherent balance.

In an earlier chapter, I described Ibn Budayr's chronicle as creatively hybrid and performative because of its infusion with the language, register, and content of the oral popular epic (*sīra*). The discussion of al-Qāsimī's editorial policies has revealed that it is precisely the elements of the *sīra* that the editor eradicates from Ibn Budayr's history. The epic qualities of the text expressed through colloquialisms, rhyme, exaggeration, and theatricality are significantly toned down. So, contrary to the statement by the editor, who claims to have "omitted the superfluous and kept the essence," it is in fact the very quintessence of the work that al-Qāsimī assails. Indeed, the editor takes out all that is epic in the book and also summarily eliminates its protagonist.

MUTING THE BARBER'S VOICE

It is worth reiterating, yet again, that one of the interesting characteristics of the contemporary chronicle is its capacity to include the self. I have shown earlier that the barber's authorial *I* presents itself as the narrator, witness, and protagonist. And because Ibn Budayr takes his role as a historian seriously and attempts to conform to the scholarly form by writing *tarjamas* (obituaries/biographies) especially of scholars and saints, he also inevitably inserts himself into these biographies as their companion, student, beloved, neighbor, and, naturally, barber. In doing so, Ibn Budayr fashions others in his shop and in his history, and fashions himself as a part of the community of Sufis and scholars. Al-Qāsimī, perhaps threatened by the very fact of the authority of Ibn Budayr, does not like the barber's "inappropriate" posturing. To the scholar's mind, the barber should know his station. So the *`ālim* undertakes to edit out most instances of the barber's appearance.

Of course, al-Qāsimī cannot escape acknowledging the authorship of Ibn Budayr. He does this by referring to the barber several times by name (which, it should be remembered, is rendered as "al-Budayrī")[80] or in statements such as "the historian said" (*qāla al-mu'arrikh*).[81] However, al-Qāsimī would admit neither the barber nor the authority that undergirds his authorship. The editor deletes from the text a number of references by Ibn Budayr to himself and his family: his place of residence while still a bachelor[82]; his having shared residence with a certain Muḥammad Ibn Makkī[83]; his moving his place of residence[84]; his moving the location of the barbershop[85]; his family trade as porters on the pilgrimage road[86]; his receiving a grandson[87]; the death of his son al-Sayyid Muḥammad,[88] and the subsequent explanation that his son was given the title al-Sayyid as "divine inspiration and without transgression"[89]; the visit to the shrine of Sayyida Zaynab with one of his sons[90]; much of Ibn Budayr's poetry[91]; the author's various complaints, including those about knee pain and bad memory[92]; and Ibn Budayr's verses about history, which were used as the opening quotation in the last chapter.[93] In short, al-Qāsimī obliterates from the text many statements that constituted clues about the barber's living and familial situations, mental and physical condition, aspirations for social mobility, some of his mundane activities, and even some of his thoughts (as expressed through his poetry). These are self-references without which I would not have been able to reconstruct the barber's life and social and intellectual biography.

Just as grave are al-Qasīmī omissions and manipulations of the obituaries included in Ibn Budayr's book. Earlier in this study, we saw the importance of the *tarjamas* in Ibn Budayr's chronicle. Not only do these biographies provide information about Ibn Budayr, his family, and friends, but they also constitute a strategy for the display and further acquisition of social capital by a proud barber. Sometimes al-Qāsimī omits entire biographies of people he deems unimportant. For example, the editor skips over the biography of a minor literati and scribe, `Uthmān b. al-Qudsī.[94] Also unworthy in the eyes of the editor are individuals who were crucial to Ibn Budayr, among them his teachers `Alī al-Ṣa`īdī [95] and Muḥammad al-Maqqār.[96] The latter was the barber's friend, a fellow artisan-historian, and the dispenser of useful supplications whom, in a previous chapter, I dubbed "the apothecary of remedies." Al-Qāsimī's most egregious omission, though, is Ibn Budayr's touching obituary for his own son, in which the father mentions the fact of the son's death by the plague and his talents, education, and apprenticeship in the craft.[97] To al-Qāsimī, the intimate proximity of these individuals to the barber and/or their influence on his life are not reason enough to keep them in the text—indeed, they apparently offer good reason to omit them!

When the biographies are of people whose social standing is sufficiently impressive in the eyes of the editor, he retains them. However, he never preserves them as presented by Ibn Budayr. Rather, he omits almost every mention of connection or association between the barber and the deceased. So in the adapted version we never learn, for example, that `Alī Kuzbar was the scholar with whom Ibn Budayr read a book of jurisprudence; indeed, al-Qāsimī does not even mention that Ibn Budayr read books at all.[98] Nor do we learn that `Alī al-Maṣrī was a teacher to the barber's son and had become a loving friend to the father thanks to the connection with the son.[99] Though Al-Qāsimī keeps the biography of the famous saint Ibrāhīm al-Jabāwī and the latter's habit of frequenting coffeehouses, the editor glosses over the saint's friendship with Ibn Budayr and visitations to the latter's shop.[100] Similarly, the editor transcribes almost verbatim Ibn Budayr's obituary of the Sufi Muḥammad Jabrī, but he conveniently expunges out of the passage Ibn Budayr's mutual affection with Jabrī and significantly the fact that he was the latter's coiffeur, hence the recipient and beneficiary of the saint's blessings.[101] Such omissions by al-Qāsimī abound in his bowdlerized version.[102] Hence most of Ibn

Budayr's convivial relations of love, companionship, and benefit with the scholars and Sufis, of which relations the barber was particularly proud, are simply erased from the text. In order for the reader to get a sense for and the effect of such alterations, let us take a few examples juxtaposing Ibn Budayr's original obituaries (two of which we encountered before) to al-Qāsimī's edition:

The first is of Ibn Budayr's cheering and cheerful visitor, "The Father of Happiness":

In Muḥarram, our *shaykh* and lover—counted among the dearest of our companions—Shaykh Muḥammad al-Azharī al-Miṣrī, known as Abū al-Surūr [the Father of Happiness], died. He was a great scholar and learned savant, unique in his age and singular in his epoch. May God, the Exalted, have mercy upon us through him and forgive him! Ours was an old friendship *(ṣuḥba qadīma)* and he had done us many a good deed. Among these is the fact that if ever he visited me while I was depressed or grieving, I would quickly be restored to happiness, and he would not leave until I was laughing. . . . [103]

Although al-Qāsimī here uncharacteristically retains the fact of Ibn Budayr's friendship with Abū al-Surūr as well as the latter's defining quality of good humor—he even adds his comment on the man as "guileless"—he does not mention the closeness of the relationship between the two; nor will he allow the reader/listener knowledge of Ibn Budayr's subjective experience of the *`ālim*'s humor:

In Muḥarram, our *shaykh* and lover, Shaykh Muḥammad al-Azharī al-Miṣrī, known as Abū al-Surūr. . . . He was knowledgeable, religious, and honorable. One of his virtues is that whoever meets him becomes joyful and happy even if he did not speak. This is the best proof of his guilelessness.[104]

In another similar example, this is how Ibn Budayr describes the famous scholar Muḥammad al-Ghazzī:

On Friday, the 20th of Muḥarram, our *shyakh*, our teacher . . . the scholar of his time, unique in his age . . . Muḥammad b. al-Ghazzī, the Muftī of the Shāfi`īs passed away. . . . I read Jurisprudence with him. We have not beheld any expression more pleasurable [than his] or meanings sweeter than in his speech.

And whatever poetry was uttered in his presence, he would be able to finish [the verses] and respond with more eloquent and better poetry.[105]

In his rendition, al-Qāsimī, in a fashion similar to how he treated Abū al-Surūr, retains al-Ghazzī's objective characteristic as an eloquent speaker but removes Ibn Budayr's expression of his own experience of al-Ghazzī's eloquence and knowledge of poetry. In other words, al-Qāsimī consistently *silences* the barber. Hence he omits the fact that the deceased was a teacher of the barber:

On Friday, the 20th of Muḥarram, the complement of notable scholars, the Muftī of the honorable Shāfi`īs, and the most eloquent of all those who spoke Arabic, Muḥammad Afandī al-Ghazzī, died.[106]

A third example is Ibn Budayr's obituary of the famous poet `Abd al-Raḥmān Bahlūl. The chronicler describes the poet's extraordinary capacity at composing chronograms, which the poet apparently put to good use in a eulogy to the Sufi `Abd al-Ghanī al-Nābulusī. In response, al-Nābulusī, probably the most important Damascene authority of his time, declared Bahlūl the poet laureate and dubbed him "the Shaykh of Literature in Damascus" (*Shaykh al-adab fī al-Shām*).[107] The foregoing report is retained in al-Qāsimī's version,[108] but he omits the sentences that immediately follow the obituary in the original version. Here is the omitted passage:

He was our companion, friend, and neighbor in the quarter . . . he remained sick for three months. We called on him and he was happy with our visit and he singled us out for his supplications. May God have mercy upon him.[109]

For al-Qāsimī, then, Ibn Budayr's interaction with Bahlūl, no matter how warm, special, or touching, is not newsworthy. It is only the elite and the relations among the more illustrious that are reportable. To the editor, the barber has no business mingling with such high-standing members of society. His shenanigans have to be deleted.

Although al-Qāsimī keeps a few biographies that relate directly to Ibn Budayr, such as those of his master barber (and the latter's relationship to the town's elite) and his mother, and of the popular epic storyteller,[110] his general strategy is unabashedly to delete the biographies of the humbler Damascenes, and to edit the barber out of the obituaries of the more select members of society—whether in regard to his social connections with them or to his having received education and blessings from them. So, though the editor is unable to entirely delete the barber from his chronicle because of the inescapable fact of the latter's authorship, whenever possible al-Qāsimī attempts to hide the barber's sources of social capital and his cultural accomplishments. In other words, his authority. This policy of *tarjama* editing by al-Qāsimī along with his tendency to omit most of Ibn Budayr's references to himself lead us to one conclusion: Muḥammad Saʿīd al-Qāsimī's has performed an operation of social castration.

On this note of the disempowerment of the barber, we have arrived at the end. Al-Qāsimī, in his opening prologue, states that his reservations about the text are of a linguistic and stylistic nature: colloquialisms, rhyme, lack of concision. These are the self-same elements we have shown to characterize the oral epic as a literary form. In extracting and eliminating these elements, the editor removes the essence of the barber's text as a hybrid of history and epic. In attempting to impose order on Ibn Budayr's text—through framing, omission, abridgement, and addition—al-Qāsimī realigns the chronicle to bring it closer to a scholarly form that celebrates high officials and the political and cultural elite, while taking away its theatrical and dramatic function. In so doing, al-Qāsimī effectively tries to reverse all the novelties that the fresh voice of the barber brought onto the scene of historiography. By editing out the voice of Ibn Budayr, whether these be self-standing references to himself or to himself as an associate of the elite, al-Qāsimī disarms the barber. The chronicle as adapted by al-Qāsimī is no longer Ibn Budayr's story; nor does it constitute a room of the barber's own.

By the time Muḥammad Saʿīd al-Qāsimī got his hands on Ibn Budayr's chronicle, the nineteenth-century reform efforts were full-fledged. The Arabic language had changed and been standardized, impelling the editor to feel the necessity to "correct" and even translate the barber's text. Also, the idea of "history" had changed. The barber's *tārīkh* was intended as a reportage of contemporary events, but for the relatively modern al-Qāsimī such a form of history was no longer current. The contemporary chronicle was now a thing of, and a source for the past. Indeed, the Nahḍa was by definition responsible for the birth of the modern idea of *turāth*, which is to be sought and recovered. So, what informs al-Qāsimī's interest in the Ibn Budayr's chronicle is an interest not so much in the barber but in the glorious past of his city, especially its "great" rulers, the `Aẓms, and their monumental accomplishments that forever changed the cityscape. It is thanks to the efforts of people like al-Qāsimī that al-`Aẓm rule in Damascus comes to be seen as having "generated a new sense of identity in the city and reinforced a style of life which was to be held as typically Damascene."[111] In other words, the scholar, al-Qāsimī, seems to have raised al-`Aẓm family on the shoulders of the barber, thus metaphorically reverting the barber back into being a "porter." It will be remembered that portering was Ibn Budyar's original family business before things "opened up" for him at the shop of his master barber in the heart of the walled city of Damascus. One wonders how many Florentine craftsmen and artisans had to be suppressed for the sake of making the Medici family famous!

Yet the barber's suppression did not happen through the same violence that brought an end to the life of the poor Friulian miller Menocchio, who was burned at the stake. It is thanks to the survival of the unique Chester Beatty manuscript of the barber's chronicle that I was able, I hope, to allow his voice to be heard more fully. I have lived with the barber's book—in two versions—for more than a decade and tried to the best of my capacity to listen. I ask forgiveness from Shihāb al-Dīn Aḥmad Ibn Budayr al-Ḥallāq, if I have attributed to him what he never intended.

Conclusion

From Nouveau Literacy to Print Journalism

I have dubbed the protagonist of this study (the barber) and his "sidekicks" (a Shīʿī farmer and his son, a Greek Orthodox priest, two soldiers, a Samaritan scribe, and a judicial court clerk) nouveau literates. "Nouveau" because their cultural wealth was newly acquired, and a consequence of a changed political and social landscape. This new landscape is exemplified by the rise and dominance of new local households, whose power allowed fresh opportunities for clientele and patronage. Each of our new authors, whether individually or as a representative of a larger community, found in this changed order a chance to gain and a possibility to lose. Thus, both eager and anxious, our new authors hoped to strategize and negotiate in uncertain times. To do this, they all employed the fact of their literacy. More strikingly, of all the Arabic literary genres, our authors chose to write in the same literary form: the contemporary chronicle.

Although it witnessed various singular appropriations by people outside the ranks of the *ʿulamāʾ*, the Arabic chronicle was historically bound up by the authority of Muslim scholars in their perpetual effort to bolster the Islamic political order. What is unusual about the phenomenon of nouveau literacy is the fact that so many people of so many differing backgrounds found in the chronicle an opportunity to write, and by the by insert themselves into history. It represents authorship by people who were not the accustomed subjects of scholarly history, and who did not habitually represent themselves in historiography. This is, then, a new kind of literacy.

What made this phenomenon possible is not only a reshuffle in the social map but also a literary form that was gradually let loose over the centuries. As the *ʿulamāʾ* ceased to conceive of history as a collective sequential exercise to be handed down from one generation of scholarly authorities to the next, the subject and the generic limits of history also changed. By the Ottoman period, the chronicle infected and was infected by other new and older forms. It now came in many guises: the Sufi dream book, the travelogue, the book of "companionship/friendship," and the diary. The chronicle became a current report of daily events. It was more focused on the mundane, more concerned with the here and now. The chronicle was the daily tabloid of local news. No longer preoccupied with previous authorities, it now turned to the self (or rather, to the events around the self).

Of those who did not miss the opportunity to represent the events of his city around himself is the Barber of Damascus, Ibn Budayr. He wrote a book of current events that documented a changing city. It was a city that was witnessing an overall "boom": an explosion in mansion and monument building, a bursting out of people onto picnic spots, and the bangs of gunfire from the rivaling going on between the janissary corps (and the roars of the occasional earthquake or flood). All of these "noises" were manifestations of the fault lines of a changing society, the tectonic shifts of a new `Aẓm regime. In other words, these were the disorders of a new order. Where there is affluence and efflorescence, there is competition and violence. In Ibn Budayr's text, we see the birth of a new Damascus, and a bloody one at that.

For the barber, the changing circumstances—whether the violence, the mansion-building activities, the appearance of prostitutes and women in the public spaces, or the involvement of people in the business of enriching themselves—reeked of corruption and moral depravity. For him, the changing order was nothing but a world "turned upside down." He longed for restoration of an idealized older order. So he used his chronicle to rebuke and tell off, to question and interrogate, to complain and whine, and to seek the help of God and His intermediaries. Ibn Budayr did so epically. Familiar with the rhyme and rhythm of the *sīra* stories recited in coffee shops (and possibly barber shops), Ibn Budayr turned his history into theater. He performed his censure and accusations, and he animated his pleas and indignation. Though the mixture of *sīra* and *tārīkh* is perhaps expected for someone who spent most of his life *in* a barbershop located *in* the elite part of town, what is remarkable about Ibn Budayr's authorship is not so much its hybridity but the extent to which the author positioned himself as his own story's protagonist. The barber,

Ibn Budayr, took it upon himself to be the interrogator and guardian of his society, and the moral compass of his community.

The barber's authorship of the chronicle allowed him moral authority, but also the freedom to use the *I*. And he used his *I* quite liberally. In addition to his helpless and self-pitying *I* of the "small people" and "commoners," Ibn Budayr had a socially ambitious *I*, which inserted itself in the society of the learned, among the scholars and Sufis of his city. Being a barber with a degree of education and penchant for cultivation, he seems to have been the favored coiffeur of the cultured elite. From them, Ibn Budayr learned the craft of *tarjama* writing and, in turn, used it as a tool for his own advancement. As Ibn Budayr fashioned his clients in his barbershop, he made certain to position himself at the center of their *tarjama* portraits. His chronicle is both a testament to and display of his social capital. The transparency of the barber's ambition to ensconce himself in the social worlds of the scholars and mystics renders him, almost literally, a nouveau literate.

It is precisely the nouveau literacy of Ibn Budayr and its manifestations, whether linguistically (the use of colloquial and rhyme) or socially (the display of elite connections) or politically (the anti-notable subversive message), that irked the scholar Muḥammad Sa`īd al-Qāsimī, more than a century later. Al-Qāsimī himself was of the nouveau variety. His own father was a barber who, when middle-aged, joined the ranks of the *`ulamā'*. Whether for the purposes of his own social climbing or out of sheer interest in his city's past (or both), al-Qāsimī undertook to edit the barber's chronicle and bowdlerize it. He did so by erasing all aspects of the barber's nouveau literacy. Through omissions, corrections, reframing, reorganization, and occasional additions, al-Qāsimī produced a relatively rhymeless, linguistically confused, politically complacent, and above all less authoritative text. By omitting the author's references to himself, and the barber's opinions and complaints, al-Qāsimī's recension is a book without author/ity.

Not all of al-Qāsimī's strategies are in the vein of the intentional suppression of a threatening nouveau literate. Some of the editor's strategies are a "product" of his own time: al-Nahḍa. This "renaissance" baptized Modern Standard Arabic as the appropriate textual language, constructed the idea of a past Golden Age, and encouraged the search for Heritage. For the editor, Ibn Budayr's chronicle, despite "its faults," was testament to a glorious Damascene past under the rule of al-`Aẓm household. It is perhaps due to the uncertainties of the modernizing Nahḍa transition that al-Qāsimī found assurance in the barber's work. The chronicle documents the pomp and clout of al-`Aẓm "great *viziers*," and their enduring mansions and public buildings. For the editor, this history is an archive, a reference guaranteeing the certainty and longevity of an identity to be found in a bygone golden time.

The shifts of the Nahḍa are significant, and Muḥammad Sa`īd al-Qāsimī is, in many ways, representative of them. He edited the work of a barber who looked to an idealized past and called for its restoration, but he produced a son, Jamāl al-Dīn, who looked to the future and called for a reorganization of society for that future. As Muḥammad Sa`īd "buried" a scribal chronicler, he gave life to a reformist, print-using son. Though the editor himself did not have any of his three works printed, his son avidly published his views in newspapers and journals of global reach. Further, Jamāl completed his father's *Dictionary of Damascene Crafts* and had it printed in Paris. Thus al-Qāsimī, the father, lived through interesting times when ideas about history and society were undergoing great transformations. He also witnessed the change in the medium in which these ideas were communicated: from scribal methods to print technology. These shifts lead us to ask the question of whether Muḥammad Sa`īd al-Qāsimī was a link between the "ages." Put differently, was there a connection at all between the barber's scribal chronicle and Jamāl al-Dīn's printed epistles? To answer this question, we need to think about the effect of the nouveau literates' chronicles and ask if nouveau literacy somehow facilitated the emergence of the protagonist of the Nahḍa, the print reformer/journalist.

I have mentioned several times that there is no evidence the chronicles of our nouveau literates circulated widely or even circulated at all. The fact that each chronicle survives in one or two manuscripts does not betoken large readership,[1] but neither does it preclude an *audience* to whom the works were recited orally. In other words, the chronicles may have had a listening public. This is especially likely in the cases of the barber and

Ibn al-Ṣiddīq, one of the Damascene soldiers in our sample. But even if the historian chooses to exercise extreme caution and avoid assumptions (as logical as they might be), the popularity of a literary genre could be gauged not only by consumption but also by production. What is interesting about the phenomenon of nouveau literacy is not so much that the chronicles were received but that they were at all conceived. It is striking that when seven "random" individuals from the Levant, who were not connected to one another, chose to exercise their literacy and translate it into authority, they did so in the same literary form. The fact of the production of these chronicles suggests that the genre itself—and not necessarily a specific example of it—was "in the air." These random authors were familiar with the form of the chronicle; hence it must have been a popular form. After all, the chronicle had become "user friendly." All it took was an observing person, who knew how to read and write. More importantly, these new authors wrote precisely because they envisioned an audience (with the exception of al-Makkī, whose text was conceived as a private diary). So even if our specific chronicles did not meet success, an audience for chronicles of nouveau literates did exist. In other words, despite the absence of evidence for the reception of our specific chronicles, their very existence indicates a larger cultural phenomenon, a general readiness to read/listen to chronicles by "random" authors.

The authority of these random voices in these eighteenth-century Levantine chronicles is the most crucial aspect of the phenomenon. Here, in a pre-egalitarian society, where everyone is supposed to observe his or her station, we are not in the company of the *`ālim* performing his traditional duty of "commanding the right and forbidding the wrong"; we are listening to a motley crew. Consider how Ibn al-Ṣiddīq, the janissary solider, exposes and ridicules the sycophancy of one of the most important Damascene *`ulamā'*; how Ibn Budayr blames the "notables" for lack of order and selfish enrichment; how Burayk chides Christian women for their impropriety; how al-`Abd, the other janissary soldier, describes the rule of successive governors as tyrannical and murderous; how al-Danafī presents his patron as one possessed by "complete manliness" despite evidence to the contrary; or how the Rukaynīs make the most disparaging statements about the Ottoman *dawla* and its representatives. These new authors dared to admonish, issue judgment, and proclaim corrective measures. The new "historians" did so as a part of keeping a record of "current events."

Under the guise of "event" the chronicle of the nouveau literate relentlessly located problems and offered diagnoses. The eighteenth-century chronicle, in other words, read remarkably like a local community newspaper. It informed the public of current events of both political and social import, and it contained severe admonishments, gratuitous advice, and urgent pleas to both fellow "citizens" and the powers that be. The chronicle clearly served as an expression of public conscience and consciousness. And who was its author? Not the *ʿālim*, but the "random" author. Are these nouveau literates, then, pre-print journalists?[2] Let us revisit the Nahḍa in order to understand the significance of the question.

One of the most noted aspects or characteristics of al-Nahḍa in Egypt and Syria is the explosion onto the scene of newspapers and journals,[3] and the rise of the figure of the journalist, columnist, or publicist. This figure is, in many instances, a reformer (whether Islamist or secularist or liberal), and the platform for reform is his journal and newspaper.[4] Statistics show that between 1828 and 1929 Egypt alone had a total of 1,486 newspapers and journals.[5] In the period between 1880 and 1908, Cairo and Alexandria alone produced 627 new journals and newspapers.[6] In a similar vein, a survey of newspapers and journals in the Arab World between 1828 and 1928 yields 1,615 newspapers and 971 magazines.[7] Even though the printing press was introduced at the moment of a state-impelled modernizing reform[8] in which new schools were established and "European expertise" became a valued commodity,[9] this exceptional—even passionate—and seemingly sudden involvement in print journalism cannot be attributed solely to state imposition or the encounter with the West. One does not deny the fact and effect of the importation of print technology and the significance of scientific missions to the West, or the seriousness of the intervention of a modernizing state, but the transformation wrought about by the Nahḍa would not have occurred without eager "citizenry." There was a social readiness or predisposition to plunge into the culture of print journalism, and an open space for the new figure of the public intellectual/journalist to occupy.

This wholehearted preoccupation with print journalism may be more readily explained through continuities in addition to ruptures. The continuities may have something to do with the phenomenon of nouveau literacy. First, both the scribal contemporary chronicle and the print newspaper are reports of current events that also functioned as platforms for interrogation and reform/reformation. Indeed, before the adoption of print, the chronicle happened to be the only written and public medium whose purpose was, like the print newspaper, to inform. (Otherwise, news traveled by word of mouth, or in private letters, or public oral announcements.) Second, the authors of both newspapers and chronicles are "civilian" actors, or "random" individuals. The breaking of the hegemony of the *`ālim* as the sole author of current (and even historical) reports, and his exclusive role as commentator and judge, was not an effect of the Nahḍa, but a facilitator of it. The arrival of the nouveau literates, well over a century before the "renaissance," paved the path for the emergence of the modern public intellectual. Third, the generic resemblance between the chronicle and the newspaper, where genre is defined by *time*, must have rendered the transition from scribal to print methods a process without much difficulty. Finally, even the reading and listening habits around the places associated with the scribal chronicle and the print newspaper were the same: they were both read aloud in coffee shops.[10]

Though I have been discussing the Arab Nahḍa, a contemporary Ottoman Turkish example is illustrative. Muṣṭafā Na`īmā (d. 1716) was a historian. He was the first appointee to the position of official court historian (*vak`anüvis*).[11] This court chronicler, strictly speaking, did not write history; his "duty was . . . to keep a day-by-day running record of the present."[12] In other words, Na`īmā's job was to write a contemporary chronicle similar to those treated in this study. Strikingly, the chronicle of the official historian, entitled *Ceride-i yevmiye*, finally metamorphosed into Turkey's first official newspaper, *Takvim-i vekayi*.[13] I am not proposing that the reincarnation of the scribal chronicle as a printed newspaper is direct and straightforward, yet the similarity of the role of their authors, and their use and function, becomes strikingly clear in this Turkish example.

In short, old habits die hard. Importations of technologies can be rejected, encounters with the other can be ignored, and impositions by

FIGURE 10. *Barbershop in Damascus. Source: courtesy of Camille Alexandre Otrakji, www.mideastimage.com.*

the state can be resisted. The adoption of print journalism would not have occurred if a culture for its use had not already been in place.

So, in accounting for al-Nahḍa, rather than seeing it as a moment of sudden radical rupture, a history of nonhistory, it may be more fruitful to examine it as a phenomenon with a genealogy. Instead of considering the introduction of print as an abrupt beginning that marginalized the "traditional" *`ālim* and undermined his hegemony, let us view it as a technology that was habilitated to both complete and discontinue preexisting patterns and practices. With the introduction of print, the appropriation of the chronicle was completed, but this time it was a fully transformative appropriation. The reincarnated printed version, the newspaper, rendered the chronicle eventually obsolete. Further, print changed the process of public engagement on the levels of time and space. No chronicle could achieve the "one day best-seller"[14] status of the newspaper. Few chronicles, if any, could achieve simultaneous readership in such far away places as São Paulo and Cairo.[15] Although the Nahḍa frenzy of print journalism opened global channels of communication, it is striking that after the adoption of the printing press no barber ever wrote a history.

Epilogue

Ironically, despite its overall "deletive" effect, Muḥammad Saʿīd al-Qasimī's edition is precisely the reason a barber's work became known and his memory survived—prompting someone like myself to look for the original unedited version. Aḥmad ʿIzzat ʿAbd al-Karīm's scholarly edition and publication of al-Qāsimī's manuscript in 1959 introduced the barber's chronicle to modern historians, but also significantly, it introduced the text itself to the medium of print.

The very same edition, whose readership was limited to the community of modern Ottomanists, has recently found a public audience through yet another medium: al-Qāsimī's edition served as the basis of the popular Syrian cable TV series launched in 2007, *al-Ḥuṣrum al-shāmī*, or *The Damascene Sour Grapes*.[1] The introduction to the first episode of the second season has this written introduction: "A hundred years have passed since the events of the first season. Nothing has changed in the general scene of the city except the names of the beneficiaries, and of the people of power and influence."[2] Although al-Qāsimī used the chronicle of Ibn Budayr as an archive of a glorious past, the contemporary producers of the TV series employ the text as a comment on their own society, seeing in it a genealogy *not* of a renaissance, but of tyranny. In other words, the barber continues to have his uses, and to acquire various afterlives.[3]

Toward the final stages of writing this book, the events of the Arab Spring started to unfold. I followed the news of revolutionary (in some cases, post- and counterrevolutionary) fervor, with both elation and distress, from Tunisia, Libya, Yemen, Bahrain, Egypt, and Syria. The difficult situation in Syria has unfortunately prevented me from paying a last visit to the city that I frequented with ritual regularity since I was a child. This book is in the vein of an *homage* to Damascus and the Damascenes.

Notes

INTRODUCTION

1. Cited in Michael Chamberlain, *Knowledge and Social Practice in Medieval Damascus, 1190–1350* (Cambridge and New York: Cambridge University Press, 1994), 139.

2. Cited in Dwight Reynolds, Christine Brustad, et al., *Interpreting the Self: Autobiography in the Arabic Literary Tradition* (Berkeley, Los Angeles, and London: University of California Press, 2001), 67.

3. Tarif Khalidi, *Arabic Historical Thought in the Classical Period* (Cambridge: Cambridge University Press, 1994).

4. Carlo Ginzburg, *The Cheese and the Worms: The Cosmos of a Sixteenth Century Miller*, 2nd ed., trans. John and Anne Tedeschi (New York: Dorset Press, 1989).

5. "`Ulamology is a noble science—at least we have to think so, because it is almost all the Islamic social history we will ever have." Roy P. Mottahedeh, review of R. Bulliet, *The Patricians of Nishapur, Journal of the American Oriental Society* 95 (1975): 491–495, at 495. Cited in R. Stephen Humphreys, *Islamic History: A Framework for Inquiry*, rev. ed. (Princeton: Princeton University Press, 1991), 187.

6. Shihāb al-Dīn Aḥmad Ibn Budayr al-Ḥallāq, "Ḥawādith Dimashq al-Shām al-yawmiyya min sanat 1154 ilā sanat 1176," MS Chester Beatty Library, Ar 3551/2, Dublin. I have found no evidence to confirm the statement of the distinguished cataloguer that the manuscript is an autograph; see Arthur Arberry, *The Chester Beatty Library: A Handlist of the Arabic Manuscripts*, 8 vols. (Dublin: Hodges, Figgis, 1958), 3:24. I owe the discovery of this apparently unique manuscript to Shahab Ahmed. Because the pagination was not clear in the microfilm copy that I had at my disposal, I paginated the manuscript starting with "1a." However, when I saw the copy of the manuscript at Chester Beatty Library, the first folio of the manuscript was numbered 24b. Because of this discrepancy, the citation of the images of the manuscript in this book follows the pagination found in the manuscript, while the rest of the citations follow the microfilm copy pagination starting with 1a.

7. Thus Ibn Budayr differed from Menocchio in that the latter was a literate miller who resided among a mostly illiterate peasant population. Also, Menocchio's problem was embodied in the Church and its practitioners, the clergymen, while Ibn Budayr, we shall see soon, admired the clergy (if the *`ulamā'* could be qualified as such). Indeed, Ibn Budayr was not a critic of the clergy but their mimic. Ginzburg, *The Cheese and the Worms*, 78 and 80.

8. As such, the barber's view in this particular instance is similar to that of the Friulian miller. Ibid., 1, 9, and 16.

9. Menocchio's audacity was of a different sort. He dared to profess heterodoxies, to speak against the Church and the clergy, and to envision an entirely "new world." Ibid., 77–86.

10. With regard to the media of information, Menocchio too was situated between the oral and the written. Ibid., xii and 33.

11. In contrast, Menocchio thought Latin a tool by which the "poor . . . are crushed." Ibid., 9.

12. Herein lies the starkest difference between the Damascene barber and the Friulian miller. Menocchio's utterances were recorded in an interrogation record mediated by hostile inquisitors who determined the subject and trajectory of his speech. As such, the questions in this study are quite different from those in Ginzburg.

13. It should be mentioned at the outset that the theoretical coordinates of this book are firmly based on a number of works and studies by various scholars and thinkers who are such an established part of the canon that they need not be invoked in the main text. Much of the social and literary analysis here is inspired by Roger Chartier, in *Understanding Popular Culture: Europe from the Middle Ages to the Nineteenth Century*, ed. Steven L Kaplan (Berlin; New York: Mouton, 1984), 229–253; idem., *The Order of Books: Readers, Authors and Libraries in Europe Between the Fourteenth and Eighteenth Centuries*, trans. Lydia G. Cochrane (Cambridge: Polity Press, 1994); Pierre Bourdieu, *The Logic of Practice* (Stanford: Stanford University Press, 1990); David Swartz, *Culture and Power: The Sociology of Pierre Bourdieu* (Chicago: University of Chicago Press, 1997); Michel de Certeau, *The Practice of Everyday Life*, trans. Steven Rendall (Berkeley: University of California Press, 1984); Hayden V. White, *The Content of the Form: Narrative Discourse and Historical Representation* (Baltimore: Johns Hopkins University Press, 1987); M. M. Bakhtin, *Rabelais and His World*, trans. Iswolsky, Helene (Cambridge, Mass: MIT Press, 1968); idem, "Epic and Novel: Toward a Methodology for the Study of the Novel," in *The Dialogic Imagination: Four Essays*, trans. Michael Holquist (Austin: University of Texas Press, 1981), 3–40; Gabrielle M Spiegel, *The Past as Text: The Theory and Practice of Medieval Historiography* (Baltimore: Johns Hopkins University Press, 1997); and Chamberlain, *Knowledge and Social Practice*.

14. See for example the following considerations of the Islamic genre of the biographical dictionaries as representative of the conditions of the *`ulamā'*: Khalidi, *Arabic Historical Thought*; Michael Cooperson, *Classical Arabic Biography: The Heirs of the Prophets in the Age of al-Ma'mūn* (Cambridge: Cambridge University Press, 2000); Wadad al-Qadi, "Biographical Dictionaries as the Scholars' Alternative History of the Muslim Community," in *Organizing Knowledge: Encyclopaedic Activities in the Pre-Eighteenth Century Islamic World*, ed. Gerhard Endress (Leiden: Brill, 2006), 23–75. Similarly, see how poetic elegies in pre-Islamic and the early Islamic period are gender-determined; Marlé Hammond, "Qasida, Marthiya, and Differance," in *Transforming Loss into Beauty: Essays on Arabic Literature and Culture in Honor of Magda Al-Nowaihi*, ed. Dana Sajdi and Marlé Hammond (Cairo: American University In Cairo Press, 2008), 143–184; and Dana Sajdi, "Revisiting Layla al-Akhyaliyya's Trespass," in *Transforming Loss into Beauty*, 185–227.

15. "States generally have an interest in ensuring the predictable and regular discharge of their functions, and this is why they employ bureaucrats to establish, document and even broadcast dates and schedules." Chase Robinson, *Islamic Historiography* (Cambridge: Cambridge University Press, 2003), 21. On the development of chronography in the form of lists of rulers, see ibid., 46–47.

16. On the marking of the Islamic calendar with the event of the flight of the Prophet Muḥammad from Mecca to Medina in 622 CE, Robinson exclaims, "[what] is striking about the early Islamic case is how quickly dating caught on . . . early Muslims came to agree that it [the Islamic calendar] should start with the Hijra." Ibid., 21.

17. This is admittedly a simplistic statement; much of early Islamic historiography was also associated with the advancement of various contenders to the throne along with the promotion of the different and conflicting branches of knowledge and their methods. However, it remains true that chronicles are usually associated with the state.

18. Of course, this means neither that the relationship between rulers and the *`ulamā'* was always a happy one nor that chronicles did not contain criticism of the rulers. However, on an abstract level, the relationship between the two prongs in Islamic society is of an essential nature.

19. The exceptional circumstances of the Shī`īs of Jabal `Āmil will be discussed in detail in a later chapter.

20. For the fact of different degrees and varieties of technical literacy in the premodern period, see Nelly Hanna, "Literacy and the 'Great Divide' in the Islamic World, 1300–1800," *Journal of Global History* 2, no. 2 (2007): 175–193. For the rise in popular authorship from the thirteenth century onward, see Konrad Hirschler, *The Written Word in Medieval Arabic Lands: A Social and Cultural History of Reading Practices* (Edinburgh: Edinburgh University Press, 2012), especially 175–193.

21. Aḥmad al-Budayrī al-Ḥallāq *Ḥawādith Dimashq al-yawmiyya 1154–1175/1741–1762*, in the recension of Muḥammad Sa`īd al-Qāsimī, ed. Aḥmad `Izzat `Abd al-Karīm (Cairo?: Maṭba`at Lajnat al-Bayān al-`Arabī, 1959). I am using the second edition, which is under the same title but with a study by Muḥammad Jamīl Ṣulṭān (Damascus: Dār Sa`d al-Dīn, 1997). The chronicle has been translated into Turkish by Hasan Yüksel as Şeyh Ahmet el-Bediri el-Hallak, *Berber Bediri'nin Günlüğü 1741–1762, Osmanlı Taşra Hayatına İlişkin Olaylar* (Ankara: Akçağ, 1995). There are two short studies on the chronicle of the barber, both of which are descriptive and based on the printed bowdlerized edition: George Haddad, "The Interests of an Eighteenth Century Chronicler of Damascus," *Der Islam* 38.3 (1963): 258–271; and Antonino Pellitteri, "Imagine Donna in *Ḥawādith Dimashq al-yawmiyya (1741–1762)* di Aḥmad al-Budayrī al-Ḥallāq," in *Verse and the Fair Sex: Studies in Arabic Poetry and in the Representations of Women in Arabic Literature*, ed. Fredrick de Jong (Utrecht: M.Th. Houtsma Stichting, 1993), 153–170. In his recent book, Eugene Rogan also uses the barber's chronicle: *The Arabs: A History* (New York: Basic Books, 2009), 39–40 and passim. Rogan seems to have been unaware of my previous publications on Ibn Budayr. Steve Tamari has translated Ibn Budayr's entry for the year 1162/1749: "The Barber of Damascus: Ahmad Budayri al-Hallaq's Chronicle of the Year 1749," in eds. Camron M. Amin, Benjamin C. Fortna, and Elizabeth Frierson, *The Modern Middle East: A Sourcebook for History* (Oxford: Oxford University Press, 2006), 562–568. For a comparison of the form and content of the several chronicles in our sample, see my "Peripheral Visions: The Worlds and World-views of Commoner Chroniclers in the eighteenth-Century Ottoman Levant" (Ph.D. diss., Columbia University, 2002).

22. Ibn Budayr, *Ḥawādith Dimashq*. Henceforth, in the notes, I will distinguish the published version by referring to the author as al-Budayrī (as opposed to Ibn Budayr) and the book as *Ḥawādith Dimashq al-yawmiyya* (as opposed to *Ḥawādith Dimashq*).

23. For example, Ibn Budayr, *Ḥawādith Dimashq*, 60b–61a, 64a, and 79a.

24. Ibid., 26a.

25. My answer is in emulation of a witty retort to a challenge posed to a modern scholar concerning the originality of the Quran. Apparently, the scholar was asked why he thought the Quran was really a product of the pre-Islamic Arabian environment. The

answer was, "There is just not enough camel in it." The camel is as essential to desert life as the ship is to the Homeric maritime context.

26. The best example is the classic study by Abdul-Karim Rafeq, *The Province of Damascus, 1723–1783* (Beirut: Khayats, 1966).

27. Ibn Budayr, *Hawādith Dimashq*, 50b.

28. Ibid., 35b.

CHAPTER 1

1. For the story of Salamūn, Ibn Budayr, *Ḥawādith Dimashq*, 25a–25b.

2. One of the first studies to explain (rather than merely note) this phenomenon is Rifa'at Ali Abou-El-Haj, *Formation of the Modern State: The Ottoman Empire, Sixteenth to Eighteenth Centuries* (Albany: State University of New York Press, 1991).

3. Rifa`at `Ali Abou-El-Haj, "The Ottoman Vezir and Pasa Households, 1683–1703: A Preliminary Report," *Journal of the American Oriental Society* 94.4 (1974): 438–447. See also, Christoph K. Neumann, "Political and Diplomatic Developments," in *The Cambridge History of Turkey*, vol. 3, *The Later Ottoman Empire, 1603–1839*, ed. Suraiya Faroqhi (Cambridge: Cambridge University Press, 2006), 53–54.

4. The rise of both central and provincial "notables" (*a`yān*) has been seen as the hallmark of the eighteenth century. For a summary, Bruce McGowan, "The Age of the Ayāns, 1699–1812," in *An Economic and Social History of the Ottoman Empire, 1600–1914*, 2 vols., eds. Halil Inalcik, Suraiya Faroqhi, Bruce McGowan, Donald Quataert, and Şevket Pamuk (Cambridge: Cambridge University Press, 1994), 2: 639–645. See also Carter Vaughn Findley, "Political Culture and the Great Households," in *The Cambridge History of Turkey*, 3: 65–80; and Jane Hathaway, "The Household: An Alternative Framework for the Military Society of Eighteenth-Century Ottoman Egypt," *Oriente Moderno* 18 (1999): 57–66. (This is a special issue of the journal entitled *The Ottoman Empire in the Eighteenth Century*, edited by Kate Fleet.) The classic essay on the notables of Syria is Albert Hourani, "Ottoman Reform and the Politics of the Notables," in *The Beginnings of Modernization in the Middle East: The Nineteenth Century*, eds. William Polk and R. Chambers (Chicago, 1968), 41–68.

5. The "excesses" of the family are best exemplified by As`ad Pasha al-`Aẓm (r. 1743–1757), whose new palace and celebrations are described in detail by the chroniclers of the period. See below. The *locus classicus* for the Province of Damascus in the eighteenth century and al-`Aẓm family is Rafeq, *The Province of Damascus*. See also Karl K. Barbir, *Ottoman Rule in Damascus, 1708–1758* (Princeton: Princeton University Press, 1980). A very useful description of the rise of al-`Aẓms is Dick Douwes, *The Ottomans in Syria: A History of Justice and Oppression* (London : I. B. Tauris, 2000), 45–49. The classic study on the province in the fifteenth and sixteenth centuries is Abdul-Rahim Abu-Husayn, *Provincial Leaderships in Syria, 1575–1650* (Beirut: American University of Beirut Press, 1985).

6. Ariel Salzmann, "An Ancien Regime Revisited: Privatization and Political Economy in Eighteenth-Century Ottoman Empire," *Politics and Society* 21, no. 4 (1993): 393–423; Linda T. Darling, "Public Finances: The Role of the Ottoman Center," in *The Cambridge History of Turkey*, 3: 126–130; Suraiya Faroqhi, "Introduction," in *The Cambridge History of Turkey*, 3: 11. For al-`Aẓm's connections to the *mālikane* of Ḥamā, see Douwes, *Ottomans in Syria*, 49.

7. "*Al-māl yajurru al-māl wa al-qaml yajurru al-sībān.*" The second half of the proverb translates as "lice pulls along its larvae." It is another way of saying, "the rich get richer and the poor get poorer."

8. For investments in *mālikānes* on the provincial level for the Syrian case, see Jean-Pierre Thieck, "Décentralization Ottomane et affirmation urbaine à Alep à la fin du XVIIIème siècle," in *Mouvement communautaires et éspaces urbaines au Machreq*, eds. Mona Zakaria, Dochchâr Chbarou, and Waddah Charâra (Beirut: Centre d'Études et Recherches sur le Moyen-Orient Contemporain, 1985), 116–178; Margaret Meriwether, "Urban Notables and Rural Resources in Aleppo, 1770–1830," *International Journal of Turkish Studies* 4 (1987): 55–73; and Abdul-Karim Rafeq, "Economic Relations between Damascus and the Dependent Countryside, 1743–71," in *The Islamic Middle East, 700–1900*, ed. A. L. Udovitch (Princeton: Princeton University Press, 1981), 653–685.

9. Thomas Philipp, *Acre: The Rise and Fall of a Palestinian City, 1730–1831* (New York: Columbia University Press, 2001); Bruce Alan Masters, *The Origins of Western Economic Dominance in the Middle East: Mercantilism and the Islamic Economy in Aleppo, 1600–1750* (New York: New York University Press, 1988).

10. The best study on al-`Umar is Philipp, *Acre*. See also Amnon Cohen, *Palestine in the 18th Century: Patterns of Government and Administration* (Jerusalem: Magnes Press, Hebrew University, 1973), and Douwes, *Ottomans in Syria*, 51–55.

11. Philipp expresses al-`Umar's style nicely when he describes the end of al-`Umar's career as he faced the Egyptian army of `Alī Bey al-Kabīr in 1770 (to be dealt with briefly below): "`Ali Bey al-Kabir . . . set the stage for the last of Ẓāhir al-`Umar's rule in Acre, five years which in human greed, hubris, and bravery, in dramatic, unforeseen turns of events, and in grandeur and catastrophe lacked nothing of Greek tragedy." Philipp, *Acre*, 41.

12. Thomas Philipp, *The Syrians in Egypt, 1725–1975* (Stuttgart: Franz Steiner Verlag Wiesbaden, 1985), 1–34. For the relationship between Christians and Jews, see also Thomas Philipp, "Jews and Arab Christians: Their Changing Positions in Politics and Economy in Eighteenth-Century Syria and Egypt," in *Egypt and Palestine : A Millennium of Association (868–1948)*, eds. Amnon Cohen and Gabriel Baer (New York: St. Martin's Press, 1984), 150–166; idem, "The Farhi Family and the Changing Position of the Jews in Syria, 1750–1860," *Middle Eastern Studies* 20, no. 4 (October 1984): 37–52. See also Rafeq, *Province of Damascus*, 19–20.

13. On the families of Damascus, the classic study is Linda Schatkowski Schilcher, *Families in Politics: Damascene Factions and Estates of the 18th and 19th Centuries* (Wiesbaden: F. Steiner, 1985). See also the discussion about the household structure and constitution of families with political ambitions in Margaret Lee Meriwether, *The Kin Who Count: Family and Society in Ottoman Aleppo, 1770–1840* (Austin: University of Texas Press, 1999). For the elite households of the towns of Ḥamā, see Douwes, *Ottomans in Syria*, 72–75.

14. Jane Hathaway, *The Arab Lands Under Ottoman Rule, 1516–1800* (Harlow, England: Pearson Longman, 2008), 14.

15. See Chapter 5.

16. Unlike Aleppo and Istanbul, Damascus has not yet received a monographic treatment that tackles public urban culture, which relates the literary, architectural, and the social. However, Shirine Hamadeh's excellent recent work on eighteenth-century Istanbul confirms many of my impressions about changes in sociability and public culture in Damascus in the same period; see Shirine Hamadeh, *The City's Pleasures: Istanbul in the Eighteenth Century* (Seattle: University of Washington Press, 2008). Given the relative positions of the cities, Istanbul being the capital of a huge empire, the changes in Damascus are on a smaller scale.

17. On domestic architecture and decoration in eighteenth-century Damascus, see Annie-Christine Daskalakis, "Damascus 18th and 19th Century Houses in the *Ablaq-`Ajamī* Style of Decoration: Local and International Significance," (Ph.D. diss., New York University, 2004); idem. (under the last name Daskalakis Mathews), "A Room of 'Splendor and Generosity' from Ottoman Damascus," *Metropolitan Museum Journal* 32 (1997): 111–139; Gerard Robine, *Palais et demeures de Damas au XVIIIe siècle* (Damascus: Institut Français de Damas, 1990); Stefan Weber, "Der Anfang vom Ende: Der Wandel bemalter Holzvertäfelungen in Damaskus des 18. und 19. Jahrhunderts," in *Angels, Peonies, and Fabulous Creatures: The Aleppo Room in Berlin*, eds. Julia Gonnella and Jens Kröger (Münster: Museum für Islamische Kunst, 2008), 153–164; Bernard Maury, "La Maison damascène au VIIIe et au début du XIXe siècle," in *L'habitat traditionnel dans les pays musulmans autour de la Méditerranée I: L'Heritage architectural, formes et fonctions* (Cairo: Institut Français d'Archéologie Orientale, 1988), 1–42; Marwan Musallamānī, *al-Buyūt al-Dimashqiyya, al-qarn 18–19 mīm* (Damascus: Zuhayr Wafā, 1979); and Brigid Keenan, *Damascus: Hidden Treasures of the Old City* (New York: Thames & Hudson, 2000). Although Stefan Weber's monumental study on Damascus is primarily focused on the long nineteenth century, he does include sections about the history of the city; *Damascus: Ottoman Modernity and Urban Transformation (1808–1918)*, 2 vols. (Aarhus, Denmark: Aarhus University Press, 2009), 227–246. On Damascene houses in the Ottoman period in general, see Abū al-Faraj `Ashash, "al-Dūr al-athariyya al-khāṣṣa fī Dimashq," *Annales archéologiques de Syrie*, 3, 8–9 (1953): 47–58; and `Abd al-Qādir al-Rīḥāwī, *Madīnat Dimashq: Kitāb yabḥath fī tārīkh Dimashq wa taṭawwuri-hā al-`umrānī wa fī al-funūn wa al-āthār al-latī ḥafilat bi-hā fī madā thalāthat ālāf `ām* (Damascus: n.p., 1969). This book is translated into English as *Damascus: Its History, Development and Artistic Heritage*, trans. Paul E. Cheveden (Damascus: n.p., 1977). Abd al-Razzaq Moaz looks at a specific neighborhood, Sūq Sārūjā, to make an argument similar to the one I am making for the Central Rectangle in the eighteenth century, "Domestic Architecture, Notables, and Power: A Neighbourhood in Late Ottoman Damascus," in *Art turc: Actes de 10e Congrès international d'art turc, Genève, 17–23 septembre 1995/ Turkish Art: Proceedings of 10th International Congress of Turkish Art, Geneva, 17–23 September 1995*. (Geneva: Foundation Max Van Berchem, 1998), 489–495.

18. For changes of elite residential patterns in Cairo, André Raymond, *Arab Cities in the Ottoman Period: Cairo, Syria and the Maghreb* (Aldershot: Ashgate, 2002), 160–162 and 256–258. See also Tülay Artan, "Arts and Architecture," in *The Cambridge History of Turkey*, 3: 470–471. For Istanbul, see Hamadeh, *The City's Pleasures*, 17–47; and Artan, "Arts and Architecture," 465–467.

19. Dorothée Sack, *Damaskus: Entwicklung und Struktur einer orientalisch-islamischen Stadt* (Mainz am Rhein: P. von Zabern, 1989); The Arabic translation of this book is *Dimashq: Taṭawwur wa-bunyān madīna mashriqiyya Islāmiyya*, trans. Qāsim Ṭuwayr, Nazīh Kawākibī, and Arynānā Aḥmad (Damascus: Institut Français de Damas, 2005), Map appendix 7 (I will be using the Arabic version throughout). It should be noted that Sack's information on the Ottoman period is based on standing structures and not textual references. As such, the comparison between the eighteenth century and earlier centuries may be slightly misleading. Having stated this, I note that scholars generally agree that Damascus witnessed an urban and cultural efflorescence, including in domestic architecture and interior decoration. Annie-Christine Daskalakis, "Damascus 18th and 19th Century Houses," 72; and Jean-Paul Pascual, "Du Notaire au propriétaire par l'expert: Descriptions de la 'maison' damascène au XVIIIe siècle," in *L'habitat traditionnel*,

387–403, at 389. This is also true for public buildings: Stefan Weber, "The Creation of Ottoman Damascus: Architecture and Urban Development of Damascus in the 16th and 17th centuries," *Aram*, 9/10 (1997–1998): 431–470, at 449.

20. Schilcher, *Families in Politics*, 13.

21. Ibid.

22. Shimon Shamir, "As'ad Pasha al-'Aẓm and Ottoman Rule in Damascus (1743–58)," *Bulletin of the School of Oriental and African Studies* 26, no. 1 (1963): 1–28.

23. Ibn Budayr, *Ḥawādith Dimashq*, 63a.

24. Ibid., 58b–59a and 60b. On al-`Aẓm palace see, Michel Ecochard, "Le Palais Azem de Damas," *Gazette des beaux-arts: courrier européen de l'art et de la curiosité* 13 no. 6 (1935): 230–241, cited in Rafeq, *Province of Damascus*, 181; and F. Daulte, "Le Palais Azem à Damas," *L'Oeil* 337 (1983): 62–63.

25. Ibn Budayr, *Ḥawādith Dimashq*, 58b.

26. Rafeq, *Province of Damascus*, 181–182.

27. Daskalakis, "Damascus 18th and 19th Century Houses"; Daskalakis Mathews, "A Room of 'Splendor and Generosity' from Ottoman Damascus"; Weber, "Der Anfang vom Enḍe." In her discussion of the topic, Hathaway characterized the architecture of the period as "al-`Aẓm style"; see her *The Arab Lands*, 108. It should be mentioned that both Cairo and Aleppo showed similar trends of a new style that constituted reworkings of older Mamluk architectural trends. For Aleppo, see Heghnar Zeitilian-Watenpaugh, *The Image of the Ottoman City: Imperial Architecture and Urban Experience in Aleppo in the 16th and 17thCenturies* (Leiden: Brill, 2004). For Cairo, Doris Behrens-Abouseif, "The Abd al-Rahmān Katkhudā style in 18th Century Cairo," *Annales Islamologiques* 26 (1992): 117–126. See also André Raymond, *The Great Arab Cities in the 16th–18th Centuries: An Introduction* (New York: New York University Press, 1984), 72–74. Schilcher is right to consider al-`Aẓm's social and cultural attitude that of "patrician cosmopolitanism." However, she claims that they were the model for later generations when in fact they were also models to other Damascene families in the eighteenth century, as will become clear in various parts of this study. Schilcher, *Families in Politics*, 35.

28. For example, the "Damascus Room" in the Cincinnati Art Museum is dated 1711–12; the "Syria-Lebanon Room" in the "Cathedral of Learning" at the University of Pittsburg is dated 1782; a no-longer-existing room from the Victoria and Albert Museum dated back to 1782; the "Syrian *Qā`a*" of the Jamīl Mardam Bek House is in the Damascus National Museum is dated 1737; various remnants of grand eighteenth-century rooms are found in the Pharaon House Museum in Beirut; the "Quwwatli Room" at the Kevorkian Center for Near Eastern Studies, New York University, is dated 1797; and the "Nūr al-Dīn Room" at the Metropolitan Museum of Art is dated 1707, among others. (See Daskalakis Mathews, "A Room of 'Splendor and Generosity'," 138, n. 91).

29. Daskalakis offers many examples of expressions of wonder by travelers who were awestruck by Damascus' natural beauty, Damascene domestic architecture, and the citizens' penchant for good living, see her "Damascus 18th and 19th Century Houses," 52 passim.

30. The treasurer of Damascus, Fatḥī al-Daftardār, also built a new reception hall in his residence; Rafeq, *Province of Damascus*, 150.

31. Muḥammad Ibn Kannān al-Ṣāliḥī, "al-Ḥawādith al-yawmiyya li-tārīkh aḥada `ashara wa alf wa miyya" ("Daily Events from 1111 AH"), MSS 9479 We. 1114 and 9480 We. 1115, Arabic Collection, Staatsbibliothek zu Berlin, Berlin. Because there are two volumes, when

relevant I will follow the title with "MS Berlin 9479" and "MS Berlin 9480" to distinguish the parts. The published edition is abridged: Muḥammad Ibn Kannān al-Ṣāliḥī, *Yawmiyyāt shāmiyya*, ed. Akram Aḥmad al-`Ulabī (Damascus: Dār al-Ṭabbā`, 1994). I will use both the manuscript and the published edition throughout this study. "Elegant furniture" is my translation of a three-word phrase that is difficult to decipher in the manuscript, the first two words of which seem to be *alṭaf athāth*. Ibn Kannān, *al-Ḥawādith al-yawmiyya*, MS Berlin 9479, 159a. Al-`Ulabī transcribes this as *al-ṭawanāt* (*yawmiyyāt shāmiyya*, 291), which does not appear in Muḥammad Muḥammad Amīn and Laylā `Alī Ibrāhīm, *al-Muṣtalaḥāt al-mi`māriyya fī al-wathā'iq al-mamlūkiyya:1250–1517* (Cairo: American University in Cairo Press, 1990).

32. Ibn Kannān, *Yawmiyyāt shāmiyya*, 13 and 170.

33. Ibid., 365.

34. Ibid., 172–173. This description is also mentioned in James Grehan, *Everyday Life and Consumer Culture in 18th-Century Damascus* (Seattle: University of Washington Press, 2007), 180 and 184.

35. On the increase in consumption in the eighteenth century, Madeline Zilfi, "Goods in the Mahalle: Distributional Encounters in Eighteenth-Century Istanbul," in *Consumption Studies and the History of the Ottoman Empire, 1550–1922: An Introduction*, ed. Donald Quataert (Albany: State University of New York Press, 2000), 289–311; Faroqhi, "Introduction," 16.

36. Hathaway, *Arab Lands*, 107. Between 1699 and 1780, seven new colleges were built in Damascus. See Stephen Edmond Tamari, "Teaching and Learning in 18th-Century Damascus: Localism and Ottomanism in an Early Modern Arab Society" (Ph. D. diss., Georgetown University, 1998), 55. For the increase in public buildings, Raymond, *Arab Cities in the Ottoman Period*, 225.

37. Sack, *Dimashq*, Map Appendix 7.

38. Raymond, *Great Arab Cities*, 51–52.

39. Rafeq, *Province of Damascus*, 150–151.

40. The mosque's decoration, however, is "profoundly influenced by Syro-Mamluk traditions," Raymond, *Great Arab Cities*, 101–102. On Fatḥī's connections to Istanbul, see Barbir, *Ottoman Rule in Damascus*, 86–89, and Hathaway, *Arab Lands*, 98.

41. That Damascenes had always enjoyed going out on picnics is attested in medieval sources. See Nicola A. Ziadeh, *Urban Life in Syria Under the Early Mamluks* (Beirut: American University of Beirut Press, 1953), 83.

42. Ibn Kannān, *Yawmiyyāt shāmiyya*, 452. My emphasis.

43. Dana Sajdi, "Ibn Kannan," in *Historians of the Ottoman Empire*, www.Ottomanhistorians.com, eds. Cornell Fleischer, Cemal Kafadar, and Hakan Karateke.

44. This is the cover illustration of Grehan, *Everyday Life*. Many of the coffeehouses were either outdoors or had an outdoor section; see "Daskalakis, "Damascus 18th and 19th Century Houses," 60–64.

45. Schilcher, *Families in Politics*, 15.

46. For example, in his topography of the Levant, Ibn Kannān writes the following: "And of the picnicable mosques of the city, is al-Bardabakkī. It is built on the river Baradā and it has 8 windows, two to the east, four to the south, and two the west." *Al-Mawākib al-islāmiyya fī al-mamālik wa al-maḥāsin al-shāmiyya*, 2 vols. Edited by Ḥikmat Ismā'īl (Damascus: Wazārat al-Thaqāfa, 1993), 1: 248. See also his statement, "And of the beauties of Damascus is Tunkuz Mosque and the Sufi Lodge attached to

it on the lower side. The river Banyās runs through this mosque, and there is no other mosque in Damascus in which a river runs." Ibid., 1: 249. For more on Ibn Kannān's descriptions of Damascus and his general preoccupation with picnics, see Sajdi, "Ibn Kannan." The charm of Damascus and the "amenities and establishments for personal comfort and pleasure" did not escape travelers (Daskalakis, "Damascus 18th and 19th Century Houses," 65).

47. Ibn Kannān, *Yawmiyyāt shāmiyya*, 486.

48. See Chapter 2.

49. Shirine Hamadeh, "Public Space and the Garden Culture of Istanbul in the Eighteenth Century," in *The Early Modern Ottomans: Remapping the Empire*, eds., Virginia H. Aksan and Daniel Goffman (Cambridge: Cambridge University Press, 2007), 227–312; André Raymond, *Arab Cities in the Ottoman Period*, 258–259.

50. The cemetery as a public space for all to congregate in dates back to older times; see for example Ohtoshi Tetsuya, "Cairene Cemeteries as Public Loci in Mamluk Egypt," *Mamluk Studies Review* 10.1 (2006): 83–116, especially 113–114. See also foreign travelers' comments about eighteenth-century Istanbul cemeteries as "favored areas for women's recreation and for prostitutes," Hamadeh, *City's Pleasures*, 283 n. 53.

51. Ibn Budayr, *Ḥawādith Dimashq*, 58b.

52. Mīkhā'īl Burayk al-Dimashqī, *Tārīkh al-Shām* (The History of Damascus), *1720–1782*, ed. Aḥmad Ghassān Sabānū (Damascus: Dār Qutayba, 1982), 74–75. My emphasis. This chronicle will be a focus of discussion in Chapter 3. Ottoman sartorial structure (as opposed to fashion) remains largely the same during the eighteenth century, but there is documentary and pictorial evidence that cuts of garments and sizes and shapes of headgear change dramatically in Istanbul. It is also noted that luxury dress items begin to be consumed by new classes in the early part of the century. See Hamadeh, *City's Pleasures*, 167–170; Filiz Çağman, "Women's Clothing," *9000 Years of Anatolian Women*, ed. Gunsel Renda (Istanbul: Ministry of Culture of the Turkish Republic, 1993): 256–291, at 258; and Charlotte Jirousek, "The Transition to Mass Fashion System Dress," in *Consumption Studies*, 201–241, at 209–210.

53. Burayk, *Tārīkh al-Shām*, 74–75.

54. Though our empirical evidence for the increase of prostitution comes from a study on Aleppo, it confirms previous impressionistic scholarship on Damascus. On Aleppo, see Elyse Semerdjian, *"Off the Straight Path": Illicit Sex, Law, and Community in Ottoman Aleppo* (Syracuse: Syracuse University Press, 2008), 105. See also, Abdul-Karim Rafeq, "Public Morality in 18th-Century Ottoman Damascus," *Revue des Mondes Musulmans et de la Méditerranée* 55–56, no. 1–2 (1990): 180–196.

55. Ibn Budayr, *Ḥawādith Dimashq*, 25b.

56. Ibid., 46a–46b.

57. See the discussion of the chronicle of Mikhā'īl Burayk in Chapter 3.

58. Sack, *Dimashq*, 53. Interestingly, there are no new great Christian mansions in the walled city in the eighteenth century. It is only in the nineteenth century, once the Greek Catholics successfully eclipsed the Damascene Jews as financiers, that the city witnesses the erection of new palaces in the Christian neighborhood; ibid., 92.

59. Schilcher, *Families in Politics*, 34.

60. The capacity of the al-`Aẓms to provision Damascus with wheat was one of the main factors for their rise and success to their gubernatorial position. Douwes, *Ottomans in Syria*, 49.

61. Schilcher, *Families in Politics*, 16–18. See also Brigitte Marino, *Ḥayy al-Maydān fī al-`asr al-`uthmānī*, trans. Māhir al-Sharīf (Damascus: Dār al-Madā li-al-Thaqāfa, 2000), 21–24.

62. Rafeq, *Province of Damascus*, 26–33. On the change of character of the Janissaries in Istanbul, see Cemal Kafadar, "Yeniçeri-Esnaf Relations: Solidarity and Conflict," (M.A. diss, McGill University, 1981).

63. Rafeq, *Province of Damascus*, 33.

64. Details are provided by Marino, *Ḥayy al-Maydān*, 21–23; and Rafeq, *Province of Damascus*, 26–35.

65. Rafeq, *Province of Damascus*, 150–151.

66. Ibid.

67. Ibid.

68. Marino, *Ḥayy al-Maydān*, 22–24.

69. Schilcher, *Families in Politics*, 31; Marino, *Ḥayy al-Maydān*, 24.

70. Hamadeh, *The City's Pleasures*. For violence and the janissaries in Istanbul, see Cemal Kafadar, "Janissaries and Other Riffraff of Ottoman Istanbul: Rebels without a Cause?" in *Identity and Identity Formation in the Ottoman World*, eds. Baki Tezcan and Karl K. Barbir (Madison: University of Wisconsin Press, 2007), 113–134.

71. See Hamadeh's chapter "In and Out of the Poetic Canon," *The City's Pleasures*, 139–170; Hatice Aynur, "Ottoman Literature" in *The Cambridge History of Turkey*, 3: 481–520; and Fikret Turan, "Synthesizing the Novelties within Old Structures: Voicing New Trends in Old Genres in the 18th-Century Ottoman Poetry," *Archivum Ottomanicum* 25 (2008): 151–171. On the poet Nedim, see Kemal Silay, *Nedim and the Poetics of the Ottoman Court: Medieval Inheritance and the Need for Change* (Bloomington: Indiana University Press, 1994), especially 57–89.

72. Hamadeh, *The City's Pleasures*, 159–167.

73. In the seventeenth century, a genre of history emerged in the vein of advice for rulers. This genre of *nasihatname* (Mirrors for Princes) has been the subject of many studies, but Abou-el-Haj's *Formation of the Modern State* remains a classic. The study looks at the emergence and development of the genre of *nasihatname* (advice literature, or Mirrors for Princes) as reflective of the socioeconomic and political changes between the sixteenth and eighteenth centuries. See also Douglas A. Howard, "Genre and Myth in the Ottoman Advice for Kings Literature," in *Early Modern Ottoman World*, 137–166; Carter Vaughn Findley, "Political Culture and the Great Households," 71–73; and Rhoads Murphey, *Essays on Ottoman Historians and Historiography* (Istanbul: Eren, 2009), 121–142. Studies that are not particularly focused on advice literature in Ottoman Historiography are Gabriel Piterberg, *An Ottoman Tragedy: History and Historiography at Play* (Berkeley: University of California Press, 2003); and Murphey, *Essays on Ottoman Historians*, especially "Ottoman Historical Writing in the Seventeenth Century: A Survey of the General Development of the Genre after the Reign of Sultan Ahmed I," 89–119.

74. Lewis V Thomas, *A Study of Naima*, ed. Norman Itzkowitz (New York: New York University Press, 1972), 36–42.

75. Baki Tezcan, "The Politics of Early Modern Ottoman Historiography," in *Early Modern Ottomans*, 167–198, especially 180–196.

76. Tezcan, "Politics of Early Modern Ottoman Historiography," 192–193.

77. This will be a subject of discussion in Chapter 4.

78. Edhem Eldem, "Urban Voices from Beyond: Identity, Status and Social Strategies in Ottoman Funerary Epitaphs of Istanbul (1700–1850)," *Early Modern Ottomans*, 233–255, at 239–240.

79. Nelly Hanna, *In Praise of Books: A Cultural History of Cairo's Middle Class, Sixteenth to the Eighteenth Century* (Syracuse: Syracuse University Press, 2003).

80. Ibid., 128–136.

81. Ibid., 140.

82. As per the subtitle of her book: *In Praise of Books: A Cultural History of Cairo's Middle Class.*

83. Hamadeh, *The City's Pleasures*, 79. See also Artan, "Arts and Architecture," 471–473. For Cairo, see Raymond, *Arab Cities in the Ottoman Period*, 255–256.

84. Hamadeh, *The City's Pleasures*, 79.

85. Ibid., 81. My emphasis.

86. Ibid., 256.

87. It is significant that the eighteenth century was the age of "free-standing libraries" both in Istanbul and in some of the provinces; "small-scale, often autonomous library buildings were easily recognisable" (Artan, "Art and architecture," 471). To the best of my knowledge, the Syrian provinces did not witness the same phenomenon. Egypt, on the other hand, saw the proliferation of private book collections (not necessarily library buildings as such); Hanna, *In Praise of Books*, 85–86.

CHAPTER 2

1. Schilcher, *Families in Politics*, 16. See the detailed description of the area, 12–14.

2. Cairo seems to have also been characterized by a geographical concentration of elite colleges. See Carl Petry, *The Civilian Elite of Cairo in the Later Middle Ages* (Princeton: Princeton University Press, 1981), 160; and idem., "Educational Institutions as Depicted in the Biographical Literature of Mamluk Cairo: The Debate over Prestige and Venue," *Medieval Prosopography*, 23 (2002): 101–123, especially 106–108.

3. It is on the death of his second cousin that Ibn Budayr mentions his family business: "the son of my cousin, al-Sayyid Aḥmad, known as Ibn al-Bawārishī, died. He stood on Mount `Arafāt 51 times, may God have mercy on him. He used to carry pilgrims on the Syrian pilgrimage route. His father, al-Sayyid Muḥammad [did the same work] prior to him, so did our grandfather, and our father." Ibn Budayr, *Ḥawādith Dimashq*, 44a–44b. According to the late nineteenth-century dictionary of arts and crafts of Damascus composed by Muḥammad Sa'īd al-Qāsimī, *`akkāmūn* were hired by camel entrepreneurs (*muqawwimūn*) during the pilgrimage season to accompany and attend to both the camel and the pilgrim-traveler. Muḥammad Sa`īd al-Qāsimī, *Qāmūs al-ṣinā`āt al-shāmiyya*, compiled with Jamāl al-Dīn al-Qāsimī and Khalīl al-`Aẓm, edited by Ẓāfir al-Qāsimī (Damascus: Dār Ḥlās, 1988), under "`akkām," 318–319. On the camel entrepreneurs, see ibid., "muqawwim," 465; and "shayyāl," 263. See also Suraiya Faroqhi, *Pilgrims and Sultans: The Ḥajj under the Ottomans* (London: I. B. Tauris, 1994), 48–51.

4. Ibn Budayr's express mention of the number of times that his second cousin went on pilgrimage betrays pride in the fact. See note above.

5. Ibn Budayr, *Ḥawādith Dimashq*, 23b–24a.

6. Schilcher, *Families in Politics*, 16–19.

7. Colette Establet and Jean-Paul Pascual, *Familles et fortunes à Damas : 450 foyers damascains en 1700* (Damascus: Institut Français de Damas, 1994), 139.

8. "We had bought a new house in Ta`dīl, so we were constrained in those days"; Ibn Budayr, *Ḥawādith Dimashq*, 5b.

9. Too numerous to cite, but a few examples are ibid., 2a–2b, 51a–51b, 56a.

10. ". . . I worked at his shop in the craft of barbership and met with goodness and blessing. It is thanks to him that things opened up to me." Ibid., 7a–7b.

11. Establet and Pascual, *Familles et fortunes*, 179–187.

12. Al-Qāsimī, *Qāmūs al-ṣinā`āt*, "`akkām," 318.

13. Faroqhi, *Pilgrims and Sultans*, 54–73.

14. Al-Qāsimī mentions that barbering is "one of the most common professions"; *Qāmūs al-ṣinā`āt*, "Ḥallāq," 104.

15. Ibid., 103–104; and "Ḥajjām," 92–93.

16. Bernard Heykal, "Dissembling Descent, or How the Barber Lost His Turban: Identity and Evidence in Eighteenth-Century Zaydī Yemen," *Islamic Society and Law* 9.2 (2002): 205–206. See also *Encyclopaedia of Islam*, 2nd ed., *s.v.* "Ḥallāḳ" (by M.A.J. Beg).

17. The scholarship on artisans and guilds is a fast-growing field in Ottoman studies. For a recent review of the scholarship on guilds in Syria and Egypt, see Nelly Hanna, "Guilds in Recent Historical Scholarship," in *The City in the Islamic World*, ed. Renata Holod, Attilio Petruccioli, and André Raymond, 2 vols. (Leiden: Brill, 2008), 2: 895–920. However, the locus classicus is André Raymond, *Artisans et commerçants au Caire au XVIIIe siècle* (Damascus: Institut Français de Damas, 1973). Burçak Evren and especially Suraiya Faroqhi have written a lot on the topic. See Burçak Evren, *Osmanlı esnafı* (Istanbul: Doğan Kitapçılık, 1999); and idem., *Osmanlı'da esnaf ve örgütleri* (Istanbul: n.p., 1997). Suraiya Faroqhi, *Artisans of Empire: Crafts and Craftspeople Under the Ottomans* (London: I. B. Tauris, 2009); and idem. with Randi Deguilhem, eds., *Crafts and Craftsmen of the Middle East: Fashioning the Individual in the Muslim Mediterranean* (London: I. B. Tauris, 2005). See also Eunjeong Yi, *Guild Dynamics in Seventeenth-Century Istanbul: Fluidity and Leverage*, (Leiden: Brill, 2004). For Syria, Amnon Cohen, *The Guilds of Ottoman Jerusalem* (Leiden: Brill, 2001); Charles L Wilkins, *Forging Urban Solidarities: Ottoman Aleppo 1640–1700* (Leiden: Brill, 2010), 205–286; Abdul-Karim Rafeq, "Craft Organizations and Religious Communities in Ottoman Syria (16th–18th Centuries)," in *Convegno sul tema: La Shi`a nell'impero Ottomano (Roma, 15 aprile 1991)*, (Rome: Accademia nazionale dei Lincei, 1993), 25–56; idem., "Law-Court Registers of Damascus, with Special Reference to Craft-Corporations during the First Half of the Eighteenth Century," in *Les Arabes par leurs archives : XVIe–XXe siècles*, eds. Jacques Berque and Dominique Chevallier, 555 (Paris: CNRS, 1976); and Abraham Marcus, *The Middle East on the Eve of Modernity: Aleppo in the Eighteenth Century* (New York: Columbia University Press, 1989), 162–194.

18. Gabriel Baer, *Egyptian Guilds in Modern Times* (Jerusalem: Israel Oriental Society, 1964), 38–39; and Ira M Lapidus, *Muslim Cities in the Later Middle Ages* (Cambridge: Cambridge University Press, 1984), 82–83.

19. Al-Qāsimī, *Qāmūs al-ṣinā`āt*, 103–104. A couple of caveats about al-Qāsimī's information need to be stated. First, he was writing in the late nineteenth century, a good hundred years later than the period in question. Second, the author may be a little prejudiced by the fact that he himself was a son of a barber, and hence his description may have arisen out of defensiveness. Interestingly, even though al-Qāsimī associates barbering with cupping and bloodletting, he sees cupping (not barbering) as "without honor" (*laysa bi-sharīf*). This is in contradistinction to those professions that he categorizes as "with honor" or positively "base" (*danī'*), ibid., 28–29.

20. Ibn Budayr, *Ḥawādith Dimashq*, 7a–b.

21. On `Abd al-Ghanī al-Nābulusī, see Barbara Rosenow von Schlegell, "Sufism in the Ottoman Arab World Arab World: Shaykh 'Abd al-Ghanī al-Nābulusī (d. 1143/1731)" (Ph. D. diss., University of California, Berkeley, 1997); Elizabeth Sirriyeh, *Sufi Visionary of Ottoman Damascus: 'Abd al-Ghanī al-Nābulusī, 1641–1731* (London: Routledge Curzon, 2005); and Samer Akkach, *`Abd al-Ghani al-Nabulusi: Islam and the Enlightenment* (Oxford: Oneworld, 2007).

22. Al-Shaykh Murād al-Kasīḥ (d. 1720) is the eponymous founder of the Murādīs, the most influential scholarly family in Damascus; see Karl Barbir, "All in the Family: The Muradis of Damascus," *Archivum Ottomanicum* 6 (1980): 327–353.

23. For the Shāfi`ī jurist, Muḥammad al-`Ajlūnī, see Muḥammad Khalīl al-Murādī, *Silk al-durar fī a`yān al-qarn al-thānī `āshar*, 4 vols. (Cairo: Dar al-Kitāb al-Islāmī, n.d.), 4: 38–39.

24. Ibn Budayr, *Ḥawādith Dimashq*, 7a–7b.

25. After 1754, Ibn Budayr moved his shop first shortly to Sūq al-Darwīshiyya, and then to Sūq al-Sinānіyya. Between 1754 and 1762, which is the last entry in the chronicle, there is no mention of further moves; ibid., 76b and 77b, respectively. Both of the aforementioned markets were immediately outside the city walls in "localist" areas according to Schilcher, *Families in Politics*, 16 and 214.

26. Between 1741, the year the chronicle begins, and 1754.

27. Personal communication to me by Shahab Ahmad, who learned this in a conversation with the current overseer of *awqāf* (Islamic public endowments) in Fez. For a concept of literacy that avoids the polarity between technical literacy and illiteracy, see Hanna, "Literacy and the 'Great Divide'," 175–193.

28. Ibn Budayr, *Ḥawādith Dimashq*, 27a.

29. Ibid., 16b.

30. Aḥmad al-Sābiq seems to have been especially celebrated as a poet rather than for his knowledge in the religious sciences. Al-Murādī also records that he was a Sufi, and that he wrote an abridgment of Jalāl al-Dīn al-Suyūṭī's *al-Itqān fī-`ulūm al-Qur'ān* ("Perfection in the Science of the Qu'rān") See *Silk al-durar*, 1:179–181.

31. Ibn Budayr, *Ḥawādith Dimashq*, 76a.

32. Schilcher, *Families in Politics*, 169–174.

33. Ibn Budayr, *Ḥawādith Dimashq*, 76a. For al-Ghazzī, see al-Murādī, *Silk al-durar*, 4: 53–58.

34. Ibn Budayr, *Ḥawādith Dimashq*, 69a–6b. `Alī b. Aḥmad b. `Alī, known as Ibn Kuzbar, has his own entry in *Silk al-durar*, 3: 205, where he is introduced by al-Murādī with the titles "the magnanimous imam, the Proof, the Journey/Reference, the Blessing, the erudite *`ālim*, the teacher of Quran" and described as "one of the best and most famous scholars and jurists of Damascus and an outstanding master of many fields of learning." On `Alī Kuzbar and his family, see Schilcher, *Families in Politics*, 207–209.

35. Schilcher, *Families in Politics*, 207.

36. Ibn Budayr, *Ḥawādith Dimashq*, 69a.

37. Ibid. The book in question is Taqiyy al-Dīn Abū Bakr b. Muḥammad al-Ḥusyanī al-Ḥiṣnī (d. 1425), *Kifāyat al-akhyār fī ḥall ghāyat al-ikhtiṣār*, edited by `Alī `Abd al-Ḥamīd Abū Khayr and Muḥammad Wahbī Sulaymān (Damascus: Dār al-Khayr, 1996).

38. Abū Shujā` al-Iṣfahānī, *Ghāyat al-ikhtiṣār aw al-Ghāya wa al-taqrīb*, edited by Sayyid Muḥammad Sayyid `Abd Allah `Āqilzada (Saudi Arabia: s.n. 2001). An English

translation of this work was carried out by Anwar Ahmad Qadri under the title *A Sunni Shafi`i Law Code* (New Delhi: Islamic Book Services, 1992). It is also worth noting that the book is a relatively common title in the book legacies of eighteenth-century Damascus; see Colette Establet and Jean-Paul Pascual, "Les Livres des gens à Damas vers 1700," *Revue des Mondes Musulmans et de la Méditerranée* 87–88 (1999): 143–175.

39. Al-Ḥiṣnī, *Kifāyat al-akhyār*, 13.

40. It should be noted that formulas are formulas for a reason—they tend to be true.

41. In the cited quotation from al-Ḥiṣnī the literal translation of the phrase "*Mulāzamat al-khalq*" is "continuous company of people," however, in the context of knowledge it means the company of scholars.

42. Ibn Budayr, *Ḥawādith Dimashq*, 57a–57b. These terms appear in the context of an obituary to a Sufi.

43. Thus Ibn Budayr's reading knowledge confirms Establet and Pascual's findings that books on Sufism and Jurisprudence were among those most widely read in eighteenth-century Damascus; see their "Livres des gens," 157, and 161–164.

44. The latter had more than one Sufi affiliation; see von Schlegell, "Sufism in the Ottoman Arab World," 133–148.

45. Schilcher, *Families in Politics*, 18–19. The biography of the founder of the order, `Abd al-Qādir al-Gilānī (d. 1166), is found among the titles of the book legacies of eighteenth-century Damascus; Establet and Pascual, "Livres des gens," 163.

46. Tamari, "Teaching and Learning."

47. Ibn Budayr, *Ḥawādith Dimashq*, 16b.

48. J. Spencer Trimingham, *The Sufi Orders in Islam*, 2nd ed., with a new foreword by John O. Voll (London: Oxford University Press, 1998), 24–25 and 225–226.

49. For the inner workings of two Syrian guilds, namely, the butchers' and the tanners' guilds of Aleppo in the seventeenth century, see Wilkins, *Forging Urban Solidarities*, 205–286.

50. Hirschler, *Written Word*.

51. Adam Sabra, "Illiterate Studies and Learned Artisans: The Circle of Abd al-Wahhab al-Sharani," in *Le Développement du Soufisme en Égypte à l'époque mamelouke*, eds. Richard J. A. McGregor and Mireille Loubet (Cairo: Institut Français d'Archéologie Orientale, 2006), 153–168.

52. In his survey specifically of college teachers in eighteenth-century Damascus, Tamari found that 20 percent of them had a distinct and clear Sufi affiliation; however, only a few were institutionally enmeshed in the order or resided in the related Sufi lodge. See Tamari, "Teaching and Learning," 133–134.

53. Chamberlain, *Knowledge and Social Practice*.

54. Ibid., 64.

55. Robert Darnton, "A *Bourgeois* Puts His World in Order," in his *Great Cat Massacre and Other Episodes in French Cultural History* (Vintage Books: New York, 1985), 114. On the size of turban as indicative of identity, and on the preference for the color white by the scholars, see James Grehan, *Everyday Life*, 192–194 and 217.

56. I borrow the image of the chain from Ahmet T. Karamustafa in his study of antinomian Sufi groups. See his *God's Unruly Friends* (Salt Lake City: University of Utah Press, 1994), 87–89.

57. On the social use of oral transmission in establishing authority, see Chamberlain, *Knowledge and Social Practice*, 138–142.

58. *Encyclopaedia of Islam*, 2nd ed., *s.v.* "*Idjāza*" (by G. Vajda). On the social uses of *ijāza*, see Chamberlain, *Knowledge and Social Practice*, 87–90 and 143.

59. *Thabat* has no entry in *Encyclopaedia of Islam*; however, see its near-equivalent term, "*fahrasa*," in ibid. See Tamari's use of the *thabat* as a source of intellectual history and his construction of an "Islamic Canon" through the *thabat* of a famous Damascene scholar, "Teaching and Learning," 148–174.

60. Ibid., 155.

61. Chamberlain sees the genre of biography not only as a storehouse of memory and reflection of politics but also as a guide map to the future elite. *Knowledge and Social Practice*, 18–21 and 149–150.

62. Ibid., 111–122.

63. Of course, this does not mean that all scholars loved one another. As Chamberlain demonstrated, *fitna*, or strife, is at the heart of the *`ulamā'* world in their struggles for positions, hence resources and privilege. On the other hand, collegial relations and social bonds, as represented by rhetoric of love and benefit, had to be established and renewed for the purpose of elite reproduction. On *fitna*, see ibid., 92–100.

64. Tamari, "Teaching and Learning," 128, table 4.9. Interestingly, the same table indicates that of those teachers who held other jobs, very few had so-called secular occupations.

65. Chamberlain, *Knowledge and Social Practice*, 116–122.

66. I have reconstructed Ibn Kannān's biography in my "Peripheral Visions," 90–112. Also, a full chapter is devoted to Ibn Kannān in Tamari, "Teaching and Learning," 180–219; and idem., "Biography, Autobiography, and Identity in Early Modern Damascus," in *Auto/Biography and the Construction of Identity and Community in the Middle East*, ed. Mary Ann Fay (New York: Palgrave, 2001) 37–49. See also Sajdi, "Ibn Kannan."

67. Both Tamari ("Teaching and Learning," 190–197) and Ḥikmat Ismā`īl (editor's introduction to Ibn Kannān's *al-Mawākib al-islāmiyya fī al-mamālik wa-al-maḥāsin al-shāmiyya*, 2 vols., ed. Ḥikmat Ismā`īl, Damascus: Wizārat al-Thaqāfa, 1992) have studied Ibn Kannān's educational background. The Khalwatiyya order, which was not a popular order in Damascus, was famed for its annual retreat. Peter Gran has established a connection between the Khalwatiyya ritual of retreat and the high social positions of its members, implying that it was material comfort that allowed these individuals to develop a ritual withdrawal from income-generating work; see his *Islamic Roots of Capitalism: Egypt 1760–1840*, 2nd ed. (Syracuse: Syracuse University Press, 1998), 46–47. For an introduction to the order, see B. G. Martin, "A Short History of the Khalwatī Order of Dervishes," in *Scholars, Saints, and Sufis*, ed. Nikki R. Keddie (Berkeley: University of California Press, 1978), 275–305.

68. See the list of Ibn Kannān's works in *al-Mawākib islāmiyya*, 1: 148–152.

69. Ibn Kannān, *Yawmiyyāt shāmiyya*. Since the published edition is abridged, I have also used the Berlin manuscript, Ibn Kannān, *al-Ḥawādith al-yawmiyya*, MSS. 9479 and 9480. See Chapter 1.

70. Such as Ibn Kannān, *Yawmiyyāt shāmiyya*, 367, 371, 374, 375, and 383. Tamari uses this point nicely to show the process of teaching and learning that took place outside institutions of formal education; "Teaching and Learning," 206–212. For example, Ibn Kannān, *al-Ḥawādith al-yawmiyya*, MS Berlin 9480, 87a.

71. Such as Ibn Kannān, *Yawmiyyāt shāmiyya*, 12, 340, and 486.

72. For an example of a reference to "the season of the roses," see Ibn Kannān, *Yawmiyyāt shāmiyya*, 442.

Frequent picnicking by the *`ulamā'* is evidenced by the activities `Abd al-Ghanī al-Nābulusī and his circle. See von-Schlegell, "Sufism in the Ottoman Arab World," 67. See also my "Peripheral Visions," 98–99 and 297–300.

73. Ibid. For a stimulating article on poetry becoming a primary means of *`ulamā'* communication and a sign of their distinction, see Thomas Bauer, "Mamluk Literature: Misunderstandings and New Approaches," *Mamluk Studies Review* 10.2 (2005): 105–132. See also Chamberlain, *Knowledge and Social Practice*, 85–86.

74. In this regard, see the section entitled "calculated performance" about informal scholarly gatherings; Akkach, *`Abd al-Ghani al-Nabulusi*, 26–27. See also Sirriyeh, *Sufi Visionary*, 13.

75. This not to say that scholars never frequented coffeehouses, but there is evidence that the elite considered them places for the socially inferior; see Alan Mikhail, "The Heart's Desire: Gender, Urban Space and the Ottoman Coffeehouse," in *Ottoman Tulips, Ottoman Coffee: Leisure and Lifestyle in the Eighteenth Century*, ed. Dana Sajdi (London and New York: I. B. Tauris, 2007), 142–143; and Ali Çaksu, "Janissary Coffeehouses in Late Eighteenth-Century Istanbul," in ibid., 122.

76. Karamustafa, *God's Unruly Friends*, 86–87.

77. As reflected in the titles of modern studies on Sufi saints; Jonathan Glustrom Katz, *Dreams, Sufism, and Sainthood: The Visionary Career of Muhammad al-Zawāwī* (Leiden: Brill, 1996); and Sirriyeh, *Sufi Visionary of Ottoman Damascus*.

78. See an overview of Ottoman visionary diaries and their antecedents in Derin Terzioğlu, "Man in the Image of God in the Image of the Times: Sufi Self-Narratives and the Diary of Niyāzī-i Mıṣrī (1618–94)," *Studia Islamica*, 94 (2002): 139–165. For a general introduction to Islamic oneirocritical literature, see J. C. Lamoreaux, *The Early Muslim Tradition of Dream Interpretation* (New York: SUNY Press, 2002).

79. Von Schlegell, "Sufism in the Ottoman Arab World," 181.

80. See Chapter 4.

81. Von Schlegell, "Sufism in the Ottoman Arab World," 43–45; Sirriyeh, *Sufi Visionary of Ottoman Damascus*, 16–17; Akkach, *'Abd al-Ghani al-Nabulusi*, 27–28.

82. This is my own interpretation of al-Nābulusī's career. Both von Schlegell and Akkach discuss the environment of rivalry and controversy surrounding academic careers; see "Sufism in the Ottoman Arab World," 44–45; and *'Abd al-Ghani al-Nabulusi*, 18–19 and 27–30, respectively.

83. `Abd al-Ghanī al-Nābulusī, "Munājāt al-ḥakīm wa munāghāt al-qadīm," MS. *al-Ẓāhiriyya* 733, al-Asad National Library, Damascus.

84. For a discussion of the book and the saint's visionary career, see von Schlegell, "Sufism in the Ottoman Arab World," 70–72; and Sirriyeh, *Sufi Visionary*, 57–83. See also a similar interpretation of the diary of the seventeenth-century Sufi Niyāzī Mıṣrī, in Terzioğlu, "Man in the Image of God," 147.

85. For an analysis of al-Zawāwī's book and career, see Katz, *Dreams, Sufism and Sainthood*.

86. `Abd al-Ghanī b. Ismā`īl al-Nābulusī, *Ta`ṭīr al-anām fī tafsīr al-manām* (Cairo: al-Maṭba`a al-Azhariyya al-Miṣriyya, 1906).

87. To make things even more complicated: al-Nābulusī attested to the legitimacy of receiving *ijaza*s from one's teachers through dreams. Rosenow von Schlegell, "Sufism in the Ottoman Arab World," 187.

88. Chamberlain, *Knowledge and Social Practice*, 162.

89. Tamari, "Teaching and Learning," 101–102. The fact remains that most Levantine biographical dictionaries in the Ottoman period were devoted to *`ulamā'*; see Naila

Takieddine Kaidbey, "Historiography in Bilād al-Shām: The Sixteenth and Seventeenth Centuries," (M.A. thesis, American University of Beirut, 1995), Kaidbey, 151–152.

90. I excluded from the survey the category of the "possessed" saints (*al-majādhīb*). Possessed saints, by definition, generally led eccentric, nonnormative lives, for which they were venerated. More often than not, *majādhīb* had no jobs at all and lived off the charity of others, as with the saint known as "Tishtish" (Al-Murādī, *Silk al-durar*, 2:183), or held what was considered demeaning work, as with "Ibrāhīm, the garbage collector" (Al-Murādī, *Silk al-durar*, 1:43).

91. Al-Murādī, *Silk al-durar*, 1: 82–96.

92. Ibid., 3: 11, 3: 108, and 1: 52.

93. Ibid., 1: 113–116.

94. Ibid., 1: 229–230; 3: 58–59 and 4: 231.

95. Ibid., 3: 132–133.

96. Ibid., 1: 43; and 2: 77.

97. Ibid., 4: 13–14.

98. One grammarian did other various odd jobs; ibid., 2: 19–26. See also ibid., 2: 82, 3: 133, and 4: 235.

99. Ibid., 2: 30–31, and 1: 256–258.

100. "*Muwaffar al-dawā`ī muraffah al-bāl*," ibid., 2: 30.

101. "*Yuḥammiq wālida-hu wa yaṣ`ub `aly-hi*," ibid., 1: 257.

102. It is worth noting that research on the academy in Istanbul in the seventeenth century shows remarkably variant trends in terms of social origins of members, more than does that on the eighteenth century. In the seventeenth century, entry by people from artisanal backgrounds seems to have been rather high; however, in the eighteenth century, the academy was entirely aristocratized. For seventeenth-century Istanbul, see Denise Klein, *Die osmanischen Ulema des 17. Jahrhunderts Eine geschlossene Gesellschaft?* (Berlin: Klaus Schwartz, 2007). For the eighteenth century, see Madeline C. Zilfi, *The Politics of Piety: The Ottoman Ulema in the Post-classical Age, 1600–1800* (Minneapolis: Bibliotheca Islamica, 1988).

103. Schilcher, *Families in Politics*, 162; and Tamari, "Teaching and Learning," 112–115.

104. Madeline C. Zilfi, "Elite Circulation in the Ottoman Empire: Great Mollas of the Eighteenth Century," *Journal of the Economic and Social History of the Orient* 26, no. 3 (1983): 318–364; and idem., *Politics of Piety*, 43–81.

105. Ibn Budayr, *Ḥawādith Dimashq*, 25b, 82b, 5b, and 10a. Ibn Budayr does not mention his wife, as was the habit of most male authors. See my "Peripheral Vision," 340–353.

106. For example, see Ibn Budayr, *Ḥawādith Dimashq*, 9b–10a; 15a; 17a–17b; 27a; 27a–27b; 43b–45a; 58a; 45; 65a; 66b; 69a–69b.

107. Ibid., 43b. My emphasis.

108. Ibid., 17a–17b. My emphasis.

109. Ibid., 76a.

110. Ibid., 62b. My emphasis.

111. Ibid., 9b–10a. My emphasis.

112. Ibid., 18a–19a, and 21b, respectively.

113. Grehan, *Everyday Life*, 197.

114. Al-Murādī, *Silk al-durar*, 3: 193.

115. Ibn Budayr, *Ḥawādith Dimashq*, 28b.

116. Ibid., 57a–57b.

117. Ibid., 58b and 72a.

118. The line is *mallā khamīs mā ṣādafa-hu arzāl*. ***Arzāl*** is the plural of the colloquial ***rizl*** (formal Arabic, *radhl*), which usually denotes an ill-mannered person but can be colloquially used to describe a bad day, "*yawm* ***rizl***."

119. Ibn Budayr, *Ḥawādith Dimashq*, 58b.

120. Though he deals specifically with the Egyptian *mawwāl*, Pierre Cachia's treatment of the genre is instructive; see his "The Egyptian Mawwal: Its Ancestry, Its Development, and Its Present Forms," *Journal of Arabic Literature* 8 (1977): 79.

121. Turan, "Synthesizing the Novelties within Old Structure"; and Aynur, "Ottoman Literature," 488. See also the previous chapter on the significance of the vernacularization of Ottoman-Turkish poetry.

122. Ibn Budayr, *Ḥawādith Dimashq*, 26a.

123. For an example of a major trend of "Sayyidization," see Hülya Canbakal, *Society and Politics in an Ottoman Town: `Ayntab in the 17th Century* (Leiden: Brill, 2007), 77–83.

124. Ibn Budayr, *Ḥawādith Dimashq*, 26a.

125. It is noteworthy that Ibn Budayr had another son also bearing a Prophetic title, al-Sayyid Muṣṭafā, who lived long enough to marry and have a son of his own in 1757. Ibn Budayr, *Ḥawādith Dimashq*, 82b.

126. This is inspired by Pierre Bourdieu's *Distinction* as delineated by Swartz's discussion of "class, habits, and tastes"; *Culture and Power*, 163–176.

127. Ibn Budayr, *Ḥawādith Dimashq*, 29b.

128. Muḥammad b. Jum`a b. al-Maqqār, *al-Bashāt wa al-quḍat*, in *Wulāt Dimashq fī al-`ahd al-`uthmānī*, ed. Ṣalāḥ al-Dīn al-Munajjid (Damascus: n.p., 1949), 1–71. This edition by al-Munajjid also includes a book by Raslān Ibn al-Qārī, *al-Wuzarā' al-ladhīna ḥakamū bi-Dimashq*.

129. According to the editor of al-Maqqār's book, al-Munajjid, the sobriquet of the author, *al-maqqār* indicative of a craft, which al-Munajjid sites as *al-maqāra*. I have found no such craft nomenclature, but given that *qār* is tar, the author could have done something to do with tar.

130. Ibn Budayr, *Ḥawādith Dimashq*, 27a–27b.

131. Ibid., 18b–19a.

132. Ibid., 21a–21b.

133. Ibid., 70b.

134. Ibid., 12b.

135. Ibid., 72a.

136. For the mention of Ibn Budayr's mother and daughter see ibid., 5b and 10a, respectively.

137. Ibid., 59b and 71a–71b.

138. Ibid., 69b–70a.

139. Ibid., 56b–57a.

140. Quran, 36: 82, and 2: 46, respectively. Ibn Budayr, *Ḥawādith Dimashq*, 25b. On plague in the eighteenth-century Middle East including the Levant, see Michael W. Dols, "The Second Plague Pandemic and Its Recurrences in the Middle East, 1347–1894," *Journal of Economic and Social History of the Orient* 22, no. 2 (1979), 162–189.

141. This might be *al-Durr al-thamīn fī al-munāqasha bayna Abī Ḥayyān wa al-Samīn* by Badr al-Dīn al-Ghazzī (d. 1576), Muftī of Damascus in the early Ottoman period. See Ḥajjī Khalīfa Kātib Çelebi, *Kashf al-ẓunūn `an asāmī al-kutub wa al-funūn*,

6 vols., eds. Şerifettin Yaltkaya and Kilisli Rifat Bilge (Istanbul: Maarif Matbaasi, 1941), 1: 730–731.

142. Ahmad Hikmat Sharkas, *Badr al-Dīn al-Ghazzī (904/1499–984/1577), and His Manual on Islamic Scholarship and Education*, al-Durr al-Nadīd (Cambridge, Mass.: Harvard University Press, 1976).

143. Al-Murādī, *Silk al-durar*, 1: 155. It is important to note that despite al-Murādī's bad judgment of the poet, the author holds the poet in affection and mentions that his own father used to receive the poet in his assemblies, despite the latter's social impropriety.

144. Ibn Budayr, *Ḥawādith Dimashq*, 82a.

145. These are the popular epics of al-Ẓāhir Baybars, Sayf Ibn Dhī Yazan, and `Antara b. Shaddād and his lover, `Abla. The genre of the epic will be discussed in a later chapter.

146. Ibn Budayr, *Ḥawādith Dimashq*, 11b.

CHAPTER 3

1. Burayk, *Tārīkh al-Shām* (The History of Damascus), 17. There is an earlier edition of Burayk's chronicle: Mīkhā'īl Burayk al-Dimashqī, *Tārīkh al-Shām, 1720–1782*, ed. Quṣṭanṭīn al-Bāshā (Harisa: Maṭba`at al-Qiddīs Būluṣ, 1930). The history exists in two manuscripts, neither of which is an autograph: MS *Tārīkh* 2213, Taymūriyya Collection, Dār al-Kutub, Cairo; and MS 9786. Pet. 188 and MS 9787. Pet. 188, Arabic Collection, Staatsbibliothek zu Berlin, Berlin. Burayk wrote a church history as well, *Ḥaqā'iq al-waḍiyya fī tārīkh al-kanīsa al-urthudhūksiyya*, also known as *Tārīkh al-ābā' baṭārikat Anṭākiya*, which is a defensive history seeking to establish the antiquity of the Greek Orthodox church; it is extant in manuscript. See Usāma `Ānūtī, *al-Ḥaraka al-adabiyya fī Bilād al-Shām khilāl al-qarn al-thāmin `ashar* (Beirut: Lebanese University Press, 1970), 218. Burayk also wrote a universal history (a history that starts with the moment of Creation). The latter is a genre that had long gone out of fashion with his Muslim counterparts, the *`ulamā'*. See Burayk's "Tawārīkh al-zamān wa zahrat a`ājīb al-kawn wa al-awān," MS *Tārīkh* 5453, al-Asad National Library, Damascus. `Umar Riḍā Kaḥḥāla mistakenly identified Burayk as a Lebanese; see his *Mu`jam al-mu`allifīn*, 4 vols. (Beirut: Mu'assasat al-Risāla, 1993), 3: 943–944.

2. Burayk speaks about himself only when it comes to his promotion in the ecclesiastical hierarchy. In 1741, Burayk mentions being ordained as deacon (*shammās*) and then ten days later as a priest (*qassīs*). Three months after being ordained as priest, Burayk was allowed to hear confession (Burayk, *Tārīkh al-Shām*, 35). In 1750, Burayk was promoted to the rank of *brūṭūbābās* (Greek, *protopapas*), the highest level of priesthood; he was also appointed to the administrative responsibilities of a vicar (*wakīl*; Burayk, *Tārīkh al-Shām*, 38). It is not clear how long he remained a vicar following this appointment, as he mentions becoming a vicar once again in 1767. He speaks of his second vicarship in a self-congratulatory tone: his predecessor seems to have been "uncompassionate and unmerciful," and when Burayk took over "the church matters calmed down and spiritual matters were put in order and the Christians were happy with that" (Burayk, *Tārīkh al-Shām*, 95–96). The last upward step in Burayk's career came a year later when he was invited by the Patriarch of Antioch to become the archimandrite and vicar of the revered Ṣīdnāyā Monastery, one of the most prestigious ecclesiastical appointments in the Levant. However, he resigned after only a year's service at Ṣīdnāyā, citing "excessive burdens and an absence of organization" (Burayk, *Tārīkh al-Shām*, 102). On the history and importance of the Ṣīdnāyā Monastery, see Ḥabīb al-Zayyāt, *Khabāya al-zawāya min tārīkh Ṣīdnāyā*, in *Wathā'iq*

tārīkhiyya li-al-kursī al-milkī al-anṭākī, ed. Ilyās Andrāwus al-Būluṣī (Harisa: Maṭba`at al-Qiddīs, 1937), where Mīkhā'īl Burayk is briefly mentioned, 248.

3. Only one other Greek Orthodox historian is known for this period, and he wrote one work to Burayk's three; see Georg Graf, *Geschichte der christlichen arabischen Literatur*, 4 vols. (Vatican City: Bibliotheca Apostolica Vaticana, 1951), 4: 152–154.

4. Burayk, *Tātīkh al-Shām*, 17.

5. Ibid., 85. For discussions of Burayk's use of "Arab," see Bruce Masters, "The View from the Province: Syrian Chronicles of the Eighteenth Century," *Journal of American Oriental Society* 114 (1994): 359–360; Rafeq, *Province of Damascus*, 24; Hayat Bualuan, "Mikha'il Breik: A Chronicler and a Historian in 18th Century Bilad al-Sham," *Parole de l'Orient* 21 (1996): 67–68; Barbir, *Ottoman Rule in Damascus, 1708–1758*, 59; and my "Peripheral Visions," 247–248.

6. Burayk, *Tārīkh al-Shām*, 81, 90, and 28, respectively.

7. Ibid., 73.

8. Ibid., 73–74. See also his report on how, in 1762, the *muftī* of Damascus ordered the reconstruction of the Ṣidnāyā Monastery, which had been destroyed by an earthquake. Burayk reads it as a direct inspiration of the *muftī* by the Virgin Mary. Ibid., 83.

9. Ibid., 73.

10. For example, he severely berates some richer members of the community who hired gunmen to ward off the poor during wedding celebrations and says, "May God punish the one who introduced it [the custom]." Ibid., 31.

11. Ibid., 74–75.

12. Ibid., 109. In another instance, he mentions excessive public consumption of meat by church officials during Christmas celebrations. Ibid., 94–95.

13. "The Orthodox leaders would every now and then complain to the local Ottoman officials [*al-ḥukkām*] about the Catholics, and the officials would force the Catholics to pay an additional tax." In 1747, "the infighting amongst the vicars and the leaders of the Orthodox sect and their followers, and the lack of affection between them" allowed the Catholics to "seize the opportunity" and bribe the Ottoman officials to impose an additional tax on the Orthodox as well. Ibid., 32.

14. Ibid., 88.

15. Ibid., 102.

16. The chronicle was first serialized in the Shī`ī journal *al-`Irfān*: "*Jabal `Āmil fī qarn*," (Jabal `Āmil in a Century) *al-`Irfān* 27 (1938): 525–527, 626–628, 735–736, 814–815; 28 (1939): 54–56, 158–159, 255–256, 350–351, 453–454, 727–728, 830–832, 951–954; 29 (1939): 73–76, 187–188, 303–304, 678–683. Unfortunately, the original manuscript seems to have been lost, as both subsequent editions are based on the serialized version: Ḥaydar Riḍā al-Rukaynī, *Jabal `Āmil fī qarn*, ed. Aḥmad Ḥuṭayṭ (Beirut: Dār al-Fikr al-Lubnānī, 1997); and Ḥaydar Riḍā al-Rukaynī, *Jabal `Āmil fī qarn*, ed. Ḥasan Muḥammad Ṣāliḥ (Beirut: Dār al-Jumān, 1998). I am using the 1997 Ḥuṭayt edition in this study. Ḥasan Ṣāliḥ claims that al-Rukaynī Jr.'s name was Ḥasan; however, he does not tell us how he came to that conclusion. See his edition of *Jabal `Āmil fī qarn*, 16. It is important to note that the chronicle offers no indication as to the transfer of authorship from father to son. I have elsewhere tried to approximate the point at which the son takes over authorship, on the basis of literary style and interests. See my "Peripheral Visions," 134–137.

17. A recent study on the Shī`īs of Lebanon, Matāwila, and otherwise is Stefan Winter, *The Shiites of Lebanon Under Ottoman Rule, 1516–1788* (Cambridge: Cambridge University

Press, 2010). One of the best studies on the history of the Matāwila community is Mounzir Jaber, "Pouvoir et société au Jabal `Āmil de 1749 à 1920 dans la conscience chiite et dans un essai d'interprétation" (Ph.D. diss., Université Paris IV-Sorbonne, 1978). A published but inadequate history is Muḥammad Jābir Āl al-Ṣafā, *Tārīkh Jabal `Āmil*, 2nd ed. (Beirut: Dār al-Nahār li-al-Nashr, 1981). See also the treatment of the Matāwila in Cohen, *Palestine in the 18th century.* The appellation "al-Matāwila" makes its first appearance in the seventeenth century; see Muḥammad Kāẓim al-Makkī, *Munṭalaq al-ḥayāh al-thaqāfiyya fī Jabal `Āmil* (Beirut: Dār al-Zahrā', 1991), 65; see also Jaber, "Pouvoir et société," 1.

18. Cohen, *Palestine in the 18th Century*, 123–124.

19. See Jaber, "Pouvoir et société," xv. It may be that other such chronicles have yet to be discovered in the private libraries of Jabal `Āmil, on which see al-Sayyid Muḥsin al-Amīn, *Khiṭaṭ Jabal `Āmil*, 2 vols., ed. Ḥasan al-Amīn (Beirut: Maṭba`at al-Inṣāf, 1961), 1: 158–160.

20. On the Shī`ī scholarly tradition of Jabal `Āmil, see Kamal Salibi, *A House of Many Mansions: The History of Lebanon Reconsidered* (Berkeley: University of California Press, 1988), 144–145; and Moojan Momen, *An Introduction to Shī`ī Islām: The History and Doctrines of Twelver Shi`ism* (New Haven: Yale University Press, 1985), 123. It will be remembered that when the Safavid dynasty was established in Iran at the beginning of the sixteenth century, the Safavid state imported scholars from Jabal `Āmil to assist in entrenching Twelver Shī`ism in their domains.

21. On the *madrasa*-building activity in Jabal `Āmil in the eighteenth century, see al-Amīn, *Khiṭaṭ Jabal `Āmil*, 150–153; and Muḥammad Kāẓim al-Makkī, *al-Ḥaraka al-fikriyya wa al-adabiyya fī Jabal `Āmil*, with an introduction by Fu'ād Afrām al-Bustānī (Beirut: Dār al-Andalus, 1963), 140.

22. For the Matāwila's rise to power, see Winter, *The Shiites of Lebanon*,117–145. For earlier scholarship on the immediate circumstances, see Cohen, *Palestine in the 18th century*, 14, n. 26, and 83; and Jaber, "Pouvoir et société," 193.

23. Winter, *Shiites of Lebanon*, 92–96.

24. According to Winter, "the Druze-Maronite condominium would establish a political and narrative title to all 'Lebanon' in which the Shi`a was left little room." Ibid., 115.

25. Of the various Shī`ī groups, those of Jabal `Āmil were the most associated with Ottoman Empire's own archenemy, Safavid Iran.

26. Quran 7: 136.

27. Quran 51: 45 (in reference to the Thamūd).

28. Al-Rukaynī, *Jabal `Āmil*, 65–66.

29. Ibid., 105.

30. Raḍiyy al-Dīn Ibn Ṭāwūs (d. 1265), *al-Tashrīf bi al-minan fī al-ta`rīf bi-al-fitan* (Qom: Mu'assasat Ṣāḥib al-Amr, 1995), 371–372.

31. See also al-Rukaynī, *Jabal`Āmil*, 64, 69, and 73.

32. Ibid., 95–97.

33. Ibrāhīm al-Danafī (al-Sāmirī), *Ẓāhir al-`Umar wa ḥukkām Jabal Nāblus, 1185–1187/1771–1773* ("al-Ẓāhir al-`Umar and the Rulers of the Mount of Nablus, 1771–1772") ed. Mūsā Abū Diyya (Nablus: Jāmi`at al-Najāḥ, 1986), 32. I will henceforth use *Jabal Nāblus* as the title for convenience. A Hebrew translation of the chronicle was done by Reuven Shiloah and published in I. Ben Zvi, *The Book of the Samaritans* (Tel Aviv: Magnes Press, 1970), 331–340. The chronicle was first extensively quoted by Iḥsān al-Nimr, *Tārīkh Jabal Nāblus wa al-Balqā'*, 2 vols. (Damascus: Ibn Zaydūn, 1938), 1: 142–149. Thereafter, al-Nimer edited and published it along with the Nablus section of `Abd al-Ghanī al-Nābulusī's

travelogue as *al-Mukhtār min kitāb al-ḥaḍra al-unsiyya fī al-riḥla al-qudsiyya wa yalī-hi kurrās `an hujūm al-Ẓāhir al-`Umar `alā Nāblus* (n.p., n.d.), 69–82. It is worth noting that the sole existing manuscript of the chronicle was found in the family papers of the Ṭūqān family in Nablus and is now in the Department of History and Archeology at al-Najāḥ University.

34. The nickname "al-`Ayyā" was self-bestowed; see editor's introduction, *Jabal Nāblus*, 13–14. See entry on "Ibrāhīm al-`Ayyā" by Nathan Schur in *A Companion to Samaritan Studies*, ed. Alan D. Crown, Reinhard Pummer, and Abraham Tal (Tubingen: J.C.B. Mohr, 1993). For a summary of the chronicler's life, see Edward Robertson, "Ibrhaim al-`Ayyah: A Samaritan Scholar of the Eighteenth Century," in *Essays in Honour of the Very Rev. Dr. J. H. Hertz, Chief Rabbi of the United Hebrew Congregations of the British Empire, on the Occasion of His Seventieth Birthday, September 25, 1942 (5703)*, ed. Isidore Epstein et al. (London: E. Goldston, 1942), 341–350. For a list of documents and manuscripts, which was drafted by Ibrāhīm al-Danafī or on which he signed his name, see Alan David Crown, *Samaritan Scribes and Manuscripts* (Tübingen: Mohr Siebeck, 2001), 411.

35. Among the nineteenth-century Western travelers who were interested in the Samaritans were John Wilson, *The Lands of the Bible* (Edinburgh: William While, 1847); Ulrich Jasper Seetzen, *Reisen durch Syrien, Palästina, Phönicien, die Transjordan-länder, Arabia Petrea und Unter-Agypten*, ed. Fr. Kruse, 4 vols. (Berlin: G. Reimer, 1854–1859); H. H. Petermann, *Reisen im Orient* (Leipzig: Verlag von Veit & Co., 1860–1861); and John Mills, *Three Months Residence in Nablus and an Account of the Modern Samaritans* (London: John Murray, 1861). A useful summary on the history, doctrines, and literature of the Samaritans is the entry "al-Sāmira," *Encyclopaedia of Islam*, 2nd ed., *s.v.*, (by Noja Noseda). Among the modern scholarly works on the Samaritans are Moses Gaster, *The Samaritans, Their History, Doctrine, and Literature* (Oxford: Oxford University Press, 1925); and I. Ben Zvi's *The Book of the Samaritans*. There is also Nathan Schur, *History of the Samaritans*, 2nd rev. ed. (Frankfurt: Peter Lang, 1992). Though the latter is one of the more comprehensive works on the Samaritans, it should be used with caution, as it is an ideologically laden work.

36. Schur, *History of the Samaritans*, 123 and 152–153, respectively; see also editor's introduction, al-Danafī, *Jabal Nāblus*, 13; "al-Sāmira," n.1.

37. Schur, *History of the Samaritans*, 123.

38. Ibid., 211.

39. See "al-Sāmira"; "Samaritans as a Jewish Sect," in *Companion to Samaritan Studies*; and editor's introduction, al-Danafī, *Jabal Nāblus*, 13, n. 1.

40. "al-Sāmira."

41. Schur, *History of the Samaritans*, 228.

42. This was the population estimate of the Western traveler U. J. Seetzen, who visited Nablus in 1806 (20 years after al-Danafī's death); see ibid., 152.

43. Ibid., 135. The contents al-Danafī's letters to European scholars are devoted to the explication of Samaritan doctrine. He signed one of the letters as "Abraham, the son of Jacob, of the sons of Danaftah"; see Gaster, *Samaritans, Their History*, 164. See also Robertson, "Ibrahim al`Ayyah," 343.

44. Al-Danafī seems to have also related his dreams in writing. See Robertson, "Ibrahīm al-`Ayyah," 347–350.

45. Ibid., 342.

46. Abū al-Fatḥ, *The Kitāb al-tārīkh of Abu 'l-Fath*, ed. Paul Stenhouse (Sydney: University of Sydney Press, 1985). Anonymous *dhayl* additions later continued the *Kitāb*

al-tārīkh up to 1853. Based on Abū al-Fatḥ's history and other sources, an anonymous chronicle (dubbed "Chronicle Adler") was compiled in 1900 for the benefit of contemporary Western scholars interested in the Samaritans. See Gaster, *Samaritans, Their History*, 156–158; James Montgomery, *The Samaritans, the Earliest Jewish Sect: Their History, Theology, and Literature* (New York: Ktav, 1907), 300–310; and Schur, *History of the Samaritans*, 116–119.

47. Al-Danafī, *Jabal Nāblus*, 10.

48. Schur, *History of the Samaritans*, 125.

49. See the observations of Henry de Beavau on the Ghazzan Samaritans cited in ibid., 127.

50. Al-Danafī, *Jabal Nāblus*, 48.

51. Ibid., 33–34. For another such episode also described in rhymed prose, see 28–29.

52. Ibid., 28.

53. Ibid., 35. The only instance where the Sultan is called by his title is when al-Danafī cites almost verbatim a letter sent by the governor of Damascus, ibid., 45.

54. Ibid., 36–37.

55. Ibid., 44.

56. Ibid., 45–46.

57. Ibid., 47–48 (I am reading *fa-inghamma* for *fa-an`ama*).

58. Ibid., 39, 42, 43 and 44.

59. Ibid., 44.

60. "On that day, over a thousand of them fell, while of *our* forces (*min jam`i-nā*) only two men were killed. Towards noon, they retreated and the fighting ended. *Our* forces entered the city and were received with joy and celebration." Ibid., 34, my emphasis; see also 28, 30, and elsewhere in the chronicle.

61. Schur, *History of the Samaritans*, 137.

62. Muḥammad b. `Abd al-Sayyid al-Makkī, *Tārīkh Ḥimṣ: yawmiyyāt Muḥammad ibn al-Sayyid ibn al-Ḥājj Makkī ibn al-Khanqāh* ("The History of Ḥimṣ: The Diary of Muḥammad ibn al-Sayyid ibn al-Ḥājj Makkī ibn al-Khanqāh"), ed. `Umar Najīb al-`Umar (Damascus: al-Ma`had al-`Ilmī al-Firansī li-al-Dirasāt al-`Arabiyya, 1987). The editor of the chronicle confused the name of the author in the title of this chronicle; his correct name is Muḥammad b. `Abd al-Bāqī b. al-Sayyid al-Makkī as per the manuscript cited below. Al-Makkī's manuscript, which is not an autograph, was originally a part of the private collection of `Īsā Iskandar al-Ma`lūf and is now in the collection of the American University of Beirut under the title of "Mudhakkarāt aḥad abnā` Ḥimṣ" ("The Diary of a Person from Ḥimṣ"), MS 792. Another copy is reported to have been spotted in the author's hometown, Ḥimṣ. See editor's note, al-Makkī, *Tārīkh Ḥimṣ*, 15 *mīm*.

63. We know nothing about the workings of the courts in Ḥimṣ, not even if there was only one court or several. Al-Makkī once refers to *al-Maḥkama al-`ulyā* ("the high court"); however, all other references are simply to *al-maḥkama* ("the court"). See al-Makkī, *Tārīkh Ḥimṣ*, 51, and numerous references at 72–73. The likelihood is that there was only one court. Unfortunately, in their valuable documentary study on Ḥimṣ, Muḥammad `Umar al-Sibā`ī and Na`īm Salīm al-Zahrāwī do not even mention courts in their *Ḥimṣ, dirāsa wathā'iqiyya, al-ḥiqba min 1256–1337h/1840–1918m* (Ḥimṣ: n.p., 1992).

64. Elsewhere, I have demonstrated how I came to this conclusion about al-Makkī's profession; see my "Peripheral Visions," 90–93.

65. Al-Makkī, *Tārīkh Ḥimṣ*, 94.

66. Ibid., 72, further examples occur at 72–74 and throughout the chronicle.

67. Ibid., 75.

68. Ibid., 86.

69. Al-Makkī sometimes appears as a witness in these transactions. Unfortunately, we have no knowledge about the criteria for the selection of witnesses in the Ḥimṣ court.

70. An indication of the remarkable number of people mentioned by al-Makkī is the fact that the editor of the chronicle includes in the index of names only those people whose are mentioned more than once. Presumably, a survey of all the names would have considerably lengthened an already substantial list; al-Makkī, *Tārīkh Ḥimṣ*, 275–285.

71. See below.

72. Al-Makkī, *Tārīkh Ḥimṣ*, 227.

73. Ibid., 231.

74. Ibid., 231.

75. Ibid., 259.

76. See the entry for Ibrāhīm Āghā in the index of names prepared by the editor. Ibid., 275.

77. See, for example, ibid., 71, and 39–40, respectively.

78. Ibid., 41–42, and 47, respectively.

79. Ibid., 11. See other instances in which al-Makkī notes the politicking trips of Ibrāhīm Āghā and various other figures to Tripoli and Istanbul and even Ḥamāh, 28, 45, 52, 89, and 212.

80. Ibid., 97.

81. Ibid., 46–47.

82. Ibid., 16.

83. Ibid., 30.

84. Ibid., 40.

85. The singular manuscript of this chronicle is now lost, but a microfilm exists: MS 1136, Majma` al-Lugha al-`Arabiyya, Damascus. There is one edition of the chronicle: Ḥasan Āghā al-`Abd, *Tārīkh Ḥasan Āghā al-`Abd: ḥawādith Bilād al-Shām wa al-imbaraṭūriyya al-`uthmāniyya* ("The History of Ḥasan Āghā al-`Abd: The Events of the Levant and the Ottoman Empire"), ed. Yūsuf Nu`aysa (Damascus: Dār Dimashq li-al-Ṭibā'a wa al-Nashr, 1986).

86. The index of names in *Tārīkh Ḥasan* contains about 16 entries with the title *afandī*, which denotes an official position in the religio-judicial-academic institution. The entries with the title *āghā* are approximately 50. This is aside from numerous other entries with military titles such as *tafakjī, shurbajī, shāwīsh bāshī*, etc., which are all military titles.

87. There seem to be similar cases from seventeenth-century Aleppo. In this regard, Charles Wilkins's construction of the biographies of two highly placed soldiers from archival sources is instructive. One of the cases is of a certain `Alī b. Shabīb (fl. 1678), who managed to enrich himself spectacularly (probably like our al`Abd). The other, `Alī Aghā b. `Abdullāh (fl. 1673), started off well but ended with a large debt that his children would inherit. See Wilkins, *Forging Urban Solidarities*, 185–192, and 192–196, respectively.

88. Ṭannūs al-Shidyāq (d. 1861), *Akhbār al-a`yān fī Jabal Lubnān*, 2 vols. ed. Buṭrus al-Bustānī, (Beirut: n.p., 1859), reprinted with an updated edition by Mārūn Ra`d and indexed by Ilyās Ḥannā (Beirut?: Dār Nāẓir `Abbūd, 1993), 2: 251–252; and Mīkhā'īl Mishāqa (d. 1888), *Mashhad al-`ayān bi-ḥawādith Sūriyya wa Lubnān*, ed. Milḥim Khalīl `Abdū and Andrāwus Ḥannā Shakhashīrī (Cairo: n.p., 1908), 79.

89. Bruce Masters suggests that al-`Abd might be the ancestor of a family that acquires prominence in the nineteenth century, see his "View from the Province," 355. For the al-`Abd family, see Schilcher, *Families in Politics*, 153–156.

90. Halil Inalcik, "Centralization and Decentralization in Ottoman Administration," in *Studies in Eighteenth Century Islamic History*, ed. Thomas Naff and Roger Owen (Carbondale: Southern Illinois University Press, 1977), 35.

91. Al-`Abd, *Tārīkh Ḥasan*, 156.

92. For a useful study of the Damascus janissaries, see Barbir, *Ottoman Rule in Damascus*, 89–97. That both the local and the imperial janissary corps were employed on the pilgrimage route is established in ibid., 91. Al-`Abd's involvement in the construction of forts along the pilgrimage route might well have been in such a posting. It seems chronologically probable that the construction project of which al-`Abd was a part was the one carried out by Kurjī `Uthmān, who was governor of Damascus from 1760 to 1771; ibid., 139–140.

93. Al-`Abd, *Tārīkh Ḥasan*, 156. An *Arpa Emini* is a commissioner in charge of the supply of fodder to the stables; see Harold Bowen and H.A.R. Gibb, *Islamic Society and the West: A Study of the Impact of Western Civilization on Moslem Culture in the Near East*, 2 vols. (London, New York: Oxford University Press, 1950), 1: 85.

94. Though the author is silent about his life during his tenure as a *mutasallim* of al-Biqā`, which was not a peaceful area, there are a few passing references to him during that period in a couple of chronicles. The famous Lebanese historian Ṭannūs al-Shidyāq informs us that while al-`Abd was *mutasallim* of al-Biqā` he visited the village of `Ummayq, whose inhabitants refused to receive him and kicked him out. Al-`Abd is reported to have retaliated by plundering the villagers' livestock. This report is not critical of al-`Abd; rather, it presents him as the victim of the insolence of the villagers. Al-Shidyāq, *Akhbār al-a`yān*, 2:252. However, in the chronicle of Mīkhā'īl Mishāqa, al-`Abd is portrayed as a corrupt and extortative ruler who was driven out of al-Biqā` on account of his transgressions. Mishāqa, *Mashhad al-`ayān*, 79–80.

95. Though the result of the battle was indecisive, al-`Abd was able to return bearing the severed heads of some of the enemy along with letters from the governor of Sidon. Al-`Abd, *Tārīkh Ḥasan*, 175. The sable fur was given by the governor as a symbol of official appointment, or as a sign of approval on the part of the governor for the individual's services.

96. Al-`Abd, *Tārīkh Ḥasan*, 180.

97. Ibid., 22, 61, 84, and 135.

98. I have excluded the governors mentioned in the first few years covered by the chronicle since al-`Abd mentions only the dates of their respective appointments and depositions without comment; see ibid., 3–10. The only governor al-`Abd seems to like in the pre-1817 portion of the chronicle is Ḥusayn Pasha al-Baṭṭāl (1787–88), 11.

99. Ibid., 97.

100. Ibid., 61.

101. Ibid., 135.

102. Ibid., 61.

103. Factional wars and intrigues saturate the chronicle, but see especially ibid., 13–17, 73–77, 79–80, 108–110, 121, and 124–126.

104. Ibid., 46.

105. A few examples are ibid., 81, 111, 125–126.

106. Ibid., 111 and 129, respectively.

107. Ibid., 59 and 83.

108. Ibid., 53. For reports on the French advance in Egypt, see ibid., 36, 37, 38; on Palestine, 49, 51; for al-Jazzār's campaign against the French, 52 and 54; and on the final departure of the French from Egypt, 61 and 66.

109. See ibid., 131–133 and 144. For other reports on the Wahhābīs and the Damascus Hajj caravan, see 85–86, 122, 149–150.

110. Ibid., 132.

111. Ibid., 157, 158.

112. Ibid., 161.

113. Ibid., 163.

114. Previous quotation, ibid., 165. Current quotation, ibid., 163–164.

115. Ibid., 164.

116. George John Koury, "The Province of Damascus, 1783–1832" (Ph.D. diss., University of Michigan, 1970), 113. See the chapter entitled "The Province of Damascus from the Death of Aḥmad Pasha al-Jazzār to the Egyptian Occupation of Syria in 1832," at 112–198.

117. Al-`Abd, *Tārīkh Ḥasan*, 182. For a narrative account of the disbanding of the janissary corps, see Godfrey Goodwin, *The Janissaries* (London: Saqi Books, 1994), 214–228.

118. Masters, "View from the Province," 361.

119. Ḥasan Ibn al- Ṣiddīq, *Gharā'ib al-badā'i` wa `ajā'ib al-waqā'i`* ("Strange Marvels and Wondrous Events"), ed. Yūsuf Nu`aysa (Damascus: Dār al-Ma`rifa, 1988). The editor does not tell us about the provenance of the manuscript from which he worked; however, there is a copy in Berlin: MS 9832, WE 417, Arabic Collection, Staatsbibliothek zu Berlin.

120. Rafeq, *Province of Damascus*, 323.

121. Ibn al-Ṣiddīq, *Gharā'ib al-badā'i'*, 15. My emphasis.

122. Ibid., 14. This also leads Rafeq to believe that Ibn al-Ṣiddīq was of the janissary corps; see Rafeq, *Province of Damascus*, 323.

123. *Encyclopaedia of Islam*, 2nd ed., *s.v.* "`Adjā'ib" (by C. E. Dubler).

124. Rafeq, *Province of Damascus*, 323.

125. Ibid. My emphasis.

126. Jane Hathaway, *The Politics of Households in Ottoman Egypt: The Rise of the Qazdağlis* (Cambridge: Cambridge University Press, 1997), 101.

127. The details of this event are found in Rafeq, *Province of Damascus*, 251–282.

128. Ibn al-Ṣiddīq, *Gharā'ib al-badā'i'*, 30.

129. Ibid., 82–83. Actually, the story is narrated almost with disbelief at the favor that Ṭūqān received from the governor, who not only hosted the beg but also obliged his request to have an enemy of his killed.

130. This episode has been noted before in Hayat Bualuan, *Mu'arrikhū Bilād al-Shām fī-al-qarn al-thāmin 'ashar* (Beirut: al-Furat, 2002), 122.

131. The two epistles are *Ḥulūl al-ta`ab wa al-ālām bi-wuṣūl Abī al-Dhahab ilā Dimashq al-Shām* ("The Coming on of Affliction and Pain by the Arrival of Abū al-Dhahab to Damascus") ed. Ṣalāḥ al-Dīn al-Munajjid (n.p.: Dār al-Kitāb al-Jadīd, 1962); and *al-Baghī wa al-tajarrī fī ẓuhūr Ibn Jabrī* ("Infringement and Insolence on Account of the Appearance of Ibn Jabrī"). I was not able to locate a copy of the epistle.

132. For the full story of Ibn Jabrī's escape and the possible motivations, see Rafeq, *Province of Damascus*, 267–268.

133. Ibn al-Ṣiddīq, *Ghara'ib al-badā'i`*, 58.

134. Ibid., 23–24.

135. Al-`Abd, *Tārīkh Ḥasan*, 10.

136. Al-Rukaynī, *Jabal 'Āmil*, 28.

137. Burayk, *Tārīkh al-Shām*, 11.

138. Al-Makkī, *Tārīkh Ḥimṣ*, 13 *mīm*.

139. Ibn Budayr, *Ḥawādith Dimashq*, 23.

140. Al-Danafī, *Jabal Nāblus*, 10.

141. For one of the first debates on "the problem of Arabic," see the Egyptian literary journal *al-Muqtaṭaf*, 6 (1881): 352–354, 494–495. That the problem still continues today is evidenced by the titles of relatively recent works that are in the nature of polemic manifestos, among them Nufūsa Zakariyya Sa'īd, *Tārīkh al-da'wa al-'āmmiyya wa atharu-hā fī Misr* ("The History of the Call to Colloquial and its Effects on Egypt," Cairo: Dār al-Mā'arif, 1964), and Nuhād Mūsā, *Qaḍiyyat al-taḥawwul ilā al-fuṣḥā fī al-'ālam al-'arabī al-ḥadīth* ("The Issue of Transformation into *Fuṣḥā* in the Modern Arab World") (Amman: Dār al-Fikr li-al-Nashr wa al-Tawzī', 1987). The locus classicus on diglossia is Charles A. Ferguson, "Diglossia," *Word* 15 (1959): 325–340; representative studies of the issue of Arabic diglossia include Salih al-Toma, *The Problem of Diglossia in Arabic: A Comparative Study of Classical and Iraqi Arabic* (Cambridge, Mass.: Harvard University Press, 1969); and S. El-Hassan, "Educated Spoken Arabic in Egypt and the Levant: A Critical Review of Diglossia and Related Concepts," *Archivum Linguisticum* 3 (1977): 112–132. A more recent treatment is Niloofar Haeri, *Sacred Language, Ordinary People: Dilemmas of Culture and Politics in Egypt* (New York: Palgrave Macmillan, 2003). Unfortunately, to the best of my knowledge no detailed study of the historical relationship between classical and colloquial in Arabic has yet been carried out; Roger Wright's edited volume *Latin and the Romance Languages in the Early Middle Ages* (London: Routledge, 1991) would provide a comparative conceptual framework for such a project.

142. On al-Ṭabarī's use of colloquial, see Li Guo, *Early Mamluk Syrian Historiography: al-Yūnīnī's* Dhayl Mir'āt al-Zāmān, 2 vols. (Leiden: E. J. Brill, 1998), 1: 94.

143. On the use of colloquial by al-Yūnīnī and his colleagues, see ibid, 1:95.

144. See Khalidi, *Arabic Historical Thought*, 188.

145. Muḥammad b. Muḥammad Ibn Ṣaṣra, *al-Durra al-muḍī'a fī al-dawla al-Ẓāhiriyya*, edited by William M. Brinner under the title *A Chronicle of Damascus, 1389–1397*, 2 vols. (Berkeley: University of California Press, 1963). On Ibn Ṣaṣra's language, see the editor's introduction, 1: xix–xx.

146. All of these examples and others are cited in the excellent work of Shākir Muṣṭafā, *al-Tārīkh al-'arabī wa al-mu'arrikhūn: dirāsa fī taṭawwur 'ilm al-tārīkh wa ma'rifat rijāli-hi fī al-islām*, 4 vols. (Beirut: Dār al-'Ilm li-al-Malāyin, 1978–1993) 3: 74–75.

147. On the use of colloquial by chroniclers in Ottoman Egypt, see Nelly Hanna, "The Chronicles of Ottoman Egypt: History or Entertainment?" *The Historiography of Egypt*, ed. Hugh Kennedy (Leiden: E. J. Brill, 2001), 237–250.

148. Cited in Nelly Hanna, "Culture in Ottoman Egypt," in *The Cambridge History of Egypt*, vol. 2, *Modern Egypt From 1517 to the End of the Twentieth Century*, ed. M. W. Daly (Cambridge: Cambridge University Press, 2001) 2: 86–111, at 111, footnote 55. A similar glossary, or language guidebook, was authored in the early nineteenth century by the Levantine Christian scholar, Mīkhā'īl al-Ṣabbāgh (d. 1816), entitled *al-Risāla al-tāmma fī kalām al-'āmma wa al-manāhij fī aḥwāl al-kalām*; see Luwīs Shaykhū, "Mīkhā'īl al-Ṣabbāgh wa usratu-hu," *al-Machriq* 8 (1905), 24–35, at 31.

149. I have elsewhere treated in detail how the authors in our sample negotiated textual and oral Arabic in their chronicles; Sajdi, "Peripheral Visions," 426–450. Because

the discussion of the language is an entirely technical matter, I have determined not to include it here in order not to lose the interest of a general academic audience. However, I will be treating some of these issues in detail as they relate to the chronicle of the barber in Chapters 5 and 6.

150. Ilham Khuri-Makdisi, *The Eastern Mediterranean and the Making of Global Radicalism, 1860–1914* (Berkeley: University of California Press, 2010), 35–59.

151. This issue will come up again in subsequent chapters.

CHAPTER 4

1. See Claude Cahen, "History and Historians," in *The Cambridge History of Arabic Literature: Religion, Learning, and Sciences in the `Abbasid Period*, eds. M.J.L. Young, J. D. Latham, and R. B. Serjeant (Cambridge: Cambridge University Press, 1990), 188–233.

2. M.J.L. Young, "Arabic Biographical Writing," in ibid., 172.

3. Khalidi, *Arabic Historical Thought*, 17–82. Michael Cooperson sees that the concern with biography of transmitters originated even before the development of Hadith with the *akhbāriyyūn* ("collectors of reports"); see his *Classical Arabic Biography*, 1–23. For differing opinions on the development of the genre of biography, see Wadad al-Qadi, "Biographical Dictionaries," 23–75; George Makdisi, "Ṭabaqāt-Biography: Law and Orthodoxy in Classical Islam," *Islamic Studies* 32, no. 4 (1993): 371–396.

4. Of course, I agree with Chase F. Robinson that ninth- and tenth-century compiler-historians such as al-Ṭabarī were indeed authors inasmuch as they imposed their own historical vision, interpretations, and values in compiling their texts; however, as we shall see below, authorship as constituted entirely from the author's own knowledge will not develop until later. In other words, I am using a specific definition of authority. Robinson, *Islamic Historiography*, 36.

5. George Makdisi, "Autograph Diary of an Eleventh Century Historian of Baghdad" (in five parts), *Bulletin of the School of Oriental and African Studies* 18.1 (1956): 9–31, 18.2 (1956): 239–260, 19.3 (1957): 13–38, 19.4 (1957): 281–303, and 19.4 (1957): 426–443.

6. Makdisi, "Autograph Diary," 18.1 (1956): 23.

7. George Makdisi, "The Diary in Islamic Historiography: Some Notes," *History and Theory* 25.2 (1986), 173–185. Technically speaking, *ta'rīkh* means the act of writing history or chronicling while *tārīkh* is history or chronicle. Although I have not distinguished between these two terms in the present disucussion of Ibn al-Bannā' work, it will become clear that the relevant text is akin to a source from which a history would be written. In other words, it is a text used for history writing. As such, even though Ibn al-Bannā's diary is a chronicle of events, it is technically a *ta'rīkh* and not a *tārīkh*.

8. When an author published a book (*akhraja-hu, kharraja-hu*, literally, "to put it out"), he would circulate his work by publicly dictating it to copyists or disciples in a concourse in a mosque or *madrasa*, or give his rough draft to a copyist to make fair copies for sale; see Johannes Pederson, *The Arabic Book*, trans. Geoffrey French (Princeton: Princeton University Press, 1984), 24–27, and 49.

9. Makdisi, "The Diary in Islamic Historiography," 185.

10. Makdisi, "The Diary in Islamic Historiography," 173.

11. Ibn Kannān, *Yawmiyyāt shāmiyya*, 340.

12. Makdisi, "The Diary in Islamic Historiography," 180–181.

13. Ibid., 176–178.

14. Ibid., 185.

15. The locus classicus of literary and generic changes in the Mamluk period is Ulrich Haarmann, "Auflösung and Bewahrung der klassischer Formen arabischer Geschichtsschreibung in der Zeit Mamluk," *Zeitschrift der deutschen Morgenländischen Gesellschaft* 121 (1971): 46–60.

16. Robinson, *Islamic Historiography*, 98.

17. Khalidi, *Arabic Historical Thought*, 200–201.

18. Reynolds, Brustad, et al. *Interpreting the Self*, 53.

19. Khalidi, *Arabic Historical Thought*, 200.

20. Cahen, "History and Historians," 216.

21. Haarmann, "Auflösung und Bewahrung."

22. Khalidi, *Arabic Historical Thought*, 182.

23. Cited in ibid., 182; emphasis mine.

24. Shākir Muṣṭafā, *al-Tārīkh al-'arabī wa-al-mu'arrikhūn*, 3: 63–67.

25. Ibid., 3: 50–53, and 3: 20–21.

26. Ibid., 3: 26.

27. See his excellent "Table comparing the time-periods covered by the historians of the Mamlūk age during 650–950/1252–1543," ibid., 3: 89.

28. Li Guo, *Early Mamluk Syrian Historiography*. On the use of colloquial by al-Yūnīnī and his colleagues, see ibid., 1: 95.29. On the *dhayl* genre, see Caesar Farah, *The* Dhayl *in Medieval Arabic Historiography* (New Haven: American Oriental Society, 1967).

30. Li Guo, *Early Mamluk Syrian Historiography*, 1: 84–85. On al-Birzālī, see Muṣṭafā, *al-Ta'rīkh al-`arabī wa al-mu'arrikhūn*, 4: 43–46.

31. That this is the same work as *al-Muqtafā* is confirmed by two of the manuscripts that are extant under this title; see Li Guo, *Early Mamluk Syrian Historiography*, 1: 85, footnote 11.

32. Donald Presgrave Little, *An Introduction to Mamluk Historiography* (Wiesbaden: Hans Steiner Verlag, 1970), 47.

33. Li Guo, *Early Mamluk Syrian Historiography*, 1: 85–86.

34. Franz Rosenthal, *A History of Muslim Historiography*, 2nd ed. (Leiden: E. J. Brill, 1968), 175.

35. Khalidi, *Arabic Historical Thought*, 182.

36. Ibid.

37. On the new institutions in the Saljūqid and Ayyūbid periods, see P. M. Holt, *The Age of the Crusades: The Near East from the Eleventh Century to 1517* (London: Longman, 1986), 77–81; and on Saladin's biographers, see 209–211.

38. Khalidi, *Arabic Historical Thought*, 200.

39. See Muṣṭafā, *al-Ta'rīkh al-`arabī wa al-mu'arrikhūn*, 3: 122–125.

40. Khalidi, *Arabic Historical Thought*, 188. Khalidi provides no biographical information about Ibn Dawādārī but implies that he was an *`ālim*—however, he provides no evidence to support this.

41. Little, *An Introduction to Mamluk Historiography*, 10.

42. Li Guo speaks of al-Dawādārī as "an important innovator" who introduced "popular motifs and themes, anecdotes, folklore, etc.," into the chronicle; see his "Mamluk Historiographic Studies: The State of the Art," *Mamluk Studies Review* 1 (1997): 40.

43. Muḥammad b. Muḥammad Ibn Ṣaṣra, *al-Durra al-muḍī'a*. On Ibn Ṣaṣra's language, see the editor's introduction, 1: xix–xx.

44. Cited by Li Guo, "Mamluk Historiographic Studies," 41. Shākir Muṣṭafā similarly notes how these historians "did not pay attention to literary style and correctness of language"; *al-Tārīkh al-`arabī wa al-mu'arrikhūn*, 3: 74–75.

45. Li Guo, "Mamluk Historiographic Studies," 32.

46. On the education of the *mamlūks* (as opposed to their descendants, the *awlād al-nās*), see Jonathan Berkey, *The Transmission of Knowledge in Medieval Cairo: A Social History of Islamic Education* (Princeton: Princeton University Press, 1992), 146–155.

47. The *awlād al-nās* were the descendants of the *mamlūks*, who were by definition excluded from important state positions, military or otherwise. Scholarship offered them a respectable career option, and some, such as Ibn Iyās and Ibn Taghribirdī, inherited much wealth. On the *awlād al-nās*, see Ulrich Haarmann, "Arabic in Speech, Turkish in Lineage: Mamluks and Their Sons in the Intellectual Life of Fourteenth-Century Egypt and Syria," *Journal of Semitic Studies* 33 (1988), 81–114. On the close connections of the Egyptian *awlād al-nās* with the Mamlūk sphere, see Li Guo, "Mamluk Historiographic Studies," 39–40.

48. Berkey, *Transmission of Knowledge*, 216–218.

49. Shihāb Aḥmad b. Muḥammad Ibn Ṭawq, *al-Ta`līq, yawmiyyāt Shihāb Aḥmad Ibn Ṭawq: mudhakkarāt kutibat bi-Dimasqh fī ākhir al-`ahd al-mamlūkī (1480–1502)*, 4 vols. ed. Ja`far al-Muhājir (Damascus: Institut Français de Damas), 2000–.

50. See editor's comments, Ibn Ṭawq, *al-Ta`līq*, 1: 9; and examples of legal transactions that the author reports in his text, ibid., 1: 171 and 184. In the latter, he includes direct speech.

51. See editor's comments, Ibn Ṭawq, *al-Ta`līq*, 1: 9; and some random examples of the mention of the scholar Taqiyy al-Dīn, ibid., 1: 40, 1: 44, 1: 50, 1: 57, 1: 115, and 1: 133.

52. Ibid., 1: 321, 1: 411, and 1: 26, respectively.

53. Li Guo, "Mamluk Historiographic Studies," 39–40, where the differences between Levantine and Egyptian historiography in this period are brought out.

54. Also, markedly fewer chronicles were produced in this period in the Levant than in Egypt; see Kaidbey, "Historiography in Bilād al-Shām," 157.

55. Edited by Muḥammad Muṣṭafā (Cairo: al-Mu'assasa al-Miṣriyya al-`Āmma li-al-Ta'līf wa al-Anbā' wa al-Nashr, 1964). Ibn Ṭūlūn has been described as a "walking encyclopedia." He wrote 746 books and epistles on subjects ranging from the religious sciences to literature, to language, to history, to topography/geography, to mathematics, to medicine; see Muṣṭafā, *al-Ta'rīkh al-`arabī wa al-mu'arrikhūn*, 4: 128–136. Ibn Ṭūlūn also wrote an autobiography, for which see Reynolds, Brustad et al., *Interpreting the Self*, 272–273.

56. Establet and Pascual, "Livres des gens," 143–169.

57. Ibn Ṭūlūn, *Mufākahat al-khillān*, 1: 112, and 199, respectively.

58. Ibid., 1: 88.

59. Kaidbey, "Historiography in Bilād al-Shām," 175. There are some personal similarities between Ibn Ṭūlūn and Ibn Kannān; Ibn Ṭūlūn also had difficulties with teaching appointments. See Kaidbey, "Historiography of Bilād al-Shām," 175.

60. On the formal model of Levantine chronicles, see Li Guo, "Mamluk Historiographic Studies," 38.

61. Ibid.,39.

62. Kaidbey, "Historiography in Bilād al-Shām," 166 (emphasis mine).

63. Ibid.,163.

64. Ibid.,171.

65. Ibid., 154.

66. The following discussion will draw heavily on the seminal article of Cemal Kafadar, "Self and Others: The Diary of a Dervish in Seventeenth-Century Istanbul and First-Person Narratives in Ottoman Literature," *Studia Islamica* 69 (1989), 121–150.

67. Kafadar speculates as to whether Seyyid Ḥasan was specifically aware of Ibn al-Bannā's "*ta'rīkh*-diary" and drew his inspiration therefrom. The foregoing discussion in the present chapter establishes, of course, that such specific inspiration was unnecessary. See Kafadar, "Self and Others," 128.

68. Ibid.,142–144.

69. In the absence of union catalogues of unpublished manuscripts, such a task would be a superhuman undertaking.

70. This was edited by `Abd Allāh b. Muḥammad al-Ḥabashī under the title *Yawmiyyāt Ṣan`ā'* (Abu Dhabi: Manshūrāt al-Majma` al-Thaqāfī, 1996).

71. *Kunnāsh Ismā'īl al-Maḥāsinī: ṣafaḥāt min tārīkh Dimashq fī al-qarn al-ḥādī `ashar*, ed. Ṣalāḥ al-Dīn al-Munajjid (Beirut: Dār al-Kitāb al-Jadīd, 1965).

72. This work was mentioned by al-Murādī, *Silk al-durar*, 4: 127–128.

73. Kafadar, "Self and Other," 128–129.

74. See Madeline Zilfi, "Diary of a Müderris: A New Source for Ottoman Biography," *Journal of Turkish Studies* 1 (1977), 157–174.

75. `Abd al-Raḥmān al-Suwaydī, *Tārīkh Ḥawādith Baghdād wa al-Baṣra 1772–1778*, ed. `Imād `Abd al-Salām Ra'ūf (Baghdad, Dār al-Shu'ūn al-Thaqāfiyya al-`Āmma, 1987).

76. Aḥmad ibn Muḥammad Ibn 'Ajība, *The Autobiography of the Moroccan Sufi Ibn Ajiba*, ed. Jean-Louis Michon, trans. David Streight (Louisville, Ky.: Fons Vitae, 1999).

77. Kerima Filan, "Life in Sarajevo in the 18th Century (According to Mulla Mustafa's mecmua)," in *Living in the Ottoman Ecumenical Community: Essays in Honour of Suraiya Faroqhi*, ed. Vera Costantini and Markus Koller (Leiden, Boston: Brill, 2008), 317–345.

78. Other Arabic contemporary chronicles from this period include the narrative account book kept by the Yemeni keeper of the public treasury, al-Mu`ayyad bi-Allāh Muḥammad Ibn Ismā`īl (fl. 1677), which has been edited by `Abd Allāh Muḥammad al-Ḥabashī as *Mudhakkarāt al-Mu'ayyad bi-Allāh Muḥammad b. Ismā`īl* (Beirut: al-Mu'assasa al-Jāmi`iyya li-al-Dirāsāt wa al-Nashr wa al-Tawzī`, 1991); and the short tract by the Tripolitan *`ālim* Muṣṭafā Jamāl al-Dīn Ibn Karāma (*fl.* 1607), describing the siege of Tripoli in 1606, and his own capture and subsequent release. This was edited and published by Muhammad `Adnan Bakhit, "Aḥdāth bilād Ṭarāblus al-Shām," *Majallat majma` al-lugha al-`arabiyya al-urdunī* 1.1 (January 1986): 171–206, and discussed by Kaidbey, "Historiography in Bilād al-Shām," 383–387.

79. For discussions of the interaction between Arabic and Turkish historiography, see Cornell Fleischer, *Bureaucrat and Intellectual in the Ottoman Empire* (Princeton: Princeton University Press, 1986), especially 253–257; and Jane Hathaway, "Sultans, Pasha, *Taqwims* and *Mühimmes*: A Reconsideration of Chronicle-Writing in Eighteenth Century Ottoman Egypt," in *Eighteenth Century Egypt: The Arabic Manuscript Sources*, ed. Daniel Crecelius (Claremont: Regina Books, 1990), 51–78.

80. The first work to have used a variation of the root *y-w-m* (day) in its title seems to have been the lost contemporary chronicle of Saladin's scribe, al-Qāḍī al-Fāḍil al-Baysānī (d. 1200), who used the word *muyāwamāt* to describe his chronicle; see Rosenthal, *A History of Muslim Historiography*, 152. However, I am unaware of the recurrence of any *y-w-m*-related title until Muḥibb al-Dīn al-Ghazzī's lost chronicle, mentioned above. The

Turkish *yevmiye* is the name now sometimes given to the genre in Turkish manuscript collections; see Madeline Zilfi, "Diary of a Müderris," 157.

81. Interestingly, no *yawmiyyāt* are known to have been produced in Egypt at this time. It is not apparent why this is the case.

82. Kafadar, "Self and Others," 127–128.

83. Ibid., 127.

84. Ibid., 127.

85. Von Schlegell, "Sufism in the Ottoman Arab World," 69 (emphasis mine).

86. Katz, *Dreams*, xvii–xviii.

87. Kafadar, "Self and Others," 128–130. Some of Hüdā'i's dreams, like those of Muḥammad al-Zawāwī, took the form of conversations with the Prophet.

88. Asiye Hātūn's dreams, however, are not dated, with the result that her dream logbook cannot properly be considered a chronicle; see Cemal Kafadar, "Mütereddit bir Mutasavvıf: Üsküp'lü Asiye Hātūn'un Rüya Defteri 1641–43," *Topkapı Sarayı Müzesi Yıllık* 5, 168–222.

89. On travelogues by Muslim scholars that are not necessarily related to shrine visitation, see Hala Fattah, "Representations of Self and Other in Two Iraqi Travelogues of the Ottoman Period," *International Journal of Middle East Studies* 30 (1998): 51–76. For some Christian travelogues of the period, see Elias Muhanna, "Ilyās al-Mawṣilī (fl. 1668–1683)," in *Essays in Arabic Literary Biography*, ed. Roger M. A. Allen et al., vol. 1, 2 vols. (Wiesbaden: Harrassowitz, 2009), 295–308; Ilyās Mawṣilī, *An Arab's Journey to Colonial Spanish America: The Travels of Elias Al-Mûsili in the Seventeenth Century*, ed. Caesar E. Farah (Syracuse: Syracuse University Press, 2003). Another chronicle-travelogue is by the Greek-Catholic merchant Yūsuf b. Dīmitrī b. Jirjis al-Khūrī `Abbūd al-Ḥalabī (fl. 1809), "al-Murtād fī tārīkh Ḥalab wa Baghdād," ed. Fawwāz Maḥmūd Fawwāz (M.A. thesis, University of Damascus, 1978).

90. See, for example, the "self-writing" of his student Muṣṭafa al-Bakrī, as discussed by Ralf Elger, *Muṣṭafā Bakrī: zur Selbstdarstellung eines syrischen Gelehrten, Sufis und Dichters des 18. Jahrhunderts* (Schenefeld: EB-Verlag, 2004).

91. Suraiya Faroqhi, *Subjects of the Sultan: Culture and Daily Life in the Ottoman Empire* (London: I. B. Tauris, 2000), 199–202.

92. Derin Terzioğlu, "Man in the Image of God."

93. Pederson, *Arabic Book*, 21.

94. Ibid., 22–23.

95. On *ṣuḥba* and *mulāzama* in Islamic education, see George Makdisi, *The Rise of Colleges: Institutions of Learning in Islam and the West* (Edinburgh: Edinburgh University Press, 1981), 128–129. See also the discussion on the subject in Chapter 2.

96. Kafadar, "Self and Others," 147.

97. Suraiya Faroqhi, *Approaching Ottoman History: An Introduction to the Sources* (Cambridge: Cambridge University Press, 1999), 163–167.

98. Kaidbey, "Historiography in Bilād al-Shām," 160.

99. The preamble to the *Mufākahat al-khillān* has not survived; thus we do not have any direct statement by Ibn Ṭūlūn as to why or for whom he wrote the chronicle.

100. See Muṣṭafā, *al-Ta'rīkh al-`arabī wa al-mu`arrikhūn*, 4: 126. However, Yūsuf al-`Ashsh has identified MS al-Ẓāhiriyya 4533 as a contemporary chronicle, and attributed the work to al-Nu`aymī; see his article "Mudhakkarāt yawmiyya duwwinat bi-Dimashq," *Majallat al-majma` al-`ilmī al-`arabī* 18 (1943): 142–154. It is not clear, however, if this is the same work as the *Tadhkirat al-ikhwān*.

101. See the next chapter.

102. Kafadar, "Self and Others," 125–126.

103. Ibid., 149. For a study of a famous "decline-conscious" Ottoman intellectual in the early post-Sulaymanic age, Muṣṭafā `Ālī (d. 1600), see Cornell Fleischer's *Bureaucrat and Intellectual.*

104. William Bouwsma, "Anxiety and the Formation of Early Modern Culture." In *After the Reformation: Essays in Honor of J. H. Hexter*, edited by Barbara Malament and William Bouwsma (Manchester: Manchester University Press, 1980), 215–246.

105. Kafadar acknowledges as much; see "Self and Others," 149, note 61.

106. For the Kadızadeli movement, see Zilfi, *Politics of Piety*, 128–181.

107. The Kadızadeli movement continued in the Arabic speaking world into the eighteenth century; see von Schlegell, "Sufism in the Ottoman Arab World," 84.

108. Ibid., 80–85.

109. Kafadar, "Self and Others," 147–148.

110. Hanna, "Chronicles of Ottoman Egypt," 247.

111. Ibid., 243–248. For al-Isḥāqī, see Muḥammad Anīs, *Madrasat al-tārīkh al-miṣrī fī al-`ahd al-`uthmānī* (Cairo: Ma`had al-Dirasāt al-`Arabiyya al-`Āliya, 1962), 20.

112. Hanna, "Chronicles of Ottoman Egypt," 245–246.

113. P. M. Holt, "Al-Jabartī's Introduction to the History of Ottoman Egypt," *Bulletin of the School of Oriental and African Studies* 25.1 (1962): 39.

114. Hathaway does not actually use the term "pasha chronicle," but this is the clear implication of her statement: "one might modify Holt's terminology slightly . . . the governor remains the protagonist of the narrative." See Hathaway, "Sultans, Pashas, *Taqwīms* and *Mühimmes*," 59.

115. Ibid., 58–59.

116. Hanna, "Culture in Ottoman Egypt," 110–111.

117. Anīs, *Madrasat al-tārīkh al-miṣrī*, 53–58.

118. The name derives from the best-known of the chronicles, that of Aḥmad al-Damurdāshī Katkhudā al-`Azabān (fl. 1756), and was given by P. M. Holt, "The Career of Küçük Muḥammad (1676–94)," *Bulletin of the School of Oriental and African Studies* 24 (1963): 269–287. See also `Abd al-Wahhab Bakr, "Interrelationships Among the Damurdāshī group of Manuscripts," in *Eighteenth Century Egypt*, 79–88.

119. Hathaway, "Sultans, Pashas, *Taqwīms* and *Mühimmes*," 60–65. Holt, "al-Jabartī's Introduction," 42, differentiated between the "sultan-pasha chronicle," which he calls "the literary chronicle," and the "soldiers' school chronicle," which he calls "the popular chronicle," but the two are so similar in regard to both structure and content that this distinction seems unfounded.

120. Bakr, "Interrelationships Among the Damurdāshī group of Manuscripts," 87.

121. This is not to say that Ottoman Egypt did not have its share of "learned" scholarly works and audiences. We have only to cite the great al-Jabartī (d. 1824), whose works, however, fall outside the scope of our review.

122. See Farah, *Dhayl*, 2.

123. Cited in Reynolds, Brustad, et al., *Interpreting the Self*, 67.

124. Establet and Pascual, "Livres des gens," 150–151.

125. On the educational tradition of Jabal `Āmil, see the previous chapter.

126. Al-Makkī, *Munṭalaq al-ḥayāh al-thaqāfiyya*, 190. See also the previous chapter.

127. I show this in my "Peripheral Visions," 139–141.

128. For a brief review of the histories written in Jabal ʿĀmil after the eighteenth century, see Jaber, "Pouvoir et société," xv–xviii.

129. Burayk, *Tārīkh al-Shām*, 17.

CHAPTER 5

1. Ibn Budayr, *Ḥawādith Dimashq*, 33b.

2. This chapter is an expanded version of an article by the same title that appeared in *The MIT Electronic Journal of Middle East Studies* 4 (2004), 19–35. The journal has since ceased publication and lost its site rights.

3. In enumerating the kindnesses of his craft master, Ibn Budayr mentions how his master shaved the poor for no fee. Ibn Budayr, *Ḥawādith Dimashq*, 7b.

4. For the social backgrounds of coffeehouse clientele, see Cengiz Kirli, "The Struggle over Space: Coffeehouses of Ottoman Istanbul, 1780–1845" (Ph.D. diss., State University of New York at Binghamton, 2001), 38–49. For politically subversive conversations in coffeehouses, ibid., 49–58.

5. Brigitte Marino, "Cafés et cafetiers de Damas aux XVIIIe et XIXe siècles," *Revue des Mondes Musulmans et de la Méditerranée* 75–76, no. 1 (1996): 280.

6. Kafadar, "Self and Others," 144.

7. For a text of a decree of closure that mentions both institutions in the same sentence, see Kirli, "Struggle over Space," 63.

8. Marino, "Cafés et cafetiers de Damas ," 285–287; and Kirli, "Struggle over Space," 153–178.

9. Khaled El-Rouayheb, *Before Homosexuality in the Arab-Islamic World, 1500–1800* (Chicago: University of Chicago Press, 2005), 42.

10. It is interesting that the epic form is usually compared to the novel, as in the examples of György Lukács, "The Epic and the Novel," in *The Theory of the Novel: A Historico-Philosophical Essay on the Forms of Great Epic Literature* (Cambridge, Mass: MIT Press, 1971), 3–69; and M. M. Bakhtin, "Epic and Novel."

11. This sentence was written some time ago. I realized recently that it constituted an "appropriation" of Hayden White's words, "the account does not so much conclude as simply terminate," in his *Content of the Form*, 17. The influence of White's scholarship is evident throughout this study. Speaking of Hayden White, I am aware of the difficulty of the distinction between fiction/plot and real/nonplot, which distinction was blurred by his works. However, I am using the distinction in terms of generic and authorial intentions. Hayden V. White, *Metahistory: The Historical Imagination in Nineteenth-Century Europe* (Baltimore: Johns Hopkins University Press, 1975). For an application of White's method on Ottoman historiography, see Gabriel Piterberg, *An Ottoman Tragedy: History and Historiography at Play* (Berkeley: University of California Press, 2003).

12. See also the discussion on the same subject in the Introduction.

13. This is especially true in the Ottoman period; see Klein, *Die osmanischen Ulema*, 73.

14. Khalidi, *Arabic Historical Thought*, 17–82. See also the previous chapter.

15. *Encyclopaedia of Islam*, 2nd ed. *s.v.* "Sīra" (by W. Raven).

16. For a survey of Arabic *sīra* literature, see Giovanni Canova, "Gli Studi sull'epica popolare araba," *Oriente Moderno* 57 (1977): 211–226. For a very useful (though difficult-to-navigate) study that includes an analysis and summary of twelve Arabic epics, as well as a comparative index of shared themes between Arabic epics and universal romances and epics, see M. C. Lyons, *The Arabian Epic: Heroic and Oral Story-Telling*, 3 vols.

(Cambridge: Cambridge University Press, 1995). Perhaps thanks to its continued performance down to the present day, *Sīrat Banī Hilāl* (of which Abū Zayd al-Hilālī is the hero) has enjoyed more scholarly attention than any other *sīra*. Two excellent studies in English are Bridget Connelly, *Arab Folk Epic and Identity* (Berkeley: University of California Press, 1986); and Dwight Fletcher Reynolds, *Heroic Poets, Poetic Heroes: The Ethnography of Performance in an Arabic Oral Tradition* (Ithaca: Cornell University Press, 1995).

17. Tarif Khalidi's discussion of the *sīra* literature, *Images of Muhammad: Narratives of the Prophet in Islam Across the Centuries* (New York: Doubleday Religion, 2009), 57–103.

18. Mohammed Shahab Ahmed, "The Satanic Verses Incident in the Memory of the Early Muslim Community: An Analysis of the Early Riwāyahs and their Isnāds" (Ph. D. diss., Princeton University, 1999), 16. My emphasis. Khalidi argues that *sīra* is an attempt at "'packaging' Muhammad to conform . . . to the prophetic type," *Images of Muhammad*, 79.

19. The *sīra* of Muḥammad went through "a new age [that is] canonizing, moralizing, exclusivist, rationalizing, and uniform"; Khalidi, *Images of Muhammad*, 175–176. The exception to the canonical *sīra* of the Prophet is that of al-Bakrī (perhaps a fictitious author), *al-Anwār*. This text bears many features of the popular epic and continued to be recited as a public performance. See Hirschler, *Written Word*, 165–166.

20. The Hilālī saga and the epic al-Ẓāhir Baybars seem to have retained some elements of historicity; see Reynolds, *Heroic Poets*, 9, and Lyons, *Arabian Epic*, 1: 105, respectively. An interesting study of the various images of al-Ẓāhir Baybars as constructed in the various memory forms, including the chronicle and the epic, is Amina A. Elbendary, "The Sultan, the Tyrant, and the Hero: Changing Medieval Perceptions of al-Zahir Baybars," *Mamluk Studies Review* 5 (2001): 141–157.

21. Some *sīra* literature was textualized around the thirteenth century and posed a threat to the authority of the *ʿulamā'*. See Hirschler, *Written Word*, 167 and 175–186. In her discussion of the origin and mode of transmission of the *Sīrat Banī Hilāl*, Connelly demonstrates that despite the existence of *siyar* in written form the epic is of oral provenance and transmission, and of oral composition as well. She concludes that such literature is generally nonfixed and without a single originator. See Connelly, *Arab Folk epic*, 36–47.

22. Reynolds, *Heroic Poets*, 7. Connelly describes the language of the written editions of *siyar* as "popular dialect corrected (often hypercorrected) so as to approach the Classical idiom"; *Arab Folk Epic*, 8.

23. For example, Ibn Budayr, *Ḥawādith Dimashq*, 51a.

24. Ibid., 68a–68b.

25. For example, he says, "The author—may God forgive him and his parents, as well as those who pray for him and for the Muslims—said, 'Sir-reader (*ya sayyid-ī al-muṭṭaliʿ*) of this sublime collection: on account of our incapacity and our unworthiness for this task, which was forced upon us by Zayd and ʿAmr (Tom, Dick [and Harry]), for the sake of God, treat me with leniency, for I am but a weak slave who seeks support in the Merciful, the Kind . . . and do not treat me with severity.'" Ibn Budayr, *Ḥawādith Dimashq*, 3a. See also 68a–68b.

26. See Ibn Budayr's references to himself as the author of the text and/or instances of addressing his readers/listeners; *Ḥawādith Dimashq*, 28b, 44b, and 57b.

27. Al-Budayrī, *Ḥawādith Dimashq al-yawimiyya*, 82.

28. "And the Sultan of the Turkish, Arab, and Persian lands is . . . the Grand Vizier is . . . the Governor [of Damascus] is . . . the *qāḍī* of Damascus is . . . the *muftī* of Istanbul is . . . the *muftī* of Damascus is . . . the teachers [of Damascus] are . . . and the Hajj

commander [in Damascus] is. . . . " Ibn Kannān, *Yawmiyyāt shāmiyya*, 7 (and almost every annual entry).

29. Ibn Budayr, *Ḥawādith Dimashq*, 2a.

30. For examples of the juxtaposition of the "big people" with the "small people" or "the poor," see ibid., 17a, and 40a.

31. Ibid., 28a–28b.

32. Ibid., 62b–63a.

33. Ibid., 63a.

34. Ibid., 11b.

35. Examples are ibid., 2a, 12b, 51a–51b, 56a. Mentions are too many to cite.

36. Ibn Kannān, *Yawmiyyāt shāmiyya*, 13, 106, 154, 382, and 473.

37. See an article that uses both Ibn Kannān and Ibn Budayr's chronicles as sources for a study on street violence in Damascus: James Grehan, "Street Violence and Social Imagination in Late-Mamluk and Ottoman Damascus (ca. 1500–1800)," *International Journal of Middle East Studies* 35.2 (2003): 214–236.

38. Steve Tamari also notes the cyclical rhythm in Ibn Kannān's chronicle in "Biography, Autobiography, and Identity," 43.

39. Ibn Budayr, *Ḥawādith Dimashq*, 80b, 81a, 86b–87a.

40. Ibid., 14b.

41. Ibid., 15a.

42. Ibid., 58b.

43. Ibid., 38b and 38a, respectively.

44. Ibid., 60b–61a.

45. Ibid., 64a.

46. Ibid., 22b.

47. For example, Ibn Kannān, *Yawmiyyāt shāmiyya*, 421, 431, 435, and 444.

48. For example, ibid., 381, 393, and 504.

49. For example, ibid., 371, 383, 391, 421, and 463.

50. For details of Ibn Kannān's professional tribulations, see Sajdi, "Ibn Kannan."

51. Ibn Kannān, *Yawmiyyāt shāmiyya*, 498.

52. Astrid Meier has noticed this tendency for solitude and melancholy among the *`ulamā'* of the period and saw it as an indication of Early Modernity. See her "Perceptions of a New Era? Historical Writing in Early Ottoman Damascus," *Arabica* 51.4 (2004): 419–434, especially 430–433.

53. Ibn Budayr, *Ḥawādith Dimashq*, 35b, 25a, 47a, and 72b, respectively.

54. Ibid., 12a.

55. Ibid., 20a.

56. About Ibn Kannān's use of colloquial, see my "Peripheral Visions," 430–431.

57. Ibn Budayr, *Ḥawādith Dimashq*, 22b.

58. Establet and Pascual, "Livres des gens," 158–159.

59. For a survey of the long tradition of the *maqāma* genre, see Jaakko Hämeen-Anttila, *Maqama: A History of a Genre* (Wiesbaden: Harrassowitz, 2002).

60. Badī' al-Zamān al-Hamadhānī, *Maqāmāt Badī' al-Zamān al-Hamadhānī* (Beirut: Dār wa-Maktabat al-Hilāl, 1993).

61. Abū Muḥammad al-Ḥarīrī, *Sharḥ Maqāmāt al-Ḥarīrī, wa huwa Abū Muḥammad al-Qāsim ibn 'Alī ibn Muḥammad ibn 'Uthmān al-Ḥarīrī al-Baṣrī* (Beirut: Dār al-Turāth, 1968).

62. On this genre, see the compelling studies of James T. Monroe, *The Art of Badī' az-Zamān al-Hamadhānī as Picaresque Narrative* (Beirut: American University of Beirut, 1983); and Abdelfattah Kilito, *Les Séances: récits et codes culturels chez Hamadhânî et Harîrî* (Paris: Sindbad, 1983); the latter was translated into Arabic as *al-Maqāmāt: al-sard wa al-ansāq al-thaqāfīya*, trans. `Abd al-Karīm al-Sharqāwī, 2nd ed. (Casablanca: Dār Tūbqāl, 2001).

63. On the structure, see Hämeen-Anttila, *Maqama*, 39–61.

64. Muhsin Al-Musawi, "Abbasid Popular Narrative: The Formation of Readership and Cultural Production," *Journal of Arabic Literature* 38 (November 2007): 270. In this article, Al-Musawi presents an interesting argument about the development of a book culture and reading publics in the Abbasid period. He does so by investigating change in literary genres and the involvement of the literate in popular narratives bringing about such interesting and mixed texts as the *Arabian Nights* and the *maqāmāt*.

65. Hämeen-Anttila, *Maqama*, 52.

66. Ibid., 46–48. See the previous chapter on the importance of Hadith and its chain of transmission in the evolution of the chronicle.

67. Monroe, *The Art of Badī' az-Zamān al-Hamadhānī*, 24. Emphasis in the original.

68. Ibid., 166. In this regard, see Kilito's interesting reading of the character of the scoundrel, which he sees as an effect of the literateur's own comment about the decline of the station of the poet in the general culture; Kilito, *al-Maqāmāt: al-sard wa al-ansāq al-thaqāfīya*, 59–70.

69. Ibid., 26.

70. On the structure of the epic, see Lyons, *Arabian Epic*, 1: 73–76.

71. Monroe, *The Art of Badī' az-Zamān al-Hamadhānī*, 37.

72. Ibid., 26–37 and passim.

73. On Arabic shadow theater, see Fārūq Sa'd, *Khayāl al-ẓill al-'arabī* (Beirut: Sharikat al-Maṭbū'āt, 1993); and Shmuel Moreh, *Live Theatre and Dramatic Literature in the Medieval Arab World* (New York: New York University Press, 1992). On its Turkish counterpart, see Helmut Ritter, *Karagös: türkische Schattenspiele*, 3 vols. (Hannover: Orient-Buchhandlung H. Lafair, 1924–1953); Metin And, *A History of Theatre and Popular Entertainment in Turkey* (Ankara: Forum Yaynlar, 1963); and idem., *Karagöz: Turkish Shadow Theatre*, 3rd ed. (Istanbul: Dost, 1987). See also Dror Ze'evi, *Producing Desire: Changing Sexual Discourse in the Ottoman Middle East, 1500–1900* (Berkeley: University of California Press, 2006), 125–128.

74. The only complete plays that survive are those of the Mamluk playwright Muḥammad Shams al-Dīn Ibn Dāniyāl (d. 1310). For his plays, or the plays of Muḥammad Ibn Dānīyāl, see *Three Shadow Plays*, trans. and eds. Paul Kahle, Derek Hopwood, and Muḥammad Muṣṭafā Badawī (Cambridge: Trustees of E.J.W. Gibb Memorial, 1992). See also Amila Buturovic, "Sociology of Popular Drama in Medieval Egypt: Ibn Dāniyāl and His Shadow Plays" (Ph.D. diss., McGill University, 1993), and idem., "'Truly, This Land Is Triumphant and Its Accomplishments Evident!' Baybar's Cairo in Ibn Daniyal's Shadow Play," in *Writers and Rulers: Perspectives on Their Relationship from Abbasid to Safavid Times*, ed. Louise Marlow and Beatrice Gruendler (Wiesbaden: Reichert, 2004), 149–168.

75. Sa'd, *Khayāl al-ẓill*, 207–231 and 657–752.

76. And *History of Theatre*, 35; Ze'evi, *Producing Desire*, 132–135.

77. For a description in Arabic shadow plays, Buturovic, "Sociology of Popular Drama," 127–136. For the Turkish counterpart, Kirli, "Struggle over Space," 160–163; and Ze'evi, *Producing Desire*, 135–138.

78. Walter G. Andrews and Irene Markoff, "Poetry, the Arts, and Group Ethos in the Ideology of the Ottoman Empire," *Edebiyat* 1, no. 1 (1987): 46.

79. In Turkish shadow theater, Karagöz and Hacivat perform functions similar to the scholar and scoundrel in the *maqāma* in that the latter represents high culture while the former is of a more common extraction. Kirli, "Struggle over Space," 158–159; and Andrews and Markoff, "Poetry, the Arts, and Group Ethos," 42 and 46–47. Buturovic's reading of Ibn Danīyāl's plays is more complex in view of her identifying multiple discourses. For the argument that Ibn Dāniyāl was reconciling various worldviews including the courtly, the plebian, and the religious, see ibid., chap. 5, "Collectivity as Dramaturgic Discourse."

80. Kirli, "Struggle over Space," 169–171; Buturovic, "Sociology of Popular Drama," 26–28; and Ze'evi, *Producing Desire*, 125–127. All three authors use the work of Mikhail Bakhtin in their readings of shadow theater, namely his *Rabelais*. Nelly Hanna also reads the works in her study in Bakhtinian terms, *In Praise of Books*, 155–156.

81. This is a difficult passage: "*wa kataba asmā' al-awlād al-maḥābīb wa arsala atā bi-him wa amara-hum bi-al-raqṣ fī ḥudūr dhālika al-maḥfal wa amara-hum an yuẓhira kull waḥid min-hum bi-mā yaqdir `alay-hi min ālāt al-munkar wa yatakallam bi-mā yurīd an yatakallam bi-al-ghunj wa* ***al-baws*** *wa al-inkhilā` bi-al-maḥdar wa kāna ḥaḍir bi-al-jam` rajul naṣrānī wakīl al-batrak* [sic] *yuqāl la-hu Ibn Tūmā fa-aṭlaqū la-hu al-ṣarāḥ fa-`amila* ***`amāyil*** *mawhūma wa lu`iba khayāl anwār wa `amila waḥid bi-ṣifat Ibn Tūmā wa kāna ghalīẓ ṭawīl wa `amila wāḥid ṣifat yahūdī wa ja`ala al-yahūdi yankiḥ ilā Ibn Tūmā al-naṣrānī fī dhālika al-jam` wa al-maḥfal wa kull min-him li-dhālika al-amr yanẓur wa yubṣir wa qad fa`alū af`āl la tāf`alu-hā al-juhhāl.*" Ibn Budayr, *Ḥawādith Dimashq*, 15a. It is not entirely clear whom Ibn Budayr means by *al-awlād al-maḥābīb* (which literally is "the beloved boys"). Given the context, I understood it as "the boys who love one another." However, these *awlād maḥābīb* might have been transvestite performers. Nor is it clear what Ibn Budayr means by *ālāt al-munkar,* which I have translated literally as "instruments of abomination." As regards the shadow play, I am reading *khayāl anwār* for the corrupt *khayāl īzār.*

82. Monroe, *Art of Badī' az-Zamān al-Hamadhānī*, 169–170, and Ṭalāl Ḥarb, *Bunyat al-sīra al-sha`biyya wa khiṭabu-hā al-malḥamī fi `asr al-Mamālīk* (Beirut: al-Mu'assassa al-Jāmi`iyya li-al-Dirāsāt wa al-Nashr, 1999), 64.

83. Bakhtin, *Rabelais*, 123. Cited in Buturovic, "Sociology of Popular Drama," 27–28.

84. His is an anxiety typical in Ottoman society in the seventeenth and eighteenth centuries; see Dana Sajdi, "'Decline' and Its Discontents and Ottoman Cultural History: By Way of Introduction," in *Ottoman Tulips,* , 30–32. For anxiety as a marker of Early Modernity, see Bouwsma, "Anxiety."

85. I was not able to determine the principle for the use of red ink. Oftentimes it is used for prepositions introducing the date "*wa fī.*" Also, the words "*wa qālā*" (he said) and "*wa qad*" (it/he/she had). Red ink is used as well in dots separating hemistichs in verses. The fact that the use of red ink is later abandoned may be indicative of expense, unavailability, or perhaps just a change of whim.

86. Though the manuscript is not by any means fancy, the relatively generous use of paper and the variety of ink (even if the red ink is later dropped) conveys that the intended user or consumer or market was not particularly poor. If it were a printed text in today's market, one would qualify it as a cheaper but respectable paperback.

87. Could the copyist have been the barber's son, whose scribal skills the father praised in the obituary for the son?

88. The page preceding the text bears the inscription "*Ḥawādith Dimashq al-Shām al-yawmiyya min sanat 1154 ilā sanat 1176 jam` al-adīb al-māhir al-bāri` Shihāb al-Dīn Aḥmad Ibn Budayr al-Ḥallāq al-Dimashqī al-Shafi`ī raḥima-hu Allāḥ*" ("The Daily Events of Damascus from the year 1154 to the year 1176 AH, compiled by the proficient and excellent literati Shihāb al-Dīn Aḥmad the Barber the Shafi`ī Damascene, may God have mercy on him").

89. The sentence is not entirely legible: *naẓara-hu fī-hi* [sic] *muta'millan ma`anī-hi wa sabara-hu kāna fī bayti-hi ḥawiyya, fī 15 Dhī al-Qa`da sanat 49.* I am unable to determine the subject, hence the meaning of *kāna fī bayti-hi ḥawiyya.* It could be "it [the book] was found as a scroll in his [the reader's] house" or "it [the book] was found in a scroll cover." The rest of the sentence is: "he read it with reflection upon its meaning and probed it . . . on the 15th of Dhī al-Qa`da in the year [AH 12]49." Ibn Budayr, *Ḥawādith Dimashq*, 52b.

90. One of them alerts the reader to the fact of the presence in the text of the "biography of `Abd al-Raḥman Bahlūl," who was a poet of relative renown (ibid., 58b). A series of notes mark the stages of the building of the palace of As`ad Pasha al-`Aẓm, which it will be remembered was and is one of the finest and most important buildings in Damascus (ibid., 58b, 59a, 60b, and 61a) The interest of this commentator/reader in the governor As`ad Pasha is also clear from the rest of his comments: one of them marks the beginning of the rule of "the deceased Ḥājj, As`ad Pasha" (ibid., 21a.), while the other two take note of parties held for the governor by Damascene notables (namely, Ḥasan Afandī al-Safarjalānī and `Alī Afandī al-Murādī (ibid., 59a and 59b).

91. Compare the hand in the margin note to samples of al-Qāsimī's writing in various manuscripts written by him; Muḥammad b. Nāṣir 'Ajamī, *Āl al-Qāsimī wa nubūghu-hum fī al-'ilm wa al-taḥṣīl* (Beirut: Dār al-Bashā'ir al-Islāmīya, 1999), 224–227. It is noteworthy that al-Qāsimī's hand in the samples provided is not always consistent.

92. The works are Zayn al-`Ābidīn b. al-Sayyid Muḥammad al-Barzanjī of Mecca (d. 1759), "Kashf al-ḥujub wa al-sutūr `an mā waqa`a li-ahl al-Madina ma`a amīr Makka Surūr" (MS Chester Beatty Library Ar. 3551/1, Dublin); and Abū al-Kamāl Muḥammad Sa`īd al-Suwaydī of Baghdād (d. 1831), *Wurūd ḥadīqat al-wuzarā bi-wurūd wazārat mawālī-him fī al-zūrā* (MS Chester Beatty Library Ar 3551/3, Dublin). For their biographies, see `Umar Riḍā Kaḥḥāla, *Mu`jam al-mu'allifīn: tarājim muṣannifī al-kutub al-`arabiyya* 4 vols. (Beirut: Mu'assassat al-Risāla, 1995), 1: 488 and 3: 316, respectively. Al-Barzanjī may be the son of the Muḥammad al-Barzanjī whose biography appears in al-Murādī, *Silk al-durar*, 4: 65–66. Curiously, al-Suwaydī mentions the reason for his composing this work being to help out al-Murādī for his compilation of the famous biographical dictionary.

93. The name appears in the following phrase as though someone is practicing his modes of address (and handwriting): *Janāb ḥaḍrat al-a`azz al-akram al-muḥtaram . . . al-sayyid Salīm Jalabī al-Sāyḥa* (his dearer and more generous and respected excellency Mr. Salīm Jalabī al-Sāyḥa); MS Chester Beatty Library Ar 3551, Dublin, end folio.

94. "*naẓara fī-hi wa ta'mmal ma`ānī-hi . . . al-Ḥājj `Abd al-Wahāb al-Tarazī*" (`Abd al-Wahāb al-Tarazī looked into it and reflected upon its meanings); MS Chester Beatty Library Ar 3551, Dublin, end folio.

CHAPTER 6

1. A history of the family is provided in 'Ajamī, *Āl al-Qāsimī*. David Dean Commins also devotes a large part of his book to the activities of the family. See his *Islamic Reform: Politics and Social Change in Late Ottoman Syria* (New York: Oxford University Press,

1990). For Muḥammad Sa'ī al-Qāsimī's biography, see 'Abd al-Razzāq Al-Bayṭār, *Ḥulyat al-bashar fī tārīkh al-qarn al-thālith 'ashar*, 3 vols. (Damascus: Majma' al-Lugha al-'Arabiyya), 2: 654–661; Muḥammad Jamīl al-Shaṭṭī, *Tarājim a'yān Dimashq fī al-qarn al-rābi' 'ashar* (Dār al-Yaqaẓa al-'Arabiyya, 1948), 81–83; Muḥammad Adīb al-Ḥiṣnī, *Kitāb muntakhabāt al-tawārīkh li-Dimashq*, 3 vols. (Damascus, al-Ḥadītha Press, 1927–1929), 2: 722; Kaḥḥāla, *Mu'jam al*-mu'allifīn,10: 34. See also excerpts of the biography of al-Qāsimī by his son, Jamāl al-Dīn, along with printed obituaries and handwritten condolence notes in 'Ajamī, *Āl al-Qāsimī*, 195–221. On the description of the manuscript of al-Qāsimī's edition, Yūsuf al-'Ashsh, *Fihris makhṭūṭat dār al-kutub al-Ẓāhiriyya*, 15 vols. (Damascus: al-Majma' al-'Ilmī al-'Arabī, 1946) 6: 145–146.

2. Commins, *Islamic Reform*, 44.

3. Much of the Commins book is on Jamāl al-Dīn al-Qāsimī and his writings. Commins, *Islamic Reform*.

4. Ibid., 60, n. 33.

5. Excerpts of which appear in 'Ajamī, *Āl al-Qāsimī*, 27–54.

6. Dominique Chevallier, "A Damas, production et société à la fin de XIXe siècle," *Annales* 19.5 (1064): 966.

Muḥammad Sa'ī al-Qāsimī's second work is *Safinat al-faraj fi mā habba wa dabba wa daraj*. Edited by Muḥammad Khayr Ramaḍān Yūsuf (Beirut: Dār al-Bashā'ir, 2004).

7. Al-Qāsimī, *Qāmūs al-ṣinā'āt*.

8. Commins, *Islamic Reform*, 86.

9. This is also an implicit argument in Chevallier, "A Damas."

10. 'Ajamī, *Āl al-Qāsimī*, 28; Commins, *Islamic Reform*, 42.

11. See Commins's discussion of the lives of al-Shaykh Qāsim and Muḥammad Sa'īd. Ibid., 42–44.

12. Ibid., 47.

13. Ibid., 43.

14. These are related by the editor of al-Qāsimī's rendition of Ibn Budayr's chronicle, Aḥmad 'Izzat 'Abd al-Karīm, on the authority of al-Qāsimī's grandchildren through the "Overseer of the National Museum," Abū al-Faraj al-'Ashsh. Al-Budayrī, *Ḥawādith Dimashq al-yawmiyya*, 23–25, and 23 notes 1 and 2.

15. Ibid., 23.

16. Commins, *Islamic Reform*, 41–42.

17. Al-Budayrī, *Ḥawādith Dimashq al-yawmiyya*, 24.

18. They were from the same reformist circles of Damascus, Commins, *Islamic Reform*, 34–48.

19. Afaf Lutfi Sayyid-Marsot, *Egypt in the Reign of Muhammad Ali* (Cambridge: Cambridge University Press, 1984).

20. For a relatively recent treatment, see Şükrü Hanioğlu, *A Brief History of the Late Ottoman Empire* (Princeton: Princeton University Press, 2008), 72–149.

21. Although the literature on al-Nahḍa is extensive, two classics are Albert Hourani, *Arabic Thought in the Liberal Age, 1798–1939* (Oxford: Oxford University Press, 1962); and Hisham Sharabi, *Arab Intellectuals and the West: The Formative Years, 1875–1914* (Baltimore: Johns Hopkins University Press, 1970).

22. For a recent contribution that focuses on the movement of radical—as opposed to religious reformist or nationalist—ideas in the period, see Ilham Khuri-Makdisi, *Eastern Mediterranean*.

23. Adrian Gully, "Arabic Linguistic Issues and Controversies of the Late Nineteenth and Early Twentieth Centuries," *Journal of Semitic Studies* XLII/I (1997): 75–120.

24. All of these issues are described in Gully, "Arabic Linguistic Issues." For an example of the direct connection between al-Nahḍa and linguistic revival as described by contemporary intellectuals, see declarations by Jurjī Zaydān (d. 1914) in the journal *al-Hilāl*, as quoted and discussed by Thomas Philipp, "Language, History, and Arab National Consciousness in the Thought of Jurjī Zaidan (1861–1914)," *International Journal of Middle East Studies* 4.1 (1973): 16.

25. The role of the printing press in the reform movements of the Nahḍa is universally acknowledged. For its role in the linguistic reform, see Gully, "Arabic Linguistic Issues," 76. For interesting recent treatments, see Ilham-Khuri Makdisi, *Eastern Mediterranean*, 35–59; and Dyala Hamzah, "From `*ilm* to *Sihāfa* or the Politics of the Public Interest (Maslaha): Muhammad Rashīd Ridā and his journal al-Manār (1898–1935)," in *The Making of the Arab Intellectual: Empire, Public Sphere, and the Colonial Coordinates of Selfhood*, ed. Dyala Hamzah (New York and Abdingon, Oxon: Routledge, 2013), 90–127.

26. al-Qāsimī, *Safīnat al-faraj*, 49.

27. Al-Budayrī, *Ḥawādith Dimashq al-yawmiyya*, 81.

28. Ibid., 82.

29. Ibn Budayr, *Ḥawādith Dimashq*, 2a.

30. Ibid.

31. See for example ibid., 78b.

32. Al-Budayrī, *Ḥawādith Dimashq al-yawimiyya*, 229.

33. Cited above.

34. Ibn Budayr, *Ḥawādith Dimashq*, 58b–59b, 60b, and 61a.

35. Al-Budayrī, *Ḥawādith Dimashq al-yawimiyya*, 184 and 194–197.

36. It should be noted that there are a couple of instances of praise for As`ad Pāsha in Ibn Budayr's text, one of which is for the governor's renovations of the Sayyida Zaynab shrine. Ibn Budayr, *Ḥawādith Dimashq*, 41b (renovations) and 77b.

37. Rhyming words are underlined: "*wa ishtarā As`ad Bāshā wālī al-Shām amlāl (sic) kathīra min dūr wa basātīn wa tawāḥīn wa ghallā al-ḥinṭa wa al-sha`īr wa al-khalq tastaghīth wa tastajīr, wa laysa li-l-khalq mulabbī (sic) wa lā mushīr*," Ibn Budayr, *Ḥawādith Dimashq*, 53a.

38. Al-Budayrī, *Ḥawādith Dimashq al-yawimiyya*, 184.

39. Ibn Budayr, *Ḥawādith Dimashq*, 63a.

40. Al-Budayrī, *Ḥawādith Dimashq al-yawimiyya*, 203.

41. Ibn Budayr, *Ḥawādith Dimashq*, 74b.

42. Al-Budayrī, *Ḥawādith Dimashq al-yawimiyya*, 222.

43. For a discussion of the Islamic consensus about great building projects by rulers and their categorization into Solomonic (pious power) vs. Nemrodian (impious excess), see Stefanos Yerasimos, *La Fondation de Constantinople et de Sainte-Sophie dans les traditions turques: légendes d'empire* (Istanbul: Institut Français d'Études Anatoliennes, 1990), 40–50.

44. This is a very common saying that is not from either the Quran or Hadith.

45. Al-Budayrī, *Ḥawādith Dimashq al-yawimiyya*, 126.

46. Examples are ibid., 98, 99, 128, 129, 131, 134, 135, and 187.

47. Ibn Budayr, *Ḥawādith Dimashq*, 30a.

48. Al-Budayrī, *Ḥawādith Dimashq al-yawimiyya*, 134. My emphasis.

49. Schilcher, *Families in Politics*, 32

50. Ibn Budayr, *Ḥawādith Dimashq*, 46a–46b.

51. *Mawlid* indicates the birth of the Prophet Muḥammad, the commemoration of which usually involves the reading of poetry and the singing of songs about the Prophet. However, such celebrations, as in this instance, may take place on the occasion of a recovery from illness or other such auspicious occurrence.

52. A tambourinelike percussion instrument, but larger and without the metal disks.

53. It is important to note that al-Qāsimī is not always consistent in his vocabulary glosses, especially when it comes to the synonyms in Arabic for "prostitute." For example, in another instance al-Qāsimī substitutes *min banāt al-khaṭā* ("one of the girls of wrongdoing"), which is still commonly used today, with *`āhira* (prostitute; Ibn Budayr, *Ḥawādith Dimashq*, 25b; al-Budayrī, *Ḥawādith Dimashq al-yawmiyya*, 127). Yet in another occurrence of the term *banāt al-khaṭā*, which is a perfectly respectable and current term, the editor decides to gloss it with the vulgar colloquial *shlikkāt*, which we have just encountered in the main body of the text and which he has just glossed! (Ibn Budayr, *Ḥawādith Dimashq*, 55b; al-Budayrī, *Ḥawādith Dimashq al-yawmiyya*, 188). The use of *shlikkāt* ("whore" rather than "prostitute") is hardly consonant with al-Qāsimī's project of language refinement. Furthermore, it is a term used only in colloquial Arabic and is of Turkish provenance (*şıllık*). We will see later in the chapter that al-Qāsimī usually translates Turkish and Arabified Turkish words into Arabic.

54. This is not to say that al-Qāsimī does not consistently fix colloquialisms. Note, for example, his changing (and switching around) the phrases "*asqā al-`aṭshān wa aṭ`am al-jī`ān*," into "*aṭ`ama al-jā'i` wa saqā al-`aṭshān*" (he gave water to the thirsty and fed the hungry). Ibn Budayr, *Ḥawādith Dimashq*, 94b; al-Budayrī, *Ḥawādith Dimashq al-yawmiyya*, 267.

55. Ibn Budayr, *Ḥawādith Dimashq*, 89a; al-Budayrī, *Ḥawādith Dimashq al-yawmiyya*, 253.

56. In two instances. See Ibn Budayr, *Ḥawādith Dimashq*, 90a and 55a; al-Budayrī, *Ḥawādith Dimashq al-yawmiyya*, 257 and 187, respectively.

57. Ibid., 56a and 189.

58. Ibid., 52a and 162.

59. Ibid., 42b and 165.

60. Ibid., 26b and 129.

61. Ibid., 2a and 82.

62. For example, compare Ibn Budayr, *Ḥawādith Dimashq*, 31a, 38b, 49a, 50a, 51a, 86b, 53a, 63a, 63a–63b, 61a, 68a, 70a, 81b, and 86b to al-Budayrī, *Ḥawādith Dimashq al-yawimiyya*, 136, 157, 176, 187, 180, 184, 199, 203, 203, 212, 214, 235, and 248, respectively.

63. Given that this section of the chapter is about abridgements by al-Qāsimī, I will indicate where the event or narrative *would have been* located in the text had al-Qāsimī preserved it in his edition by the phrase "hypothetical page number." Ibn Budayr, *Ḥawādith Dimashq*, 68a; al-Budayrī, *Ḥawādith Dimashq al-yawimiyya*, hypothetical page number 212.

64. Ibn Budayr, *Ḥawādith Dimashq*, 27a, 35a, 51a, 57b, 61a, and 75b; al-Budayrī, *Ḥawādith Dimashq al-yawimiyya*, hypothetical page numbers, 129, 149, 180, 149, 62, and 223–224, respectively.

65. For example, Ibn Budayr, *Ḥawādith Dimashq*, 53a, 62a, 65b, and 70a; al-Budayrī, *Ḥawādith Dimashq al-yawimiyya*, hypothetical page numbers 184, 202, 212, and 214, respectively.

66. For example, Ibn Budayr, *Ḥawādith Dimashq*, 93a, 95a, and 95b; al-Budayrī, *Ḥawādith Dimashq al-yawimiyya*, hypothetical page numbers 263, 268, and 269, respectively.

67. Ibn Budayr, *Ḥawādith Dimashq*, 29b, al-Budayrī, *Ḥawādith Dimashq al-yawimiyya*, hypothetical page number 133.

68. Ibid., 38b and hypothetical page number 157.

69. Ibn Budayr, *Ḥawādith Dimashq*, 22b.

70. Al-Budayrī, *Ḥawādith Dimashq al-yawimiyya*, 121.

71. Another illustrative example of rhyme and direct speech omission can be found in the familiar story of the encounter between al-Ẓāhir al-`Umar and the governor, Sulaymān Pasha al-`Aẓm, quoted in the last chapter. See ibid., 118.

72. Ibn Budayr, *Ḥawādith Dimashq*, 35b.

73. Ibid., 49a.

74. Al-Budayrī, *Ḥawādith Dimashq al-yawimiyya*, hypothetical page number 176.

75. *wa fī kull waqt yaṣīr faz`a wa* **taskīr** *ḥattā intaqalat ghālib al-dūr al-latī fī khārij al-madīna ilā dākhili-hā wa ilā al-qal`a wa fī kull ḥāra wa maḥalla taṣīr al-jam`iyyāt fī al-layl wa al-sahar wa al-akl wa al-shurb wa al-ḍaḥik wa al-`ab* [sic] *wa kharj al-ahwāl lākin ma` al-khawf wa al-faza`*, Ibn Budayr, *Ḥawādith Dimashq*, 51a.

76. Al-Budayrī, *Ḥawādith Dimashq al-yawimiyya*, 187.

77. Compare Ibn Budayr, *Ḥawādith Dimashq*, 50a–51a; al-Budayrī, *Ḥawādith Dimashq al-yawimiyya*, 178–179.

78. Compare for example, Ibn Budayr, *Ḥawādith Dimashq*, 14b–15b, 17a–17b, 20b, 31a–31b, 54a–55a, and 77a; al-Budayrī, *Ḥawādith Dimashq al-yawimiyya*, 111–112, 114, 119, 137, 187, and 227, respectively.

79. More examples are Ibn Budayr, *Ḥawādith Dimashq*, 68a, 69b, 73a, 78b; al-Budayrī, *Ḥawādith Dimashq al-yawimiyya*, hypothetical page numbers 212, 214, 218, and 228, respectively. It should be noted that with some minor changes, al-Qāsimī is exceptionally faithful in his rendition of Ibn Budayr's report of the famous 1171/1757 pilgrimage disaster, when the entire caravan was raided by nomadic tribes. Al-Budayrī, *Ḥawādith Dimashq al-yawimiyya*, 246–249; Ibn Budayr, *Ḥawādith Dimashq*, 86a, and 86b–87a, respectively.

80. Al-Budayrī, *Ḥawādith Dimashq al-yawimiyya*, 88, 176, 177, 217, and 192.

81. Al-Budayrī, *Ḥawādith Dimashq al-yawimiyya*, 101, 123, 153, 212, and 217.

82. Ibn Budayr, *Ḥawādith Dimashq*, 29a; al-Budayrī, *Ḥawādith Dimashq al-yawimiyya*, hypothetical page number 133.

83. Ibid., 65a and hypothetical page number 207.

84. Ibid., 76b and hypothetical page number 226.

85. Ibid., 77b and hypothetical page number 227.

86. Ibid., 44a–44b and hypothetical page number 168.

87. Ibid., 82b and hypothetical page number 237.

88. Ibid., 25b and hypothetical page number 127.

89. Ibid., 26a and hypothetical page number 127.

90. Ibid., 59b and hypothetical page number 193.

91. Ibid., 13b and 32a, and hypothetical page numbers 110 and 138, respectively.

92. Ibid., 16a and 21a–21b and hypothetical page numbers 114 and 119, respectively.

93. Ibid., 33b and hypothetical page number 145.

94. Ibid., 59b and hypothetical page number 198.

95. Ibid., 27a and hypothetical page number 129.

96. Ibid., 27a–27b and hypothetical page number 129.

97. Ibid., 57b and hypothetical page number 127. Although al-Qāsimi retains Ibn Budayr's obituary to his mother, he offers an abbreviated version thereof; ibid., 10a and 104.

98. Ibid., 69a–69b and hypothetical page number 214.

99. Ibid., 69b–70a and hypothetical page number 214.

100. Ibid., 81b–82a and hypothetical page number 236.

101. Ibid., 57a–57b and hypothetical page numbers 191–192. Al-Qāsimī does, however, keep the "barbering" relationship Ibn Budayr had with the saint, Yūsuf al-Ṭabbākh; ibid., 28b and hypothetical page number 130.

102. Further examples are Ibn Budayr, *Ḥawādith Dimashq*, 11b–12a, 17a–17b, 29a, 42a, 43b, 56b, and 56b–57a; al-Budayrī, *Ḥawādith Dimashq al-yawimiyya*, hypothetical page numbers 107, 114, 132–133, 164, 167, 191, and 191, respectively.

103. Ibn Budayr, *Ḥawādith Dimashq*, 43b.

104. Al-Budayrī, *Ḥawādith Dimashq al-yawimiyya*, 167.

105. Ibn Budayr, *Ḥawādith Dimashq*, 76a.

106. Al-Budayrī, *Ḥawādith Dimashq al-yawimiyya*, 225.

107. Ibn Budayr, *Ḥawādith Dimashq*, 58a.

108. Al-Budayrī, *Ḥawādith Dimashq al-yawimiyya*, 192–193.

109. Ibn Budayr, *Ḥawādith Dimashq*, 58a.

110. Al-Budayrī, *Ḥawādith Dimashq al-yawimiyya*, 99–100 ,104 , and 107, respectively.

111. Schilcher, *Families in Politics*, 35.

CONCLUSION

1. The exact number of manuscripts for each work is cited in Chapter 3 on first mention of the title.

2. The following is a condensed summary of my "Print and Its Discontents: A Case for Pre-Print Journalism and Other Sundry Print Matters," *Translator*, 15.1 (2009): 105–138. Special Issue "Nation and Translation in the Middle East," edited by Samah Selim.

3. For printing history in the Ottoman empire in general, see Johann Strauss, "Who Read What in the Ottoman Empire (19th–20th Centuries)," *Middle Eastern Literature* 6, no. 1 (2003): 39–76; idem., "'Kütüp ve Resail-i Mevkute': Printing and Publishing in a Multi-Ethnic Society," in *Late Ottoman Society: The Intellectual Legacy* (London: Routledge, 2005), ed. Elisabeth Özdalga, 225–253; and Server Rifat İskit, *Türkiyede Neşriyat Hareketleri Tarihine Bir Bakış* (Istanbul: Devlet Basımevi, 1939), 1–151.

4. Hourani, *Arabic Thought*, passim.

5. Fīlīb Dī Ṭarrāzī, *Tārīkh al-ṣiḥāfa al-ʿarabiyya: yaḥtawī ʿalā akhbār kull jarīda wa majalla ʿarabiyya ẓaharat fī al-ʿālam sharqan wa gharban maʿa rusūm aṣḥābi-hā wa al-muḥarririn fī-hā wa tarājim mashāhīri-him*, 4 parts in 2 vols. (Beirut: al-Maṭbaʿa al-Adabiyya, 1914), 2: 162–243 and 274–346.

6. Ami Ayalon, *The Press in the Arab Middle East: A History* (New York: Oxford University Press, 1995), 50.

7. Dagmar Glass, Geoffrey Roper, and Hrant Gabeyan, "Arabic Book and Newspaper Printing in the Arab World," in *Middle Eastern Languages and the Print Revolution: A Cross-Cultural Encounter: A Catalogue and Companion to the Exhibition*, eds. Eval Hanebutt Benz et al. (Westhofen: WVA-Verlag Skulima, 2002), 215.

8. The first printing press in Egypt, the Būlāq Press, was established as a successor to Napoleon's printing press under the reforming regime of Muḥammad ʿAlī. The first Ottoman-Turkish printing press was set up in Istanbul by Ibrahim Müteferrika in 1728, but the

production of the press was interrupted after its owner's death. Full-fledged journalistic activities in Ottoman Turkish happened during the *Tanzimat*, Özdalga, "Introduction," in *Late Ottoman Society*, ed. Elisabeth Özdalga, 3–4; and Hanioğlu, *Brief History of the Late Ottoman Empire*, 94–97.

9. For new schools and colleges in the imperial center of Istanbul, see Hanioğlu, *Brief History of the Late Ottoman Empire*, 63 and 102–103; for Egypt, see J. Heyworth-Dunne, *An Introduction to the History of Education in Modern Egypt* (London: Cass, 1968).

10. "[T]he proliferation of the printing press . . . and the exponential increase in textual production, specifically in the form of the periodical, did not, or at least not immediately, supersede older ways of writing or reading . . . periodicals . . . were often read communally. . . . Articles were read aloud and discussed in coffeehouses." Khuri-Makdisi, *Eastern Mediterranean*, 36–37. See also Juan Cole, "Urban Islam in the Mediterranean World, 1890–1920," in *Modernity and Culture: From the Mediterranean to the Indian Ocean*, eds. by Leila Tarazi Fawaz and C. A. Bayly (New York: Columbia University Press, 2002), 350–351.

11. Thomas, *A Study of Naima*, 36–42.

12. Ibid., 38.

13. Ibid., 39. On the newspaper and the printing press for which it was especially established, İskit, *Türkiyede Neşriyat Hareketleri*, 29–31.

14. Benedict Anderson, *Imagined Communities: Reflections on the Origin and Spread of Nationalism* (New York: Verso, 1983), 39.

15. Khuri-Makdisi, *Eastern Mediterranean*, 51 passim.

EPILOGUE

1. http://www.panet.co.il/Ext/series.php?name=folder&id=292&autostart=40097&page=0, accessed June 12, 2012.

2. http://www.veoh.com/watch/v15824408rMjdpksC?h1=Al+Hosrom.Al+Shami.Ep01.

3. Even more recently, the novelist Ibrāhīm Naṣr Allāh used the bowdlerized version of Ibn Budayr's chronicle as a source for his historical novel on the life and times of al-Ẓāhir al-`Umar, *Qanādīl malik al-Jalīl* (Beirut: al-Dār al-`Arabiyyā li-al-`Ulūm, 2012).

Glossary

afandī: A title denoting an official position in the religio-judicial-academic institution, or in the modern government bureaucracy.
al-akābir (singular, *kabīr*): Literally, "the big people," the notables.
`ālim* (plural,*`ulamā'): Literally, "the one who knows," a scholar of the religious sciences.
`āmmiyya: Popular or common language referring to spoken Arabic or dialect. Usually used in juxtaposition to *fuṣḥā*.
al-aṣāghir (singular, *saghīr*): Literally, "the small people," the commoners.
ashrāf (singular, *sharīf*): A group that claims descent from the Prophet Muḥammad. The title of the individual *sharīf* is *sayyid*.
al-`awāmm: The commoners.
awlād al-nās: Literally, "the children of people," referring to the descendent of the *mamlūk* military-administrative class. See *mamlūk* and Mamluk below.
al-a`yān* (singular, *`ayn): The notables.
bāshā: Pasha. A title indicating a high-ranking political/administrative position, usually a provincial governor.
dawla: State, rule.
dhayl: Literally, "tail," a sequel to a work.
fiqh: Jurisprudence.
fuqahā' ummiyyūn: Learned illiterates.
fuṣḥā: Literally, "eloquent (language)," denotes high or textual Arabic. Usually used in juxtaposition to *`āmmiyya*.
Hadith: Reports about the behavior and speech of the Prophet Muḥammad. The second most important source of Islamic law after the Qur'ān.
ḥājj: The title of someone who has performed the pilgrimage to Mecca, the Hajj.
Hajj: Pilgrimage.
ḥakawī or *ḥakawātī*: Storyteller of popular epics.
ḥallāq: Barber.
ḥawādith yawmiyya: Literally, "daily events" referring to journals or chronicles with daily entries.
Hijrī: From *hijra*, the event of the flight of the Prophet and the nascent Muslim community from Mecca to Medina in 622 CE. This is the marker of the Islamic calendar.
ḥubb/maḥabba: Love/affection.
ijāza: An official license to transmit a book.
isnād: Literally, "support." A list of the names of the transmitters of a historical report. The authority of the individual in the list lends the report authenticity and veracity.
kātib: Scribe, secretary.
khān: Caravanserai.
khānqāh: Sufi lodge.
khaṭīb: Sermonist, or preacher.

khayāl al-ẓill (in Turkish *karagöz*): Shadow theater.
khuṭba: Preamble in a text; also the sermon at the Friday congregational prayer.
madrasa: College.
mamlūk: Literally, "possessed," indicating slave soldiers, which often constituted an elite military caste in many Islamic regimes. See Mamluk.
Mamluk: From *mamlūk,* referring to the regime that ruled Egypt and Syria 1250–1517, hence a period in Islamic history. The sultan and the political-administrative and military classes in this regime were of a slave background.
maqāma (plural, *maqāmāt*): Literally, "assembly," the picaresque narrative.
mashāyakha: Formal investment of spiritual authority akin to certificate in mystical knowledge. Also known as *silsila.*
muftī: Jurisconsult.
mulāzama: Constant companionship.
mutasallim: District or sub-district governor.
al-Nahḍa: Literally "resurgence," indicating the literary, intellectual, and social reform movements that took place in the Arabic-speaking world in the late nineteenth and early twentieth centuries. Usually translated as "the Arab Renaissance."
naqīb al-ashrāf: The head of the *ashrāf*, a group that claims descent from the Prophet Muḥammad.
nazīh: Delightful, picnicable.
qabīqūl (in Turkish, *kapıkulları*): Literally, "slaves of the Porte," referring to the imperial janissary corps as opposed to the *yarliyya.*
qāḍī: Judge.
saj`: Rhymed prose.
sayyid: See *ashrāf.*
shaykh: Elder, master. Often a title denoting advanced learning or spiritual position.
silsila: See *mashāyakha.*
sīrā (plural, *siyar*): The genre of Arabic popular epic. The epic is a fictionalized biography of a real historical personality. The term also refers to the biography of the Prophet Muḥammad.
sīrān: Picnic, promenade.
sohbet (Turkish): Conversation from the Arabic *ṣuḥba.*
ṣuḥba: Companionship, fellowship.
tārīkh: History, chronicle.
ta'rīkh: History writing, or the act of chronicling.
tarjama (plural, *tarājim*): Obituary notice or biographical entry, typically of a deceased scholar.
thabat: A list of books that a scholar has been authorized to transmit.
walī : A friend of God, a saint.
yarliyya (*yerli* in Turkish): The local janissary corps as opposed to the *qabīqūl.*
yawmiyyāt (*yevmiye* in Turkish): Daily occurrences, journal.

Bibliography

al-'Abd, Ḥasan Āghā. "Tārīkh Ḥasan Āghā al-`Abd." Microfilm MS 1136, Majma` al-Lugha al-`Arabiyya, Damascus.

———. *Tārīkh Ḥasan Āghā al-`Abd: Ḥawādith Bilād al-Shām wa al-imbaraṭūriyya al-`uthmāniyya*. Edited by Yūsuf Nu`aysa. Damascus: Dār Dimashq li-al-Ṭibā'a wa al-Nashr, 1986.

Abd al-Razzaq, Moaz. "Domestic Architecture, Notables, and Power: A Neighbourhood in Late Ottoman Damascus." In *Art turc: Actes de 10e Congrès international d'art turc, Genève, 17–23 septembre 1995/ Turkish Art: Proceedings of 10th International Congress of Turkish Art, Geneva, 17–23 September 1995*, 489–495. Geneva: Foundation Max Van Berchem, 1998.

Abou-El-Haj, Rifaat Ali. *Formation of the Modern State: The Ottoman Empire, Sixteenth to Eighteenth Centuries*. Albany: State University of New York Press, 1991.

———. "The Ottoman Vezir and Paşa Households 1683–1703: A Preliminary Report." *Journal of the American Oriental Society* 94, no. 4 (December 1974): 65–80, 438–447.

Abū al-Fatḥ. *The Kitāb al-tārīkh of Abu 'l-Fath*. Edited by Paul Stenhouse. Sydney: University of Sydney Press, 1985.

Abu-Husayn, Abdul-Rahim. *Provincial Leaderships in Syria, 1575–1650*. Beirut: American University of Beirut, 1985.

Ahmed, Mohammed Shahab. "The Satanic Verses Incident in the Memory of the Early Muslim Community: An Analysis of the Early Riwāyahs and Their Isnāds." Ph. D. diss., Princeton University, 1999.

'Ajamī, Muḥammad b. Nāṣir. *Āl al-Qāsimī wa nubūghu-hum fī al-'ilm wa altaḥṣīl*. Beirut: Dār al-Bashā'ir al-Islāmīya, 1999.

Akkach, Samer. *'Abd al-Ghani al-Nabulusi: Islam and the Enlightenment*. Oxford: Oneworld, 2007.

Altoma, Salih J. *The Problem of Diglossia in Arabic: A Comparative Study of Classical and Iraqi Arabic*. Cambridge, Mass.: Harvard University Press, 1969.

Amīn, Muḥammad, and Laylā `Alī Ibrāhīm. *Al-Muṣṭalaḥāt al-mi`māriyya fī al-wathā'iq al-mamlūkiyya:1250–1517*. Cairo: American University in Cairo Press, 1990.

al-Amīn, al-Sayyid Muḥsin. *Khiṭaṭ Jabal `Āmil*. Edited by Ḥasan al-Amīn. 2 vols. Beirut: Maṭba`at al-Inṣāf, 1961.

And, Metin. *A History of Theatre and Popular Entertainment in Turkey*. Ankara: Forum Yaynlar, 1963.

Anderson, Benedict. *Imagined Communities: Reflections on the Origin and Spread of Nationalism*. New York: Verso, 1983.

Andrews, Walter, and Irene Markoff. "Poetry, the Arts, and Group Ethos in the Ideology of the Ottoman Empire." *Edebiyat: A Journal of Middle Eastern and Comparative Literature* 1, no. 1 (1987), 41–47.

Anīs, Muḥammad. *Madrasat al-tārīkh al-miṣrī fī al-`ahd al-`uthmānī*. Cairo: Jāmi'at al-Duwal al-'Arabiyya, 1962.

Ānūtī, Usāma. *Al-Ḥaraka al-adabiyya fī Bilād al-Shām khilāl al-qarn al-thāmin `ashar*. Beirut: Lebanese University Press, 1970.

Arberry, A. J. *The Chester Beatty Library: A Catalogue of the Persian Manuscripts and Miniatures*. Dublin: Hodges, Figgis, 1959.

Artan, Tülay. "Arts and Architecture." In *The Cambridge History of Turkey*. Vol. 3: *The Later Ottoman Empire, 1603–1839*. Edited by Soraiya Faroqhi, 408–480. Cambridge: Cambridge University Press, 2006.

al-'Ashsh, Abū al-Faraj. "al-Dūr al-athariyya al-khāṣṣa fī Dimashq." *Annales archéologiques de Syrie* 3, no. 8–9 (1953): 47–58.

al-'Ashsh, Yūsuf. *Fihris makhṭūṭat dār al-kutub al-Ẓāhiriyya*. Damascus: al-Majma' al-'Ilmī al-'Arabī, 1946.

———. "Mudhakkarāt yawmiyya duwwinat bi-Dimashq." *Majallat al-majma` al-`ilmī al-`arabī* 18 (1943): 142–154.

Ayalon, Ami. *The Press in the Arab Middle East: A History*. Oxford: Oxford University Press, 1995.

Aynur, Hatice. "Ottoman Literature." In *The Cambridge History of Turkey*. Vol. 3: *The Later Ottoman Empire, 1603–1839*. Edited by Suraiya Faroqhi, 481–520. Cambridge: Cambridge University Press, 2006.

Baer, Gabriel. "Jerusalem Notables in Ottoman Cairo." In *Egypt and Palestine: A Millennium of Association (868–1948)*. Edited by Amnon Cohen and Gabriel Baer, 167–175. Jerusalem: Ben-Zvi Institute for the Study of Jewish Communities in the East, 1984.

———. *Egyptian Guilds in Modern Times*. Jerusalem: Israel Oriental Society, 1964.

Bakhtin, M. M. "Epic and Novel: Toward a Methodology for the Study of the Novel." In *The Dialogic Imagination: Four Essays*, translated by Michael Holquist, 3–40. Austin: University of Texas Press, 1981.

———. *Rabelais and His World*. Translated by Helene Iswolsky. Cambridge, Mass: MIT Press, 1968.

Bakr, `Abd al-Wahhab. "Interrelationships Among the Damurdāshī group of Manuscripts." In *Eighteenth Century Egypt: the Arabic Manuscript Sources*. Edited by Daniel Crecelius, 79–88. Claremont: Regina Books, 1990.

Barbir, Karl. "All in the Family: The Muradis of Damascus." *Archivum Ottomanicum* 6 (1980): 327–353.

———. *Ottoman Rule in Damascus, 1708–1758*. Princeton: Princeton University Press, 1980.

Bartlett, W. H., and William Purser. *Syria, the Holy Land, Asia Minor, etc., Illustrated*. London: Fisher, Son, and Co., 1836.

al-Barzanjī , Zayn al-`Ābidīn b. al-Sayyid Muḥammad. "Kashf al-ḥujub wa al-sutūr `an mā waqa`a li-ahl al-Madina ma`a amīr Makka Surūr." MS Chester Beatty Library, Ar 3551/1, Dublin.

Bauer, Thomas. "Mamluk Literature: Misunderstandings and New Approaches." *Mamluk Studies Review* 10, no. 2 (2005): 105–132.

al-Bayṭār, Abd al-Razzāq. *Ḥulyat al-bashar fī tārīkh al-qarn al-thālith `ashar*. 3 vols. Damascus: Majma` al-Lugha al-`Arabiyya, 1961–1963.

Beg, M.A.J. "Ḥallāḳ," in *Encyclopaedia of Islam*, 2nd ed.

Behrens-Abouseif, Doris. "The Abd al-Rahmān Katkhudā Style in 18th Century Cairo." *Annales Islamologiques* 26 (1992): 117–126.

Ben Zvi, Itzhak. *The Book of the Samaritans.* Tel-Aviv: Magnes Press, 1970.

Berkey, Jonathan Porter. *The Transmission of Knowledge in Medieval Cairo: A Social History of Islamic Education.* Princeton: Princeton University Press, 1992.

Bourdieu, Pierre. *The Logic of Practice.* Stanford: Stanford University Press, 1990.

Bouwsma, William. "Anxiety and the Formation of Early Modern Culture." In *After the Reformation: Essays in Honor of J. H. Hexter.* Edited by Barbara Malament and William Bouwsma, 215–246. Manchester: Manchester University Press, 1980.

Bowen, Harold, and H.A.R. Gibb. *Islamic Society and the West: A Study of the Impact of Western Civilization on Moslem Culture in the Near East.* 2 vols. London: Oxford University Press, 1950.

Bualuan, Hayat. "Mikha'il Breik: A Chronicler and a Historian in 18th Century bilad al-Sham." *Parole de l'Orient* 21 (1996): 257–270.

———. *Mu'arrikhū Bilād al-Shām fī al-qarn al-thāmin `ashar.* Beirut: al-Furāt, 2002.

al-Budayrī (al-Ḥallāq), Aḥmad. "The Barber of Damascus: Ahmad Budayri al-Hallaq's Chronicle of the Year 1749." In *The Modern Middle East: A Sourcebook for History.* Edited by Camron M. Amin, Benjamin C. Fortna, and Elizabeth Frierson, translated by Steve Tamari, 562–568. London: Oxford University Press, 2006.

———. (or Şeyh Ahmet el-Bediri el-Hallak). *Berber Bediri'nin günlüğü 1741–1762, Osmanlı taşra hayatına ilişkin olaylar.* A translation of al-Budayrī's chronicle into Turkish by Hasan Yüksel. Ankara: Akçağ, 1995.

———. *Ḥawādith Dimashq al-yawmiyya, 1154–1175 H: 1741–1762 M.* In the recension of Muḥammad Sa'īd al-Qāsimī, edited by Aḥmad 'Izzat 'Abd al-Karīm. Cairo: Maṭbū'āt Lajnat al-Bayān al-'Arabī, 1959. Second edition with a study Muḥammad Jamīl Ṣulṭān. Damascus: Dār Sa`d al-Dīn, 1997.

Burayk, Mīkhā'īl. *Tārīkh al-Shām.* Edited by Aḥmad Ghassān Sabānū. Damascus: Dār Qutaybah, 1982.

———. "Tārīkh al-Shām." MS 9786. Pet. 188, and 9787. Pet. 188, Arabic Collection, Staatsbibliothek zu Berlin, Berlin.

———. "Tārīkh al-Shām." MS Tārīkh 2213, Taymuriyya Collection, Dār al-Kutub, Cairo.

———. "Tawārīkh al-zamān wa zahrat a`ājīb al-kawn wa al-awān." MS *Tārīkh* 5453, al-Asad National Library, Damascus.

Buturovic, Amila. "Sociology of Popular Drama in Medieval Egypt: Ibn Dāniyāl and His Shadow Plays." Ph.D. diss., McGill University, 1993.

———. "'Truly, This Land Is Triumphant and Its Accomplishments Evident!' Baybar's Cairo in Ibn Daniyal's Shadow Play." In *Writers and Rulers: Perspectives on Their Relationship from Abbasid to Safavid Times.* Edited by Louise Marlow and Beatrice Gruendler, 149–168. Wiesbaden: Reichert, 2004.

Cachia, Pierre. "The Egyptian Mawwal: Its Ancestry, Its Development, and Its Present Forms." *Journal of Arabic Literature* 8 (1977): 77–103.

Çağman, Filiz. "Women's Clothing." In *9000 Years of Anatolian Women.* Edited by Günsel Renda, 256–291. Istanbul: Ministry of Culture of the Turkish Republic, 1993.

Cahen, Claude. "History and Historians." In *The Cambridge History of Arabic Literature. Religion, Learning and Science in the Abbasid Period.* Edited by M.J.L. Young, J. D. Latham, and R. B. Serjeant, 188–233. Cambridge: Cambridge University Press, 1990.

Çaksu, Ali. "Janissary Coffeehouses in Late Eighteenth-Century Istanbul." In *Ottoman*

Tulips, Ottoman Coffee: Leisure and Lifestyle in the Eighteenth Century. Edited by Dana Sajdi, 117–132. London: I. B. Tauris, 2007.

Canbakal, Hülya. "'Ayntab at the End of the Seventeenth Century: A Study of Notables and Urban Politics." Ph.D. diss., Harvard University, 1999.

———. *Society and Politics in an Ottoman Town: `Ayntab in the 17th Century*. Leiden: Brill, 2007.

Canova, Giovanni. "Gli Studi sull'epica popolare araba." *Oriente Moderno* 57 (1977): 211–226.

Çelebi, Ḥajjī Khalīfa Kātib. *Kashf al-Ẓunūn `an asāmī al-kutub wa al-funūn*. Edited by Şerifettin Yaltkaya and Kilisli Rifat Bilge. 6 vols. Istanbul: Maarif Matbaasi, 1941.

de Certeau, *The Practice of Everyday Life*. Translated by Steven Rendall. Berkeley: University of California Press, 1984.

Chamberlain, Michael. *Knowledge and Social Practice in Medieval Damascus, 1190–1350*. Cambridge: Cambridge University Press, 1994.

Chartier, Roger. "Culture as Appropriation: Popular Cultural Uses in Early Modern France." In *Understanding Popular Culture: Europe from the Middle Ages to the Nineteenth Century*, edited by Stephen L Kaplan, 229–253. Berlin: Mouton, 1984.

———. *The Order of Books: Readers, Authors and Libraries in Europe Between the Fourteenth and Eighteenth Centuries*. Translated by Lydia G. Cochrane. Cambridge: Polity Press, 1994.

Chevalier, Dominique. "A Damas, production et société à la fin de XIXe siècle." *Annales* 19, no. 5 (1064): 966–972.

Cohen, Amnon. *The Guilds of Ottoman Jerusalem*. Leiden: Brill, 2001.

———. *Palestine in the 18th Century: Patterns of Government and Administration*. Jerusalem: Magnes Press, 1973.

Cole, Juan. "Printing and Urban Islam in the Mediterranean World, 1890–1920." In *Modernity and Culture: From the Mediterranean to the Indian Ocean*. Edited by Leila Tarazi Fawaz and C. A. Bayly, 344–364. New York: Columbia University Press, 2002.

Commins, David Dean. *Islamic Reform: Politics and Social Change in Late Ottoman Syria*. London: Oxford University Press, 1990.

Connelly, Bridget. *Arab Folk Epic and Identity*. Berkeley: University of California Press, 1986.

Cooperson, Michael. *Classical Arabic Biography: The Heirs of the Prophets in the Age of al-Mamūn*. Cambridge: Cambridge University Press, 2000.

Crown, Alan David. *Samaritan Scribes and Manuscripts*. Tübingen: Mohr Siebeck, 2001.

al-Danafī, Ibrāhīm b. Yaqūb. *Ẓāhir al-'Umar wa-ḥukkām Jabal Nābulus, 1185–1187 AH/1771–1773 CE*. Edited by Mūsā Abū Diyya. Nablus: Jāmiat al-Najā al-Waanīya, 1986.

al-Danafī, Ibrāhīm b. Yaqūb, and (separately) `Abd al-Ghanī al-Nābulusī. *Al-Mukhtār min kitāb al-ḥaḍra al-unsiyya fī al-riḥla al-qudsiyya wa yalī-hi kurrās `an hujūm al-Ẓāhir al-`Umar `alā Nāblus*. Excerpts of a book by al-Nābulusī and the chronicle by al-Danafī edited by Iḥsān al-Nimr. Nablus: n.p., 1972.

Darling, Linda T. "Public Finances: The Role of the Ottoman Center." In *The Cambridge History of Turkey*. Vol. 3: *The Later Ottoman Empire, 1603–1839*. Edited by Soraiya Faroqhi, 118–131. Cambridge: Cambridge University Press, 2006.

Darnton, Robert. "A Bourgeois Puts His World in Order: The City as a Text." In *The Great Cat Massacre and Other Episodes in French Cultural History*, 107–144. New York: Basic Books, 1984.

Daskalakis (Mathews), Anne-Christine. "Damascus 18th and 19th Century Houses in the Ablaq-`Ajamī Style of Decoration: Local and International Significance." Ph.D. diss., New York University, 2004.

———. "A Room of 'Splendor and Generosity' from Ottoman Damascus." *Metropolitan Museum Journal* 32 (1997): 111–139.

Daulte, F. "Le Palais Azem à Damas." *L'Oeil* 337, no. 1983: 62–63.

Deguilhem, Randi, and Suraiya Faroqhi, eds. *Crafts and Craftsmen of the Middle East: Fashioning the Individual in the Muslim Mediterranean.* London: I. B. Tauris, 2005.

Dols, Michael W. "The Second Plague Pandemic and Its Recurrences in the Middle East: 1347–1894." *Journal of the Economic and Social History of the Orient* 22, no. 2 (May 1979): 162–189.

Douwes, Dick. *The Ottomans in Syria: A History of Justice and Oppression.* London: I. B. Tauris, 2000.

Dubler, C. E. "`Adjā'ib," in *Encyclopaedia of Islam*, 2nd ed.

Elbendary, Amina A. "The Sultan, the Tyrant, and the Hero: Changing Medieval Perceptions of al-Zahir Baybars." *Mamluk Studies Review* 5 (2001): 141–157.

Eldem, Edhem. "Urban Voices from Beyond: Identity, Status and Social Strategies in Ottoman Funerary Epitaphs of Istanbul (1700–1850)." In *The Early Modern Ottomans: Remapping the Empire.* Edited by Virginia H Aksan and Daniel Goffman, 233–255. Cambridge: Cambridge University Press, 2007.

Elger, Ralf. *Muṣṭafā Bakrī: zur Selbstdarstellung eines syrischen Gelehrten, Sufis und Dichters des 18. Jahrhunderts.* Schenfeld: EB-Verlag, 2004.

El-Hassan, S. "Educated Spoken Arabic in Egypt and the Levant: A Critical Review of Diglossia and Related Concepts." *Archivum Linguisticum* 3 (1977): 112–132.

El-Rouayheb, Khaled. *Before Homosexuality in the Arab-Islamic World, 1500–1800.* Chicago: University of Chicago Press, 2005.

Establet, Colette, and Jean-Paul Pascual. *Familles et fortunes à Damas: 450 foyers damascains en 1700.* Damascus: Institut Français de Damas, 1994.

———. "Les Livres des gens à Damas 1700." *Revue des Mondes Musulmans et de la Méditerranée* 87–88 (1999): 143–175.

Evren, Burçak. *Osmanlı esnafı.* Istanbul: Doğan Kitapçılık, 1999.

———. *Osmanlı'da esnaf ve örgütleri.* Istanbul, n.p., 1997.

Farah, Caesar E. *The Dhayl in Medieval Arabic Historiography.* New Haven: American Oriental Society, 1967.

Faroqhi, Suraiya. *Approaching Ottoman History: An Introduction to the Sources.* Cambridge: Cambridge University Press, 1999.

———. *Artisans of Empire: Crafts and Craftspeople Under the Ottomans.* London: I. B. Tauris, 2009.

———. "Introduction." In *The Cambridge History of Turkey.* Vol. 3. *The Later Ottoman Empire, 1603–1839.* Edited by Suraiya Faroqhi, 3–17. Cambridge: Cambridge University Press, 2006.

———. *Pilgrims and Sultans: The Ḥajj Under the Ottomans.* London: I. B. Tauris, 1994.

———. *Subjects of the Sultan: Culture and Daily Life in the Ottoman Empire.* London: I. B. Tauris, 2000.

Fattah, Hala. "Representations of Self and Other in Two Iraqi Travelogues of the Ottoman Period." *International Journal of Middle East Studies* 30 (1998): 51–76.

Ferguson, Charles A. "Diglossia." *Word* 15 (1959): 325–340.

Filan, Kerima. "Life in Sarajevo in the 18th Century (According to Mulla Mustafa's *Mecmua*)." In *Living in the Ottoman Ecumenical Community: Essays in Honour of Suraiya Faroqhi*. Edited by Vera Costantini and Markus Koller, 317–345. Leiden; Boston: Brill, 2008.

Findley, Carter Vaughn. "Political Culture and the Great Households." In *The Cambridge History of Turkey*. Vol. 3: *The Later Ottoman Empire, 1603–1839*. Edited by Suraiya Faroqhi, 65–80. Cambridge: Cambridge University Press, 2006.

Fleischer, Cornell H. *Bureaucrat and Intellectual in the Ottoman Empire: The Historian Mustafa Âli (1541–1600)*. Princeton: Princeton University Press, 1986.

Gaster, Moses. *The Samaritans, Their History, Doctrines and Literature*. London: Oxford University Press, 1925.

Ginzburg, Carlo. *The Cheese and the Worms: the Cosmos of a Sixteenth Century Miller*. Translated by John Tedeschi and Anne Tedeschi. 2nd ed. New York: Dorset Press, 1989.

Glass, Dagmar, Geoffrey Roper, and Hrant Gabeyan. "Arabic Book and Newspaper Printing in the Arab World." In *Middle Eastern Languages and the Print Revolution: A Cross-Cultural Encounter: A Catalogue and Companion to the Exhibition*. Edited by Eval Hanebutt Benz et al., 177–216. Westhofen: WVA-Verlag Skulima, 2002.

Goodwin, Godfrey. *The Janissaries*. London: Saqi Books, 1994.

Graf, Georg. *Geschichte der christlichen arabischen Literatur*. 5 vols. Vatican City: Biblioteca Apostolica Vaticana, 1944.

Gran, Peter. *Islamic Roots of Capitalism: Egypt 1760–1840*. 2nd ed. Syracuse: Syracuse University Press, 1998.

Grehan, James. *Everyday Life and Consumer Culture in 18th-Century Damascus*. Seattle: University of Washington Press, 2007.

———. "Street Violence and Social Imagination in Late-Mamluk and Ottoman Damascus (ca. 1500–1800)." *International Journal of Middle East Studies* 35, no. 2 (2003): 215–236.

Gully, Adrian. "Arabic Linguistic Issues and Controversies of the Late Nineteenth and Early Twentieth Centuries." *Journal of Semitic Studies* 42, no. I (1997): 75–120.

Guo, Li. "Mamluk Historiographic Studies: The State of the Art." *Mamluk Studies Review* 1 (1997): 16–43.

Haarman, Ulrich. "Arabic in Speech, Turkish in Lineage: Mamluks and Their Sons in the Intellectual Life of Fourteenth-Century Egypt and Syria." *Journal of Semitic Studies* 33 (1988): 81–114.

———. "Auflösung und Bewahrung der klassischer Formen arbischer Geschichtsschreibung in der Zeit Mamluk." *Zeitschrift der deutschen Morgenländischen Gesellschaft*, 121 (1971): 47–61.

Haddad, George. "The Interests of an Eighteenth Century Chronicler of Damascus." *Der Islam* 38, no. 3 (1963): 258–271.

Haeri, Niloofar. *Sacred Language, Ordinary People: Dilemmas of Culture and Politics in Egypt*. New York: Palgrave Macmillan, 2003.

Hamadeh, Shirine. *The City's Pleasures: Istanbul in the Eighteenth Century*. Seattle: University of Washington Press, 2008.

———. "Public Space and the Garden Culture of Istanbul in the Eighteenth Century." In *The Early Modern Ottomans: Remapping the Empire*, eds. Virginia H. Aksan and Daniel Goffman, 227–312. Cambridge University Press: Cambridge, 2007.

al-Hamadhānī, Badī' al-Zamān. *Maqāmāt Badī' al-Zamān al-Hamadhānī.* Beirut: Dār wa-Maktabat al-Hilāl, 1993.

Hämeen-Anttila, Jaakko. *Maqama: A History of a Genre.* Diskurse der Arabistik Bd. 5. Wiesbaden: Harrassowitz, 2002.

Hammond, Marlé. "Qasida, Marthiya, and Differance." In *Transforming Loss into Beauty: Essays on Arabic Literature and Culture in Honor of Magda Al-Nowaihi.* Edited by Dana Sajdi and Marlé Hammond, 143–184. Cairo: American University in Cairo Press, 2008.

Hamzah, Dyala, ed. "From `ilm to Sihāfa or the Politics of the Public Interest (Maslaha): Muhammad Rashīd Ridā and His Journal al-Manār (1898–1935)." *In the Making of the Arab Intellectual: Empire, Public Sphere, and the Colonial Coordinates of Selfhood.* Edited by Dyala Hamzah, 90–127. (New York and Abdingon, Oxon: Routledge, 2013).

Hanioğlu, Şükrü. *A Brief History of the Late Ottoman Empire.* Princeton: Princeton University Press, 2008.

Hanna, Nelly. "The Administration of Courts in Ottoman Cairo." In *The State and Its Servants: Administration in Egypt from Ottoman Times to the Present.* Edited by Nelly Hanna, 44–59. Cairo: American University in Cairo Press, 1995.

———. "The Chronicles of Ottoman Egypt: History or Entertainment?" In *The Historiography of Islamic Egypt, c. 950–1800.* Edited by Hugh Kennedy, 237–250. Leiden: Brill, 2001.

———. "Culture in Ottoman Egypt." In *The Cambridge History of Egypt: Modern Egypt from 1517 to the End of the Twentieth Century.* 2 vols. Edited by M. W. Daly, 2: 87–112. Cambridge: Cambridge University Press, 2008.

———. "Guilds in Recent Historical Scholarship." In *The City in the Islamic World.* 2 vols. Edited by Renata Holod, Attilio Petruccioli, and André Raymond, 2: 895–920. Leiden: Brill, 2008.

———. *In Praise of Books: A Cultural History of Cairo's Middle Class, Sixteenth to the Eighteenth Century.* Syracuse: Syracuse University Press, 2003.

———. "Literacy and the 'Great Divide' in the Islamic World, 1300–1800." *Journal of Global History* 2, no. 2 (2007): 175–193.

Ḥarb, Ṭalāl. *Bunyat al-sīra al-sha`biyya wa khiṭābu-hā al-malḥamī fī `asr al-Mamālīk.* Beirut: al-Mu'assassa al-Jāmi`iyya li-al-Dirāsāt wa al-Nashr, 1999.

al-Ḥarīrī, Muḥammad b. `Uthmān. *Sharḥ Maqāmāt al-Ḥarīrī, wa-huwa Abū Muḥammad Al-Qāsim ibn 'Alī ibn Muḥammad ibn 'Uthmān al-Ḥarīrī al-Baṣrī.* Commentaries by `Abd Allāh Ibn Khashshāb and `Abd Allāh Ibn Barrī. Beirut: Dār al-Turāth, 1968.

Hathaway, Jane. *The Arab Lands Under Ottoman Rule, 1516–1800.* Harlow: Pearson Longman, 2008.

———. "The Household: An Alternative Framework for the Military Society of Eighteenth-Century Ottoman Egypt." *Oriente Moderno* 18 (1999): 57–66.

———. *The Politics of Households in Ottoman Egypt: The Rise of the Qazdağlis.* Cambridge: Cambridge University Press, 1997.

———. "Sultans, Pasha, Taqwims and Mühimmes: A Reconsideration of Chronicle-Writing in Eighteenth Century Ottoman Egypt." In *Eighteenth Century Egypt: The Arabic Manuscript Sources.* Edited by Daniel Crecelius. Claremont: Regina Books, 1990.

Heykal, Bernard. "Dissembling Descent, or How the Barber Lost His Turban: Identity and Evidence in Eighteenth-Century Zaydī Yemen." *Islamic Society and Law* 9, no. 2 (2002): 194–230.

Heyworth-Dunne, J. *An Introduction to the History of Education in Modern Egypt.* London: Cass, 1968.

Hirschler, Konrad. *The Written Word in the Medieval Arabic Lands: A Social and Cultural History of Reading Practices.* Edinburgh: Edinburgh University Press, 2012.

al-Ḥiṣnī, Muḥammad Adīb. *Kitāb muntakhabāt al-tawārīkh li-Dimashq.* 3 vols. Damascus: al-Ḥadītha Press, 1927–1929.

al-Ḥiṣnī, Taqiyy al-Dīn. *Kifāyat al-akhyār fī ḥall ghāyat al-ikhtiṣār.* Edited by `Alī `Abd al-Ḥamīd Abū Khayr and Muḥammad Wahbī Sulaymān. Damascus: Dār al-Khayr, 1996.

Holt, P. M. *The Age of the Crusades: The Near East from the Eleventh Century to 1517.* London: Longman, 1986.

———. "The Career of Küçük Muḥammad (1676–94)." *Bulletin of the School of Oriental and African Studies* 26, no. 2 (1963): 269–287.

———. "al-Jabartī's Introduction to the History of Ottoman Egypt." *Bulletin of the School of Oriental and African Studies* 25, no. 1/3 (1962): 38–51.

Hourani, Albert. *Arabic Thought in the Liberal Age, 1798–1939.* 2nd ed. Cambridge: Cambridge University Press, 1983.

———. "Historians of Lebanon." In *Historians of the Middle East.* Edited by Bernard Lewis and P. M. Holt, 226–245. London: Oxford University Press, 1962.

———. "Ottoman Reform and the Politics of the Notables." In *Beginnings of Modernization in the Middle East: The Nineteenth Century.* Edited by William Roe Polk and Richard L. Chambers, 41–68. Chicago: University of Chicago Press, 1968.

Howard, Douglas A. "Genre and Myth in the Ottoman Advice for Kings Literature." In *The Early Modern Ottomans: Remapping the Empire.* Edited by Virginia H. Aksan and Daniel Goffman, 61–74. Cambridge: Cambridge University Press, 2007.

Humphreys, R. Stephen. *Islamic History: A Framework for Inquiry.* Princeton: Princeton University Press, 1991.

al-Ḥusayn, Yaḥyā b. *Bahjat al-zaman fī ḥawādith al-Yaman.* Edited by Abd Allāh b. Muḥammad al-Ḥabashī. Abu Dhabi: Manshūrāt al-Majma` al-Thaqāfī, 1996.

Ibn 'Ajība, Aḥmad ibn Muḥammad. *The Autobiography of the Moroccan Sufi Ibn Ajiba.* Edited by Jean-Louis Michon. Translated by David Streight. Louisville: Fons Vitae, 1999.

Ibn Budayr, Shihāb al-Dīn Aḥmad. "Ḥawādith Dimashq al-Shām al-yawmiyya min sanat 1154 ilā sanat 1176." MS Chester Beatty Library Ar 3551/2, Dublin.

Ibn Dānīyāl, Muḥammad. *Three Shadow Plays.* Edited by Paul Kahle, Derek Hopwood, and Muḥammad Muṣṭafā Badawī. Cambridge: Trustees of the E.J.W. Gibb Memorial, 1992.

Ibn Dīmitrī (al-Ḥalabī), Yūsuf. "al-Murtād fī tārīkh Ḥalab wa Baghdād." Edited by Fawwāz Maḥmūd al-Fawwāz. M.A. thesis. University of Damascus, 1978.

Ibn al-Husayn, Yaḥyā, *Bahjat al-zamān fī ḥawādith al-Yaman.* Edited by `Abd Allāh b. Muḥammad al-Ḥabashī under the title *Yawmiyyāt Ṣan`ā'*. Abu Dhabi: Manshūrāt al-Majma` al-Thaqāfī, 1996.

Ibn Ismā`īl, al-Mu'ayyad bi-Allāh. *Mudhakkarāt al-Mu'ayyad bi-Allāh Muḥammad b. Ismā`īl.* Edited by `Abd Allāh Muḥammad al-Ḥabashī. Beirut: al-Mu'assasa al-Jāmi`iyya li-al-Dirāsāt wa al-Nashr wa al-Tawzī`, 1991.

Ibn Kannān, Muḥammad b. Īsā. "al-Ḥawādith al-yawmiyya li-tārīkh aḥada 'ashara wa alf wa miyya." MS 9479. We. 1114 and 9480 We. 1115, Arabic Collection, Staatsbibliothek zu Berlin, Berlin.

———. *Al-Mawākib al-islāmiyya fī al-mamālik wa-al-maḥāsin al-shāmiyya*. 2 vols. Edited by Ḥikmat Ismāʿīl. Damascus: Wizārat al-Thaqāfa, 1992.

———. *Yawmīyāt shāmiyya: wa-huwa, al-tārīkh al-musammā bi-al-ḥawādith al-yawmiyya min tārīkh aḥada ʿashara wa-alf wa-miyya*. Edited by Akram Ḥasan ʿUlabī. Damascus: Dār al-Ṭabbāʿ li-al-Ṭibāʿa wa-al-Nashr wa-al-Tawzīʿ, 1994.

Ibn Karāma, Muṣṭafā Jamāl al-Dīn. "Aḥdāth bilād Ṭarāblus al-Shām." Edited by Muḥammad ʿAdnān al-Bakhīt, *Majallat majmaʿ al-lugha al-ʿarabiyya al-urdunī* 1, no. 1 (1986): 171–206.

Ibn Ṣaṣra, Muḥammad b. Muḥammad. *A Chronicle of Damascus 1389–1497: The Unique Bodleian Library Manuscript of al-Durra al-muḍīʾa fī al-dawla al-Ẓāhiriyya*. Edited, translated, and annotated by William M. Brinner. 2 vols. Berkeley: University of California Press, 1963.

Ibn al-Ṣiddīq, Hasan. *Gharāʾib al-badāʾiʿ wa ʿajāʾib al-waqāʾiʿ*. Edited by Yūsuf Jamīl Nuʿaysa. Damascus: Dār al-Maʿrifa, 1988.

———. "Gharāʾib al-badāʾiʿ wa ʿajāʾib al-waqāʾiʿ." MS 9832. We. 417, Arabic Collection, Staatsbibliothek zu Berlin, Berlin.

Ibn Ṭawq, Shihāb Aḥmad b. Muḥammad. *al-Taʿlīq, yawmiyyāt Shihāb Aḥmad Ibn Ṭawq: mudhakkarāt kutibat bi-Dimasqh fī ākhir al-ʿahd al-mamlūkī (1480–1502)*. Edited by Jaʿfar al-Muhājir. 3 vols. Damascus: Institut Français de Damas, 2000–.

Ibn Ṭāwūs, Raḍiyy al-Dīn. *al-Tashrīf bi al-minan fī al-taʿrīf bi-al-fitan*. Qom: Mu'assasat Ṣāḥib al-Amr, 1996.

Ibn Ṭūlūn, Shams al-Dīn Muḥammad b. ʿAlī. *Mufākahat al-khillān fī ḥawādith al-zamān, tārīkh Miṣr wa-al-Shām*. Edited by Muḥammad Muṣṭafā. Cairo: al-Muʾassasa al-Miṣrīya al-ʿĀmma li-al-Taʾlīf wa-al-Tarjama wa-al-Ṭibāʿa wa-al-Nashr, 1962.

Ibrāhīm, Nabīla. *Sīrat Dhāt al-Himma: dirāsa muqārana*. Riyad: Dār al-Marrīkh, 1985.

Inalcik, Halil. "Centralization and Decentralization in Ottoman Administration." In *Studies in Eighteenth Century Islamic History*. Edited by Thomas Naff and Roger Owen, 27–52. Carbondale: Southern Illinois University Press, 1977.

al-Iṣfahānī, Abū Shujā. *Ghāyat al-ikhtiṣār aw al-Ghāya wa al-taqrīb*. Edited by Sayyid Muḥammad Sayyid ʿAbd Allah ʿĀqilzada. Saudi Arabia: n.p., 2001. Translated into English by Anwar Ahmad Qadri, *A Sunni Shafiʿi Law Code*. New Delhi: Islamic Book Services, 1992.

İskit, Server Rifat. *Türkiyede Neşriyat Hareketleri Tarihine Bir Bakış*. Istanbul: Devlet Basımevi, 1939.

Jaber, Mounzer. "Pouvoir et société au Jabal ʿĀmil de 1749 à 1920 dans la conscience chiite et dans un essai d'interprétation." Ph.D. diss., Université Paris IV-Sorbonne, 1978.

Jirousek, Charlotte. "Transition to Mass Fashion System Dress in the Later Ottoman Empire." In *Consumption Studies and the History of the Ottoman Empire, 1550–1922: An Introduction*. Edited by Donald Quataert, 201–242. Albany: State University of New York Press, 2000.

Kafadar, Cemal. "Janissaries and Other Riffraff of Ottoman Istanbul: Rebels Without a Cause?" In *Identity and Identity Formation in the Ottoman World*. Edited by Baki Tezcan and Karl K. Barbir, 113–134. Madison: University of Wisconsin Press, 2007.

———. "Mütereddit bir Mutasavvıf: Üsküp'lü Asiye Hātūn'un Rüya Defteri 1641–43." *Topkapı Sarayı Müzesi Yillık* 5: 168–222.

———. "Self and Others: The Diary of a Dervish in Seventeenth Century Istanbul and First-Person Narratives in Ottoman Literature." *Studia Islamica*, no. 69 (1989): 121–150.

———. "Yeniçeri-Esnaf relations: Solidarity and Conflict." M.A. thesis, McGill University, 1981.

Kaḥḥāla, ʿUmar Riḍā. *Muʿjam al-mu'allifīn: tarājim muṣannifī al-kutub al-ʿarabiyya.* 15 vols. Damascus: al-Taraqqī Press, 1957. Another edition is *Muʿjam al-muʿallifīn.* 4 vols. Beirut: Mu'assasat al-Risāla, 1993.

Kaidbey, Naila Takieddine. "Historiography in Bilād al-Shām: The Sixteenth and Seventeenth Centuries." M.A. thesis, American University of Beirut, 1995.

Karamustafa, Ahmet T. *God's Unruly Friends.* Salt Lake City: University of Utah Press, 1994.

Katz, Jonathan Glustrom. *Dreams, Sufism, and Sainthood: The Visionary Career of Muhammad al-Zawāwī.* Leiden: Brill, 1996.

Keenan, Brigid. *Damascus: Hidden Treasures of the Old City.* New York: Thames & Hudson, 2000.

Khalidi, Tarif. *Arabic Historical Thought in the Classical Period.* Cambridge: Cambridge University Press, 1994.

———. *Images of Muhammad: Narratives of the Prophet in Islam Across the Centuries.* New York: Doubleday Religion: 2009.

Khuri-Makdisi, Ilham. *The Eastern Mediterranean and the Making of Global Radicalism, 1860–1914.* Berkeley: University of California Press, 2010.

Kilito, Abdelfattah. *al-Maqāmāt: Al-sard wa al-ansāq al-thaqāfīya.* Translated by ʿAbd al-Karīm al-Sharqāwī. 2nd ed. Casablanca: Dār Tūbqāl, 2001.

———. *Les Séances: récits et codes culturels chez Hamadhânî et Harîrî.* Paris: Sindbad, 1983.

Kirli, Cengiz. "The Struggle over Space: Coffeehouses of Ottoman Istanbul, 1780–1845." Ph.D. diss., State University of New York at Binghamton, 2001.

Klein, Denise. *Die osmanischen Ulema Des 17. Jahrhunderts: eine geschlossene Gesellschaft?* Berlin: Klaus Schwarz, 2007.

Koury, George John. "The Province of Damascus, 1783–1832." Ph.D. diss., University of Michigan, 1970.

Lamoreaux, J. C. *The Early Muslim Tradition of Dream Interpretation.* Albany: SUNY Press, 2002.

Lapidus, Ira M. *Muslim Cities in the Later Middle Ages.* Student ed. Cambridge: Cambridge University Press, 1984.

Little, Donald P. *An Introduction to Mamlūk Historiography; An Analysis of Arabic Annalistic and Biographical Sources for the Reign of al-Malik an-Nāṣir Muḥammad ibn Qalā'ūn.* Wiesbaden: Hans Steiner Verlag, 1970.

Lukács, György. "The Epic and the Novel." In *The Theory of the Novel: a Historico-Philosophical Essay on the Forms of Great Epic Literature*, 3–69. Cambridge, Mass.: MIT Press, 1971.

Lyons, M. C. *The Arabian Epic: Heroic and Oral Story-Telling.* 3 vols. Cambridge: Cambridge University Press, 1995.

Ma'oz, Moshe. "Changes in the Position and the Role of the 'Ulama in the 18th and 19th Century." In *The Syrian Land in the 18th and 19th Centuries: The Common and the Specific in the Historical Experience.* Edited by Thomas Philipp, 109–122. Stuttgart: Franz Steiner Verlag, 1992.

al-Maḥāsinī, Ismāʿīl b. Tāj al-Dīn. *Kunnāsh Ismāʿīl al-Maḥāsinī: ṣafaḥāt min tārīkh Dimashq fī al-qarn al-ḥādī ʿashar [al-hijrī].* Edited by Ṣalāḥ al-Dīn al-Munajjid. Beirut: Dār al-Kitāb al-Jadīd, 1965.

al-Maḥāsinī, Sulaymān b. Aḥmad. *Ḥulūl al-taʿab wa al-ālām bi-wuṣūl Abī al-Dhahab ilā Dimashq al-Shām*. Edited by Salāh al-Dīn al-Munajjid, Damascus?: Dār al-Kitāb al-Jadīd, 1962.

Makdisi, George. "Autograph Diary of an Eleventh-Century Historian of Baghdād in five parts." *Bulletin of the School of Oriental and African Studies, University of London* 18.1 (1956): 9–31, 18.2 (1956): 239–260, 19.3 (1957): 13–38, 19.4 (1957): 281–303, and (1957): 426–443.

———. "The Diary in Islamic Historiography: Some Notes." *History and Theory* 25, no. 2 (May 1986): 173–185.

———. *The Rise of the Colleges: Institutions of Learning in Islam and the West*. Edinburgh: Edinburgh University Press, 1981.

———. "Ṭabaqāt-Biography: Law and Orthodoxy in Classical Islam." *Islamic Studies* 32, no. 4 (1993): 371–396.

al-Makkī, Muḥammad b. Abd al-Sayyid al-Makkī. "Mudhakkarāt aḥad abnā' Ḥimṣ." MS 792, American University of Beirut, Beirut.

———. *Tārīkh Ḥimṣ: yawmiyyāt Muḥammad ibn al-Sayyid ibn al-Ḥājj Makkī ibn al-Khanqāḥ*. Edited by `Umar Najīb al-`Umar. Damascus: al-Ma`had al-`Ilmī al-Firansī li-al-Dirasāt al-`Arabiyya, 1987.

al-Makkī, Muḥammad Kāẓim. *Al-Ḥaraka al-fikriyya wa al-adabiyya fī Jabal `Āmil*. With an introduction by Fu`ād Afrām al-Bustānī. Beirut: Dār al-Andalus, 1963.

———. *Munṭalaq al-ḥayāh al-thaqāfiyya fī Jabal `Āmil*. Beirut: Dār al-Zahrā', 1991.

Manna, Adil. "Continuity and Change in the Socio-Political Elite in Palestine During the Late Ottoman Period." In *The Syrian Land in the 18th and 19th Century: The Common and the Specific in the Historical Experience*. Edited by Thomas Philipp, 69–89. Stuttgart: F. Steiner, 1992.

al-Maqqār, Muḥammad b. Jum`a, and Raslan Ibn al-Qārī. *Wulāt Dimashq fī al-`ahd al-`uthmānī wa huwa yataḍammanu: al-Bāshāt wa al-quḍāh, li-Ibn Jum`a, wa al-wuzarā' al-ladhīna ḥakamū Dimashq, li-Ibn al-Qārī, wa maṣādir `an tārīkh Dimashq ayyām al-`uthmaniyyīn*. Edited by Salāḥ al-Dīn al-Munajjid. Damascus, n.p. 1949.

Marcus, Abraham. *The Middle East on the Eve of Modernity: Aleppo in the Eighteenth Century*. New York: Columbia University Press, 1989.

Marino, Brigitte. "Cafés et cafetiers de Damas aux XVIIIe et XIXe siècles." *Revue des Mondes Musulmans et de la Méditerranée* 75–76, no. 1–2 (1996): 275–294.

———. *Ḥayy al-Maydān fī al-`asr al-`uthmānī*. Translated by Māhir al-Sharīf. Damascus: Dār al-Madā li-al-Thaqāfa, 2000.

Martin, B. G. "A Short History of the Khalwati Order of Dervishes." In *Scholars, Saints, and Sufis; Muslim Religious Institutions in the Middle East Since 1500*. Edited by Nikki R. Keddie, 276–305. Berkeley: University of California Press, 1972.

Masters, Bruce. *The Origins of Western Economic Dominance in the Middle East: Mercantilism and the Islamic Economy in Aleppo, 1600–1750*. New York: New York University Press, 1988.

———. "Ottoman Policies Toward Syria in the 17th and 18th Centuries." In *The Syrian Land in the 18th and 19th Century: The Common and the Specific in the Historical Experience*. Edited by Thomas Philipp, 11–26. Stuttgart: F. Steiner, 1992.

———. "The View from the Province: Syrian Chronicles of the Eighteenth Century." *Journal of American Oriental Society* 114 (1994): 353–362.

Maury, Bernard. "La Maison damascène au VIIIe et au début du XIXe siècle." In *L'habitat traditionnel dans les pays musulmans autour de la Méditerranée I:*

l'Heritage architectural, formes et fonctions. Cairo: Institut Français d'Archéologie Orientale, 1988.

al-Mawṣilī, Ilyās. *An Arab's Journey to Colonial Spanish America: The Travels of Elias Al-Mûsili in the Seventeenth Century.* Edited by Caesar E Farah. Syracuse: Syracuse University Press, 2003.

McGowan, Bruce. "The Age of the Ayāns, 1699–1812." In *An Economic and Social History of the Ottoman Empire, 1600–1914.* Edited by Halil İnalcık, Donald Quataert, Suraiya Faroqhi, Bruce McGowan, and Sevket Pamuk, 2 vols., 2: 637–758. Cambridge: Cambridge University Press, 1997.

Meier, Astrid. "Perceptions of a New Era? Historical Writing in Early Ottoman Damascus." *Arabica* 51.4 (2004): 419–434.

Meriwether, Margaret. *The Kin Who Count: Family and Society in Ottoman Aleppo, 1770–1840.* Austin: University of Texas Press, 1999.

———. "Urban Notables and Rural Resources in Aleppo, 1770–1830." *International Journal of Turkish Studies* 4, no. 1 (1987): 55–73.

Messick, Brinkley Morris. *The Calligraphic State: Textual Domination and History in a Muslim Society.* Berkeley: University of California Press, 1993.

Mikhail, Alan. "The Heart's Desire: Gender, Urban Space and the Ottoman Coffeehouse." In *Ottoman Tulips, Ottoman Coffee: Leisure and Lifestyle in the Eighteenth Century.* Edited by Dana Sajdi, 133–170. London: I. B. Tauris, 2007.

Mills, John. *Three Months' Residence at Nablus and an Account of the Modern Samaritans.* London: John Murray, 1864.

Mishāqa, Mīkhā'īl. *Mashhad al-`ayān bi-ḥawādith Sūriyya wa Lubnān.* Edited by Milḥim Khalīl `Abdū and Andrāwus Ḥannā Shakhashīrī. Cairo: n.p., 1908.

Momen, Moojan. *An Introduction to Shi'i Islam: The History and Doctrines of Twelver Shi'ism.* New Haven: Yale University Press, 1985.

Monroe, James T. *The Art of Badī' az-Zamān al-Hamadhānī as Picaresque Narrative.* Beirut: American University of Beirut, 1983.

Montgomery, James A. *The Samaritans, the Earliest Jewish Sect: Their History, Theology and Literature.* New York: Ktav, 1907.

Moreh, Shmuel. *Live Theatre and Dramatic Literature in the Medieval Arab World.* New York: New York University Press, 1992.

Mottahedeh, Roy P. Review of *The Patricians of Nishapur*, by Richard Bulliet. *Journal of the American Oriental Society* 95 (1975): 491– 495.

Muhanna, Elias. "Ilyās al-Mawṣilī (fl. 1668–1683)." In *Essays in Arabic Literary Biography.* 3 vols. Edited by Roger M. A. Allen, Joseph E. Lowry, Terri DeYoung, and Devin J. Stewart, 2: 295–308. Wiesbaden: Harrassowitz, 2009.

al-Murādī, Muḥammad Khalīl b. 'Alī. *Silk al-durar fī a'yān al-qarn al-thānī 'ashar.* Edited by Muḥammad 'Abd al-Qādir Shāhīn. Beirut: Dār al-Kutub al-'Ilmiyya, 1997.

Murphey, Rhoads. *Essays on Ottoman Historians and Historiography.* Istanbul: Eren, 2009.

Mūsā, Nuhād. *Qaḍīyyat al-taḥawwul ilā al-fuṣḥā fī al-ālam al-'arabī al-ḥadīth.* Amman: Dār al-Fikr, 1987.

Musallamānī, Marwān. *al-Buyūt al-Dimashqiyya, al-qarn 18–19 m.* Damascus: Zuhayr Wafā, 1979.

al-Musawi, Muhsin. "Abbasid Popular Narrative: The Formation of Readership and Cultural Production." *Journal of Arabic Literature* 38 (2007): 261–292.

Muṣṭafā, Shākir. *al-Tārīkh al-'arabī wa-al-mu'arrikhūn: dirāsa fī taṭawwur 'ilm al-tārīkh wa-ma'rifat rijāli-hi fī al-Islām*. 4 vols. Beirut: Dār al-'Ilm lil-Malāyīn, 1978.

al-Nābulusī, 'Abd al-Ghanī. *Ta'ṭīr al-anām fī tafsīr al-manām*. Cairo: al-Maṭba'a al-Azhariyya al-Miṣriyya, 1906.

———. *Mumajāt al-ḥakīm wa munāghāt al-qadīm*. MS al-Ẓāhiriyya 733, al-Asad National Library, Damascus

Neumann, Christoph K. "Political and Diplomatic Developments." In *The Cambridge History of Turkey*. Vol. 3: *The Later Ottoman Empire, 1603–1839*. Edited by Suraiya Faroqhi, 44–62. Cambridge: Cambridge University Press, 2006.

al-Nimr, Iḥsān. *Tārīkh Jabal Nāblus wa al-Balqā'*, 2 vols. Damascus: Ibn Zaydūn, 1938.

Noseda, Noja. "al-Sāmira." In *Encyclopaedia of Islam*, 2nd ed.

Özdalga, Elisabeth, "Introduction." In *Late Ottoman Society: The Intellectual Legacy*. Edited by Elisabeth Özdalga, 1–13. London: Routledge, 2005.

Panzac, Daniel, ed. *Les Villes dans l'Empire ottoman: activités et sociétes*. Paris: CNRS, 1991.

Pascual, Jean-Paul. "Du Notaire au propriétaire par l'expert: Descriptions de la "maison" Damascène au XVIIIe siècle." In *L'habitat traditionnel dans les pays musulmans autour de la Méditerranée I: l'Heritage architectural, formes et fonctions*, 387–403. Cairo: Institut Français d'Archéologie Orientale, 1988.

Pederson, Johannes. *The Arabic Book*. Translated by Geoffrey French. Princeton: Princeton University Press, 1984.

Pellitteri, Antonio. "Immagine donna in Hawadith Dimashq al-Yawmiyya (1741–1762) di Ahmad al-Budayri al-Hallaq." In *Verse and the Fair Sex: Studies in Arabic Poetry and in the Representation of Women in Arabic Literature*. Edited by Frederick De Jong, 153–170. Utrecht: M. Th. Houtsma Stichting, 1993.

Petermann, H. H. *Reisen im Orient*. Leipzig: Verlag von Veit & Co., 1860.

Petry, Carl. *The Civilian Elite of Cairo in the Later Middle Ages*. Princeton: Princeton University Press, 1981.

———. "Educational Institutions as Depicted in the Biographical Literature of Mamluk Cairo: The Debate over Prestige and Venue." *Medieval Prosopography* 23 (2002).

Philipp, Thomas. *Acre the Rise and Fall of a Palestinian City, 1730–1831*. New York: Columbia University Press, 2001.

———. "The Farhi Family and the Changing Position of the Jews in Syria, 1750–1860." *Middle Eastern Studies* 20, no. 4 (October 1984): 37–52.

———. "Language, History, and Arab National Consciousness in the Thought of Jurjī Zaidan (1861–1914)." *International Journal of Middle East Studies* 4, no. 1 (1973): 3–22.

———. "Jews and Arab Christians: Their Changing Positions in Politics and Economy in Eighteenth Century Syria and Egypt." In *Egypt and Palestine: A Millennium of Association (868–1948)*. Edited by Amnon Cohen and Gabriel Baer, 150–166. New York: St. Martin's Press, 1984.

———. "Social Structure and Political Power in Acre in the 18th Century." In *The Syrian Land in the 18th and 19th Century: The Common and the Specific in the Historical Experience*, 91–108. Stuttgart: F. Steiner, 1992.

———. *The Syrians in Egypt, 1725–1975*. Stuttgart: Steiner, 1985.

Piterberg, Gabriel. *An Ottoman Tragedy: History and Historiography at Play*. Berkeley: University of California Press, 2003.

al-Qadi, Wadad. "Biographical Dictionaries as the Scholars' Alternative History of the Muslim Community." In *Organizing Knowledge: Encyclopaedic Activities in the*

Pre-Eighteenth Century Islamic World. Edited by Gerhard Endress, 23–75. Leiden: Brill, 2006.

al-Qāsimī, Muḥammad Sa'īd. *Qāmūs al-ṣinā'āt al-shāmiyya.* Edited by Jamāl al-Dīn al-Qāsimī and Khalīl al-'Aẓm. Paris: Mouton & Co, 1960.

———. *Safīnat al-faraj fi-ma habba wa dabba wa daraj.* Edited by Muḥammad Khayr Ramaḍān Yūsuf. Beirut: Dār al-Bashā'ir, 2004.

Rafeq, Abdul-Karim. "Craft Organizations and Religious Communities in Ottoman Syria (16th–18th Centuries)." In *Convegno sul tema: La Shi'a nell'impero Ottomano,* 25–56. Rome: Accademia nazionale dei Lincei, 1993.

———. "Economic Relations Between Damascus and the Dependent Countryside." In *The Islamic Middle East, 700–1900: Studies in Economic and Social History.* Edited by Abraham L Udovitch, 653–685. Princeton: Darwin Press, 1981.

———. "The Law-Court Registers of Damascus, with Special Reference to Craft-Corporations During the First Half of the Eighteenth Century." In *Les Arabes par Leurs Archives: XVIe–XXe Siècles.* Edited by Jacques Berque and Dominique Chevallier, 141–159. Paris: CNRS, 1976.

———. *The Province of Damascus, 1723–1783.* Beirut: Khayats, 1966.

———. "Public Morality in 18th Century Ottoman Damascus." *Revue des Mondes Musulmans et de la Méditerranée* 55–56, no. 1–2 (1990): 180–196.

Raymond, André. *Arab Cities in the Ottoman Period: Cairo, Syria and the Maghreb.* Aldershot: Ashgate, 2002.

———. *Artisans et commerçants au Caire au XVIIIe siècle.* Damascus: Institut Français de Damas, 1973.

———. *The Great Arab Cities in the 16th–18th Centuries: An Introduction.* New York: New York University Press, 1984.

Reynolds, Dwight Fletcher. *Heroic Poets, Poetic Heroes: The Ethnography of Performance in an Arabic Oral Tradition.* Ithaca: Cornell University Press, 1995.

———, Kristen Brustad, et al., *Interpreting the Self: Autobiography in the Arabic Literary Tradition.* Berkeley: University of California Press, 2001.

al-Rīḥāwī, 'Abd al-Qādir. *Damascus: Its History, Development and Artistic Heritage.* Translated by Paul E. Cheveden. Damascus: n.p., 1977.

———. *Madīnat Dimashq: Kitāb yabḥath fī tārīkh Dimashq wa taṭawwuri-hā al-'umrānī wa fī al-funūn wa al-āthār al-latī ḥafilat bi-hā fī madā thalāthat ālāf 'ām.* Damascus: n.p., 1969.

Ritter, Hellmut, ed. *Karagös: türkische Schattenspiele.* 3 vols. Hannover: Orient-Buchhandlung H. Lafaire, 1924.

Robertson, Edward. "Ibrahaim al-'Ayyah: A Samaritan Scholar of the Eighteenth Century." In *Essays in Honour of the Very Rev. Dr. J. H. Hertz, Chief Rabbi of the United Hebrew Congregations of the British Empire, on the Occasion of His Seventieth Birthday, September 25, 1942 (5703).* Edited by Isidore Epstein, Joseph H. Hertz, Ephraim Levine, and Cecil Roth, 341–350. London: E. Goldston, 1942.

Robine, Gerard. *Palais et demeures de Damas au XVIIIe siècle.* Damascus: Institut français de Damas, 1990.

Robinson, Chase. *Islamic Historiography.* Cambridge: Cambridge University Press, 2003.

Rogan, Eugene. *The Arabs: A History.* New York: Basic Books, 2009.

Roper, Geoffrey. "Fāris al-Shidyāq and the Transition from Scribal to Print Culture in the Middle East." In *The Book in the Islamic World: The Written Word and Com-*

munication in the Middle East. Edited by George N. Atiyeh, 209–231. Binghamton: SUNY Press, 1995.

Rosenthal, Franz. *A History of Muslim Historiography.* 2nd ed. Leiden: Brill, 1968.

al-Rukaynī, Ḥaydar Riḍā (and his unnamed son). "Jabal ʿĀmil fī qarn." *al-ʿIrfān* 27 (1938): 525–527, 626–628, 735–736, 814–815; 28 (1939): 54–56, 158–159, 255–256, 350–351, 453–454, 727–728, 830–832, 951–954; 29 (1939): 73–76, 187–188, 303–304, 678–683.

———. *Jabal ʿĀmil fī qarn.* Edited by Aḥmad Ḥuṭayṭ. Beirut: Dār al-Fikr al-Lubnānī, 1997.

———. *Jabal ʿĀmil fī qarn.* Edited by Ḥasan Ṣāliḥ. Beirut: Dār al-Jumān, 1998.

Sabra, Adam Abdelhamid. "Illiterate Sufis and Learned Artisans: The Circle of ʿAbd al-Wahhāb al-Shaʿrānī." In *Le Développement du Soufisme en Égypte à l'époque mamelouke.* Edited by Richard J. A. McGregor and Mireille Loubet, 153–168. Cairo: Institut Français d'Archéologie Orientale, 2006.

Sack, Dorothée. *Damaskus: Entwicklung und Struktur einer orientalisch-islamischen Stadt.* Mainz am Rhein: P. von Zabern, 1989.

———. *Dimashq: Taṭawwur wa-bunyān madīna mashriqīya Islāmīya.* Translated by Qāsim Ṭuwayr, Nazīh Kawākibī, and Aryānā Aḥmad. Damascus: Institut Français de Damas, 2005.

Saʿd, Fārūq. *Khayāl al-ẓill al-ʿarabī.* Beirut: Sharikat al-Maṭbūʿāt, 1993.

al-Ṣafā, Muḥammad Jābir Āl. *Tārīkh Jabal ʿĀmil.* 2nd ed. Dār al-Nahār li-al-Nashr, 1981.

Saʿīd, Nufūsa Zakariyyā. *Tārīkh al-daʿwa al-āmiyya wa atharu-hā fī Miṣr.* Cairo: Dār al-Maʾārif, 1964.

Sajdi, Dana. "'Decline' and Its Discontents and Ottoman Cultural History: By Way of Introduction." In *Ottoman Tulips, Ottoman Coffee: Leisure and Lifestyle in the Eighteenth Century,* 1–40. London: I. B. Tauris, 2007.

———. "Ibn Kannan." In *Historians of the Ottoman Empire.* Edited by Cornell Fleischer, Cemal Kafadar, and Hakan Karateke. http://www.ottomanhistorians.com.

———. "Peripheral Visions: the Worlds and Worldviews of Commoner Chroniclers in the 18th-Century Ottoman Levant." Ph.D. diss., Columbia University, 2002.

———. "Print and Its Discontents: A Case for Pre-Print Journalism and Other Sundry Print Matters." *Translator* 15, no. 1 (2009): 105–138.

———. "Revisiting Layla al-Akhyaliyya's Trespass." In *Transforming Loss into Beauty: Essays on Arabic Literature and Culture in Honor of Magda Al-Nowaihi.* Edited by Dana Sajdi and Marlé Hammond, 185–227. Cairo: American University in Cairo Press, 2008.

———. "'A Room of His Own': The 'History' of the Barber of Damascus (fl. 1762)." *MIT Electronic Journal of Middle East Studies* 4 (2004), 19–35. (No longer available online.)

Salibi, Kamal. *A House of Many Mansions: The History of Lebanon Reconsidered.* Berkeley: University of California Press, 1988.

Salzmann, Ariel. "An Ancien Regime Revisited: Privatization and Political Economy in Eighteenth-Century Ottoman Empire." *Politics and Society* 21, no. 4 (1993): 393–423.

Sayyid-Marsot, Afaf Lutfi. *Egypt in the Reign of Muhammad Ali.* Cambridge: Cambridge University Press, 1984.

Schilcher, Linda Schatkowski. *Families in Politics: Damascene Factions and Estates of the 18th and 19th Centuries.* Wiesbaden: F. Steiner, 1985.

Von Schlegell, Barbara Rosenow. "Sufism in the Ottoman Arab World: Shaykh ʿAbd al-Ghani al-Nabulusi (d. 1143/1731)." Ph. D. diss., University of California, Berkeley, 1997.

Schur, Nathan. *History of the Samaritans*. 2nd rev. ed. Frankfurt: Peter Lang, 1992.

———. "Ibrāhīm al-`Ayyā." In *A Companion to Samaritan Studies*. Edited by Alan D. Crown, Reinhard Pummer, and Abraham Tal. Tübingen: J.C.B. Mohr, 1993.

Seetzen, Ulrich Jasper. *Reisen durch Syrien, Palästina, Phönicien, die Transjordan-länder, Arabia Petrea und Unter-Agypten*. Edited by Fr. Kruse. 4 vols. Berlin: G. Reimer, 1854.

Semerdjian, Elyse. *"Off the Straight Path": Illicit Sex, Law, and Community in Ottoman Aleppo*. Syracuse: Syracuse University Press, 2008.

Shamir, Shimon. "As'ad Pasha al-'Aẓm and Ottoman Rule in Damascus (1743–58)." *Bulletin of the School of Oriental and African Studies* 26, no. 1 (1963): 1–28.

Sharabi, Hisham. *Arab Intellectuals and the West: The Formative Years, 1875–1914*. Baltimore: Johns Hopkins University Press, 1970.

Sharkas, Hikmat. *Badr al-Dīn al-Ghazzī (904/1499–984/1577) and His Manual on Islamic Scholarship and Education, al-Durr al-Nadīd*. Cambridge: Harvard University Press, 1976.

al-Shaṭṭī, Muḥammad Jamīl. *Tarājim a`yān Dimashq fī niṣf al-qarn al-rābi` `ashar*. Damascus: Dār al-Yaqaẓa al-`Arabiyya, 1948.

Shaykhū, Luwīs. "Mīkhā'īl al-Ṣabbāgh wa usratu-hu." *al-Machriq* 8 (1905), 24–35.

al-Shidyāq, Ṭannūs. *Akhbār al-a`yān fī Jabal Lubnān*. 2 vols. Edited by Milḥim Khalīl `Abdū and Andrāwus Ḥannā Shakhashīrī, Cairo: n.p., 1908. Reprinted with an updated edition by Mārūn Ra`d and indexed by Ilyās Ḥannā. Beirut?: Dār Nāẓir `Abbūd, 1993.

al-Sibā`ī, Muḥammad `Umar, and Na`īm Salīm al-Zahrāwī. *Ḥimṣ, dirāsa wathā'iqiyya, al-ḥiqba min 1256–1337h/1840–1918m*. Ḥimṣ: s.n., 1992.

Silay, Kemal. *Nedim and the Poetics of the Ottoman Court: Medieval Inheritance and the Need for Change*. Bloomington: Indiana University Press, 1994.

Sirriyeh, Elizabeth. *Sufi Visionary of Ottoman Damascus: 'Abd al-Ghanī al-Nābulusī, 1641–1731*. London: Routledge Curzon, 2005.

Spiegel, Gabrielle M. *The Past as Text: The Theory and Practice of Medieval Historiography*. Baltimore: Johns Hopkins University Press, 1997.

Strauss, Johann. "'Kütüp ve Resail-i Mevkute': Printing and Publishing in a Multi-Ethnic Society." In *Late Ottoman Society: The Intellectual Legacy*. Edited by Elisabeth Özdalga, 225–253. London: Routledge, 2005.

———. "Who Read What in the Ottoman Empire (19th–20th Centuries)." *Middle Eastern Literature* 6, no. 1 (2003): 39–76.

al-Suwaydī, Abd al-Raḥmān. *Tārīkh ḥawādith Baghdād wa al-Baṣra*. Edited by `Imād `Abd al-Salām Ra'ūf. Baghdad: Dār al-Shu'ūn al-Thaqāfiyya al-`Āmma, 1987.

al-Suwaydī, Abū al-Kamāl Muḥammad Sa`īd. "Wurūd ḥadīqat al-wuzarā bi-wurūd wazārat mawālī-him fī al-zūrā." MS Chester Beatty Library Ar 3551/3, Dublin.

Swartz, David. *Culture and Power: The Sociology of Pierre Bourdieu*. Chicago: University of Chicago Press, 1997.

Tamari, Steve (Stephen Edmond). "The Barber of Damascus: Ahmad Budayri al-Ḥallāq's Chronicle of the Year 1749." In *The Modern Middle East: A Sourcebook for History*. Edited by Camron M. Amin, Benjamin C. Fortna, and Elizabeth Frierson, 562–568. Oxford: Oxford University Press, 2006.

———. "Biography, Autobiography and Identity in Early Modern Damascus." In *Auto/Biography and the Construction of Identity and Community in the Middle East*. Edited by Mary Ann Fay, 37–50. New York: Palgrave, 2001.

———. "Teaching and Learning in 18th-Century Damascus: Localism and Ottomanism in an Early Modern Arab Society." Ph.D. diss., Georgetown University, 1998.

Ṭarrāzī, Fīlīb Dī. *Tārīkh al-ṣiḥāfa al-'arabiya: yaḥtawī 'alā akhbār kull jarīda wa majalla 'arabiyya ẓaharat fī al-'ālam sharqan wa gharban ma'a rusūm aṣḥābi-hā wa al-muḥarrirīn fī-hā wa tarājim mashāhīri-him.* 4 parts in 2 vols. Beirut: al-Maṭba'a al-Adabiyya, 1914.

Terzioğlu, Derin. "Man in the Image of God in the Image of the Times: Sufi Self-Narratives and the Diary of Niyāzī-i Mıṣrī (1618–94)." *Studia Islamica*, no. 94 (2002): 139–165.

Tetsuya, Ohtoshi. "Cairene Cemeteries as Public Loci in Mamluk Egypt." *Mamluk Studies Review* 10, no. 1 (2006): 83–116.

Tezcan, Baki. "The Politics of Early Modern Ottoman Historiography." In *The Early Modern Ottomans: Remapping the Empire.* Edited by Virginia H. Aksan and Daniel Goffman, 167–198. Cambridge: Cambridge University Press, 2007.

Thieck, Jean-Pierre. "Décentralization Ottomane et affirmation urbaine à Alep à la fin du XVIIIème siècle." In *Mouvement communautaires et éspaces urbaines au Machreq.* Edited by Mona Zakaria, Dochchâr Chbarou, and Waddah Charâra, 116–178. Beirut: Centre d'Études et Recherches sur le Moyen-Orient Contemporain, 1985.

Thomas, Lewis V. *A Study of Naima.* Edited by Norman Itzkowitz. New York: New York University Press, 1972.

Trimingham, J. Spencer. *The Sufi Orders in Islam.* London: Oxford University Press, 1998.

Turan, Fikret. "Synthesizing the Novelties Within Old Structure: Voicing New Trends in Old Genres in the 18th-Century Ottoman Poetry." *Archivum Ottomanicum* 25 (2008): 151–171.

Vajda, G. "Idjāza." In *Encyclopaedia of Islam*, 2nd ed.

Watenpaugh, Heghnar Zeitlian. *The Image of an Ottoman City: Imperial Architecture and Urban Experience in Aleppo in the 16th and 17th Centuries.* Leiden: Brill, 2004.

Weber, Stefan. "Der Anfang vom Ende: Der Wandel bemalter Holzvertäfelungen in Damaskus des 18. und 19. Jahrhunderts." In *Angels, Peonies, and Fabulous Creatures, The Aleppo Room in Berlin.* Edited by Julia Gonnella and Jens Kröger, 153–164. Münster: Museum für Islamische Kunst, 2008.

———. "The Creation of Ottoman Damascus: Architecture and Urban Development of Damascus in the 16th and 17th centuries." *Aram* 9/10 (1997): 431–470.

———. *Damascus: Ottoman Modernity and Urban Transformation (1808–1918)*, 2 vols. Aarhus, Denmark: Aarhus University Press, 2009.

White, Hayden V. *The Content of the Form: Narrative Discourse and Historical Representation.* Baltimore: Johns Hopkins University Press, 1987.

Wilkins, Charles L. *Forging Urban Solidarities: Ottoman Aleppo 1640–1700.* Leiden: Brill, 2010.

Wilson, John. *The Lands of the Bible.* Edinburgh: William Whyte, 1847.

Winter, Stefan. *The Shiites of Lebanon Under Ottoman Rule, 1516–1788.* Cambridge: Cambridge University Press, 2010.

Wright, Roger. *Latin and the Romance Languages in the Early Middle Ages.* London: Routledge, 1991.

Yerasimos, Stefanos. *La Fondation de Constantinople et de Sainte-Sophie dans les traditions turques: légendes d'empire.* Istanbul: Institut Français d'Etudes Anatoliennes, 1990.

Yi, Eunjeong. *Guild Dynamics in Seventeenth-Century Istanbul: Fluidity and Leverage.* 27. Leiden: Brill, 2004.

Young, M.J.L. "Arabic Biographical Writing." In *The Cambridge History of Arabic Literature. Religion, Learning and Science in the Abbasid Period.* Edited by M.J.L. Young, J. D. Latham, and R. B. Serjeant, 168–187. Cambridge: Cambridge University Press, 1990.

al-Yūnīnī, Mūsā ibn Muḥammad. *Early Mamluk Syrian Historiography: al-Yūnīnī's Dhayl Mir'āt al-Zāmān.* 2 vols. Edited and introduced by Li Guo. Leiden: Brill, 1998.

al-Zayyāt, Ḥabīb. *Khabāya al-zawāya min tārīkh Ṣīdnāyā.* In *Wathā'iq tārīkhiyya li-al-kursī al-milkī al-anṭākī.* Edited by Ilyās Andrāwus al-Būluṣī. Harisa: Maṭba'at al-Qiddīs, 1937.

Ze'evi, Dror. *Producing Desire: Changing Sexual Discourse in the Ottoman Middle East, 1500–1900.* Berkeley: University of California Press, 2006.

Ziadeh, Nicola A. *Urban Life in Syria Under the Early Mamlūks.* Beirut: American University of Beirut, 1953.

Zilfi, Madeline. "Diary of a Müderris: A New Source for Ottoman Biography." *Journal of Turkish Studies* 1 (1977): 160.

———. "Elite Circulation in the Ottoman Empire: Great Mollas of the Eighteenth Century." *Journal of the Economic and Social History of the Orient* 26, no. 3 (1983): 318–364.

———. "Goods in the Mahalle: Distributional Encounters in Eighteenth Century Istanbul." In *Consumption Studies and the History of the Ottoman Empire, 1550–1922: An Introduction.* Edited by Donald Quataert, 289–311. Albany: State University of New York Press, 2000.

———. *The Politics of Piety: The Ottoman Ulema in the Post-classical Age (1600–1800).* Minneapolis: Bibliotheca Islamica, 1988.

Index

al-`Abd, Ḥasan Āghā, 96–103; al-Biqā`, 98, 239n94; family, 97, 239n90; and governors, 97–100, 102, 138, 141, 209, 239n98; janissary on pilgrimage to Mecca, 97–103, 239n92; language, 111
`Abd al-Karīm, Aḥmad `Izzat, 10–11, 213
`Abd Allāh Pasha al-`Aẓm, 34, 98
Abū al-Dhahab, Muḥammad, 105–6
Abu al-Fatḥ, 87, 143, 236–37n46
Abū al-Surūr, 61, 73, 201–2
advice literature (*nasihatname*), 224n73
Alexandria, newspapers and journals, 210
`Alī Pasha, 151, 181
`āmmiyya. *See* colloquial Arabic
Anīs, Muḥammad, 138
annalistic chronicles, 6–7, 109, 116, 118
appropriations: Ibn Budayr, 5, 60–62, 145, 150, 153, 173; nouveau literates, 6, 205; print journalism, 212
Arabic, 130; Arabization of foreign words, 179, 187, 192; Modern Standard, 108–9, 179, 187–93, 207–8; reform, 109, 179, 203–4, 207–8. *See also* classical Arabic (*fuṣḥā*); colloquial Arabic (*`āmmiyya*)
Arabic epic. *See sīra*
architecture: al-`Aẓm family, 21–23, 24*fig*, 28, 170, 183–87, 208, 221n27, 252n90; caravanserai, 27–28, 182–85; Damascus, 16, 17, 20–28, 36, 220n19, 221n27, 252n90; fountains, 35, 36–37; Mamluk, 23, 221n27; Ottoman, 27–28
As`ad Pasha al-`Aẓm, 218n5; Burayk on, 79, 81, 83; caravanserai, 28, 182–85; vs. al-Daftardār, 28, 33–34, 154, 185; Ibn Budayr on, 152, 182, 188, 255n36; vs. al-Maydān quarter, 33–34; palace, 21, 24*fig*, 170, 183, 185, 252n90; poll tax lifted from Christians, 31; al-Qāsimī edit vs. Ibn Budayr, 179–87, 188
audience: chronicles, 112–14, 119, 125–26, 128, 133–40, 162, 208–9, 247n121; popular, 136–37, 139, 209; "*ta`rīkh*-diary," 119, 128; *yawmiyyāt*, 133–35. *See also* public performance; reception
authorial I, 121–22, 130–33, 140, 148–49; al-`Abd, 141; al-Danafī and, 143; dream chronicles, 132; Ibn Budayr, 4–5, 156, 157, 158, 173, 198–99, 207; Ibn Kannān, 156–57; nouveau literates, 103, 115, 129, 157; travelogue, 132; *yawmiyyāt*, 130, 132
authority, 115–44; chains of transmission, 50–51, 57, 60, 64, 116–17; Ibn Budayr, 4, 5, 14, 61, 64, 67, 199, 202, 207; Ibn al-Ṣiddīq and, 104–5; *ijāzas*, 50, 51, 54, 56, 60, 64, 230n87; *isnād*, 116–17, 123; nouveau literates, 9, 14–37, 82, 116, 209; patriarchal, 152–53, 155; rise of, 9; *silsila*, 54, 56, 64; spiritual, 55; *thabat*, 50, 51, 54, 56, 229n59. *See also* authorial I; authorship
authorship: culture of transmission, 50–57, 60, 133–34; Ibn Budayr, 4, 38, 48, 49, 67, 145–46, 199, 206–7; nouveau literates, 205; Rukaynīs, 86, 234n16; technical literacy dissociated from, 9. *See also* authorial I; authority
autobiography, 119–20, 136; Ibn Ṭūlūn, 139–40, 244n55; Jabal `Āmil, 142
awlād al-nās, 126, 127, 137, 244nn46,47

al-`Aẓm family, 31–34, 204, 206, 208, 218n5; `Abd Allāh Pasha, 34, 98; architecture, 21–23, 24*fig*, 28, 170, 183–87, 208, 221n27, 252n90; Damascus governors, 17, 21, 34, 79, 91, 92, 98, 175, 179–87, 223n60; Muḥammad Pasha, 91, 92; al-Qāsimī edit vs. Ibn Budayr, 179–87; Sulaymān Pasha, 154–55, 159, 179–80, 182. *See also* As`ad Pasha al-`Aẓm

Bāb al-Barīd, Damascus, 2, 42–43, 44
Bahlūl, `Abd al-Raḥmān, 14, 202, 252n90
Bakhtin, Mikhail, 165, 166, 252n80
Bakr, `Abd al-Wahhab, 139
barbers: guild, 47, 71; Ibn Budayr's son, 73–74; master (Ibn al-Ḥashīsh), 41–43, 68, 76, 226n10, 248n3; al-Qāsimī's father, 176, 178, 207, 226n19; social status, 41–42. *See also* barbershops; Ibn Budayr
barbershops, 212*fig*; coffeehouse and, 74, 76; Ibn Budayr's, 4, 12–13, 41–43, 63–64, 73, 75, 147–50, 207, 227n25
Bilād al-Shām. *See* Levant
biographical dictionary: defined, 116; for the people, 128; *ta'rīkh*-diary distinguished from, 118; *`ulamā'* and, 35, 173, 230–31n89. *See also* al-Murādī, Muḥammad Khalīl, *Silk al-durar*
biographies, 12, 35, 229n61; *sīra*, 149; social and intellectual, 38–76, 176–77. *See also* autobiography; biographical dictionary; *tarjama*
al-Biqā`, 98, 239n94
al-Birzālī, `Alam al-Dīn, 120–21, 127
Brustad, Christine, 119
al-Budayrī. *See* Ibn Budayr
Burayk, Mīkhā'īl, 78–81, 233–34; al-`Aẓm rule, 79, 81, 83; Christian community, 78–81, 92, 142–43; language, 78–79, 111; women chided by, 80, 209

cafes: Damascus, 29*fig*. *See also* coffeehouses
Cahen, Claude, 120
Cairo: audience for scholarship, 126, 137; cemeteries, 223n50; colleges, 225n1; fountains, 36; literary "ordinary person," 36, 140; Mamluk architecture, 221n27; newspapers and journals, 210
caravans: pilgrimage, 11–12, 99–101, 257n79; treasury, 11, 154
caravanserais, 27–28, 182–85
Catholics, Greek, 18, 79–81, 223n58, 234n13
Çelebi, Evliyā, 132
cemeteries: biographies in, 35; outdoor pleasure, 30, 223n50
Central Rectangle, Damascus, 21, 31, 40, 42–43
chains of transmission: authority, 50–51, 57, 60, 64, 116–17; *maqāma*, 163
Chamberlain, Michael, 49, 56, 229nn61,63
"cheap" monumentality, 36–37, 77–114; defined, 104
Chester Beatty Library manuscript, Ibn Budayr, 11, 168, 172, 178, 204, 215n6, 252n86
Christians: Burayk ecclesiastical positions, 81, 233n2; Crusades, 122, 136, 149; Damascus, 31, 78–81, 113, 142–43; Greek Catholics, 18, 79–81, 223n58, 234n13; Greek Orthodox, 18, 78–81, 113, 142, 234nn3,13; Ibn Budayr, 144; schismatics, 18, 79, 80–81; Ṣidnāyā Monastery, 31, 81, 233n2, 234n8; taxes on, 31, 81m31, 81, 234n13; travelogue, 132
chronicles, 4–8; absence of intertextuality, 112–14; annalistic, 6–7, 109, 116, 118; audience, 112–14, 119, 125–26, 128, 133–40, 162, 208–9, 247n121; authors of diverse backgrounds, 7, 9–10; circulation, 112–14, 118, 127, 168, 208–9; contemporary, 6–8, 115–44, 148–49, 182, 198–99, 203–4, 205,

211; "Damurdāshī," 138–39, 141; dearth of extant copies, 112–14; defined, 148; dream, 55–56, 131–32; first, 117; as genre, 6–10, 114; history of, 114, 115–44; nouveau literates, 6–8, 16–17, 35–37, 77–114, 121, 129, 208–11; openness, 113–14; oral transmission, 113, 145–46, 167, 208–9; organization of, 6; Ottoman Egypt, 136–39, 247n121; "pasha chronicles," 138–39, 141, 247n114; for the people, 127–28; popularization, 113–14, 136–39, 144, 209; as public texts, 8–9, 35–37, 65, 78, 93, 118, 121; reception, 112–14, 167–72, 209; self-fashioning, 4–5, 8, 13, 199, 207; state/political order, 6, 148, 151, 163–64, 173, 179–87, 205, 217nn17,18; "sultan-pasha chronicle," 138, 247n119; transformations by new historians, 5, 10, 77, 117–23, 205–6; *yawmiyyāt*, 126, 130–34, 144, 180–81. *See also* authorial I; classical Arabic (*fuṣḥā*); colloquial Arabic (*`āmmiyya*); Ibn Budayr; Ibn Kannān; politics; soldier-chronicles; *tārīkh*; *ta'rīkh*-diary (chronicle-diary); *`ulamā'*

circulation, chronicles, 112–14, 118, 127, 168, 208–9

circumcision party, Ibn Budayr and, 154–55

classical Arabic (*fuṣḥā*), 108–13, 115, 127, 241n141; chronicle genre, 148; Ibn Budayr, 159–62; Ibn Kannān, 160; *sīra*, 149–50; *ta'rīkh*-diary, 139

coffeehouses, 139, 222n44; barbershop and, 74, 76; elites and, 53, 230n75; Ibn Budayr and, 74–76, 147, 200; Ibn Kannān and, 53, 74; Istanbul, 147; public performance, 164; scribal chronicle ande print newspaper, 211; storytellers, 104–5. *See also* cafes

colleges: Cairo, 225n1; Damascus, 28, 222n36; economics, 52; Ibn Budayr's education, 48, 75; Ibn Kannān, 53, 127, 156, 244n59; Ibn Ṭūlūn and, 127, 244n59; Jabal `Āmil, 82, 142; *madrasa*, 27, 75, 122–23; Sufi teachers, 47, 228n52

colloquial Arabic (*`āmmiyya*), 108–13, 115, 127–28, 139, 140, 241n141; al-`Abd, 141; chronicle genre, 148; Egypt, 125–27, 138; Ibn Budayr, 160–62, 179, 188–90, 193, 256n54; poetry, 34–35, 65–66; *sīra*, 149–50; al-Yūnīnī, 120

commoners: al-`Abd's language, 102–3; historiography by, 1–5, 20; al-Jibāwī mixing with, 75; literate, 48, 57; subjects of chronicles, 40–41, 57; and violence in Damascus, 99, 196–97. *See also* colloquial Arabic (*`āmmiyya*) "learned illiterates"; nouveau literates; the people; popularization

companionship, knowledge production and, 133–34

complaints: Caireans, 36; Ibn Budayr, 40–41, 67, 70, 153–54, 183–84, 186, 193–94, 196, 199, 206–7; nouveau literates, 16–17

contemporary chronicles, 6–8, 115–44, 148–49, 182, 198–99, 203–4, 205, 211. *See also* chronicles

conversation, knowledge production and, 133–34

cotton trade, Palestine, 18, 82–83

court chronicler, 35, 211

Crusades, 122, 136, 149

cultural capital: Ibn Budayr, 67–68; scholars, 52

culture: scholarly transmission, 50–57, 60, 133–34. *See also* architecture; cultural capital; literary culture; al-Nahḍa; public culture

curative remedies, al-Maqqār, 70, 72, 200

al-Daftardār (Fatḥī al-Falāqinsī), 28, 33–34, 154, 185, 221n30

Damascus, 14–16, 22–23*map*, 32*map*, 213, 221n29; academy,

59; architecture and decoration, 16, 17, 20–28, 220n19, 221n27, 252n90; Bāb al-Barīd, 2, 42–43, 44; barbershop, 212*fig*; cafes, 29*fig*; Central Rectangle, 21, 31, 40, 42–43; Christians, 31, 78–81, 113, 142–43; colleges, 28, 222n36; disorder, 16, 20–34, 98–103, 151–52, 154, 206; earthquake, 151, 158, 181, 206, 234n8; economics, 8, 16–18, 20–21, 31–34; Egyptian occupation, 105–7; Ibn Budayr and, 14, 37, 206; intramural, 31–34, 32*map*; Jews, 18, 25*fig*, 30–31, 223n58; "learned illiterates," 140; literacy, 140; localist areas, 40, 227n25; al-Maydān, 31–34, 32*map*; Muslims, 21, 30–31, 79–80, 142; new order, 16–17, 28, 79–80, 81, 103, 206; new social topography, 16–18; Ottoman importance, 2, 14–16; outdoor culture, 28–31; politics, 31–34; residences, 21–28, 22–23*map*, 24*fig*, 25*fig*, 27*fig*, 31; from above Salahyeh, 15*fig*; Sufism, 47, 54; Turkish Divan, 26*fig*; violence, 31–34, 98–99, 154, 196–97. *See also* al-`Aẓm family; Damascus governors; Ibn Budayr; public culture; Umayyad Mosque

Damascus governors: al-`Abd and, 97–100, 102, 138, 141, 209, 239n98; `Alī Pasha, 151, 181; al-`Aẓm family, 17, 21, 34, 79, 91, 92, 98, 175, 179–87, 223n60; al-Danafī and, 90; Ibn al-Ṣiddīq and, 105; al-Maqqār's list, 69; pilgrimage managed by, 97–101; *qabīqūl* troops, 33–34; al-Qāsimī edit vs. Ibn Budayr, 179–87; residences, 21, 28; Rukaynīs and, 83–84; tax farms, 17; and treasurer of the province, 28, 33–34, 154, 185; and Ṭūqāns, 88, 91, 92; `Uthmān Pasha, 83, 106

"Damurdāshī chronicles," 138–39, 141

al-Danafī, Ibrāhīm, 86–93, 111; authorial I, 143; Ottomans, 88–93, 94–95, 143; patronage, 92–93, 95, 105, 143, 209; Samaritans, 86–93, 105, 111, 236n43

Darnton, Robert, 49–50

al-dawla: al-Danafī and, 90, 91; al-Qāsimī edit, 190; Rukaynīs and, 83–85, 90, 209

death: of guild leaders, 71–72; Ibn Budayr and, 153, 155–56, 160–61, 166–67, 194–95; minaret suicide, 155–56, 160–61, 166–67, 194–96. *See also* cemeteries; *tarjama*

dhayl (supplementary history), 115, 120, 123–24, 127, 139, 237–38n46

dialogue form, 133

diary, 36–37; dream, 131–32; Ibn Ṭawq, 126, 130–31; al-Maḥāsinī (Ismā`īl), 129; al-Makkī, 9, 93–96, 111, 126, 133, 143–44, 209, 237nn62,63, 238nn69,70,79. *See also ta'rīkh*-diary; *yawmiyyāt*; *yevmiye*

dictionary: dream interpretation, 56; Ibn Ḥanbal al-Ḥanafī, 110–11; al-Qāsimī work, 41, 175–76, 208. *See also* biographical dictionary

disorder: Damascus, 16, 20–34, 98–103, 151–52, 154, 206; humorous, 165; Ibn Budayr, 20, 30–31, 65–66, 151–56, 165, 166–67, 173, 174–75, 180–87, 194–98, 206; literary, 34–37, 77, 167, 173, 174–75, 180

divine blessing, 62–64

drama, history as, 107–8

dreams and visions: Ibn Budayr, 66–67; Sufi, 54–56, 66–67, 131–32, 230n87, 246n88

Drūz, Jabal `Āmil, 83, 85, 235n24

earthquake, Damascus, 151, 158, 181, 206, 234n8

economics: Damascus, 8, 16–18, 20–21, 31–34; Ibn Budayr, 59, 60, 67–68; knowledge-related careers, 52, 57–59; nouveau riche, 10, 36–37, 68, 194. *See also* nouveau riche; patronage; prices; taxes; trade

education: culture of transmission, 133–34; Ibn Budayr, 44–48, 72–73, 75,

200; Ibn Budayr's children, 72–73; Ibn Kannān, 52. *See also* colleges; knowledge; scholars
Egypt: `Alī Beg al-Kabīr, 90–91, 105, 219n11; barbering, 42; colloquial Arabic, 125–27, 138; Damascus occupation, 105–7; "Damurdāshī chronicles," 138–39, 141; "Egyptian Treasury" caravan, 11; Ibn al-Dawādārī, 110, 124–26, 136, 137, 141, 243nn40,42; *mamlūk* households, 137, 139; Mamluk period, 127, 137; middle class emergence, 36; Muḥammad `Alī, 101, 178, 258n8; al-Nahḍa, 210; Napoleon, 99, 258n8; newspapers and journals, 210; Ottoman, 99, 136–39, 247n121; "pasha chronicles," 138–39, 141; printing press, 258n8; private book collections, 225n87; al-Sakhāwī, 110; Syria conquered by (1832), 101; `Uthmān Pasha as governor, 90. *See also* Cairo
elites: chronicles, 7; and coffeehouses, 53, 230n75; Ibn Budayr's barbershop and, 43, 44, 145; Ibn Budayr's biographies, 61–62; Ibn Kannān and, 156; knowledge, 49, 57; al-Qāsimī and, 176. *See also* governors; households; scholars; Sufis; *`ulamā`*
entertainment: chronicles as, 137–38, 139; humorous, 163–65. *See also* public performance
epic, Arabic. *See sīra*
Events of Damascus (Ibn Budayr). *See* Ibn Budayr

al-Falāqinsī, `Abd al-Mu`ṭī, 24–27
al-Falāqinsī, Fatḥī (al-Daftardār), 28, 33–34, 154, 185, 221n30
family patronage, 19
Fārḥī family, 18, 25*fig*, 31
farmers: chronicle by, 82–86, 141–42; literacy of, 82
Faroqhi, Suraiya, 132, 134
first-person narratives, 54, 128–36. *See also* authorial I; diary
food prices, Ibn Budayr and, 11, 153–54, 181
fountains, 35, 36–37
fuṣḥā. *See* classical Arabic

Gaybī, Ṣun`ullah, 131
al-Ghazzī, Badr al-Dīn, 73, 232n141
al-Ghazzī, Muḥammad, 44, 47, 61–62, 201–2
al-Ghazzī, Muḥibb al-Dīn, 129, 245n80
governors, 97; Egypt, 90–91; Ḥimṣ, 94, 95, 96; Ibn Budayr and, 181–82; Nablus, 88; Ṣafad, 97, 98, 102; Sidon, 85. *See also* Damascus governors
Great Mosque. *See* Umayyad Mosque
Greek Catholics, 18, 79–81, 223n58, 234n13
Greek Orthodox, 18, 78–81, 113, 142, 234nn3,13
guilds, 226n17; barbers, 47, 71; Ibn Budayr on death of guild leaders, 71–72

Haarman, Ulrich, 120
Hadith, 116, 131, 148, 163, 242n3
Hajj. *See* pilgrimage to Mecca
al-Ḥakawātī, Aḥmad Shākir, 74, 75–76, 233n143
ḥakawī or *ḥakawātī*. *See* storytellers
al-Ḥakawī, Sulaymān Ibn al-Ḥashīsh, 75–76, 153
Hanna, Nelly, 137–38, 252n80
Ḥasan, al-Shaykh, 58–59
Hathaway, Jane, 138–39, 221n27, 247n114
Hātūn, Asiye, 54, 132, 246n88
heritage, 175, 181, 187, 204, 208
Hijrī, 6–7, 11, 116, 148, 216n16
al-Hilālī, Abu Zayd, 149, 249n20
Ḥimṣ, 93–96, 144, 237n63, 238n69
al-Ḥiṣniyya, 44–46, 48, 59
history, 115–44; Arabic-Islamic historiography, 35, 116, 119–44, 217n17; of chronicle, 114, 115–44;

as drama, 107–8; Ibn Budayr, 38, 70, 107–8, 145, 150, 173; al-Maqqār's list, 70; *nasihatname*, 224n73; by non-scholars, 1–10, 57, 77–114, 136–44; Ottoman historiography, 35, 127–28, 224n73; popularization of, 113–14, 136–39, 144; supplementary (*dhayl*), 115, 120, 123–24, 127, 139, 237–38n46. *See also* chronicles; social history; *tārīkh*
Holt, P. M., 138, 247nn114,119
homes. *See* residences
households, rise of notable, 8, 16, 34, 79, 88, 95, 218n4; Damascene academy, 59; Egyptian *mamlūk*, 137, 139; externalization of sultan's authority to, 17, 35; gubernatorial, 17, 186; new authors' entries into, 78, 205; patronage and, 19, 205; residences, 21–28; tax-farming system and, 17; "vizier-pasha," 17, 208. *See also* al-`Aẓm family
Hüdā'ī, Maḥmūd, 131–32, 133
humor, 73, 162–67, 201
al-Ḥusayn, Yaḥyā b., 129

Ibn `Ajība, Aḥmad, 130
Ibn al-Bannā', 117–21, 126, 135, 242n7, 245n67
Ibn Budayr, Shihāb al-Dīn Aḥmad, 10–13, 38–76, 145–73, 206; absence of conclusion, 12; absence of preamble, 12, 168; appropriation, 5, 60–62, 145, 150, 153, 173; As`ad Pasha al-`Aẓm, 152, 182, 188, 255n36; auction story of acquisition, 177–78; audience, 113, 162; authorial boldness, 38, 66; authorial I, 4–5, 156, 157, 158, 173, 198–99, 207; authority, 4, 5, 14, 61, 64, 67, 199, 202, 207; authorship, 4, 38, 48, 49, 67, 145–46, 199, 206–7; barbershop, 4, 12–13, 41–43, 63–64, 73, 75, 147–50, 207, 227n25; beginning, 150–51; birth, 39–40; "al-Budayrī" name, 10–11; Chester Beatty Library manuscript, 11, 168, 172, 178, 204, 215n6, 252n86; circulation, 168–72; codex, 170, 172; coffeehouses, 74–76, 147, 200; complaints, 40–41, 67, 70, 153–54, 183–84, 186, 193–99, 206–7; credibility, 13; cultural formation, 3–4; cutting, 148, 174–204; Damascus, 14, 37; dating chronicle, 6, 11, 12, 148; discovery, 2; disorder, 20, 30–31, 65–66, 151–56, 165, 166–67, 173, 174–75, 180–87, 194–98, 206; economics, 59, 60, 67–68; education, 44–48, 72–73, 75, 200; epic aspect, 157–62, 166, 167, 173, 198, 203, 206; family business (portering), 40, 41, 204, 225nn3,4; family members, 66–67, 72–74, 199, 200, 231n105, 232n125, 258n97; fingerprints on manuscript, 170, 171–72; history, 38, 70, 107–8, 145, 150, 173; Ibn Kannān compared with, 146–47, 150, 151, 153–54, 156; intellectual itinerary, 43–48; language and registers, 158–62, 179, 187–98, 256n54; later reincarnation, 174–204; "learned illiterate," 43–48, 57, 59–60; literary devices, 150; marginal notes, 12, 168–72, 171*fig*; master barber to, 41–43, 68, 76, 226n10, 248n3; and Menocchio, 2, 204, 215n6, 216n12; "middling sort," 41; missing parts, 12; moral outrage, 66, 165–66, 167; nouveau literate status, 5–6, 48, 57, 60, 67, 68, 207; original text, 174–204; for the people, 128, 151, 152; performativeness, 159–60, 162, 167, 173, 196, 198; picnics, 28, 64–66, 71–72, 155; places of residence, 40–41, 226n8; poetry, 12, 65–66, 158, 199; politics, 11, 148, 151–52, 159, 162, 173, 175, 179–87; on prices, 11, 152, 153–54, 181, 183; al-Qāsimī abridgements, 193–98; al-Qāsimī edit, 12, 146, 150–51, 174–204, 207–8, 213, 256–58, 259n3; al-Qāsimī

manuscript, 150–51, 168–72, 169*fig*, 171*fig*, 176–78; reception, 167–72; residences, 40–41, 226n8; rhymed prose, 158–62, 179, 183, 191–98, 255n37; self-editing and self-fashioning, 4–5, 13, 199, 207; on sexual indiscretions, 12, 155–56, 165–66; social biography, 38–76; social mobility, 39–43, 59–60, 167; sons' titles, 66–67, 199, 232n125; storytelling, 113, 153, 162; Sufism, 46–47, 48, 62–63, 66–67; al-Ta`dīl, 40–41; *tarjama*, 12, 60–64, 71, 150, 153, 157, 199–203, 207; texts, 146–47; "title markers," 168–70; *yawmiyyāt*, 133, 144, 180–81
Ibn al-Dawādārī, Abū Bakr b. `Abd Allāh, 110, 124–26, 136, 137, 141, 243nn40,42
Ibn Dhī Yazan, Sayf, 149, 233n145
Ibn Ḥanbal al-Ḥanafī, 110–11
Ibn al-Ḥashīsh: Aḥmad (barber master), 41–43, 68, 76, 226n10, 248n3
Ibn al-Ḥashīsh al-Ḥakawī, Sulaymān (storyteller), 75–76, 153
Ibn Iyās, 125–26, 129, 137, 244n47
Ibn Jabrī, 106
Ibn al-Jawzī, 118–19
Ibn Kannān, 52–53, 77, 117, 118, 124, 130, 143; audience, 119, 135; and coffeehouses, 53, 74; colleges, 53, 127, 156; comparison with Ibn Budayr, 146–47, 150, 151, 153–54, 156; education, 52; homes, 23–24, 53; Ibn Ṭūlūn and, 244n59; language, 160; picnics, 28–29, 31, 53, 64–65, 222–23n46
Ibn Sa`d, 116
Ibn Ṣaṣra, 110, 125, 136
Ibn Shaddād, `Antar, 149, 233n145
Ibn al-Ṣiddīq, Ḥasan, 103–8, 111, 113, 141, 167, 208–9
Ibn Taghribirdī, 126, 137, 244n47
Ibn Ṭawq, 126, 130–31, 143
Ibn Ṭūlūn, Shams al-Dīn, 1, 5, 134–35, 244n55; autobiography, 139–40, 244n55; and Ibn Kannān, 127, 244n59; *Mufākahat al-khillān*, 127–29, 134–35, 246n99; and the people, 128
Ibn Tūmā, 165
Ibn Zunbul al-Rammāl, 138, 141
Ibrāhīm Āghā, 94–96, 126, 238n79
ijāzas, 50, 51, 54, 56, 60, 64, 230n87
intertextuality, 112–14, 130
Iran, Safavid, 235nn20,25
al-Iṣfahānī, `Imād al-Dīn al-Kātib, 120, 122
al-Isḥāqī al-Munūfī, Muḥammad b. `Abd al-Mu`ṭī, 137–38, 139
Ismā`il al-Ḥā'ik, al-Shaykh, 58–59
isnād (chain of authority), 116–17, 123. *See also* chains of transmission
Israel, Samaritans, 86–87
Istanbul: academy, 59, 231n102; barbershops, 147; cemeteries, 223n50; coffeehouses, 147; fountains, 36–37; Ḥimṣ and, 95–96; libraries, 225n87; new order, 34–35; Ottoman capital, 8, 16, 90, 219n16; printing press, 258–59n8; and violence in Damascus, 34; "vizier-pasha" households, 17

Jabal `Āmil: Matāwila, 82–86, 89, 90, 105, 235n17; Shī`īs, 82–86, 142, 235nn20,25
al-Jabāwī, Ibrāhīm, 200
Jabrī, Muḥammad, 64, 200
Jabri house, 27*fig*
janissaries: As`ad Pasha al-`Aẓm encounter, 185–86; Damascus occupation, 106–7; Ibn Budayr and, 194; and pilgrimage to Mecca, 97–103, 239n92; *qabīqūl*, 33–34, 99; *yarliyya*, 33–34, 99, 103. *See also* military
al-Jazā'irī, Ṭāhir, 177–78
al-Jazzār Pasha, 85, 98
Jews: Damascus, 18, 25*fig*, 30–31, 223n58; Fārḥī family, 18, 25*fig*, 31; and Samaritans, 87. *See also* Judaism
al-Jibāwī, Ibrāhim, 73, 74–75
journalism, 210–12. *See also* newspapers

Judaism: Samaritans and, 87. *See also* Jews

al-Kabīr, `Alī Beg, 90–91, 105, 219n11
Kadızadeli movement, 136, 247n107
Kafadar, Cemal, 128, 131, 134, 135–36, 245n67
Kaidbey, Naila, 127–28, 134–35
Karagöz (in Turkish) / Karākūz (in Arabic). *See* shadow theater
Khalidi, Tarif, 1, 119–23, 136, 243n40, 249n18
Khalwatiyya order, 52, 229n67
knowledge: culture of transmission of, 50–57, 60, 133–34; economics and, 52, 57–59; elite, 49, 57; experiential, 49, 53–54; religious, 148, 149; textually based, 49. *See also* authority; education
Koury, George, 101
Kuzbar, `Alī, 44–45, 47, 200, 227n34

land, private ownership, 8, 17
language, 241–42n149; Ibn Budayr, 158–62, 179, 187–98, 256n54; nouveau literates, 6, 77, 108–12, 113, 115, 120, 125–27, 148; Persian, 130; al-Qāsimī edit of Ibn Budayr, 10–11, 12, 146, 150–51, 174–204, 207–8, 213, 256–58; reform, 109, 179, 192, 207–8. *See also* Arabic; classical Arabic (*fuṣḥā*), colloquial Arabic (*`āmmiyya*); Turkish
laughter, 162, 165, 166–67. *See also* humor
law. *See* Shāfi`ī
"learned illiterates," 140–41; Ibn Budayr, 43–48, 57, 59–60; Ibn Budayr's son, 74; al-Maqqār, 69. *See also* nouveau literates
Lebanon, 82, 235n24
Leighton, Frederick, 23, 25*fig*, 31
leisure time, 46, 52, 53, 59, 60
Levant (Bilād al-Shām), 1, 3*map*, 14–37, 110–11, 115–44; colloquial language, 110–12, 127–28; Egyptian conquest of Syria (1832), 101; Ottoman, 2, 8, 14–37, 128–39. *See also* chronicles; Damascus
Li Guo, 120–21, 125, 127, 243n42
libraries, 225n87
literacy: Damascus, 140; of farmers, 82; new, 9–10, 205; technical, 6, 9, 48, 227n27. *See also* literary culture; nouveau literates
literary culture, 9–10, 162–63; "ordinary person" as topic, 36; public, 34–37, 53, 71–72. *See also* nouveau literates
literary disorder, 34–37, 77, 167, 173, 174–75, 180
Little, Donald, 121
localist areas, Damascus, 40, 227n25

madrasa, 27, 75, 122–23. *See also* colleges
al-Maḥāsinī, Ismā`īl, 129
al-Maḥāsinī, Sulaymān b. Aḥmad, 105–6
al-Mahdī, Muḥammad, 66, 73
Maḥmūd Khān, 101, 151, 181
Makdisi, George, 117–19
al-Makkī, Muḥammad, 199; diary, 9, 93–96, 111, 126, 133, 143–44, 209, 237nn62,63, 238nn69,70,79
mālikāne, 17
Mamluk period: architecture and decoration, 23, 221n27; Egypt, 127, 136–37; Ibn Ṭawq diary, 126, 130–31, 136; language of chronicles, 109–10, 126–27, 136–37, 148; al-Ẓāhir Baybars, 149
mamlūk (slave soldier), 244n47; chronicle authors, 124–26, 137, 138–39; `Alī Beg al-Kabīr, 105. *See also* military
maqāma (picaresque narrative), 162–67, 252n79
al-Maqqār, Muḥammad Ibn Jum`a, 69–70, 72, 200, 232n129
Maronites, Jabal `Āmil, 83, 235n24
master barber (Ibn al-Ḥashīsh), 41–43, 68, 76, 226n10, 248n3
Masters, Bruce, 102, 239n89
Matāwila, Jabal `Āmil, 82–86, 89, 90, 105, 235n17
mawāliya, 65

al-Maydān, Damascus, 31–34, 32*map*
Menocchio, 1, 2, 204, 215–16nn7,9,10,11,12
military: al-ʿAbd, 96–103, 141; Ibn al-Dawādārī, 124–25; Ibrāhīm Āghā, 94–96; Matāwila, 84, 86. *See also* janissaries; *mamlūk* (slave soldier); soldier-chronicles
minaret suicide, 155–56, 160–61, 166–67, 194–96
minorities, religious, 31, 79
al-Miṣrī, ʿAlī, 72, 73, 200
al-Miṣrī, Muḥammad al-Azharī (Abū al-Surūr), 61, 73, 201–2
Mışrī, Nıyāzı-i, 133
Mitwālīs. *See* Matāwila
Mongols, 122, 136, 149
monumentality: "cheap," 36–37, 77–114; public, 78
moral outrage: Burayk, 80, 234nn10,12; Ibn Budayr, 66, 165–66
mosques: Ibn Kannān, 222–23n46; minaret suicide, 155–56, 160–61, 166–67, 194–96; Qaymariyya mosque/college, 28. *See also* Umayyad Mosque
Muḥammad al-ʿAjlūnī, 42, 61, 68
Muḥammad ʿAlī, Egypt, 101, 178, 258n8
al-Murādī, Muḥammad Khalīl, *Silk al-durar*, 57–59, 61, 69, 253n92; and coffeehouses, 74, 75; Ibn Budayr's teachers, 44, 51, 227n30; and Ibn Kannān, 118–19; and the poet Shākir, 233n143; on al-Ṭabbākh, 63
Muslims: Damascus, 21, 30–31, 79–80, 142. *See also* mosques; Prophet Muḥammad; *ʿulamāʾ*
Muṣṭafā, Mulla, 130
Muṣṭafā, Shākir, 120, 244n44
Muṣṭafā, Ṣidḳī, 130
mysticism. *See* Sufis

Nablus, 113, 235–36nn33,42; governors, 88; Ṭūqāns, 87–93, 94–95, 105, 143, 236n33; al-ʿUmar, 86, 88, 89–91, 143. *See also* al-Danafī, Ibrāhīm
al-Nābulusī, ʿAbd al-Ghanī, 42; Bahlūl eulogy to, 202; barber of, 42; book as power, 1, 9; Damascus, 14, 29; dreams, 55, 56, 67, 131–32, 230n87; Ibn Budayr and, 62, 68; and Kadızadelis, 136; picnics, 229n72; Qādiriyya Sufi order, 47; travelogue, 132
al-Nahḍa (Arab Renaissance), 5, 112, 210–12; print journalism and, 210–12, 255n25; al-Qāsimī edit of Ibn Budayr and, 10–11, 178–79, 193, 204, 207–8
Naʿīmā, Muṣṭafā, 211
Napoleon, Egypt, 99, 258n8
nasihatname (advice literature), 224n73
al-Naṣṣār, Naṣīf, 82, 85
Nedim, 34–35, 65
new order: Damascus, 16–17, 28, 79–80, 81, 103, 206; Istanbul, 34–35; Ottoman Levant, 17–20, 34–35, 103
newspapers, 175, 179, 208, 210, 211, 212
non-scholars: chronicles by, 1–10, 57, 77–114, 136–44. *See also* commoners; "learned illiterates"; nouveau literates
nouveau literates, 5–10, 49, 77–114, 205, 208–11; arrival of, 139–44; authorial I, 103, 115, 129, 157; authority, 9, 14–37, 82, 116, 209; chronicles, 6–8, 16–17, 36–37, 77–114, 121, 129, 208–11; defined, 6, 10; Ibn Budayr status, 5–6, 48, 57, 60, 67, 68, 207; language, 77, 108–12, 113, 115, 120, 125–27, 148; and new order, 19, 79–80, 81, 103; al-Qāsimī edit of Ibn Budayr and, 175, 207; texts as public displays, 17, 36–37, 65. *See also* Ibn Budayr; "learned illiterates"
nouveau riche, 10, 36–37, 68, 194
al-Nuʿaymī, ʿAbd al-Qādir, 127, 135, 246n100

obituaries/biographies. *See tarjama*
oral transmission: chronicles, 113, 145–46, 167, 208–9; *sīra*, 149–50, 249n21. *See also* storytellers
order: political, 6, 148, 151, 163–64, 173, 179–87; al-Qāsimī edit vs. Ibn

Budayr, 179–87. *See also* disorder; new order
Ottomans: al-`Abd on, 99–103; architecture, 27–28; court chronicler, 211; Damascus importance in, 2, 14–16; al-Danafī and, 88–93, 94–95, 143; Egypt, 99, 136–39, 247n121; first-person narratives, 135–36; fiscal and political devolution from center to provinces, 8; historiographical tenor and form, 35, 127–28, 224n73; Istanbul as capital, 8, 16, 90, 219n16; Levant, 2, 8, 14–37, 128–39; Matāwila and, 82–86; new order, 17–20, 34–35, 103; newspapers, 211; printing press, 258–59n8; al-Qāsimī edit and, 182; vs. Safavid Iran, 235n25; semi-independent rule, 8; *Tanzimat*, 178, 259n8; and Ṭūqāns, 88; vs. al-`Umar, 18, 82–83, 88, 90–91. *See also al-dawla*; Jabal `Āmil; janissaries
outdoor culture: biographies in, 35; cemeteries, 30, 223n50; Damascus, 28–31. *See also* picnics; public culture

Palestine, cotton trade, 18, 82–83
"pasha chronicles," 138–39, 141, 247n114
patriarchal authority, Ibn Budayr and, 152–53, 155
patronage: al-`Abd, 98; al-Danafī and, 92–93, 95, 105, 143, 209; family, 19; fountains, 36–37; Ibn Ṭawq, 126; al-Makkī and, 94–95, 126; nouveau literates, 78
Pederson, Johannes, 133
the people: chronicles for, 127–28; Ibn Budayr in voice of, 128, 151, 152. *See also* colloquial Arabic (*`āmmiyya*); commoners
performativeness: Ibn Budayr, 159–60, 162, 167, 173, 196, 198. *See also* public performance
Persian, 130
Petry, Carl, 125
picnics: Damascene, 28–29, 64–66, 222n41; Ibn Budayr, 28, 64–66, 71–72, 155; Ibn Kannān, 28–29, 31, 53, 64–65, 222–23n46; literary, 53, 56, 65, 71–72
pilgrimage to Mecca: caravans, 11–12, 99–101, 154, 257n79; in chronicles, 154; Damascus governors managing, 97–101; Damascus as point of departure, 16; janissaries and, 97–103, 239n92; portering as Ibn Budayr's family business, 40, 225nn3,4
poets/poetry, 230n73, 251n68; Bahlūl, 14, 202, 252n90; colloquial forms, 34–35, 65–66; Ibn Budayr, 12, 65–66, 158, 199; *mawāliya*, 65–66; al-Qāsimī, 176; al-Sābiq, 227n30; Shākir, 74
politics, 6, 163; al-`Abd, 97–103; Damascus, 31–34; Ḥimṣ, 95; Ibn Budayr, 11, 148, 151–52, 159, 162, 173, 175, 179–87; Islamic, 6, 148, 180–87; *maqāma*, 162–64; Ottoman, 8; of patronage, 92–93, 95; shadow theater, 162; Shī`īs of Jabal `Āmil, 82–86; *`ulamā'* and, 6, 148, 151, 163–64, 173, 179–87, 205. *See also* al-`Aẓm family; governors; power
popularization: of chronicles, 113–14, 136–39, 144, 209. *See also* commoners; the people
portering, Ibn Budayr's family business, 40, 41, 204, 225nn3,4
"possessed" saints, 231n90
power: al-`Abd and, 97–103; book as, 1, 9; Central Rectangle, 40; knowledge as, 49; new dominant urban households, 28; Shī`īs of Jabal `Āmil, 82–86; Sufis, 50; *`ulamā'*, 50. *See also* cultural capital; military; politics; social capital; social status
prices, Ibn Budayr and, 11, 152, 153–54, 181, 183
print, 174, 179, 208; Ibn Budayr, 213; journalism, 210–12; newspapers, 175, 179, 208, 210, 211, 212

printing press, 179, 210, 212, 255n25, 258–59nn8,10
private ownership, land, 8, 17
Prophet Muḥammad, 66–67, 95, 163, 216n16; *mawlid*, 256n51; *sīra*, 149, 249nn18,19; titles, 66–67, 232n125
prostitutes, 14, 30, 188–90, 223nn50,54, 256n53
public culture: Damascus, 20, 28–31, 219n16; literary, 34–37, 53, 71–72; public intellectual of al-Nahḍa, 5. *See also* coffeehouses; outdoor culture; picnics; public displays
public displays: Ibn Budayr's book, 60; power of new dominant urban households, 28; texts as, 8–9, 17, 35–37, 65, 78, 93, 118; by women, 30, 31, 65–66, 80, 155, 188–89, 223n50. *See also* public performance
public performance: shadow theater, 162, 164–66, 251n74, 252nn79,80,81; *sīra*, 164. *See also* entertainment; oral transmission; performativeness; storytellers

qabīqūl, 33–34, 99
Qādiriyya Sufi order, 47, 48, 228n45
Qāsim, al-Shaykh, 175, 176
al-Qāsimī, Jamāl al-Dīn, 174, 175, 177, 179, 208
al-Qāsimī, Muḥammad Sa`īd, 174, 175, 179, 207; barber father, 176, 178, 207, 226n19; edit of Ibn Budayr, 10–11, 12, 146, 150–51, 174–204, 207–8, 213, 256–58, 259n3; manuscript of Ibn Budayr, 150–51, 168–72, 169*fig*, 171*fig*, 176–78; and portering, 41, 204, 225n3; works, 41, 175–76, 208
Qaymariyya mosque/college, Damascus, 28
al-Qubaybāt, 39–40, 160, 195
al-Qudsī, `Uthmān b., 200
quotidian here and now, 130–31, 140, 144

reception: chronicles, 112–14, 167–72, 209. *See also* audience
red ink, 168, 252nn85,86
reform: language, 109, 179, 192, 203–4, 207–8; al-Nahḍa (Arab Renaissance), 112; print and, 210; al-Qāsimī's son and, 174, 208; *salafiyya*, 174, 176
residences: Damascus, 21–28, 22–23*map*, 24*fig*, 25*fig*, 27*fig*, 31; Damascus governors, 21, 28; Ibn Budayr, 40–41, 226n8
responsa format, 133
Reynolds, Dwight, 119
rhymed prose, Ibn Budayr, 158–62, 179, 183, 191–98, 255n37
Robinson, Chase F., 119, 216n16, 242n4
Rosenthal, Franz, 122, 136
Rukaynīs, 89, 90, 105, 141–42, 209, 234n16; Ḥaydar Riḍā (al-Rukaynī Sr.), 82–86, 111, 234n16; al-Rukaynī Jr., 82–86, 234n16

al-Sābiq, Aḥmad b. Muḥammad b. `Alī, 44, 47, 227n30
Safavid Iran, 235nn20,25
al-Ṣa`īdī, `Alī, 200
al-Sakhāwī, 110
Saladin, 120, 122, 245n80
salafiyya reform movement, 174, 176
Salamūn, 14, 30
Samaritans, 94–95, 105, 113, 143, 236–37nn35,46; al-Danafī, 86–93, 105, 111, 236n43; "the Good Samaritan," 86, 93
sayyid title, 66–67, 199, 232n125
schismatics: Greek Catholics, 18, 79, 80–81; Samaritans, 87
scholars: chronicles, 7, 12; culture of transmission, 50–57, 60, 133–34; Shāfi`ī, 44–45, 72. *See also* colleges; "learned illiterates"; non-scholars; *`ulamā*
self-authorship. *See* authorial I
self-fashioning, 4–5, 8, 13, 199, 207
sexual indiscretions: Ibn Budayr and, 12, 155–56, 165–66. *See also* prostitutes
Seyyid Ḥasan, 129, 131, 133, 134, 135, 136, 245n67

shadow theater, 162, 164–66, 251n74, 252nn79,80,81
Shāfi`ī: law code, 228n38; legal rite, 42, 45; *muftī*, 44, 61, 201; scholars, 44–45, 72
al-Sha`rānī, `Abd al-Wahhāb, 48
Shihābī family, 83, 85
Shī`īs, 235n24; Jabal `Āmil, 82–86, 142, 235nn20,25
Ṣidḳī, Muṣṭafā, 130
Ṣidnāyā Monastery, 31, 81, 233n2, 234n8
Sidon, al-Jazzār Pasha, 85, 98
silsila, 54, 56, 64
sīra (Arabic epic), 233n145, 248–49; Ibn Budayr, 157–62, 166, 167, 173, 198, 203, 206; *maqāma* and, 164; *tārīkh* and, 148–50, 167, 206
social biography: of chroniclers, 7–8; Ibn Budayr, 38–76; al-Qāsimī, 176–77
social capital, Ibn Budayr's, 200–202, 207
social disorder: Ibn Budayr and, 65–66, 152–56, 166–67, 180–87, 194–98, 206; patriarchal authority threatened by, 152–53, 155; women's publicness, 30, 31, 65–66, 80, 155, 188–89
social history: `ulamology, 1, 215n5. *See also* social biography
social mobility, 7, 19–20; al-`Abd, 97–103; of chroniclers, 8, 16–17, 104; Ibn Budayr, 39–43, 59–60, 167
social status: barbers, 41–42; Ibn Budayr's book and, 60–64, 66–67, 75, 155; al-Murādī's biographic subjects, 58–59, 74, 75; nouveau literates, 78. *See also* elites; social mobility
social topography: public culture, 20, 28–31, 35, 36; reshuffling, 16–20
soldier-chronicles, 138–39, 141; Ibn al-Ṣiddīq, 103, 141, 209. *See also* al-`Abd, Ḥasan Āghā; military
storytellers, 76; guild, 71–72; Ibn Budayr, 113, 153, 162; Ibn al-Ṣiddīq, 104–5, 113, 167. *See also* oral transmission
Sufis, 46–47, 131–33, 140; college teachers, 47, 228n52; dreams and visions, 54–56, 66–67, 131–32, 230n87, 246n88; Ibn Budayr, 46–47, 48, 62–63, 66–67; and Kadızadeli movement, 136; orders, 47, 48, 52, 228n45, 229n67; al-Sābiq, 47, 227n30; social and discursive practices and material conditions, 49–57; travel literature, 132; *walī*, 54; *yawmiyyāt*, 131–33. *See also* al-Nābulusī, `Abd al-Ghanī
suicide, minaret, 155–56, 160–61, 166–67, 194–96
"sultan-pasha chronicle," 138, 247n119
sultans, Ibn Budayr and, 181–82
al-Suwaydī, `Abd al-Raḥmān, 130
Syria. *See* Damascus; Levant (Bilād al-Shām)

al-Ṭabarī, 109, 116, 242n4
al-Ṭabbākh, Yusuf, 63, 64, 258n101
al-Ta`dīl, Ibn Budayr's homes, 40–41, 226n8
Tamari, Steve, 50, 228n52, 229nn59,70
Tanzimat, Ottoman, 178, 259n8
tārīkh, 8; Ibn Budayr, 145, 148–50, 167, 203–4, 206; vs. *sīra* (Arabic epic), 148–50, 167, 206; and *ta'rīkh*, 118, 242n7. *See also* chronicles; history
ta'rīkh-diary (chronicle-diary), 115, 117–19, 123, 139; al-Birzālī, 120–21, 127; Ibn al-Bannā', 117–21, 126, 135, 242n7, 245n67; Ibn Ṭūlūn, 127–28; Seyyid Ḥasan, 129, 131, 133, 134, 135, 136, 245n67
tarjama, 39, 51, 52, 56; Ibn Budayr, 12, 60–64, 71, 150, 153, 157, 199–203, 207; Ibn Kannān, 153
taxes: on Christians, 31, 81, 234n13; Ottoman campaign against Napoleon, 99; tax farms (*mālikāne*), 17
teachers. *See* colleges; scholars
technical literacy, 6, 9, 48, 227n27
Tel-Aviv, Samaritans, 86–87
Telḥīsī Muṣṭafā Efendi, 129–30
Terzioğlu, Derin, 133
thabat, 50, 51, 54, 56, 229n59

theater, shadow theater, 162, 164–66, 251n74, 252nn79,80,81
trade: cotton, 18, 82–83; global, 17–18; grain, 31–33
travelogue, 132
treasurer of the province, al-Daftardār, 28, 33–34, 154, 185
treasury caravans, 11, 154
Tripoli, Ḥimṣ and, 95
Ṭūqāns, 87–93, 236n33, 240n129; Aḥmad Beg, 89–90, 91; Muṣṭafā Beg/Pasha, 88, 90–92, 94–95, 105, 143
turāth, 181, 204. *See also* heritage
Turkish, 128–33, 187, 192; printing press, 258–59n8; shadow theater, 164, 252n79
Turkish Divan, Damascus, 26*fig*
TV series, Syrian, 213

`ulamā`, 1–2, 6, 215n5; and biographical dictionary, 35, 173, 230–31n89; chronicles for the people, 127–28; and coffeehouses, 74; collegial relations, 51, 61, 229n63; Egypt, 136; Ibn Budayr and, 166, 215n7; Ibn al-Dawādārī and, 125, 243n40; Ibn Ṭūlūn's colleagues, 135; Jabal `Āmil, 142; language of chronicles, 6, 111–12, 127; and political order, 6, 148, 151, 163–64, 173, 179–87, 205, 217n18; as primary authors of chronicles, 6, 9–10, 77, 148, 205, 211; al-Qāsimī family position, 176; shared discourse, 112; and *sīra*, 249n21; social and discursive practices and material conditions, 49–57; tendency for solitude and melancholy, 156–57, 250n52; transformation within class of, 122–24; `ulamology, 1, 215n5. *See also* Burayk, Mīkhā'īl; Ibn Kannān; al-Qāsimī, Muḥammad Sa`īd
al-`Umar, al-Ẓāhir, 18, 219n11, 259n3; cotton trade in Palestine, 18, 82–83; Ibn Budayr and, 159; Ibn al-Ṣiddīq and, 105; Matāwila and, 82–84, 86, 105; Nablus, 86, 88, 89–91, 143
Umayyad Mosque, 15*fig*, 21, 22*map*, 39, 40; Ibn Budayr's education at, 44, 47–48, 72–73; Ibn Budayr's manuscript in auction sale, 177–78; al-Maḥāsinī, 105–6
`Uthmān Pasha al-Maṣrallī, 83, 90–91, 106

vernacular. *See* colloquial Arabic (*`āmmiyya*)
violence, Damascus, 31–34, 98–99, 154, 196–97
visions. *See* dreams and visions

Wahhābī revolt, 99
wedding, Ibn Budayr and, 154
White, Hayden, 248n11
women: Burayk chiding, 80, 209; prostitutes, 14, 30, 188–90, 223nn50,54, 256n53; publicness, 30, 31, 65–66, 80, 155, 188–89, 223n50

yarliyya, 33–34, 99, 103
yawmiyyāt, 126, 130–34, 138, 143–44, 180–81. *See also yevmiye*
yevmiye, 130, 133, 134, 211, 245–46n80. *See also yawmiyyāt*
al-Yūnīnī, 109–10, 120, 125

al-Ẓāhir Baybars, 149, 233n145, 249n20
al-Zawāwī, Muḥammad, 55–56
Zilfi, Madeline, 59

The authorized representative in the EU for product safety and compliance is:
Mare Nostrum Group
B.V Doelen 72
4831 GR Breda
The Netherlands

www.ingramcontent.com/pod-product-compliance
Lightning Source LLC
Chambersburg PA
CBHW031759220426
43662CB00007B/459
* 9 7 8 0 8 0 4 7 9 7 2 7 6 *